Every *Sunset Magazine* recipe and
food article from 1994

By the Editors of *Sunset Magazine* and Sunset Books

Summer Salmon and Corn Relish with Basil Vinaigrette (page 157)

Sunset Publishing Corporation ■ Menlo Park, California

SUNSET BOOKS

President and Publisher
Susan J. Maruyama

Director, Finance and Business Affairs
Gary Loebner

Director, Manufacturing and Sales Service
Lorinda Reichert

Western Regional Sales Director
Richard A. Smeby

Eastern Regional Sales Director
Richard M. Miller

Editorial Director
Kenneth Winchester

Coordinating Editor
Cornelia Fogle

Assistant Editor
Kevin Freeland

SUNSET PUBLISHING CORPORATION

Chairman
Jim Nelson

President/Chief Executive Officer
Robin Wolaner

Chief Financial Officer
James E. Mitchell

Publisher
Stephen J. Seabolt

Circulation Director
Robert I. Gursha

Editor, Sunset Magazine
William R. Marken

Managing Editor
Carol Hoffman

Executive Editor
Melissa Houtte

Senior Editor, Food and Entertaining
Jerry Anne Di Vecchio

Cover: Low-fat Chicken Tamales, page 42. Design by Image Network, Inc. Photography by Peter Christiansen. Photo styling by Hilary Doubleday.

Back cover:
Insalata di Mare, page 157. Photography by Michael Skott.

First printing January 1995

Copyright © 1995 Sunset Publishing Corporation, Menlo Park, CA 94025. First edition. All rights reserved, including the right of reproduction in whole or in part in any form.

ISBN 0-376-02696-0.
ISSN 0896-2170.
Printed in the United States.

Material in this book originally appeared in the 1994 issues of *Sunset Magazine*. All of the recipes were developed and tested in the Sunset test kitchens.

Sunset Recipe Annual was produced by Sunset Books. If you have comments or suggestions, please let us hear from you. Write us at:

Sunset Books
Cook Book Editorial
80 Willow Road
Menlo Park, CA 94025

If you would like to order additional copies of any of our books, call us at 1-800-634-3095 or check with your local bookstore.

Gingered Peach and Goat Cheese Tart (page 121)

A Banquet of Ideas

Once again we present our yearly feast—the *Sunset Recipe Annual*. Our eighth annual collection, like its predecessors, contains every food article and recipe from the past year's issues of *Sunset Magazine*.

In this 1995 edition, you'll discover the latest food trends from around the West. If you've been curious about the boom in farmers' markets, wondering what's new in Western goat cheeses, or looking for sources for artisan-style breads, you'll find what you need to know in these pages. We offer plenty of ideas from chefs and food experts as well: spit-roasting tips, advice on cooking salmon perfectly, recipes for outstanding regional salads and great veggie burgers, and more. You'll find entertaining plans suited to your busy lifestyle. There are suggestions for dining out, too—look for our features on Portland eateries and great San Francisco breakfast spots.

New this year is the monthly *Food Guide*, a stimulating collection of recipes, food ideas, cooking tips, and advice on wines. And of course, our popular regular features are still going strong: *Sunset's Kitchen Cabinet*, *Chefs of the West*, and *Why?*

Contents

A Letter from Sunset

DEAR READER,

As you leaf through this 1995 *Recipe Annual*, you'll notice some exciting changes. Leading off each month's chapter is a new feature, the *Food Guide*. I'm having a grand time putting it together, sharing the tips and tricks I've gathered in my three decades as a food editor. And I'm sharing some fond memories, too: look to May's chapter, for example, for happy recollections of a picnic I enjoyed with the late M. F. K. Fisher. Of course, I'm collecting plenty of new ideas as well. Lending advice and inspiration each month are many of my friends and colleagues, among them California fisherman Pietro Parravano and great chefs like Elka Gilmore, Wolfgang Puck, and Michael Roberts.

The *Food Guide* always begins with *A Taste of the West*—one great recipe. Sometimes we offer a seasonal idea: there's a pomegranate tart in October, for example, and Dungeness crab sauced Singapore-style in January. In other months, I've simply selected a special personal favorite, such as February's zabaglione (made with the West's delicious late-harvest white wines) or May's double rabbit roast.

Besides serving up that tempting taste of the West, the *Food Guide* covers the latest news on kitchen tools, food-related books, unusual ingredients, and more. And anyone who likes wine will cheer Bob Thompson's monthly column, *Bob Thompson on Wine*. Bob's an old friend, an international authority on wines, and an author whose refreshingly direct style makes a sometimes-intimidating subject eminently accessible. Wondering what wine to serve with burgers? See July's advice. Not sure just what a "sweet" wine is? Check June's column. Looking for the perfect complement to the holiday turkey? November's discussion suggests some lively wines made the nouveau fashion.

Even more so than in previous years, our latest *Recipe Annual* features in-depth essays on Western foods and food trends. "The Bread Rush" (January) reports on the booming popularity of artisan-style loaves; "Revolution in Your Salad Bowl" (April) tells you all about ready-to-use salad greens. In June, we travel to farmers' mar-

MEMBERS OF *Sunset's food team gather in our test kitchens: (front row) Linda Lau Anusasananan, Bernadette Hart, Elaine Johnson, Jerry Anne Di Vecchio; (back row) Eligio Hernandez, Barbara Goldman, Betsy Reynolds Bateson, and Christine Weber Hale.*

KEEPSAKE EDITIONS *of Sunset recipes include The Best of Sunset, published in 1987, and seven editions of the Sunset Recipe Annual, each containing a full year's food articles and recipes.*

1987
1988
1989
1990
1991
1992
1993
1994

kets throughout the West; in November, we discover how Westerners celebrate Thanksgiving.

Of course, you'll still find a bounty of what you demand most: wonderful recipes. Some are presented as party menus; there's a Shanghai New Year's dinner in February, a Cinco de Mayo fiesta in May, and a summertime barbecued turkey feast in June, for example. Other recipes are designed to address your continued interest in low-fat and vegetarian cuisine. Try lightened-up Mexican favorites (March), veggie burgers in variety (January), a broccoli lovers' supper (June), and dozens of other choices.

If you're hunting for ways to present new or unfamiliar foods, you'll find those, too. We offer farm-raised sturgeon recipes in March, ideas for cooking pea tendrils in May, and a discussion of California rices—from sweet to wild—in October. And no *Recipe Annual* would be complete without that trio of long-time favorites: *Sunset's Kitchen Cabinet, Chefs of the West,* and *Why?* (answers to your cooking questions).

Welcome to great cooking—and a good read, too!

Jerry DiVecchio

Senior Editor, Food and Entertaining
Sunset Magazine

TO USE OUR NUTRITION INFORMATION

Sunset recipes contain nutrition information based on the most current data available from the USDA for calorie count; grams of protein, total fat (including saturated fat), and carbohydrates; and milligrams of sodium and cholesterol.

This analysis is usually given for a single serving, based on the largest number of servings listed for the recipe. Or it's for a specific amount, such as per tablespoon (for sauces) or by a unit, as per cookie.

The nutrition analysis does not include optional ingredients or those for which no specific amount is stated (salt added to taste, for example). If an ingredient is listed with an alternative, the figures are calculated using the first choice or a comparable food. Likewise, if a range is given for the amount of an ingredient (such as ½ to 1 cup butter), values are figured on the first, lower amount.

Recipes using regular-strength chicken broth are based on the sodium content of salt-free homemade or canned broth. If you use canned salted chicken broth, the sodium content will be higher.

FOOD GUIDE

Crab Singapore via Seattle... mighty mustard seed, clever cleaver, and more

By Jerry Anne Di Vecchio

Even though live tanks in supermarkets and fish markets keep Dungeness crab available year-round, this month's abundance and quality demand attention.

Right now, recently molted Dungeness crab are packed with a new growth of sweet meat, and the catch is in full swing from Alaska to central California. I find Dungeness, in its prime, to be a superb value, and I always cook it myself for some very good reasons: (1) Fresh-cooked crab tastes best. Commercially cooked crab is often overcooked and oversalted. (2) Time is crab's enemy. In hours the quality slides from superlative to acceptable, and after a day or so, right on down to smelly. (3) Crab is easy to cook and done in 20 minutes or less. (4) I love the golden crab "butter" (which contains what little fat the crab stores) and the creamy white "fat" (actually a delicate protein rather like egg white) that you get only when you cook and clean your own crab.

Unquestionably, fresh-cooked Dungeness crab, warm or cool, stands on its own with little more than a squeeze of lemon juice (chilling on ice, although popular, cuts the flavor). However, this crab is no shrinking violet around bold flavors; it holds its own magnificently with pronounced seasonings, from cioppino to the wonderful, potent crab Singapore that senior writer Linda Lau Anusasananan discovered at Wild Ginger Asian Restaurant and Satay Bar in Seattle.

Here, Ann and Rick Yoder present classic dishes from Southeast Asia and China in a contemporary setting that includes a tank of live Dungeness crab. Chef Jeem Han Lock in-

sists that these Western shellfish be kicking when he pulls them out to use. (I also demand a demonstration of liveliness before I buy crab; avoid those that dangle their legs listlessly when fetched for inspection.)

At Wild Ginger, tiny, explosively hot Thai chilies go into Lock's Singapore sauce. However, you can use any

chili that suits your heat tolerance—Fresno and jalapeño chilies measure medium-hot. Salted fermented black beans, a standard condiment in Chinese markets and many supermarkets, contribute a complex pungency to the dish.

Lock serves crab Singapore with hot cooked rice and stir-fried bok choy splashed with garlic oil.

PETER CHRISTIANSEN

Crab Singapore

1 freshly cooked Dungeness crab (2 to 2½ lb.), cleaned and cracked, including back shell if available (purchased or prepared according to "Back to basics," below left)

3 cloves garlic

1 tablespoon chopped fresh ginger

1 tablespoon salad oil

Singapore chili sauce (recipe follows)

Fresh cilantro (coriander) sprigs (optional)

2 cups hot cooked long-grain white rice

Rinse crab back shell and set aside with crab.

Pound garlic and ginger into a paste with a mortar and pestle or mince.

Set a wok or 5- to 6-quart pan on high heat; add oil. When oil is hot, add garlic-ginger paste; stir until golden, 30 seconds to 1 minute. Add Singapore chili sauce and crab; stir with a wide spatula until crab is hot and sauce is boiling, 3 to 4 minutes. Arrange crab on a hot platter; lay crab back shell onto crab pieces. Garnish with cilantro. Serve with rice. Makes 2 servings.

Per serving: 503 cal. (18 percent from fat); 30 g protein; 10 g fat (1.4 g sat.); 70 g carbo; 903 mg sodium; 109 mg chol.

Singapore chili sauce. Rinse and drain 1 tablespoon **salted fermented black beans** (or use 1 tablespoon soy sauce). Wearing kitchen gloves, cut stems and seeds from 2 or 3 **fresh red** or green **chilies,** such as Thai, serrano, Fresno, or jalapeño. Mince chilies. In a bowl, smoothly blend 1 teaspoon **cornstarch** with ¾ cup **regular-strength chicken broth** and ¼ cup **catsup;** stir in the beans and chilies.

BACK TO BASICS

From live to cracked crab

If you're squeamish or terribly pressed for time, a fresh-cooked and cleaned market crab is a fair trade-off. But if it was cooked the day before, rinse it before using.

You will be most rewarded if you cook your own. Once you get the crab home, you can keep it loosely covered in the refrigerator up to 12 hours; longer is risky because when a crab dies, it almost instantly begins to deteriorate and get stinky.

First, select a pan by putting the live crab in it to check fit. Take the crab out of the pan and fill it with enough water to cover the crab by 2 or 3 inches. I generally cook no more than six crab at a time in a pan because they cool the water down so much that cooking time is hard to judge, and any more than six makes the pan too heavy for me to lift.

Cover the pan and bring water to boiling over high heat. Do not salt the water;

crab is naturally salted.

 1 Grasp crab from the back, between the legs **(1)**; plunge it headfirst into water and cover pan. If you're cooking more than one, add the rest quickly.

 2 Start timing the minute the last crab hits the water. It takes 15 minutes to cook a panful of crab that weigh 2 to 2½ pounds each (the most common size);

 3 allow 20 minutes to cook larger crab (3-lb. size). When boil resumes, reduce heat to simmering. Drain crab and rinse briefly with

 4 cold water to cool enough to handle.

To clean and crack crab, pull off and discard triangular-shaped flap from belly side of crab **(2)**. Turn crab over; pulling

 5 from rear end, lift top shell up and free **(3)**. Drain and discard liquid from back shell. Scoop soft golden crab butter and white crab fat from the shell into a small

 6 bowl **(4)**. Save to eat by the spoonful with crab or to stir into a dipping sauce. Break bony section (mouth) from front side of shell and

 7 discard. Rinse back shell well and let drain.

On the body section, lift off and discard reddish membrane that covers the center **(5)**. Sometimes it

8 comes off with the back. Also

LUCY I. SARGEANT

pull out and discard anything else that's loose, except the golden butter; put it into the bowl. Pull off and discard spongy gills on body. Rinse body with cool water.

Break legs from body **(6)**; with a nutcracker or hammer, slightly crack the shell of each leg and claw section **(7)**. With a knife, cut the body into quarters **(8)**.

Serve warm or cool; to chill, cover crab, back shell, and crab butter mixture and refrigerate. For finest flavor, serve within 6 hours; you can get by with 24 hours.

The handiest picking tool is built in; use the tip of the crab legs to pull meat from the shells. Enjoy crab plain or season with lemon juice, melted butter, or mayonnaise mixed with enough Dijon mustard to give it a little bite and enough lemon juice to add tang. A 2- to 3-pound crab makes 1 or 2 servings.

Per serving plain crab: 111 cal. (15 percent from fat); 22 g protein; 1.9 g fat (0.2 g sat.); 0 g carbo; 303 mg sodium; 109 mg chol.

SEASONAL NOTE

Winter sunshine jam

One striking example of the worldwide movement of foods is the summer fruit we get in winter from the Southern Hemisphere. Seeing these peaches, plums, apricots, and cherries only emphasizes gray-cold days and makes me yearn for an old-fashioned summer favorite—sunshine jam. The beauty of this jam is how the pieces of fruit—literally baked in the hot sun for several days—retain their shapes while growing plump and succulent with sweetness.

What would happen, I wondered, if I duplicated some of the sun's quiet action by other means? I experimented with peaches from Chile, and the results turned rather average fruit into low-sugar jam that made a sensational summer-ripe impression on toasted

English muffins.

Peach winter-sun jam. To make a small batch of about 1½ cups, start with 1 to 1¼ pounds firm-ripe **peaches.** Dunk them in boiling water to cover just long enough to loosen skins (5 to 10 seconds), then pull off and discard skins.

Cut peaches into about ½-inch-thick slices into a shallow casserole (about 8 by 12 in.; it must be both microwave- and oven-safe) and mix with 2 or 3 tablespoons **lemon juice** (to prevent darkening) and ½ cup **sugar** (this is about half the sugar used for regular jam).

Heat peaches, uncovered, in a microwave oven on full power (100 percent) until juices begin to bubble, 6 to 8 minutes. Turn slices over with a spatula and let mixture stand until cool, at least 1 hour or up to 3 hours.

Microwave again until juices bubble, 6 to 8 minutes. Turn slices over and let cool at least 2 hours, or cover and chill up to 1 day. Microwaving gets the fruit to juice and then soak up the syrup.

Then, to duplicate the sun's drying effects, bake peaches, uncovered, in a 400° oven until syrup is covered with big, shiny bubbles, about 30 minutes (about 5 minutes more if chilled). The fruit wants to brown, but you don't want it to—so spoon syrup over slices and also turn slices over occasionally. The syrup around the peaches will be

thinner than jam, but it thickens as it cools. Serve warm or cool. If making ahead, spoon into a jar, cover airtight, and chill up to 4 days.

Per tablespoon: 23 cal. (0 percent from fat); 10 g protein; 0 g fat; 5.8 g carbo; 0.3 mg sodium; 0 mg chol.

TOOLS OF THE TRADE

Clever cleaver

I can't remember when I last sharpened my big French knife. No, it doesn't have a miracle edge. It just doesn't get used anymore. Usurping its dominance in my kitchen is a Chinese cleaver with a 3- by 8-inch blade. The cleaver and a 3-inch paring knife make an all-purpose team for most of my cutting chores.

A guest from Japan brought me my first cleaver as a gift. Courtesy prompted me to use it—I wanted my thank-you note to be honest. But the convenience of scooping chopped ingredients onto the wide blade quickly became a habit. The short, rectangular blade also gave me more leverage for chopping and slicing than my long French knife; its balance felt good in my hand.

This cleaver was carbon steel, and it readily took a sharp edge, but its natural behavior of discoloring and leaving a metallic flavor on foods like artichokes, lemons, and onions got to be a nui-

FRESH JAM *made with peaches from Chile captures the essence of summer.*

PETER CHRISTIANSEN

AMPLE GRIP, *blunt end, and wide blade give the cleaver its edge over a French knife.*

sance. I decided to switch to a high-carbon stainless steel cleaver. In doing so, I also opted for a larger blade. Resulting pluses included more knuckle room, finer cutting control, more scooping space, easier maintenance (no rust), and no aftertaste or staining. A few strokes on my knife steel now and then keep the edge well honed.

Both the Chinese and Japanese are masters of the cleaver, and cookware and hardware stores in the Chinatowns and Japantowns in large cities offer a great range of choices. Three of my favorite stores for cleaver shopping and kitchen tool browsing just happen to be Japanese.

Los Angeles: Anzen Hardware, 353 E. First Street. Hours: 9:30 to 6 Mondays through Fridays, to 7 on Saturdays, and 11 to 3 on Sundays; (213) 628-7600 or 628-2068.

San Francisco: Soko Hardware, 1698 Post Street. Hours: 9 to 5:30 Mondays through Saturdays; (415) 931-5510.

Seattle: Uwajimaya, 519 Sixth Avenue S. Hours: 9 to 8

daily; (206) 624-6248.

Prices for lightweight carbon steel cleavers with unfinished wooden handles start at about $7; magnificent tools can cost as much as $400. Stainless steel cleavers start at about $10; top of the line at Uwajimaya's is $78.

Martin Yan, host and chef for television's "Yan Can Cook" show, offers a high-carbon stainless steel cleaver like mine for $44.95 plus tax and postage. Call (415) 341-5133 to order by mail.

The mighty mustard seed

It took me years to realize that those delicious, pop-with-bite seeds that I fished out of my great-aunt Nora's bread-and-butter pickles were the same ones that made hot mustard. Since then, it has become my mission to share this tasty discovery.

First of all, mustard seed purchased in bulk is a much better value. I get yellow mus-

tard seed (also called white, and milder than black/brown seed) for $1.20 a pound at San Francisco Herb Company, Dept. S, 250 14th St., San Francisco 94103. For a catalog, call 861-7174 in the city, (800) 227-4530 elsewhere. There is a $30 minimum on mail orders. For other sources, check under Spices in the telephone directory yellow pages. Keep mustard seed in tightly closed jars; the seed is reputed to last forever.

The combination of moisture and heat neutralizes the hot taste in mustard seed; soaking also softens them. The result is a surprisingly delicate flavor and an intriguing texture.

One of my favorite salads makes generous use of mustard seed, cracked wheat, and grapefruit, which is excellent this month. The salad holds well if you want to make it a day ahead. It's hearty enough to be a main dish, and just by chance, it also happens to be quite low in fat.

As for the seed itself, 1 tablespoon has 53 calories (54 percent from fat), 2.8 grams protein, 3.2 grams fat (0.2 grams saturated fat), 3.9 grams carbohydrates, 0.6 milligrams sodium, and no cholesterol.

Grapefruit and cracked wheat salad with mustard seed. In a 3- to 4-quart pan, combine 4 cups **regular-strength chicken broth,** ¼ cup yellow **mustard seed,** 1

teaspoon **cumin seed,** 1 teaspoon **coriander seed,** 1 teaspoon **crushed dried hot red chilies,** 1 teaspoon **dried thyme leaves,** ½ teaspoon **cardamom seed** (hulled), and 2 tablespoons minced **fresh ginger.** Cover and bring to a boil over high heat; let simmer about 5 minutes. Uncover and stir in 2 cups **cracked wheat** (bulgur); cover pan and remove from heat. Let stand 10 minutes. Drain off and save juices; let wheat and liquid cool, uncovered. If making ahead, cover and chill both up to 2 days.

Meanwhile, with a sharp knife, cut peel and membrane from 4 large (each 1 lb.) **grapefruit;** cut between membranes to release fruit segments into a bowl. Squeeze juice from membranes into bowl. Drain juice into another, small bowl; add ⅓ cup **rice vinegar,** ¼ cup **fish sauce** (*nam pla* or *nuoc mam,* or use reduced-sodium soy sauce), and 1 tablespoon **sugar;** mix sauce with cracked wheat mixture and ½ cup minced **fresh basil leaves** or mint leaves. If desired for moistness, also stir in some of the reserved cooking liquid. Arrange grain mixture in a shallow salad bowl; top with grapefruit sections and garnish with more fresh herb leaves. Makes about 6 cups, 6 servings.

Per serving: 308 cal. (15 percent from fat); 12 g protein; 5.3 g fat (0.7 g sat.); 58 g carbo; 48 mg sodium; 0 mg chol. ■

Rieslings for crab

Most, perhaps all, of the great pairings of wine and food are personal, born of and magnified by experience. One such for me is a young, not quite bone-dry Riesling and Dungeness crab. A ripe, round Riesling waffles back and forth between tart berries and riper ones. Dungeness crab meat has an unbeatable sweet succulence. The flavors of the two—and their tex-

tures—each make the other more intense and pleasurable. The number of times they have come together with welcome company at picnics on beautiful seacoasts counts for a lot of bonus points.

Cold cracked crab, a baguette of sourdough, and a chilled bottle of Riesling are the perfect match, but there are many other options. It takes a heavy sauce that masks the crab flavor to push Riesling out of the picture.

Riesling goes by several

names, including White or Johannisberg Riesling. All are made from the same grape, and the wines are most refreshing in their youth. Right now you'll find 1991 and 1992 vintages in their prime.

The following fruit-foremost wines are reliably outstanding with Dungeness crab. Each costs less than $10.

From California: Firestone Vineyard Santa Ynez Valley Johannisberg Riesling, Greenwood Ridge Vineyards Anderson Valley White Riesling,

Navarro Vineyards Anderson Valley White Riesling, and Smith-Madrone Napa Valley Riesling.

From Oregon: Adelsheim Oregon Dry Riesling and Elk Cove Dry Riesling.

From Washington: Kiona Yakima Valley White Riesling and The Hogue Cellars Johannisberg Riesling.

If you like Riesling with crab, then try it with clams or shrimp. However, shellfish as sweet as lobster grows cloyingly so with it.

The Bread Rush

Artisan loaves are setting a new standard. Here's what to look for and where to buy the best loaves in the West. On page 16, try your hand at a few recipes.

By Elaine Johnson

SUSAN WERNER

REX RYSTEDT

B read is back—crackling hot from the oven at the new corner bakery, wrapped in linen at all the best restaurants, in rustling paper bags at the supermarket. Not just good bread, but fabulous bread—loaves with flavorful, chewy interiors and crusts to sink your teeth into, with decorative slashes and rustic shapes that look a little different every time.

The new breads go by old-fashioned names, like artisan-style, hearth, and country breads. You could also say they've redefined progress: the machine-made, plastic-wrapped white slices we grew up with are losing out to loaves that are handmade and purchased daily from a bakery that is part of the community.

What's fired the renewed interest in the staff of life? It's a story of our increasing interest in good food and nutrition, and in freshness. It's also the story of dedicated bakers all over the West who are committed to their craft, learning age-old European methods and adding their own twists.

Why bread is the new nifty food

R ustic loaves fit nicely into the lifestyle of many '90s "cocooners" who are going out less and eating better at home. For some, a stop for bread may even be part entertainment. The scene at Grace Baking in Oakland, California, is typical: the predinner rush brings a steady stream of customers who can choose from 40 kinds, including 20 different baguettes.

Customers have come to appreciate the handcrafted appearance of today's loaves. Says Nancy Silverton, owner of La Brea Bakery in Los Angeles, "When we started four years ago,

11

people didn't really understand our bread. They would say, 'There's dirt all over your bread'—it was the residual flour. One lady, trying to be helpful, said, 'I love your bread, but did you know it's full of holes?' It took some education, but now the bread gives people a lot of joy." Michael Rose, of Semifreddi's in the San Francisco Bay Area, adds that at the new bakeries, "You can buy something handmade for just a few dollars—which you can't say about much else."

The new rustic breads have lots of flavor without butter or toppings that add calories. Bread gets high marks as a good-for-you food, a great source of the complex carbohydrates that nutritionists advise we eat more of, and the trend is toward using more whole grains and organic flours. Bakers want to create food that's healthful and substantial.

A slice of bread history

A handful of bakers in Berkeley started the current bread craze in the 1970s, but the stage was set long before. During the California Gold Rush, miners who congregated in San Francisco took a prized possession with them to the fields: a sourdough starter. In those days before commercial yeast, the starter (a blend of flour, water, and helpful bacteria that lasted indefinitely, if cared for) meant the miners could bake leavened bread in camp. And the starter added a nice tang.

In 1849, Isidore Boudin founded San Francisco's first French bakery. Lore has it that Boudin borrowed some starter from a "sourdough," as the miners were called, and mixed it into a batch of dough. The West's most popular bread was born.

Did San Francisco invent sourdough bread? Not by a long shot. This interaction of bacteria and yeast actually goes back to the ancient Egyptians. Though European bakers have used sourdough

techniques for centuries, Westerners were the first to cultivate the sour flavor.

Fast-forward to Berkeley in 1979. At Chez Panisse, a restaurant known for its obsession with quality, owner Alice Waters was frustrated that she couldn't get good bread. She asked Steve Sullivan, a Chez Panisse cook and passionate hobbyist baker, to make its baguettes.

"There were bakeries making flavorful, chewy baguettes (back then we were only interested in the baguette shape)," says Sullivan. "The problem was, they would get bought up and go downhill. Or as they got more successful, they got bigger and sped up the processes, and got worse. There were others that were baking a wide variety but weren't interested in selling at wholesale prices to restaurants and stores. The restaurant and the whole eating community had a need for good bread."

Sourdough was so much a part of the local scene that Sullivan knew it had to be a component of his breads. After honeymooning in France at harvesttime, he got the idea to inoculate a sourdough starter with the yeast from wine grapes. In 1983 Sullivan and his wife, Susie, took his crusty, dense loaves and started Acme Bread Company. Bread lovers still cite Acme's hand-formed loaves as the benchmark for artisan bread.

Around this time, others fired up their ovens. Le Panier in Portland and Boulangerie in Seattle began baking traditional French bread. Zen Center students in San Francisco started Tassajara Bread Bakery, known for its whole-grain loaves. The first Il Fornaio bakery, which opened in San Francisco, licensed a concept from a company in Milan that was founded to preserve authentic Italian breads. (Il Fornaio now has 16 retail bakeries, 10 restaurants, and 6 production bakeries in California.)

How to tell your baguette from your bâtard

Do the cute foreign signs at the neighborhood bakery leave you confused? Here's a guide to today's most common breads and baking terms.

Baguette. A long skinny loaf with attractive slashes

Bâtard. A fat, log-shaped bread

Biga. A yeast-based starter (as opposed to a sourdough starter) that adds an extra fermentation and more complexity in flavor and texture

Bâtard

Baguette

Ficelle. Literally, string; like a mini baguette, good for sandwiches

Focaccia. Flat bread with a dimpled surface and toppings from olive oil to roasted vegetables

Boule. Literally, ball. A round loaf

Ciabatta. "Slipper" in Italian. A flat bread with a coarse, chewy interior and floury crust

Épi. Bread in a wheat-sheaf shape

Ciabatta

Still, getting these special breads in the early '80s often meant driving for miles, then standing in line, perhaps only to find when your turn came that the bakery had sold out.

Ten years later, great bread is everywhere. At the heart of the movement is the return of the local bakery, now a gathering point like the village pub. Leslie Mackie, whose Macrina Bakery Cafe is in the Belltown section of Seattle,

speaks for many bakers: "What I want to create is a bakery that's part of the community. Bread is an incredible part of life, and I want the neighborhood to have it."

Flavors pure to playful

Bread options pretty much fall into three camps: the plain, the earthy, and the flavored. Some bakeries concentrate on one kind; some do a few of each. Sourdough gets woven into everything.

Épi

Fougasse. A flat bread from Provence, France, with herbs, olive oil, and decorative slashes, usually in a tree shape

Grissini. Italian for bread sticks

Focaccia

Pain au levain. French method for making sourdough bread with a firm levain (or mother) type starter that gets built up over several days

Pain aux noix. Walnut bread, made in many shapes

Pain complet. Like pain ordinaire (at right), but with whole-grain flour

Pain de campagne. A dense country loaf made with part whole-wheat flour and sometimes part rye

Pain de seigle. Country-style French rye bread

Pain ordinaire. Classic French yeast-leavened bread (usually baguette shape) with a soft interior and crisp thin crust

Pan bigio. The round, classic rustic bread of the Italian countryside. Bigio is dialect for *grigio*—gray—or part whole-wheat

Pan di mais. Polenta (coarse cornmeal) bread from Lombardy, Italy

Fougasse

Pane all'uva. Raisin bread

Pane di Como. A round, domed bread from Lake Como, Italy, with a honey-combed texture, floury crust, and well-developed flavor

Pane all'uva

Pain aux noix

Pane francese. Literally, "French bread"; coarse but soft, flour-coated cylinders from Lake Como; the ancestor of ciabatta and pane di Como

Pane pugliese. A bread from Apulia (Puglia in Italian), round with a moist, open texture and crunchy crust

Panini. Italian rolls in various shapes

Panini

The earthy breads take the wholesome multiple grains we learned to love in the '60s and add a more rustic appearance and defined crust. Breads from bakeries like Greenwood and Ballard in Seattle typify this style.

Where plain breads may be the backdrop for a meal, some of the flavored ones become the focus. Innovative choices such as sun-dried tomato and spinach-parmesan at Grace Baking, and rosemary–olive oil and Valrhona chocolate–cherry at La Brea, make one believe that man—and woman—really can live on bread alone.

How bakers create our daily bread

It's 7 P.M. on a Friday at Acme Bread Company in Berkeley. Most of us knocked off from work awhile ago, but the team of bakers at Division One and Two, a few miles apart, are hitting their stride. They'll be getting covered in a fine coating of flour until 3 or 4 A.M. Then fresh crews will arrive to fill Acme's retail shelves, whisk bread off to grocery stores and top restaurants, and start the next day's doughs.

The smell is magical. And the cooling loaves sound like a thousand bowls of Rice Krispies when milk hits them. The bakers could be ballet dancers (though the music at the moment is Led Zeppelin): mixing, weighing, shaping, and pulling bread in and out of ovens in graceful harmony.

It takes a lot of skill to be a baker. When bakers of the new vanguard got their start, they didn't even have a good cookbook to turn to. Most learned through trial and error. Some combed villages in

Where to buy the West's best artisan-style bread

Knowing that one person couldn't eat her way through all the West's artisan-style bakeries, *Sunset* asked bread experts to nominate their regions' best bakeries. We limited the options to bakeries with at least one retail outlet, even though some restaurants, grocery stores, and wholesale bakeries are making outstanding bread.

Our top bakeries range from counter-service only, to cafés and counters within a restaurant. For each, we list the most popular loaf.

SUSAN WERNER

Alaska

Anchorage. **Europa Café Boulangerie,** 601 W. 36th Avenue; (907) 563-5704. Como.

Arizona

Scottsdale. **Pierre's Pastry Café,** 7119 E. Shea Boulevard; (602) 443-2510. French baguette.

Northern California

Berkeley. **Acme Bread Company,** 1601 San Pablo Avenue; (510) 524-1327. Sourdough baguette.
The Cheese Board, 1504 Shattuck Avenue; 549-3183. Sourdough baguette.
Capitola. **Gayle's Bakery and Rosticceria,** 504 Bay Avenue; (408) 462-1127. Francese.
Healdsburg. **Downtown Bakery & Creamery,** 308A Center Street; (707) 431-2719. Sourdough French and sourdough wheat-rye.
Kensington. **Semifreddi's,** 372 Colusa Avenue; (510) 596-9935. Three-seeded baguette.
Oakland. **Grace Baking,** 5655 College Avenue, (510) 428-2662; 1127 Solano Avenue, Albany, 525-0953. Pugliese.
St. Helena. **The Model Bakery,** 1357 Main Street; (707) 963-8192. Sourdough.
San Francisco. **Fran Gage Pâtisserie Française,** 4690 18th Street; (415) 864-8428. Pain au levain.

Southern California

Los Angeles. **La Brea Bakery,** 624 S. La Brea Avenue; (213) 939-6813 (shown above). Sourdough baguette.
Santa Barbara. **D'Angelo Bread,** 24 Parker Way; (805) 962-5466. Sourdough ficelle.
Santa Monica. **Il Fornaio,** 3110 Main Street, (310) 450-2030; 1627 Montana Avenue, 458-1562. Ciabatta. Bread is also sold at other Southern and Northern California locations.
Rockenwagner, 2435 Main Street; 399-6504. Rudolph Steiner health bread.
Tustin. **Zov's Bistro,** 17440 E. 17th Street; (714) 838-8855. Ciabatta, sourdough, olive-rosemary.

Colorado

Denver. **Bluepoint Bakery,** 1307 E. Sixth Avenue; (303) 839-1820. Dakota.

Hawaii

Maui. **Pikake Bakery,** 300 Ohukai Road, C-305, Kihei (in Kihei commercial center), (808) 879-7295; 505 Front Street, Lahaina, 661-5616. Sun-dried tomato.

Idaho

Boise. **Cristina's Bakery & Coffee Bar,** 504 Main Street; (208) 385-0133. Pane rustico.

Montana

Helena. **Park Avenue Bakery,** 44 S. Park Avenue; (406) 449-8424. Classic French.
Missoula. **Mammyth Bakery Café,** 131 W. Main Street; 549-5542. Italian peasant, semolina.

Nevada

Las Vegas. **The Beach Café** in the Rio Suite Hotel and Casino, 3700 W. Flamingo Road; (702) 252-7787. Ciabatta, pane al parmigiano.

New Mexico

Albuquerque. **Black Dog Baking,** 7638 Louisiana Boulevard N.E.; (505) 821-0881. Green chile sourdough.
Fred's Bread and Bagel, 3009 Central Avenue N.E.; 266-7323. Green chile cheese.
Santa Fe. **Cloud Cliff Bakery Cafe Artspace,** 1805 Second Street; 983-6254. Levain.

Oregon

Portland. **B. Moloch The Heathman Bakery & Pub,** 901 S.W. Salmon Street; (503) 227-5700. Pesto, San Francisco sourdough.
Elephants Delicatessen, 13 N.W. 23rd Place; 224-3955. Tuscan-style sourdough.
Neighborhood Baking Company (also called Delphina's Bakery), 3310 N.W. Yeon Avenue; 221-1829. Delphina's Italian loaf.

Utah

Salt Lake City. **Pierre Country Bakery,** 3239 E. 3300 South; (801) 486-0900. French country.

Washington

Seattle. **Ballard Baking Company/BBC Café,** 5909 24th Avenue N.W., (206) 781-0091; and **The Greenwood Bakery Café,** 7227 Greenwood Avenue N., 783-7181. Jointly owned bakeries produce breads jointly. Organic whole-wheat sourdough.
Grand Central Retail Bakery, 214 First Avenue S.; 622-3644. Como loaf.
Macrina Bakery Cafe, 2408 First Avenue; 448-4032. Giuseppe loaf.

Wyoming

Wilson. **Patty-Cake Patisserie,** 1230 Ida Lane; (307) 733-7225. French baguette.

Europe, where artisanal baking remains strong, for ideas and inspiration.

Formal training programs are still in their infancy, but there are now enough artisan bakers to share knowledge. In fact The Bread Bakers Guild of America was formed in 1993 specifically for this purpose. Founder Tom McMahon notes that California has more members than any other state, but the group's 450 bakers are spread over the country.

Better equipment, especially ovens, helps today's artisan bakers create high-quality loaves. A rack oven gives baguettes and rolls an even, thin, crisp crust: bakers roll an entire 6-foot-high rack full of loaves into a baking chamber, where it is picked up and rotated, and a convection fan blows hot air over the loaves. In a deck oven, bread bakes free-form directly on a hearth, or deck (the floor of the oven), which can be brick, stone, masonry, or even metal. The direct heat transfer creates thick, chewy crusts on country breads. Both rack and deck ovens use steam to help lean doughs expand evenly, and to give breads a crackly, shiny, deeply colored crust.

High-tech equipment aside, bread baking is still an art. And no aspect of the craft shows modern bakers' skill like sourdough. They're learning that really good sourdough—with a complex flavor, open grain, and golden crust—requires a slow process from mixing to baking.

Bakers' methods are intuitive and subject to endless variation. The starter (the mixture of flour and liquid which provides sourness and leavening, and is taken from and added to for each day's baking) can be a soupy mixture or a firm piece of dough, called a mother dough ("mama" to some) or *levain.* Some bakers keep half a dozen different starters going; one might be a soupy white flour starter fermented 12 hours, another a firmer rye flour starter built up over several days. An Italian yeast starter, or *biga,* doesn't create a sour flavor but does contribute a similarly interesting texture and complex flavor.

If you'd like to delve more into sourdough and other artisan baking techniques, two excellent books are *The Village Baker,* by Joe Ortiz (Ten Speed Press, Berkeley, 1993; $24.95), and *The Italian Baker,* by Carol Field (Harper & Row, New York, 1985; $30). On page 100, we give three recipes from top Western bakeries.

A fleeting life

After a lifetime of plastic-wrapped breads with a long shelf life, many of us are baffled when the glorious moist crumb and crisp crust of the rustic loaf become dry and hard in a day or two. (And after spending up to $10 a loaf, we may be more than baffled.) The best way to retain the loaf's magical qualities, of course, is to eat the bread the day you buy it.

For her customers who just aren't that hungry, Fran Gage of Fran Gage Pâtisserie Française in San Francisco says this. "There are two schools of thought. If you wrap the bread in plastic, it will keep longer, but you will destroy the crust we go to great lengths to produce. Leave the bread in the paper bag. It will get harder, but you can revive it on the rack of a moderate oven for a few minutes, or toast it."

Loaves made with sourdough starter stay moist longer than ones leavened with yeast. Some bakeries will sell you half-loaves. And many bread lovers get best results freezing bread (well wrapped), then reviving it in the oven. If all else fails, day-old artisan bread makes exceptional croutons.

Occasionally, progress means a giant step backward. Our modern rustic breads, handcrafted slowly with no preservatives, bring old-fashioned flavor and texture back to the table. ■

THE WEST'S BEST SOURDOUGH: A SUNSET TASTE-OFF

It was nothing but bread and water for the judges of 28 sourdough loaves.

The contenders came from the West's top bakeries (see page 68), minus those in Arizona and Wyoming, which don't make sourdough, and not counting those in Alaska and Hawaii, where long flights prohibit fresh delivery and a fair assessment. Bakeries were allowed to submit one loaf in the plain or flavored category.

All breads were baked the morning of the contest. Bakeries outside the Bay Area flew their loaves to San Francisco on same-day service. Judging was blind.

Our judges were bread experts and people with great palates: Bruce Carey, owner and general manager of Zefiro restaurant in Portland; Regina Cordova of Cocina Associates, specializing in food development and communications for the Hispanic marketplace; Narsai David, Food and Wine Editor, KCBS Radio, San Francisco; Jerry Anne Di Vecchio, senior editor at *Sunset;* Carol Field, author of *The Italian Baker* and other books; Danielle Forestier, French master baker; Elaine Johnson, food writer at *Sunset;* and Tom McMahon, founder and executive director of The Bread Bakers Guild of America.

A GOOD SOUR SMELL? *Juror Bruce Carey of Portland evaluates one of 28 loaves.*

Winning breads shone for their skillful and attractive shaping, crisp crusts, resilient textures, and complex and balanced sourdough flavor.

AND THE WINNERS ARE...

Plain Sourdough

1 *Grand Central Bakery, Seattle.* Sour white round. Narsai David summed up the judges' feelings: "Phenomenal crust, great texture, fine sour flavor." Grand Central's head baker, David Norman, says of his hatch-patterned bread, "This is one of the loaves I've worked on the hardest to improve."

2 *Macrina Bakery Cafe, Seattle.* Macrina Casera. Judges gave kudos to the beautiful, crisp crust and mild sour flavor. Before opening Macrina in August 1993, owner Leslie Mackie was head baker at Grand Central for 3½ years.

3 *Neighborhood Baking Company, Portland.* Nature's pain de campagne. This tic-tac-toe slashed bread has an exceptional chewy texture. As bakers for numerous Portland stores and restaurants, Neighborhood sells it under the Nature's label and as Alfredo's pain de Cuneo.

Flavored Sourdough

A *Acme Bread Company, Berkeley, California.* Levain walnut. Judges gave

PETER CHRISTIANSEN

exceptionally high marks for the crackly crust and superbly balanced walnut and sourdough flavors. Co-owner Steve Sullivan says the goals with this loaf were the balance in flavor, and an open, irregular structure that is strong enough to hold the nuts.

B *La Brea Bakery, Los Angeles.* Olive bread. This extremely handsome loaf full of pungent black olives has a wonderful dense texture.

C *Semifreddi's, Kensington, California.* Three-seeded baguette. This golden loaf coated with fennel, poppy, and sesame seeds has been a Semifreddi's mainstay since the bakery started in 1984.

Secrets, and recipes, of top bread bakers

Professionals' tips help produce dramatic results

PETER CHRISTIANSEN

ASK TODAY'S ARTISAN BAKERS WHAT MAKES THEIR bread so good, and the first tip they mention is a slow rise. By letting dough proof at room temperature (70° to 75°) rather than up to 85° as is typical with most bread recipes, the bread develops a much more complex flavor and interesting texture. Some bakers mix up part of the dough ahead, in a sponge or Italian yeast starter (called a *biga*) to enhance flavor and texture even more.

The catch, of course, is that the extra steps and slower rises require more time. But for a truly satisfying home-baked loaf, it's well worth a little patience.

Another tip for home bakers is a baking stone, also called a pizza stone, used to duplicate professionals' thicker, crisper crusts. Baking stones are sold with gourmet cookware. (Or you can use a regular baking sheet.)

Professional bakers have one more secret: beautiful shaping. Each of these loaves is exceptionally attractive.

The recipes come from top Western bakeries (see page 14): Fran Gage Pâtisserie Française in San Francisco, Il Fornaio of California, and Grand Central Bakery in Seattle.

When you make a loaf, pick a day when your schedule is relaxed. For rising, choose a draft-free corner of your kitchen; you can place the dough under a lamp if the kitchen is very cool.

For kneading, use one of these methods:

If using an electric mixer with dough hook, beat on high speed until dough no longer feels sticky and pulls cleanly from bowl, about 8 minutes; if necessary, add more bread flour 2 tablespoons at a time until dough meets both tests.

If mixing by hand, turn onto a lightly floured board and knead, adding more bread flour as required to prevent sticking, until dough is smooth and no longer sticky, 10 to 15 minutes.

plastic wrap. Let rise at 70° to 75° until doubled, 1¼ to 1½ hours. Punch down dough and knead briefly on a lightly floured board to expel air. Divide in half. On floured board, shape each piece into a triangle ¾ inch thick and 6 inches on a side. Place on a well-floured baking sheet.

Cover lightly with plastic wrap and let rise at 70° to 75° until loaves are puffy and hold a faint impression when lightly pressed, about 1 hour. At least 30 minutes before baking, place a 14- by 16-inch baking stone or 12- by 15-inch baking sheet in the oven and heat to 400°.

Place a ruler flat down center of a loaf and sprinkle uncovered parts with ¾ teaspoon bread flour. Remove ruler and press 4 walnut halves into unfloured portion. Repeat with other loaf.

Slide loaves onto stone and bake until deep golden, about 30 minutes. Lift loaves to a rack to cool. Makes 2 loaves, each 14 ounces.

Per ounce: 100 cal. (48 percent from fat); 2.6 g protein; 5.3 g fat (0.5 g sat.); 11.2 g carbo.; 119 mg sodium; 0 mg chol.

Il Fornaio's Panmarino

This recipe is an adaptation of one from Franco Galli's *The Il Fornaio Baking Book* (Chronicle Books, 1993).

¾ teaspoon active dry yeast

1 cup cool tap water

¼ cup biga (recipe follows) at room temperature

2 tablespoons milk

1 tablespoon coarsely chopped fresh rosemary

¾ teaspoon regular salt

3 to 3¼ cups unbleached bread flour

½ teaspoon coarse salt

In the large bowl of an electric mixer, or in another bowl, sprinkle yeast over water and let stand until dissolved, about 5 minutes. Add biga, milk, rosemary, regular salt, and 2 cups flour. With dough hook or spoon, mix in ¾ cup more flour.

Beat with dough hook or knead by hand, as directed above.

Place dough in an oiled bowl, turn over to oil top, and

cover with plastic wrap. Let rise at 70° to 75° until doubled, 1¼ to 1½ hours. Punch down and knead briefly on a lightly floured board to expel air. Repeat rising in oiled bowl until doubled, 1 to 1¼ hours. Punch down dough and knead briefly.

On a floured board, shape dough into a smooth 5-inch ball. Place on a well-floured baking sheet. Cover lightly with plastic wrap and let rise until dough is puffy and holds a faint impression when lightly pressed, about 25 minutes. At least 30 minutes before baking, place a 14- by 16-inch baking stone or 12- by 15-inch baking sheet in an oven and heat to 400°.

With a razor blade or very sharp knife, slash an asterisk about ¼ inch deep and 6 inches across into top of dough. Sprinkle slash with coarse salt.

Using a spray bottle, mist loaf and walls of oven (avoid light bulb). Slide bread onto stone, remist oven, and bake until bread is deep golden, about 35 minutes. Lift loaf to a rack to cool. Makes 1 loaf, about 1½ pounds.

Per ounce: 65 cal. (7 percent from fat); 2.1 g protein; 0.5 g fat (0.1 g sat.); 12.7 g carbo.; 86 mg sodium; 0.2 mg chol.

Biga. In a bowl, sprinkle ¼ teaspoon **active dry yeast** over ½ cup cool **water.** Let stand until yeast is dissolved, about 5 minutes. Stir in 1 cup **unbleached bread flour** until combined. Chill airtight at least 24 hours or up to 2 weeks. Makes 1 cup.

Grand Central's Yeasted Corn Loaf

1½ teaspoons active dry yeast

1½ cups cool tap water

3¼ to 3½ cups unbleached bread flour

1 tablespoon extra-virgin olive oil

Fran Gage's Pain aux Noix

1 package active dry yeast

1¼ cups cool tap water

¼ cup salad oil

1½ teaspoons salt

1 cup walnut pieces

1⅓ cups whole-wheat flour

About 1⅔ cups unbleached bread flour

8 walnut halves

In the large bowl of an electric mixer, or in another bowl, sprinkle yeast over water and let stand until dissolved, about 5 minutes. Add oil, salt, walnut pieces, whole-wheat flour, and 1⅓ cups bread flour. Mix with paddle attachment or a spoon until blended.

Beat with dough hook or knead dough by hand, as directed above.

Place dough in an oiled bowl, turn over to oil top, and cover with

1 teaspoon salt

1 cup polenta or cornmeal

In the large bowl of an electric mixer, or in another bowl, sprinkle ¾ teaspoon yeast over ¾ cup water and let stand until dissolved, about 5 minutes. Add 1 cup flour. Mix with paddle attachment or a spoon until smooth.

Cover airtight and let stand at 70° to 75° until sponge bubbles actively and smells like alcohol, about 24 hours. (If making ahead, let sponge stand at 70° to 75° for 2 hours, then chill about 3 days; to use, bring to room temperature.)

Sprinkle remaining ¾ teaspoon yeast over ¾ cup water and let stand until dissolved, about 5 minutes; add to sponge mixture with oil, salt, and polenta; mix, using paddle or spoon. With dough hook or spoon, mix in 2¼ cups more flour. Beat with dough hook or knead by hand, as directed at left.

Place dough in an oiled bowl, turn over to oil top, and cover with plastic wrap. Let rise at 70° to 75° until double, 1 to 1¼ hours. Punch down dough and knead briefly on a lightly floured board to expel air. Repeat rising in oiled bowl until doubled, 30 to 45 minutes. Punch down dough and knead briefly.

On a floured board, shape dough into a smooth, 10-inch log with pointed ends. Place on a well-floured baking sheet. Cover lightly with plastic wrap and let rise until dough is puffy and holds a faint impression when lightly pressed, 25 to 30 minutes. At least 30 minutes before baking, place a 14- by 16-inch baking stone or 12- by 15-inch baking sheet in an oven and heat to 425°.

With a razor blade or very sharp knife, cut 4 lengthwise ¼-inch-deep slashes slightly apart in dough; start slashes 1 inch in from each long side of loaf and 2 inches in from the ends.

Using a spray bottle, mist loaf and walls of oven (avoid light bulb). Slide bread onto stone, remist oven, and bake until bread is deep golden, 35 to 40 minutes.

Lift loaf to a rack to cool. Makes 1 loaf, 1 pound 14 ounces.

Per ounce: 76 cal. (11 percent from fat); 2.2 g protein; 0.9 g fat (0.1 g sat.); 14.5 g carbo.; 69 mg sodium; 0 mg chol. ∎

By Elaine Johnson

SEMISWEET CHOCOLATE *curls crumple from warmth of rich bread pudding.*

Bread pudding with Mexican connections

It's the chocolate

INTENSELY DARK AND rich with spiced Mexican chocolate, bread pudding in the hands of Blair Awbrey, former pastry chef for Garibaldi's restaurants in San Francisco, is transformed from homey to luxuriant.

Spiced Chocolate Bread Pudding

6 cups crust-trimmed cubes (1½ to 2 in.) sourdough bread

2 cups milk, half-and-half (light cream), or whipping cream

Mexican chocolate (directions follow)

4 ounces bittersweet chocolate, coarsely chopped

⅓ cup raisins

2 large eggs

¼ cup sugar

¼ teaspoon ground cinnamon

2 cups semisweet chocolate curls (optional)

Spread out bread cubes and let stand until dried and firm, 12 to 24 hours. Or spread in a 10- by 15-inch pan and bake in a 175° oven until dried and firm, about 1¼ hours.

In a 1- to 2-quart pan over medium-high heat, stir milk often until steaming, about 5 minutes. Remove from heat; add Mexican and bittersweet chocolates and raisins. Stir often until chocolate melts.

In a bowl, beat eggs, sugar, and cinnamon to blend. Stir in milk mixture and bread. Let stand until bread is saturated (tear a piece to check), 20 to 30 minutes; stir often.

Scrape mixture into a buttered shallow 2- to 2½-quart casserole; cover tightly with foil. Set in a pan that is at least 2 inches deep and 2 inches wider than casserole. Put on rack in 350° oven. Pour 1 inch boiling water into pan. Bake for 15 minutes. Uncover and bake until pudding center is set when dish is gently shaken and bread feels slightly firm when pressed, 15 to 20 minutes longer. Serve hot or warm; top with chocolate curls. Serves 8.

Per serving: 286 cal. (35 percent from fat); 8.5 g protein; 11 g fat (5.6 g sat.); 43 g carbo.; 253 mg sodium; 62 mg chol.

Mexican chocolate. Chop 1 ounce **Mexican chocolate** (cinnamon-flavored round cakes from Hispanic groceries); or mix 1 ounce chopped bittersweet chocolate with 2 table-spoons sugar and ¼ teaspoon ground cinnamon. ∎

By Elaine Johnson

City Bakery's Chutney Burgers

How about a veggie burger?

"WHY WOULD ANYONE eat a veggie burger when you could have a nice juicy hamburger?" pondered a panelist about to dig into the first of 30 meatless burgers.

His task, and that of the other seven *Sunset* panel members, was to choose the best of the vegetarian burger recipes submitted in response to a query in the magazine's April 1993 Open House feature. The most skeptical of our panelists, the aforementioned meat lover, was determined not to like any of them.

We argued a lot that day. Some tasters agreed with Mr. Skeptic. "These are like a

'Star Trek' Klingon banquet, only there's no Scotty to beam you up," said one.

Others were just as insistently in favor of the veggie burgers. "They're delicious. I could never pick just one," said another panelist.

Some conversations verged on the philosophical: why more people choose not to eat meat these days, whether a burger chock-full of high-fat ingredients like nuts and cheese can be better for you than one of meat—or if you can even call it a burger (veggie "patty" would be more accurate, insisted some).

In the end, the discussion boiled down to just one ques-

tion: Do they taste good? Even our grumpy tester had to admit, though he wouldn't put it in writing, that these five winning veggie burgers were all delicious.

On page 20, we list the three restaurants that received the greatest number of votes for their veggie burgers from respondents to our query.

City Bakery's Chutney Burgers

Our tasters' favorite veggie burger—and a hit with customers at the City Bakery in Ventura, California—is made with potatoes and has a tart-sweet chutney made from banana, ginger, and dried fruit.

Columbia Bar and Grill's Grain and Cheese Burgers

1   cup chopped onion
1   teaspoon minced garlic
2   tablespoons butter or margarine
½   teaspoon *each* ground cumin and ground ginger
1   cup *each* coarsely chopped mushrooms and cooked thin-skinned potatoes
1   cup carrots diced in ¼-inch pieces
2   tablespoons chopped fresh cilantro (coriander)
⅓   cup all-purpose flour
2   large eggs, lightly beaten
1   cup soft whole-wheat bread crumbs

PETER CHRISTIANSEN

Two Women's Zucchini–Wheat Germ Burgers

Rhonda's Broccoli Burgers

Columbia Bar and Grill's Grain and Cheese Burgers

Tracy McIntosh of Newport Beach led us to these veggie burgers of toasted rice, oats, and cheese. When the burgers were on the menu at the Columbia Bar and Grill in Hollywood, they were a favorite with vegetarian customers.

1½ cups chopped mushrooms

½ cup chopped green onions

1 tablespoon butter or margarine

½ cup regular rolled oats

½ cup cooked brown rice

⅓ cup *each* shredded mozzarella and cheddar cheeses, or all of 1 kind

3 tablespoons chopped walnuts

3 tablespoons low-fat cottage or ricotta cheese

2 large eggs

2 tablespoons chopped parsley

Salt and pepper

Toasted buns or bread

Mayonnaise, red onion rings, and lettuce

Salt and pepper

1 to 2 teaspoons salad oil

Toasted buns or bread

Ginger-banana chutney (recipe follows)

Lettuce, tomato, white onion slices, and cilantro sprigs

In a 10- to 12-inch nonstick frying pan over medium heat, cook onion and garlic in butter, stirring often, until onion is golden, about 8 minutes. Add cumin and ginger; stir for 1 minute. Add mushrooms, potatoes, carrots, and chopped cilantro; stir often until carrots are tender to bite, about 7 minutes. Add flour and stir for 3 minutes. Remove from heat; let cool slightly then mix in eggs and bread crumbs. Add salt and pepper to taste.

On plastic wrap, shape vegetable mixture into 4 patties, each ⅓ inch thick. Swirl

Lia's Walnut Burgers

1 teaspoon oil in a clean 10- to 12-inch nonstick frying pan over medium heat. Place patties in pan (2 at a time, if needed) and cook until deep golden on bottom, 4 to 5 minutes. Turn, add remaining oil if needed, and brown other side.

Spread buns with chutney and serve burgers with lettuce, tomato, onion, and cilantro sprigs. Makes 4.

Per burger with chutney, without bun: 348 cal. (28 percent from fat); 8.6 g protein; 11 g fat (4.7 g sat.); 59 g carbo; 203 mg sodium; 122 mg chol.

Ginger-banana chutney. In a 1- to 2-quart pan, combine ½ cup mashed **banana,** ⅓ cup chopped **onion,** ⅓ cup chopped **dried dates,** ⅓ cup **pineapple juice,** ¼ cup **dried currants,** ¼ cup **cider vinegar,** 3 tablespoons minced **pickled ginger,** and ½ teaspoon **curry powder.** Simmer mixture, stirring often, until chutney has the consistency of thick jam, about 30 minutes. Use warm or cool. If making chutney ahead, cool, cover, and chill for up to 3 days.

In a 10- to 12-inch nonstick frying pan over medium heat, cook mushrooms and green onions in butter, stirring often, until vegetables are limp, about 6 minutes. Add oats and stir for 2 minutes. Remove from heat; let cool slightly, then stir in cooked rice, mozzarella, cheddar, walnuts, cottage cheese, eggs, and parsley. Add salt and pepper to taste.

On an oiled 12- by 15-inch baking sheet, shape into 4 patties, each ½ inch thick. Broil 3 inches from heat until deep golden, turning once, 6 to 7 minutes total. Serve on bread with mayonnaise, onion, and lettuce. Makes 4.

Per burger without bun: 248 cal. (54 percent from fat); 12 g protein; 15 g fat (6.3 g sat.); 17 g carbo; 203 mg sodium; 132 mg chol.

Readers' choice: best veggie burger joints

Last April, Barbara Baker of Alpine, California, wrote to Open House regarding our February 1993 report on the West's best hamburgers. "Get with the times, *Sunset!*" she said. "If you really want to do us all a favor, dedicate an article to the West's best 'veggie' burgers."

We took up Barbara's challenge and invited other veggie-minded readers to send recipes or nominate restaurants. Of the 53 restaurants named, three were clear favorites.

Good Earth Restaurant

Each restaurant in this chain of about 20 independently owned and operated eateries in Oregon, California, and Arizona makes the bean and grain patties for its Planet Burger from scratch. It's served on 10-grain bread with a slice of Muenster cheese, and typically costs $5.95. For a list of restaurants, write to Good Earth Restaurants, 1058 Elwell Court, Palo Alto, Calif. 94303.

Humdinger Drive-In

Feeling nostalgic? This Portland burger joint is a '50s throwback, with a menu of burgers, fries, and shakes (39 different kinds). The mostly oats and rice veggie burger comes with the works and costs $2.95. Humdinger is at 8250 S.W. Barbur Boulevard; phone (503) 246-8132.

Sunflower Natural Foods Drive-In

This no-nonsense Sacramento-area drive-in is on a busy street corner and has just five outside picnic tables, but its $3.85 nut burgers and millet and mushroom burgers have a dedicated following. Sunflower is at 10344 Fair Oaks Boulevard in Fair Oaks; phone (916) 967-4331.—*Jeff Phillips*

Rhonda's Broccoli Burgers

Rhonda Wrobel of Portland is proud to name mayor Vera Katz among the aficionados of her broccoli burgers. Wrobel's company, The Higher Taste, now distributes vegetarian fare to 40 stores, but it used to cater parties occasionally. At two such functions, Katz sampled these burgers and pronounced them superb.

    2 large eggs
 1¾ cups chopped broccoli
  ½ cup chopped toasted
        almonds
  ¾ cup chopped red onion
  ½ cup seasoned dry bread
        crumbs
  ¼ cup water
       Salt and pepper
       Toasted buns or bread
       Mayonnaise and lettuce

In a bowl, beat eggs to blend. Stir in broccoli, almonds, onion, bread crumbs, and water. Add salt and pepper to taste. On an oiled 12- by 15-inch baking sheet, shape mixture into 4 patties, each ¾ inch thick.

Bake in a 375° oven, turning halfway through cooking, until each side is golden on bottom, about 25 minutes total. Serve on buns with mayonnaise and lettuce. Makes 4.

Per burger without bun: 211 cal. (47 percent from fat); 10 g protein; 11 g fat (1.7 g sat.); 20 g carbo; 444 mg sodium; 106 mg chol.

Two Women's Zucchini–Wheat Germ Burgers

We realized that we had a winning combination when Laurie Kirkland of Laguna Beach and Dorothy Pinson of Borrego Springs, California, who have never met, sent us nearly identical recipes for zucchini patties with wheat germ and herbs. Shred the zucchini just before using it.

    2 large eggs
  ¾ cup toasted wheat germ
  ½ cup shredded jack
        cheese
  ¼ cup chopped
        mushrooms
    3 tablespoons minced
        onion
  ½ teaspoon *each* dried
        thyme leaves and
        crumbled dried
        rosemary leaves
 1½ cups long shreds
        zucchini
       Salt and pepper
    1 to 2 teaspoons salad oil
       Toasted buns or bread
       Unflavored yogurt,
        catsup, mustard, lettuce
        or alfalfa sprouts, and
        tomato slices

In a bowl, beat eggs to blend. Stir in wheat germ, cheese, mushrooms, onion, thyme, rosemary, and zucchini. Add salt and pepper to taste. On plastic wrap, shape zucchini mixture into 4 patties, each ¾ inch thick.

Swirl 1 teaspoon oil in a 10- to 12-inch nonstick frying pan over medium heat. Place patties in pan and cook until deep golden on bottom,

4 to 5 minutes. Turn, add remaining oil if needed, and brown other side, about 4 minutes. Serve on buns with yogurt, catsup, mustard, lettuce, and tomato. Makes 4.

Per burger without bun: 193 cal. (47 percent from fat); 13 g protein; 10 g fat (3.8 g sat.); 13 g carbo; 110 mg sodium; 121 mg chol.

Lia's Walnut Burgers

Two children at once was one too many for Lia Azgapetian, and in 1986 she closed the Mill Creek Station restaurant in Forest Falls, California, to spend more time with her infant. But former customers still rave about the burgers.

    2 large eggs
  ⅔ cup soft whole-wheat
        bread crumbs
  ½ cup chopped walnuts
  ½ cup sliced green onions
  ½ cup toasted wheat germ
  ½ cup small-curd cottage
        cheese
    2 tablespoons chopped
        parsley
    1 teaspoon dried basil
  ½ teaspoon dried oregano
        leaves
  ½ teaspoon paprika
       Garlic salt
    4 slices (⅛ in. thick, 3 oz.
        total) jack cheese
       Toasted buns or bread
       Thousand Island
        dressing, tomato and
        white onion slices, and
        lettuce

In a bowl, beat eggs to blend. Stir in crumbs, walnuts, green onions, wheat germ, cottage cheese, parsley, basil, oregano, and paprika. Add garlic salt to taste.

On an oiled 12- by 15-inch baking sheet, shape mixture into 4 patties, each ½ inch thick. Broil 3 inches from heat until deep golden, turning once, about 6 minutes total. Top with jack cheese and broil until melted, about 30 seconds more.

Serve burgers on buns with Thousand Island dressing, tomato, white onion, and lettuce. Makes 4.

Per burger without bun: 321 cal. (59 percent from fat); 19 g protein; 21 g fat (6.4 g sat.); 16 g carbo; 301 mg sodium; 133 mg chol. ■

By Elaine Johnson

BROAD

Cassoulet parade takes a sensible turn

And tofu comes in yet another guise

A UTHENTIC FRENCH cassoulet is so complex to prepare and contains so many ingredients, it's little wonder that simpler versions with well-seasoned beans (never to be omitted) and minor rosters of meats are abundant. Dietary overload has led to deletion of items like pig's knuckles, *confit* (duck or goose preserved in fat), and salt pork—the arteries clog with mere contemplation. And then it takes two days to prepare.

A more sensible and healthful cassoulet is one suggested by James Adams. He uses lean poultry and sausage, and adds no fat. Because he uses canned beans, preparation is cut to a mere hour.

Streamlined Cassoulet

1 large (½ lb.) onion, chopped

2 large (about ½ lb. total) carrots, thinly sliced

1 small (about ¼ lb.) red bell pepper, stemmed, seeded, and cut into julienne strips

3 cloves garlic, minced or pressed

1 can (14½ oz.) stewed tomatoes

1¾ cups (14½ oz. can) regular-strength chicken broth

⅔ cup dry red wine

1 teaspoon dried thyme leaves

1 dried bay leaf

¼ teaspoon pepper

¼ teaspoon liquid hot pepper seasoning

2 cans (each 14 oz.) white kidney beans (cannellini), drained

2 whole chicken breasts (each about 1 lb.), skinned, boned, and cut into 1-inch cubes

½ pound turkey kielbasa sausage, cubed

Salt

In a 5- to 6-quart pan over high heat, combine onion, carrots, bell pepper, garlic, and ½ cup water. Stir often until browned bits stick in pan. Add another ½ cup water, scrape browned bits free, and boil until vegetables begin to brown. Repeat 1 or 2 more times, until vegetables are richly browned. Add tomatoes, broth, wine, thyme, bay, pepper, and liquid pepper; simmer, covered, for 45 minutes to blend flavors.

Add beans and simmer, uncovered, 10 minutes. Add chicken and sausage; simmer gently until chicken pieces are white in the center (cut to test), about 10 minutes. Ladle into bowls; add salt to taste. Serves 6 to 8.

Per serving: 242 cal. (16 percent from fat); 29 g protein; 4.3 g fat (1.1 g sat.); 22 g carbo.; 581 mg sodium; 62 mg chol.

Mar Vista, California

I N 1981, A *NEW YORKER* cartoon showed a woman with a platter bearing a boar's head, complete with apple in mouth. Her husband, with a look of wild surmise, was exclaiming, "Tofu in yet another guise?"

Andrew Dillman sends a recipe that is much easier to put together than a boar's head and more flavorful.

Mabu Tofu and Rice

1 pound soft tofu, rinsed

6 medium-size (about ⅓ oz., ¾ cup) dried shiitake mushrooms

6 to 8 green onions, ends trimmed

¼ pound ground turkey, ground lean beef, or ground lean pork

1 teaspoon minced fresh ginger

½ teaspoon pepper

1 tablespoon sugar

¼ cup reduced-sodium or regular soy sauce

½ cup sake

2 teaspoons cornstarch blended with 1 tablespoon water

4 cups hot cooked rice

Cut tofu into ½-inch chunks and drain on towels.

In a small bowl, pour 1 cup boiling water over mushrooms; let stand until soft, 15 to 20 minutes. Lift out mushrooms; discard stems. Thinly slice caps; return to water.

Thinly slice green onions, keeping white and green parts separate.

Crumble meat into a 10- to 12-inch frying pan over medium-high heat. Add white part of onions; stir often until meat is browned. Add ginger, pepper, sugar, soy, sake, mushrooms with their water, and cornstarch mixture. Stir until boiling; add tofu, simmer until hot, about 5 minutes. Spoon mixture onto rice and top with green part of onions. Serves 4.

Per serving: 453 cal. (12 percent from fat); 17 g protein; 5.8 g fat (0.7 g sat.); 73 g carbo.; 645 mg sodium; 21 mg chol.

Seattle

By Joan Griffiths, Richard Dunmire

PETER CHRISTIANSEN

Hot and hearty in 30 minutes

Effortless meals for harried holiday moments

DINNER'S ON THE TABLE *in 30 minutes when you serve baked chicken with spicy instant black beans over lettuce.*

SMOKED PORK CHOPS *bake atop instant polenta with corn.*

TWO SECRET ingredients provide quick dinner solutions during the holiday rush. Black beans and polenta—popular foods that normally take a long time to cook—are now available precooked and dried. They need only liquid, heat, and a few minutes to make them ready to eat.

Mix either of these instant foods with liquid in a shallow baking dish, arrange meat on top, and then pop the dish into the oven. In about half an hour, dinner's ready. What's more, you'll have only one pan to wash.

Look for the instant black bean mix and polenta in many supermarkets and natural-food stores.

Chicken and Black Bean Bake

1 package (7 oz.) or 1⅔ cups instant black bean mix

2 cups boiling water

⅓ to ½ cup dry sherry (or more water)

4 large (about 1½ lb. total) skinned and boned chicken breast halves, rinsed

2 quarts shredded iceberg lettuce

½ cup shredded jack cheese

1 fresh red or green jalapeño chili, thinly sliced crosswise into rings (optional)

Cherry tomatoes

Unflavored nonfat yogurt or reduced-fat sour cream

In a shallow 2- to 2½-quart baking dish, stir together bean mix, boiling water, and sherry (use larger amount if you prefer a saucelike consistency). Lay chicken breasts slightly apart on the beans.

Bake, uncovered, in a 400° oven until chicken is no longer pink in center of thickest part (cut to test), about 20 minutes. Stir any excess liquid around the chicken into the beans.

Mound shredded lettuce on 4 dinner plates; top with equal portions of beans and chicken. Sprinkle with shredded jack cheese and sliced chili, and garnish with cherry tomatoes. Offer yogurt to add to taste. Makes 4 servings.

Per serving: 469 cal. (16 percent from fat); 54 g protein; 8.5 g fat (3 g sat.); 36 g carbo.; 597 mg sodium; 114 mg chol.

Smoked Pork Chops with Polenta

3½ cups boiling regular-strength chicken broth

1 cup instant polenta

1 can (8½ oz.) cream-style corn

4 smoked pork chops (about 1¼ lb. total)

About 2 tablespoons grated parmesan cheese

2 tablespoons chopped parsley

Pour broth into a shallow 2½- to 3-quart baking dish. Gradually and smoothly stir in polenta; mix in corn. Lay pork chops on top of polenta mixture.

Bake in a 350° oven until pork chops are hot in thickest part, 25 to 30 minutes. Sprinkle meat with grated parmesan cheese and chopped parsley. Serves 4.

Per serving: 331 cal. (20 percent from fat); 25 g protein; 7.5 g fat (2.5 g sat.); 40 g carbo.; 1,609 mg sodium; 46 mg chol. ■

By Linda Lau Anusasananan

SUNSET'S KITCHEN CABINET

Creative ways with everyday foods—submitted by *Sunset* readers,
tested in *Sunset* kitchens, approved by *Sunset* taste panels

Garlic and Artichoke Bread

Jeanie Low, San Francisco

All-purpose flour

1 loaf (1 lb.) frozen white bread dough, thawed

1 jar (6 oz.) marinated artichoke hearts; save marinade and chop artichokes

1¼ cups (about 5 oz.) grated parmesan cheese

4 cloves garlic, minced or pressed

1½ teaspoons *each* dried basil leaves and dried oregano leaves

On a floured board, roll dough into a 12- by 18-inch rectangle (let rest 5 minutes if springy). Brush ½ the marinade over dough; sprinkle with artichokes, 1 cup cheese, garlic, basil, and oregano. From a long edge, roll dough into a snug log; pinch seam to seal.

On a greased 12- by 15-inch baking sheet, shape log into a ring; pinch ends together to seal. Brush ring with remaining marinade. Lightly cover with plastic wrap; let stand in a warm place until puffy, about 30 minutes.

Bake, uncovered, in a 375° oven for 15 minutes; sprinkle top with remaining cheese. Bake until bread is golden brown, 10 to 15 minutes longer; transfer to a rack. Serve hot or cool. When cool, store airtight up to 2 days; freeze to store longer. Makes 1 loaf, 1½ pounds.

Per ounce: 64 cal. (42 percent from fat); 3.4 g protein; 3 g fat (1.3 g sat.); 6 g carbo.; 192 mg sodium; 5.1 mg chol.

SCATTER *marinated artichoke pieces over dough; roll up dough and bake.*

Oven-Fried Chicken Tahini

Deborah Morgan, Albuquerque

⅓ cup canned tahini (sesame butter)

⅓ cup unflavored nonfat yogurt

3 tablespoons lemon juice

2 cloves garlic, minced or pressed

2 tablespoons minced parsley

1 cup herbed stuffing mix (not cubes)

1 tablespoon sesame seed

1 frying chicken (4 to 4½ lb.) rinsed, cut up, and skinned

Lemon wedges, salt, and pepper

In a large bowl, combine tahini, yogurt, lemon juice, garlic, and parsley. In another bowl, mix stuffing with sesame seed. Coat chicken pieces with tahini mixture. Lift out and lay meatiest side in stuffing mix. Place pieces, crumbs up, in a single layer in a 10- by 15-inch pan. Bake in a 375° oven until meat at thigh bone is no longer pink (cut to test), about 45 minutes. Accompany with lemon wedges, salt, and pepper to add to taste. Serves 4.

Per serving: 474 cal. (36 percent from fat); 53 g protein; 19 g fat (3.4 g sat.); 21 g carbo.; 461 mg sodium; 153 mg chol.

CRISP COATING *on baked chicken is stuffing mix; tahini makes crumbs stick.*

Chocolate Caramel Pecan Bars

Barbara Morkus, Carbondale, Colorado

About 1 cup (½ lb.) butter or margarine, cut into chunks

1 cup firmly packed brown sugar

1 large egg yolk

2 teaspoons vanilla

2 cups all-purpose flour

2 cups chopped pecans or almonds

Caramel filling (recipe follows)

2 cups (12 oz.) semisweet chocolate baking chips or chunks

In a bowl, beat to blend 1 cup butter, brown sugar, egg yolk, and vanilla; add flour and mix well. Press mixture evenly over bottom and sides of a buttered 10- by 15-inch pan. Sprinkle nuts over dough. Bake in a 350° oven until crust is golden brown, about 25 min-

utes. Pour caramel into crust and spread evenly; sprinkle with chocolate. When chocolate softens, about 5 minutes, spread smooth. Let cool. Cut into 30 squares, then cut each in ½ diagonally. If making ahead, cover and chill up to 1 day; freeze to store longer. Makes 60.

Per piece: 141 cal. (54 percent from fat); 1 g protein; 8.4 g fat (3.8 g sat.); 17 g carbo.; 51 mg sodium; 15 mg chol.

Caramel filling. In a 2- to 3-quart pan over high heat, melt 6 tablespoons **butter** or margarine. Add ¾ cup *each* firmly packed **brown sugar** and **light corn syrup;** stir until mixture reaches 240° (soft-ball stage) on a thermometer, about 5 minutes. Use hot.

Compiled by Paula Freschet

THREE-LAYER COOKIES *have a crust base, caramel center, and chocolate topping.*

FOOD GUIDE

Western zabaglione in minutes . . . garlic like candy, greens with a fresh bite

By Jerry Anne Di Vecchio

ow and then my cupboard gets mighty bare, but rarely is it without the three ingredients that can become one of the world's great desserts—zabaglione. Essentials are eggs, sugar, and wine, and even these few elements are flexible. I use only the yolks of the eggs because I like the creamy density they give the dessert. The wines I prefer in zabaglione are sweet, so I usually start with a small amount of sugar, then taste the cooked zabaglione and add more sugar if it is needed. The wines I like best are from the West: intensely fruity late-harvest Riesling (Johannisberg or white), Gewürztraminer, or Chenin Blanc, or the aromatic sweet white wines made from muscat grapes. Their delicacy is, to my palate, the perfect match for the dessert's fragile texture.

I've also made enjoyable zabagliones with orange juice, tangerine juice, sherry, madeira, dry vermouth, and all kinds of other white wines. High-alcohol liqueurs, such as anisette, Frangelico, and rum, keep the yolks from foaming, but a little can be added for flavor.

Zabaglione is unquestionably Italian, and it was immigrant Italian chefs who firmly established this dessert in the cuisine of San Francisco's flamboyant early days. A few 19-century restaurants, like Jack's (615 Sacramento Street, 415/986-9854) and Fior d'Italia (601 Union Street, 986-1886), still have zabaglione on their menus. My first taste of it was at the long-gone Vanessi's on Broadway; sitting at the counter, I watched, fascinated, as the chef whipped up some just for me.

Because zabaglione comes together so quickly, it makes a fascinating one-act show. Never one to minimize theatrics, I often make this dessert at the table over a portable flame. Be-

fore dinner, I gather on a roomy tray a zabaglione pan (see the section on tools, following), a wire whisk, a portable gas burner (you can also use the alcohol burner of a chafing dish; an electric unit also works, but it's slower), whole eggs in a small bowl, a little bowl of sugar, and a bottle of wine.

Working from the tray, I

begin my performance. First, I crack the eggs, separating whites into the bowl (save them for something else) and dropping yolks (1 to 1½ for a serving) into the pan. Then I use an emptied eggshell to measure the wine, allowing a generous half-shellful for each yolk (a large egg's half-shell holds a little more than 1 tablespoon); with the same

Late-harvest Zabaglione

3 to 4 tablespoons black raspberry liqueur or crème de cassis (optional)

About ½ cup whipped cream (optional)

4 large egg yolks

4 to 6 tablespoons late-harvest white wine such as Riesling, Gewürztraminer, or Chenin Blanc; or a muscat wine such as Muscat Canelli or Essensia

1 to 2 tablespoons sugar

Pour equal amounts of the liqueur into 3 or 4 stemmed glasses (about ¾-cup size), then drop equal amounts of the whipped cream onto the liqueur.

In a zabaglione pan (2½ to 3 qt.), or the top of a double boiler, combine egg yolks, the 4 to 6 tablespoons wine (I like to splash rather than measure at the table), and 1 tablespoon sugar.

With a wire whisk, whip mixture to blend well. Set zabaglione pan over medium-high gas heat or high electric heat (set double boiler over simmering water) and whisk vigorously until the mixture is thick enough to retain a slight peak when whisk is lifted from the foam and no liquid remains in pan bottom, 3 to 4 minutes. Remove from heat and taste quickly. Whisk in the remaining sugar if you wish. At once, while scraping pan, pour hot zabaglione into the glasses (it continues to thicken) and serve. Serves 3 or 4.

Per serving plain zabaglione: 82 cal. (56 percent from fat); 2.8 g protein; 5.1 g fat (1.6 g sat.); 3.5 g carbo.; 7.9 mg sodium; 213 mg chol.

Per serving with liqueur and cream: 156 cal. (56 percent from fat); 3.1 g protein; 9.7 g fat (4.5 g sat.); 7.3 g carbo.; 1.3 mg sodium; 229 mg chol.

PETER CHRISTIANSEN

shell, I scoop up 1 to 3 teaspoons of sugar for each egg yolk. With the whisk, I blend ingredients, then set the pan over the flame and whisk rapidly until the mixture multiplies 3 to 4 times in volume to make a thick, hot foam. One housekeeping secret: tilt the pan away as you whip. Less gets on you, and if you whip with some caution,

guests are usually out of spatter range. As soon as the zabaglione is ready, it must be poured into waiting glasses; leave it too long on the heat and the foam collapses into scrambled yolks.

A dramatic impression is guaranteed if you've practiced. However, shy cooks can retreat to the kitchen; panless cooks can use a dou-

ble boiler there, too.

For such a simple mixture, zabaglione (pronounced za-by-*own*-ee) has a long history. Sicilians put zabaglione on the map; the classic version uses their nutty, fortified Marsala wine. Renaissance Italians favored it more often as a restorative than as a dessert. Recipes for old English and early American remedies include similar brews. The French adopted zabaglione as sabayon; the Austrians and Germans have whole-egg chaudeau for sipping. Contemporary chefs are dropping the sugar and adding herbs and vinegar or lemon to make savory zabaglione sauces.

TOOLS OF THE TRADE

Zabaglione pan, formed for function

A zabaglione pan is a bowl with a handle. Even though I'd value mine if it were used for nothing more than the dessert, I once sorely underrated how useful it could be.

Long ago when I made my purchase, only one size was available at the Italian cookware store. Fortunately, my pan holds 3 quarts and is just right for whipping 1 to 8 egg yolks into an equal number of zabaglione servings.

Stirring or whipping action follows the pan's contours efficiently. It's perfect for any dish that needs constant mixing as it cooks, like cooked versions of hollandaise and béarnaise sauces, or stirred custard. Because mixing is so thorough, I can cook these temperamental foods over direct heat. But if you want to, you can nest the zabaglione

FOOD GUIDE COLUMNIST
Jerry Di Vecchio's simple zabaglione tools allow her to fix dessert for eight in minutes.

pan in a pan of hot water.

Unsupported, this round-bottomed pan tilts; don't fill it too high.

Although zabaglione pans are now widely available, you still need to seek them out. For local sources, check under Cooking Utensils or Gourmet Shops in the yellow pages of your telephone directory. Williams-Sonoma cookware stores, located in many cities, have copper zabaglione pans priced at about $60. You can call (800) 541-2233 to locate the store nearest you.

In Seattle, Sur La Table, 84 Pine Street, in the Pike Place Public Market area, has a zabaglione set (copper pan and whisk) for about $70. Call (800) 243-0852 to place an order.

In Pasadena, copper pans cost $52 to $68 at Bristol Farms Cook 'N' Things, 606 Fair Oaks Ave., South Pasadena, Calif. 91030; (818) 441-5588.

BACK TO BASICS

Roasting garlic

The remarkable sweetness garlic releases when carefully roasted is a very uncomplicated process—but technique is everything.

If heads of garlic are baked whole, the cloves steam inside the skin and turn soft and mild. But if you cut the heads in half and bake them cut side down in a little olive oil, the bottoms of the cloves brown and caramelize, becoming deliciously sticky-sweet and chewy. It's a fine line between perfectly browned and bitterly scorched, so you have to keep an eye (and nose) on garlic as it bakes.

1. Choose firm **heads of garlic.** Discard loose layers of skin. Cut heads in half horizontally (through the cloves), keeping each half intact as much as possible; you'll probably need to fit some of the cloves back into their skins.

2. Pour enough **olive oil** into a baking pan (nonstick is

ROASTED GARLIC *is simple and makes a bold appetizer or snack with crusty bread and parmesan cheese.*

PETER CHRISTIANSEN

best if you want more of the caramelized brown surface to stick to the garlic than to the pan) to make about a $\frac{1}{16}$-inch layer. Lay garlic cut side down in pan, allowing about $\frac{1}{2}$ inch around each piece.

3. Set pan on rack in center or slightly above center of a 375° oven. Bake, uncovered, until garlic is browned on bottom and oozing at clove edges, 35 to 40 minutes. Now and then, lift edges of garlic with a spatula to check color. Rotate pan if browning is not even; keep in mind that few tastes are more bitter than burnt garlic—the smell will warn you of impending danger. As oil is absorbed, replenish it at least once with another $\frac{1}{16}$-inch layer (generally, you use about 1 tablespoon oil for each head of garlic).

4. Serve garlic hot, warm, or cool. If making ahead, cover when cool and let stand up to 1 day. With a wide spatula, transfer garlic carefully to plates or a platter. Using a fork, pick out few cloves of garlic at a time, and add **salt** to taste. Eat plain, spread on bread or toast, tucked into a sandwich, or with roast or grilled meats. Allow $\frac{1}{2}$ to 1 head for a serving.

Per head: 227 cal. (56 percent from fat); 4.6 g protein; 14 g fat (1.9 g sat.); 24 g carbo.; 12 mg sodium; 0 mg chol.

SEASONAL NOTE

Mustard greens, stir-fried

Where winter days are mildly cool in the West, leafy

greens flourish. Right now, produce sections are piled high with ruffled fresh choices—Swiss chards and bok choys, cabbages and kales, the broccoli bunch, and the mustards. Among the latter, you'll find tiny tender leaves (green or red tinged) in salad mixes, furled-edge standard mustard greens, Chinese flat-leaf mustard (or garden variations of these), and sometimes the thick-ribbed Chinese broad-leaf mustard.

It's the slightly bitter-hot flavor of the skinny-ribbed large-leaf mustards I find especially appealing with many cold-weather foods.

Stir-fried mustard greens make a forthright companion for roast pork and mashed potatoes, richly glazed spareribs, and smoked pork chops. They also make a grand topping for hot boiled pasta, along with a little olive oil and grated parmesan.

The furled standard and Chinese flat-leaf mustards are a little too coarse to eat raw. But when cooked just enough to wilt, the leaves are tender, and their nippy flavor is slightly tamed.

To stir-fry mustard greens. Rinse leafy **mustard greens** and drain; cut off and discard tough center ribs, then stack leaves and cut crosswise into strips 1 to 2 inches wide.

For ¾ to 1 pound mustard greens, you need a wok (about 14 in. wide) or 12-inch frying pan; greens are voluminous, but wilt quickly, like spinach. Place pan on high heat; when it's hot, add 1 to 2 tablespoons **olive oil.** When oil is hot, stir in mustard greens and, if you like, about ½ teaspoon **crushed dried hot red chilies.** Stir-fry until leaves wilt, 3 to 4 minutes; if they start to scorch, add 1 to 2 tablespoons **water.** Serve hot, seasoned to taste with **salt, soy sauce,** and a few drops of **Oriental sesame oil.** Makes 2 or 3 servings.

Per serving: 67 cal. (63 percent from fat); 2.9 g protein; 4.7 g fat (0.6 g sat.); 5.2 g carbo.; 26 mg sodium; 0 mg chol.

Cooking with a French accent

When Michel Richard burst onto the Los Angeles food scene in the late '70s with a pastry shop at Third and Robertson, what struck me most were his heavy French accent and his technical mastery of great-tasting pastries and breads.

Later, when Michel opened his restaurant, Citrus, on Melrose, I was again impressed by the skillful execution of the dishes, but taken even more with his innovative, often amusing breaks from the hidebound rigors of French cuisine.

Now he is sharing his wisdom and techniques in a new book, *Michel Richard's Home Cooking with a French Accent.* A better title would be hard to imagine; he brings his French-born philosophy to bear on the West's great variety of foods and cultural influences. Many dishes from Citrus are in the book, including a complex thousand-layer smoked salmon terrine. Although he cautions you to "tackle it during a relaxed period," his very specific steps make the dish achievable for the patient cook. Many of Michel's recipes reflect his sensitivity to his customers' interest in dishes with less fat and more fresh produce, and his own awareness of popular tastes—best indicated by his turkey corn dogs. His practical, home-cook approach shows up in dishes like quiche-in-a-potato.

Altogether, this entertaining book (with Judy Zeidler and Jan Weimer, William Morrow and Company, Inc., 1993; $30) has earned its place on my ladened cookbook shelves. ∎

VOLUMINOUS *curly standard mustard greens or Chinese flat-leaf mustard wilt like spinach when stir-fried. Both have a nippy flavor.*

Ah, bleak winter. Clouds right down to the bill of your cap, hiding snow in the hills. Hard winds rattling bare branches in the trees, and bringing the chance to open a few bottles of burly reds to serve with soul-warming soups and stews.

A proper red for wintry dinners needs three qualities: robust enough flavors to taste good out of a tumbler, plenty of body, and enough tannins to feel firm in the face of a braised lamb shank. When so balanced, the rich tenderness of the meat is cleansed by the wine (the more fat in a meal, the more tannin is needed for this purpose).

One of the darker, firmer Cabernet Sauvignons is not entirely miscast as a wine for a dark and stormy night if the setting is fancy. But for a dinner suited to flannel shirts and hunting boots, one of the orphan varietals—in the vein of Petite Sirah and Barbera, or a Zinfandel—is fashionably correct. People who remember satisfying jugs of budget-priced California burgundies from another era actually are recalling wines blended mostly from Petite Sirah and Zinfandel. A few such wines are still around, augmented by fancier successors with hefty proportions of Syrah, Mourvèdre, and their peers.

The following suggestions start with ones appropriate for middling cold days and descend with the temperature to the really sturdy stuff. Prices range from $8 to $18.

For middling cold: Sebastiani Sonoma County Barbera, Foppiano Vineyards Sonoma County Petite Sirah.

For cold: A. Rafanelli Dry Creek Valley Zinfandel, Sausal Alexander Valley Zinfandel, Christopher Creek Russian River Valley Petite Sirah, Louis M. Martini Napa Valley Petite Sirah Reserve, Bonny Doon California Le Cigare Volant, Cline Cellars California Cotes D'Oakley (mostly Carignane).

For as cold as it gets: Ridge California Geyserville (a one-vineyard blend of Zinfandel, Petite Sirah, and others), Santino Zinfandel Shenandoah Valley of California Grandpere Vineyard.

MORE THAN TASTE *dictates which foods to serve for a hot pot dinner. Artfully arranged ingredients—clams, eggs, noodles, green vegetables, rice, meat, and fish—and their containers have symbolic meanings. For good luck, end meal with tangerines.*

Shanghai New Year's dinner

Usher in the year 4692 with a menu of good omens

WHEN YOU WALK INTO Sue Yung Li's home to celebrate Chinese New Year—which begins on February 10 this year and lasts two weeks—she stacks the deck in favor of good fortune. Symbols of luck, wealth, long life, and prosperity surround her guests.

She capitalizes on her dramatic flair as a filmmaker and landscape architect to display these omens. A shower of coins covers the thick rug, baskets of gold-wrapped sweets shine, red ribbons bind the stems of white narcissus, and branches of red quince blossoms mass in profusion.

Coins and shiny wrappers portend wealth in the new year. Sprouting bulbs represent new life; red is the color of happiness. Homonyms are also omens; in Li's Shanghai dialect, the word for *tangerine* sounds like the one for *good luck.*

Hot pot menus Li serves during this two-week period reinforce the symbolism. Although hot pot dishes are common in China for cold winter days, they are particularly significant at New Year's because food shared from the round pot, at a circular table, surrounded by family and friends emphasizes unity and togetherness.

Foods also have special meaning.

Want a raise? Eat spring rolls because they look (sort of) like gold bars, or eggs because their yolks are golden.

Want silver? Slurp shiny transparent noodles because they resemble silver chains.

Wish for prosperity? Eat fish; in Shanghainese, *fish* is *yu,* which also sounds like the word for *surplus* and *abundance.*

Looking for new opportunities? Cook clams and hope they pop open.

WIRE SKIMMERS, *large or small, hold small portions of foods as they cook quickly in hot broth—which grows richer in flavor as the meal progresses. Foods foretell the future: Opened clams signify new opportunities ahead, long cellophane noodles promise silver for your pocket, and green vegetables signal growth in business. For adroit diners, offer chopsticks.*

Time to expand the business? Green vegetables represent healthy growth.

Want enough to eat? Finish the meal with *felicity rice;* it's short-grain white rice cooled and seasoned with sliced Chinese sausage (*lop chong*) and green-stem (Shanghai) or baby bok choy. This dish ensures a full belly for the year to come.

For happy relationships, present foods on round plates.

If you have a traditional charcoal-burning Chinese hot pot with a chimney in the center, you can use it for this meal—with certain precautions. You must have plenty of fresh air ventilation, and you must sit the unit in a rimmed container of cool water so the pot will not scorch or burn the table.

An easier arrangement, which Li uses, is a pan on a portable burner. Or use an electric wok or frying pan.

As guests do their own cooking, they need easy access to the cooking pan, and six is the optimum number for comfort. But this meal readily multiplies if you duplicate the setup.

Many foods can be prepared in advance. Li freezes the thinly sliced meats, arranged in overlapping circles, ahead, ready to pull out for instant parties. Chinese condiments are staples in her kitchen. Asian markets sell wire skimmers and baskets.

For each person, allow about ¼ pound total of meat, fish (plus 2 clams in shell),

SHANGHAI NEW YEAR'S DINNER
Spring Rolls
Shanghai Hot Pot for 6
Felicity Rice
Warm Shaoxing (Chinese Rice Wine)
Sesame Cookies
Tangerines
Iron Goddess of Mercy Tea

poultry, or tofu, and ¼ pound vegetables. Buy spring rolls and the cookies.

Shanghai Hot Pot for 6

¼ pound boned and fat-trimmed pork loin or tenderloin

¼ pound boned and skinned chicken breast

¼ pound fat-trimmed beef flank steak

¼ pound skinned and boned white-fleshed fish

⅓ pound large (31 to 35 per lb.) shrimp, peeled and deveined

¼ pound squid mantles (optional)

About ½ pound bean thread (*sai fun* or cellophane) noodles

12 small hard-shell clams, suitable for steaming, scrubbed

6 small brown eggs

1 carton (about 14 oz.) firm tofu, drained and cut into ½-inch cubes

½ pound napa cabbage, cut into thin shreds

½ pound spinach, stems removed, rinsed and drained

6 ounces chrysanthemum greens, tough stems

trimmed, rinsed and cut into 2-inch lengths

6 green onions, ends trimmed, cut into 2-inch lengths

Fresh cilantro (coriander) sprigs and/or red radishes

Condiments (choices follow)

3½ to 5 quarts regular-strength chicken broth

Freeze pork, chicken, beef, and fish until firm but not completely frozen, 1 to 1½ hours; thinly slice foods across the grain (if cutting ahead, arrange slightly overlapping slices on waxed paper–lined round plates; freeze until hard, then transfer meat on paper to freezer bags; seal and freeze up to 2 weeks). Cut shrimp in ½ lengthwise. Cut squid mantles in ½ lengthwise and crosswise; score each piece lightly in a crosshatch pattern. Arrange pork, chicken, beef, fish (freshly cut or frozen), shrimp, and squid in overlapping circles on round plates; group each food together. If arranging ahead, cover plates and chill up to 1 day.

Soak noodles in hot water to cover until pliable, about 10 minutes. Drain well.

Arrange noodles, clams, eggs, tofu, cabbage, spinach, chrysanthemum greens, and onions on platters. If arranging ahead, cover containers and chill up to 1 day .

At each table setting, arrange a small plate, small bowl, spoon, chopsticks, and small wire basket with handle.

Uncover foods, garnish with cilantro or radishes, and place on table. Gather condiments onto a small tray.

Fill a wide, handsome 5- to 8-quart pan about ⅔ with broth; in kitchen, bring to boiling over high heat. Place on a portable burner in table center; turn heat high. In kitchen, in a 1½- to 2-quart pan, keep remaining broth, covered, hot over low heat; as liquid in pan at table concentrates, replenish with the extra broth.

Pass condiments, inviting each guest to mix a dipping sauce to taste in the small bowl. Using wire baskets or chopsticks, each person adds a few bites of food at a time to boiling broth. Most foods are ready in 1 to 2 minutes: meats and fish should be opaque in the center, greens should be wilted, and other foods should be hot; clams may take 10 minutes to open (discard if they don't).

Lift foods from broth, dip into sauce, and eat; repeat as desired.

Add more hot broth to pan as needed. To poach eggs, crack, 1 at a time, into a large ladle; immerse in broth until as firm as you like. Slide or scoop egg into a sauce bowl. Ladle rich broth and remaining tidbits into sauce bowl; eat and sip. Serves 6.

Per serving: 514 cal. (32 percent from fat); 45 g protein; 18 g fat (4.2 g sat.); 44 g carbo.; 317 mg sodium; 240 mg chol.

Condiments: Pour into small bowls or pitchers ½ cup soy sauce, ¼ cup **Oriental sesame oil**, ¼ cup **rice vinegar**, ½ cup **rice wine**, and ¼ cup **chili oil**. Put 1 cup **fresh cilantro** (coriander) **leaves** in a small bowl. ■

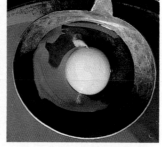

SMALL BOWL *holds individually blended seasonings to use as dipping sauce for foods from hot pot. To control egg's shape, break it into a ladle and poach in broth.*

By Linda Lau Anusasananan

RECTANGULAR AND ROUND *pizzas start with prepared crusts. Above, olives, feta, and mint make a Greek version on frozen bread dough. At right, taco sauce, black beans, cheese, and avocado become Mexican pizza on a bread shell.*
PETER CHRISTIANSEN

Pizza with a head start

Tailor-made, but not quite from scratch

THE BIGGEST stumbling block in making pizza for dinner is the crust. But designer pizza is a breeze if you start with a ready-made crust, using one of the pizza bases you can buy, then top it with your favorite foods.

Since overloading the pizza is a temptation, the cooking chart below will help you keep things in proportion.

A basic pizza is a crust coated with a thin layer of thick sauce topped with meat and/or vegetables and then cheese—to hold things together. If you want to embellish your pizza with foods that don't heat well, lay them on after the pizza is baked. And if you don't see a favorite ingredient—experiment.

Crust. Check supermarket bread shelves, refrigerators, and freezers for one of the following: baked bread shells or pizza crusts, plain or with cheese; focaccia, plain or with herbs; frozen bread dough (white or whole wheat—use a 1-lb. thawed loaf for a 3- to 6-serving pizza, or a ½ loaf to make a 1- to 2-serving pizza; pat out in an oiled pan and use at once); or refrigerated pizza dough (a 10-oz. tube makes a 3- to 6-serving pizza).

Sauce. Select a prepared pizza sauce (canned or in a squeeze dispenser), a thick tomato pasta sauce (canned or from the deli section), or a canned salsa or taco sauce.

Toppings. Meats or fish include cooked sausage (Italian, Polish, pepperoni), lightly browned ground meat, thin-sliced cooked ham, chunks of cooked chicken or turkey, and drained canned clams or anchovy fillets.

Vegetable choices might include sliced onions, bell peppers, tomatoes, and mushrooms; cooked broccoli florets; drained canned beans; and oil-packed dried tomatoes that are drained and chopped.

Popular extras are crushed dried hot red chilies, minced or pressed garlic, olives, and chopped fresh or crumbled dried herbs such as basil, dill, oregano, rosemary, and sage.

Cheeses to use because they melt include shredded or thinly sliced jack (plain or flavored), mozzarella, provolone, Swiss, and teleme. Nonmelting cheeses that add a piquant accent include freshly grated parmesan or romano and crumbled feta or cotija.

California pizza. Use **pizza sauce, fresh basil** and **oregano, yellow bell pepper** slices, and **mozzarella** and **parmesan cheeses.** Top baked pizza with **cherry tomato** halves.

Greek pizza. Use **pizza sauce, onion** slices, pitted **calamata olives,** and **feta.** Sprinkle baked pizza with chopped **fresh mint.**

Mexican pizza. Use **taco sauce, canned black beans, cumin-flavor jack cheese, tomato** slices, and **feta** and **mozzarella cheeses.** When baked, add **avocado** slices and **lime juice.** ∎

By Betsy Reynolds Bateson

What it takes to make a fast pizza: Bake pizza in the lower half of a 450° oven until crust is browned on bottom and toppings are sizzling hot, 15 to 20 minutes.

Crust	Sauce	Toppings			Servings
		cooked meat	vegetable	cheese	
6- to 7-in. round	¼ cup	2 oz. (½ cup)	½ cup	½ cup	1
9- to 10-in. round	½ cup	4 oz. (1 cup)	1 cup	1 cup	2
8- or 9-in. square	½ cup	4 oz.	1 cup	1 cup	2
12-in. round	¾ cup	6 oz. (1½ cups)	1½ cups	1½ cups	3 to 4
9- by 13-in.	¾ cup	6 oz.	1½ cups	1½ cups	3 to 4
14 in. round	1 cup	8 oz. (2 cups)	2 cups	2 cups	5 to 6
10- by 15-in.	1 cup	8 oz.	2 cups	2 cups	5 to 6

SQUEEZE SOFT PURÉE *of fish into barely simmering water; cut lengths with a small knife. Skim out gnocchi and drain.*

TINY FISH GNOCCHI *are lightly sauced.*

French dumplings get an Italian look

You make fish "pasta," serve with tomato sauce

A PLAYFUL TWIST ON the classic French fish dumplings, quenelles, turns them into new-wave Italian gnocchi. The fresh look of the dish comes from forming the fish base into tiny, pastalike shapes and serving them with a fresh tomato sauce.

Because the gnocchi are not hand-formed, they are easier for the novice cook. But the dish takes a little organization. Purée fish mixture and make tomato sauce ahead; have butter sauce ingredients ready to heat when you start to poach the gnocchi.

Gnocchi, Fisherman-style

1 pound boned and skinned firm-texture, light color fish such as halibut, rockfish, or swordfish, cut into chunks

2 large eggs

⅔ cup whipping cream

Warm tomato mince (recipe follows)

White butter sauce (recipe follows)

About ¼ cup shredded parmesan cheese

Fresh basil leaves (optional)

Salt and pepper

In a food processor, smoothly purée fish, adding eggs 1 at a time. Pour in cream with motor running. (If using a blender, smoothly purée fish and eggs; scrape container sides. Add cream with motor running.) If making ahead, cover and chill up to 3 hours.

Spoon about ½ the purée into a pastry bag fitted with a ⅜- to ½-inch-wide plain tip; cover and chill remainder.

In a deep 10- to 12-inch frying pan over high heat, bring about 1½ inches water to boiling. Reduce heat to keep water at a simmer. Twist top of pastry bag tightly shut, then continue to twist and press, forcing fish mixture out in ½- to ¾-inch-long segments; cut from tip, as formed, with a blunt knife and drop into the water. Make 30 or 40 gnocchi at a time (do not crowd pan or pieces will stick together); gently run a spoon under them if they start to stick to pan bottom. Cook until gnocchi feel firm when lightly pressed, 2 to 3 minutes, then lift out with a slotted spoon and place on towels to drain briefly. At once, transfer gnocchi to a large warm platter, cover with foil, and keep warm in a 150° oven. Repeat to cook remainder.

Spoon tomato mince equally onto 8 warm plates. Mound gnocchi in center; evenly spoon white butter sauce over them. Sprinkle with parmesan and garnish with basil leaves. Offer salt and pepper to add to taste. Makes 8 first-course or 4 main-dish servings.—*Henri Delcros, The Restaurant at Meadowood Resort, St. Helena, California*

Per main-dish serving: 488 cal (59 percent from fat); 33 g protein; 32 g fat (17 g sat.); 18 g carbo.; 356 mg sodium; 223 mg chol.

Warm tomato mince. Rinse, core, and chop 2 pounds firm-ripe **Roma-type tomatoes;** mix with 1 tablespoon minced **fresh basil leaves** and 1 teaspoon each minced **fresh oregano leaves** and **marjoram leaves** (or use 2 teaspoons dried basil leaves and ½ teaspoon each dried oregano leaves and dried marjoram leaves).

In a 10- to 12-inch nonstick frying pan over high heat, combine 1 large (about ½ lb.) **onion,** chopped; ½ cup **regular-strength chicken broth;** and 2 cloves **garlic,** minced or pressed. Stir occasionally until liquid evaporates and browned bits or film stick in pan. Deglaze pan by adding ¼ cup broth and scraping free the browned bits. Stir often until liquid evaporates and brown bits form again, 8 to 10 minutes total. Add tomato mixture and stir often until liquid evaporates, about 15 minutes. If making ahead, chill airtight up to a day; use hot.

White butter sauce. In a 10- to 12-inch frying pan, mix ½ cup **regular-strength chicken broth** with 1 teaspoon **cornstarch.** Stir on high heat until boiling. Turn heat to low and add ¼ cup (⅛ lb.) **butter** or margarine in a lump; stir until butter is melted and smoothly blended into sauce. Serve, or keep warm up to 30 minutes and stir before using. ■

By Betsy Reynolds Bateson

Why?

Why do baked goods rise?

It's almost like magic. You place a pan of runny cake batter into a hot oven, then open the door a short time later to find the shapeless mass has taken on a proud profile.

What's the secret? The lift comes from air, steam, and carbon dioxide, which are trapped by gluten, a stretchy protein in wheat flour. Picture millions of tiny balloons captured in an elastic network. Baking stabilizes this porous structure.

The gas bubbles get into batter or dough in several ways. You incorporate air as you beat ingredients, and it expands during baking. Also, steam (water vapor) forms when batter is heated (cream puffs and popovers rely on it for leavening). Carbon dioxide is produced by the addition of yeast, baking powder, or baking soda.

Why do some recipes call for baking soda, some for baking powder, and some for both?

It depends upon whether your recipe contains acid ingredients, and upon the product's characteristic texture.

Baking soda (sodium bicarbonate), an alkaline substance, needs acid to work, so it's used primarily in batters containing acid ingredients such as buttermilk, citrus juice, fruit, chocolate, vinegar, or large amounts of honey or molasses. When soda comes in contact with a wet acid, it neutralizes the acid quickly, producing carbon dixoide bubbles. (The bubbles tend to be large and to stick together, creating a fairly coarse texture.)

Baking soda produces no additional leavening effect when the batter is heated. Therefore, when a finer texture is desired, baking powder is sometimes used in combination with baking soda.

Baking powder contains components that are alkaline (sodium bicarbonate) and acid (dry acids, usually tartaric and citric). It works well in recipes that do not include acid ingredients.

Around the turn of the century, most baking powder was single-acting (containing just one acid, which was activated by moisture). Today, almost all baking powder is double-acting. It contains two kinds of acid—one that is activated by moisture (it breaks down the sodium bicarbonate base), another by heat (it slowly releases more gas when you place the batter in the oven, forming many tiny bubbles, which help create a fine texture).

Why does my cake or quick bread sink?

There's more than one reason, but in a formula with an acidic ingredient, the cause is often an imbalance of acid and alkali.

Most recipes from reliable sources have correct proportions. If a recipe doesn't work, make sure you've measured the ingredients accurately before you change anything in the recipe.

If you do change recipe proportions, it's often a matter of trial and error. Too much baking powder, for instance, may result in a sunken bread. Or, products that call for a generous amount of acid may need more baking soda to balance it.

Why does my applesauce cake have a gummy layer?

A gummy layer in a fruit (or other high-acid) cake may indicate that the fruit particles are not suspended uniformly in the batter. To improve the suspension, try adding a little more baking soda to increase carbon dioxide production, or decrease the amount of fruit. Check other recipes with similar ingredients for their proportion of leavening to fruit.

Why do you adjust leavening when baking at high altitudes?

At high altitudes, there is less atmospheric pressure to hold the carbon dioxide bubbles inside the batter or dough. The batter may rise too much, creating overstretched bubbles with a coarse texture, or bubbles may dissipate quickly, causing the baked product to fall. To set batter before bubbles explode, compensate by decreasing the leavening and increasing the baking temperature. ∎

By Linda Lau Anusasananan

LEMON CAKES, *each made with ½ cup lemon juice, show the effects of different leavening agents on an acidic batter. Left to right: high volume, coarse texture (1½ teaspoons baking soda); high volume, fine texture (1 teaspoon baking soda plus ½ teaspoon baking powder); poor volume, gummy texture (1½ teaspoons baking powder).*

NORMAN A. PLATE

Alaska enchilada is hearty fare

And Idaho shrimp are considerate of calories

ALASKAN WINTER nights are often made glorious by the aurora borealis, usually referred to as the northern lights. Robert Hartzler's Anchorage dinner table is likewise made glorious by his Northern Lights Layered Enchilada Casserole, which takes its sunny flavor from the Mexican ingredients. It remains light by using beans and corn without meat, and by softening the corn tortillas in enchilada sauce instead of frying them.

Being light is not the same as being dainty, though; this dish is substantial fare. It is to be commended for this no less than for Hartzler's orthography, a good example to the young, who have seen "lite" so often that they are in mortal danger of forgetting the proper spelling.

Northern Lights Layered Enchilada Casserole

1   small (about ¼ lb.) onion, chopped

1   small (about ¼ lb.) green bell pepper, stemmed, seeded, and chopped

1   clove garlic, minced or pressed

1   can (15 oz.) red kidney beans, drained

1   package (9 to 10 oz.) frozen whole kernel corn

1   can (8 oz.) tomato sauce

1   can (4 oz.) diced green chilies

1½ teaspoons ground cumin

1   teaspoon chili powder

2   cans (each 10 oz.) red enchilada sauce

12 corn tortillas (6- to 7-in. size)

½   pound jack cheese, shredded

1   can (2¼ oz.) sliced ripe olives, drained

⅓   cup thinly sliced green onions, including tops

    Unflavored nonfat yogurt

    Prepared salsa

In a 3- to 4-quart pan, combine onion, green pepper, garlic, and ¼ cup water. Boil on high heat, stirring often until liquid evaporates and vegetables are slightly browned, 8 to 10 minutes.

Stir in kidney beans, corn, tomato sauce, chilies, cumin, and chili powder; stir well. Bring to a boil, then gently simmer, uncovered, about 15 minutes to blend flavors. Remove from heat.

Pour about ½ cup enchilada sauce into a 9- by 13-inch pan; pour remainder into a bowl. Dip 4 tortillas, 1 at a time, into bowl of sauce to coat. Overlap in pan to cover bottom.

Top with ½ of the kidney bean and corn mixture. Dip 4 more tortillas into sauce; cover mixture in pan. Top tortillas with remaining bean mixture. Dip remaining 4 tortillas into sauce and arrange over bean mixture. Spoon sauce in bowl evenly over tortillas; sprinkle with cheese and olives.

Bake, uncovered, in a 350° oven until hot through and cheese is melted, about 20 minutes. Sprinkle casserole with green onions. Scoop out portions and accompany with yogurt and salsa to taste. Makes 6 servings.

Per serving: 445 cal. (32 percent from fat); 21 g protein; 16 g fat (0.2 g sat.); 60 g carbo.; 1,749 mg sodium; 33 mg chol.

Robert Hartzler

Robert Hartzler
Anchorage

AN OLD PROVERB, thought to be Polish in origin, states that fish, to be properly prepared, should swim three times: first in water, then in butter, and finally in wine. James Kircher is more considerate of our calories. His shrimp take a dry run the first time in the pan, then bask in a reduction of chicken broth and wine. Only a dot of butter or margarine serves to develop bouquet in the confetti of celery, shallots, garlic, and red bell pepper that enlivens the sauce.

Shrimp Sauté

¾ pound large (31 to 35 per lb.) shrimp

½ cup minced celery

¼ cup minced shallots

2 cloves garlic, minced or pressed

½ cup finely chopped red bell pepper

1 cup regular-strength chicken broth

½ teaspoon butter or margarine

½ cup fruity white wine such as Johannisberg Riesling

Shell, devein, and rinse the shrimp.

In a 10- to 12-inch frying pan, combine celery, shallots, garlic, bell pepper, broth, and butter. Stir often over high heat until liquid evaporates and vegetables are faintly tinged with brown, about 10 minutes.

Add shrimp to pan; stir often just until shrimp turn pink and are opaque but moist-looking in center, 3 to 4 minutes. With a slotted spoon, lift shrimp from pan; keep warm. Add wine to pan; boil over high heat, stirring often, until about ⅔ of the liquid has evaporated. Mix shrimp with vegetables; spoon onto plates. Makes 4 first-course servings.

Per serving: 120 cal. (16 percent from fat); 15 g protein; 2.1 g fat (0.6 g sat.); 4.7 g carbo.; 137 mg sodium; 107 mg chol.

Burley, Idaho

By Joan Griffiths, Richard Dunmire

SAUTEED SHRIMP *warm up in a seasoned wine bath.*

SMOOTH NORWEGIAN PUDDING *tops stewed apricots for dessert or brunch.*

Norwegians save it for weddings

But it's grand with tart fruit

RØMMEGRØT, A slightly tart-sweet cream pudding, is traditionally served at Norwegian weddings, topped with raisins, sugar, and cinnamon. It's rather rich, but served sparingly as a warm dessert sauce, this pudding complements fruits like stewed dried apricots and fresh pineapple.

Norwegians use cultured whipping cream; you can use crème fraîche or culture your own cream with buttermilk. For the first round of slow cooking, thicken the pudding with flour; for the velvety finish, use cornstarch.

Rømmegrøt with Stewed Apricots

2 tablespoons all-purpose flour

1 tablespoon sugar

2 cups milk

1 cup crème fraîche or Norwegian soured cream (directions follow)

2 tablespoons cornstarch blended with 2 tablespoons water

Stewed apricots (recipe follows)

Ground cinnamon (optional)

In a 2- to 3-quart pan, stir together flour and sugar; mix in the milk and crème fraîche. Stir over medium-high heat until boiling. Reduce heat until mixture bubbles very gently; stir often until reduced to about 2¾ cups, about 20 minutes. If making ahead, let cool, cover, and chill up to 2 days; reheat, stirring.

Mix cornstarch mixture into pudding. Stir over medium-high heat until boiling. Ladle apricots into bowls, top with pudding, and dust lightly with cinnamon. Serves 8.

Per serving: 325 cal. (33 percent from fat); 4.9 g protein; 12 g fat (7.1 g sat); 54 g carbo.; 47 mg sodium; 42 mg chol.

Norwegian soured cream. Warm 1 cup **whipping cream** to 100° to 110° in a 1- to 1½-quart pan over medium heat, or in a microwave-safe bowl in a microwave oven.

Remove from heat and stir in 1 tablespoon **buttermilk.** Cover and store at room temperature until mixture is thick enough to just hold its shape (like yogurt) when scooped onto a spoon, 24 to 30 hours. Use, or cover and chill up to 1 week.

Stewed apricots. Cut ¾ pound **dried apricots** in ½. Put in a 1- to 1½-quart pan with 2 cups **orange** juice, ½ cup **sugar,** and 1½ tablespoons grated **orange peel.** Bring to a boil on high heat. Simmer until fruit is plump and soft, about 20 minutes. Serve hot to cool. ■

By Christine Weber Hale

FLOAT APPLE SLICES *on velvet-textured apple soup; serve with spiced croutons.*

NORMAN A. PLATE

Creamy soups without cream

Apples, squash, and yams get the credit

SMOOTH, HOT, AND soothing bowls of soup fit many menu niches on chilly days. These two soups have a sweet side that comes from apples, or yams and squash, balanced by tangy ingredients and spices to keep the taste refreshing and inviting.

Both soups are deceptive: the fruit and vegetables thicken the soups and give them an illusion of richness, yet the amount of fat is low, and the soups are quite satisfying. As a surprise, try the apple soup for breakfast with toast and sausages.

Apple Soup with Spiced Croutons

2½ pounds tart apples

1 small (about ¼ lb.) onion, chopped

5 cups regular-strength chicken broth

1 cup apple juice or cider

1 tablespoon grated lemon peel

¼ cup lemon juice

1 teaspoon coriander seed

Thin apple slices (optional)

Spiced croutons (recipe follows)

Peel, core, and coarsely chop whole apples. In a 5- to 6-quart pan, combine chopped apples, onion, broth, apple juice, lemon peel, lemon juice, and coriander. Cover and bring to a boil over high heat; simmer gently until apples are soft enough to mash easily, about 30 minutes. If making ahead, cool, cover, and chill up to 2 days.

Smoothly purée apple mixture, a portion at a time, in a blender or food processor. Return to pan and stir often on high heat until steaming, 3 to 4 minutes (6 to 8 minutes, if chilled). Ladle soup into bowls; garnish with apple slices and add croutons to taste. Makes 8 cups; 5 to 8 servings.

Per serving: 110 cal. (11 percent from fat); 1.8 g protein; 1.4 g fat (0.3 g sat.); 24 g carbo.; 36 mg sodium; 0 mg chol.

Spiced croutons. Cut half of a ½-pound **baguette** crosswise into 20 equally thick slices; reserve remaining bread for another use. Arrange slices on a 12- by 15-inch baking sheet. Evenly brush 1 tablespoon melted **butter** or margarine onto top of slices. Dust lightly with a mixture of ½ teaspoon **ground cinnamon** and ¼ teaspoon **ground nutmeg.**

Bake in a 300° oven until lightly browned, about 20 minutes. Serve warm or cool; wrap cool croutons airtight and hold at room temperature up to 2 days.

Per slice: 22 cal. (29 percent from fat); 0.5 g protein; 0.7 g fat (0.3 g sat.); 3.2 g carbo.; 40 mg sodium; 1.9 mg chol.

Squash and Yam Soup with Prosciutto

1 medium-size or 1 piece (about 1¾ lb.) butternut or other gold-flesh squash

2 large (about 1¾ lb. total) yams or sweet potatoes

7 cups regular-strength chicken broth

¼ cup balsamic vinegar

2 tablespoons firmly packed brown sugar

1 tablespoon minced fresh ginger

¼ to ½ teaspoon crushed dried hot red chilies

1 tablespoon butter or margarine

6 ounces thinly sliced prosciutto, cut into thin slivers

Cut off peel and discard seeds from squash; peel yams. Cut vegetables into 1-inch pieces and put into a 5- to 6-quart pan. Add broth, vinegar, sugar, ginger, and chilies. Cover and bring to a boil over high heat; simmer gently until squash and yams are soft enough to mash easily, about 30 minutes. If making ahead, let cool, cover, and chill up to 2 days.

Smoothly purée soup mixture, a portion at a time, in a food processor or blender. Return to pan and stir often over high heat until steaming, about 5 minutes (about 10 minutes, if chilled).

Meanwhile, melt butter in an 8- to 10-inch frying pan over medium-high heat. Add prosciutto and stir often until meat is lightly browned and crisp, 6 to 8 minutes. Drain on towels. Ladle soup into bowls; top equally with prosciutto. Makes about 12 cups; 6 to 9 servings.

Per serving: 205 cal. (19 percent from fat); 8 g protein; 4.4 g fat (1.7 g sat.); 34 g carbo.; 479 mg sodium; 15 mg chol. ■

By Christine Weber Hale

SUNSET'S KITCHEN CABINET

Creative ways with everyday foods—submitted by *Sunset* readers,
tested in *Sunset* kitchens, approved by *Sunset* taste panels

Baked Cake Doughnuts

Barbara Elbing, Palm Desert, California

1½ cups all-purpose flour

About ¾ cup sugar

2 teaspoons baking powder

¼ teaspoon *each* salt and nutmeg

1 large egg

½ cup milk

About ½ cup (¼ lb.) melted butter or margarine

½ teaspoon vanilla

2 tablespoons jelly or marmalade

½ teaspoon ground cinnamon

In a bowl, mix flour, ½ cup sugar, baking powder, salt, and nutmeg. In another bowl, beat egg to blend with milk, ⅓ cup butter, and vanilla; add flour mixture and stir just to moisten.

Equally spoon ½ the batter into 12 buttered 2½-inch muffin cups; add ½ teaspoon jelly to each. Top equally with remaining batter. Bake in a 400° oven until deep golden, 18 to 20 minutes.

Mix ⅓ cup sugar and cinnamon. Brush doughnuts with 3 tablespoons butter and roll in sugar. Serve warm or cool. If making ahead, cool, then store airtight up to 1 day. Makes 12.

Per piece: 204 cal. (42 percent from fat); 2.6 g protein; 9.5 g fat (5.7 g sat.); 27 g carbo.; 227 mg sodium; 42 mg chol.

ROLL HOT, BAKED *muffin-shaped doughnuts in cinnamon and sugar.*

Valentine Vegetable Borscht

Desirée Witkowski, Buellton, California

2 medium-size (¾ lb. total) thin-skinned potatoes

2 medium-size (¾ lb. total) beets

1 can (15 oz.) tomatoes

¼ cup cider vinegar

2 tablespoons sugar

2 tablespoons unflavored nonfat yogurt

Thinly sliced green onion

Salt and pepper

Peel potatoes and beets, rinse, and coarsely chop. In a 2- to 3-quart pan over high heat, bring potatoes, beets, and 1 quart water to a boil. Simmer, covered, until potatoes mash easily when pressed, 15 to 18 minutes. Add tomatoes, vinegar, and sugar; simmer for 5 minutes. Smoothly purée soup, a portion at a time, in a blender or food processor. Pour into 6 bowls.

Seal yogurt in a small unpleated zip-lock plastic freezer bag; snip off 1 corner to make an ⅛-inch hole. Squeeze yogurt onto soup in ¾-inch rounds; draw a knife tip through center of each round to form a heart. Sprinkle with onion; season to taste with salt and pepper. Serves 6.

Per serving: 93 cal. (2.9 percent from fat); 2.5 g protein; 0.3 g fat (0 g sat.); 21 g carbo.; 150 mg sodium; 0.1 mg chol.

FOR A ROMANTIC TOUCH, *pull dollops of yogurt into hearts with a knife tip.*

Pork and Sauerkraut Stew

Ann Bartos Rushton, Denver

1 pound boned pork shoulder or butt, fat trimmed, and cut into 1-inch chunks

1 can (1 lb.) sauerkraut, drained

¼ cup tomato paste

2 tablespoons sugar

3 tablespoons paprika

1 pound carrots, peeled and cut diagonally ⅓ inch thick

1 package (10½ oz. or about 2 cups) dried spaetzle or fettuccine

Chopped parsley

In a 5- to 6-quart pan over medium-high heat, cook pork and ¼ cup water, covered, for 10 minutes. Uncover; boil on high heat until liquid evaporates and drippings are well browned; stir often. Add 3 cups water, sauerkraut, tomato paste, sugar, and paprika. Simmer, covered, for 1 hour. Add carrots; cook until pork is tender when pierced, about 30 minutes longer.

Meanwhile, fill a 4- to 5-quart pan ⅔ full with water; bring to a boil over high heat. Add spaetzle; cook, uncovered, until tender to bite, about 10 minutes (7 minutes for fettuccine); drain. Spoon spaetzle and stew onto plates and scatter with parsley. Serves 4 to 6.

Per serving: 377 cal. (21 percent from fat); 23 g protein; 8.7 g fat (2.6 g sat.); 52 g carbo.; 349 mg sodium; 98 mg chol.

Compiled by Elaine Johnson

CARROTS AND PAPRIKA *add their sweetness to hearty pork stew.*

FOOD GUIDE

Growing up with artichokes, tackling oysters, making nonfat cheese, and a case for Semillon

By Jerry Anne Di Vecchio

Artichokes and I are both transplants to the central California coast, but they settled in many years before my family first drove over Kings Mountain and down into Half Moon Bay, the northern tip of artichokes' American domain. There to greet us were fog-draped, ocean-edged fields where neat rows of large silver-green plants covered the earth. Even to my inexperienced eye, artichokes, with their dramatically jagged leaves, looked like gigantic thistles.

Naturally, we stopped to examine this curiosity. At the tip of each plant's strong, tall main stem was the biggest of the many green, thorny thistle buds. Beneath it, growing along the main stem, were additional stems, each tipped with a fleshy bud; the farther from the top of the plant, the smaller the bud, graduating down to the tiny, but equally mature, babies or hearts. My cousin, who had seen it all, had me gaping with her gustatory dissertation about how—and especially why—to eat an artichoke. By the time she had finished, I couldn't wait to be initiated.

But in those days, finding a restaurant with artichokes on the menu was nearly impossible. Even in Castroville, the center of artichoke production—with a banner over Main Street proclaiming it to be the artichoke capital of the world—our initial hunger went unappeased. But not for long.

Once we had settled into our canyon home south of Half Moon Bay, friendly farmer neighbors made a habit of dropping gunnysacks of artichokes at the back door. Spurred by a need to vary the family's favorite recipe (and still mine—artichokes boiled whole in water with a little vinegar or sliced lemon and, usually, a handful of seasonings including bay leaf, peppercorns, fennel seed, a few allspice, basil, and thyme), I set out to find new approaches. The best source was the growers, Portuguese- or Italian-born or first-generation, and their wives. Talking about ways to cook artichokes became a great social diversion, opening doors and giving real focus to my blossoming interest in food reporting.

Recently, staff writer Christine Hale did the same kind of food exploring while down in Castroville and Watsonville. Sampling artichoke dishes (times do change), she was captivated by the compatibility of artichokes and eggs in a frittata. She was also fascinated to find that those tiny mature ar-

tichokes, well trimmed, can be eaten whole because their fuzzy centers (which become magnificent purple blossoms if allowed to flower) are insignificant enough to ignore—unlike those of their larger peers.

Back in *Sunset*'s test kitchens, she combined the best of several frittata recipes she had tasted, and used the tiny artichokes as the crowning touch. The result was this handsome dish for supper, brunch, or lunch. With salad, bread, and fruit, you also have an informal party menu.

Although artichokes are available year-round, their natural inclination is to bud slowly and sweetly during the

PETER CHRISTIANSEN

12 large eggs

About ½ cup grated parmesan cheese

2 tablespoons minced fresh or 2 teaspoons crumbled dried basil leaves

Salt and pepper

In an ovenproof frying pan (10-in. diameter or 12-in.-long oval), combine seed from artichokes with broth and cornstarch. Stir over high heat until boiling; scrape sauce into a large bowl.

Rinse frying pan, and in it combine 1 tablespoon oil, onion, and parsley. Stir often over medium-high heat until onion is limp, about 10 minutes. With a slotted spoon, transfer vegetables to bowl with sauce. To pan, add bell pepper and 2 tablespoons water; stir often over medium-high heat until pepper strips are limp, about 5 minutes. Remove peppers from pan and set aside. Pour remaining ½ tablespoon oil into pan.

To bowl with sauce, add eggs, ¼ cup cheese, and basil; beat to blend well. Pour egg mixture into frying pan. Over medium-low heat, scrape eggs from pan bottom with a wide spatula as they firm. When eggs are almost set but still very creamy on top, remove from heat. Quickly arrange artichokes, cut sides up, on eggs. Broil about 6 inches from heat until eggs are firm to touch and lightly browned, about 5 minutes. Garnish with reserved artichoke leaves and bell pepper strips. Serve hot, warm, or cool; scoop from pan and accompany with remaining cheese, salt, and pepper. Serves 6.

Per serving: 274 cal. (53 percent from fat); 18 g protein; 16 g fat (4.9 g sat.); 14 g carbo; 304 mg sodium; 430 mg chol.

Cooked baby artichokes. Select 1¼ pounds **baby artichokes** (20 about 1½ in. wide or 30 about 1 in. wide). With a knife, cut artichoke stems flush with bottoms. Break off leaves down to pale, tender ones. If desired, reserve a handful of leaves for garnish; discard remainder.

Cut off the top ⅓ of each artichoke to remove thorny tips. With a small, sharp knife, smoothly trim fibrous portions from bottoms.

In a covered 5- to 6-quart pan over high heat, bring to boiling about 3 quarts water with 1 tablespoon **mustard seed,** 1 tablespoon **coriander seed,** and 1 thinly sliced **lemon.** Add artichokes; cover and boil gently until they are very tender when pierced, 15 to 20 minutes. After 10 minutes, add reserved leaves. Pour artichokes and leaves into a colander to drain; when cool enough to touch, discard lemon and cut artichokes in ½ lengthwise. Set aside leaves; save seed.

cool of fall and winter, and then rush to produce the most buds from March through May.

BACK TO BASICS

The art of oyster opening

One chore I've always been willing to leave to a professional is oyster shucking. But one afternoon, while admiring the smooth action of Michael Watchorn of Hog Island Oyster Co., in Marshall, California, I began to quiz him about his technique. He made it sound so simple, I finally ventured to

TASTE OF THE WEST

Baby Artichoke Frittata

Cooked baby artichokes (recipe follows)

⅔ cup regular-strength chicken broth

1 tablespoon cornstarch

1½ tablespoons olive or salad oil

1 large (about ½ lb.) onion, chopped

2 tablespoons minced Italian parsley

1 medium-size (about 6 oz.) red bell pepper, stemmed, seeded, and cut into thin strips

PETER CHRISTIANSEN

PRICE of oyster knives starts at about $3 and escalates depending on materials and workmanship.

follow his advice, with the payoff of oysters on demand.

It is foolhardy to claim that oyster shucking is a snap, but with patience and a sturdy oyster knife (long or short blade, with or without guard—found in most cookware stores), and by starting at the right place, it takes surprisingly little force to pry open an oyster's shell.

The trick is to find the hinge; of the four oyster species readily available fresh—Eastern, European flats, the tiny Olympia, and Pacifics—the curvy rippling shell of Pacifics probably does the best job of concealing its hinge.

But before launching into shucking, I want to insert a fussy preference that professional shuckers usually ignore. Oysters, even if rinsed, usually have mud or grit in their crevices, so I first scrub them with a stiff brush under cool running water. At the same time, any gaping oysters that refuse to close when tapped get tossed.

Keep oysters cold at all times, partly for safety and very much to enhance flavor and texture. I have a rimmed tray filled with ice cubes ready to hold the opened oysters. Now the lesson:

1. Grasp the curved end of the **oyster** with a gloved hand (garden gloves work fine) and sit it, cupped side down, on a thick towel. Keep oyster as level as possible to save juices.

2. With the tip of an oyster knife, trace around the hinged (most pointed) end of the oyster to locate its hinge; you may have to do a little scraping and prying.

3. Move knife just a hair to one side of the hinge; push knife tip firmly between top and bottom shell, then twist. An almost silent pop, then a little seeping moisture means success. The lid of the shell is still firmly attached.

4. Through the gap, slide a long-bladed knife into the oyster along the underside of the top shell (to avoid damaging the oyster) until you hit the adductor muscle (there's one on each side of the oyster so it can open and close its shell). Push the blade down and under the adductor to cut the oyster free. Lift off the top shell.

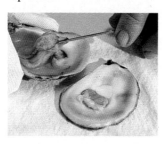

5. Holding bottom shell steady, slide knife under oyster to cut it free from bottom adductor muscle. Eat oyster, or cradle it in its shell on ice.

For some, plain oysters are the ultimate; others like to add a squeeze of lemon, a nugget of horseradish, or a drizzle of mignonette sauce. I relish this smooth version based on rice wine: For 2 to 3 dozen oysters, mix ½ cup **rice vinegar** with 2 tablespoons **fish sauce** (*nuoc mam* or *nam pla*), 1 tablespoon minced **shallots** or onion, 1 teaspoon minced **fresh ginger,** and ½ teaspoon *each* **freshly ground black pepper** and **sugar.** Makes about ⅔ cup.

Per tablespoon: 11 cal. (25 percent from fat); 0.5 g protein; 0.3 g fat (0.1 g sat.); 1.5 g carbo; 2.2 mg sodium; 0 mg chol.

GREAT INGREDIENT
Yogurt cheese

In Middle Eastern markets, you often find a cool, tangy, fresh white cheese that spreads like soft cream cheese. I first came across it by its Lebanese name, *lebnah* or *lebni.* The shopkeeper said it was just yogurt, drained in a cloth for several days. Since then, in *Sunset* recipes we've drained nonfat yogurt many times to make refreshing, lean options for rich mascarpone, cream cheese, whipped cream, and mayonnaise.

However, not all yogurts behave the same. Those that contain gelatin drain very little and won't work for making this simple cheese.

Draining yogurt emphasizes its character, so pick a brand you like. Whole-milk yogurts taste richest; mild-flavored yogurts taste smoothest; tangy yogurts taste tart. Tart nonfat yogurts make the tangiest cheese.

I keep nonfat yogurt cheese on hand for many uses, including a snack that tastes especially good after a workout. I spread the cheese thickly on *vollkornbrot* (a dense dark bread), sprinkle it lightly with kosher salt and generously with crushed dried hot red chilies. Several tall glasses of cool water are the perfect companion as I refresh and rehydrate.

I've also made excellent cheesecake using nonfat yogurt, drained for about 4 days, in place of cream cheese.

Yogurt cheese. Line a colander or a fine strainer with 2 layers of **cheesecloth** or 1 layer of muslin. Spoon **yogurt** (made without gelatin) into cloth, and then fold cloth over it.

Set colander in a pan or bowl; the bottom of the yogurt should be suspended at least 1 inch above pan bottom. Enclose colander and pan with plastic wrap, making it reasonably airtight. Chill; pour off whey as it accumulates so yogurt can drain freely. After about 4 days, the yogurt stops draining and is at maximum thickness.

Yields vary with the brand, but after 24 hours, 1 quart nonfat or low-fat yogurt usually makes 1½ to 2 cups cheese, and regular (whole milk) yogurt makes 1½ to 2¼ cups. Scoop cheese from cloth; use or chill in an airtight container up to 10 days, or as long as the flavor is fresh and there is no sign of spoilage.

Per tablespoon unflavored nonfat yogurt cheese: 10 cal. (0 percent from fat); 1.1 g protein; 0 g fat; 1.1 g carbo; 10 mg sodium; 0 mg chol.

Per tablespoon unflavored low-fat yogurt cheese: 12 cal. (30 percent from fat); 1.4 g protein; 0.4 g fat (0 g sat.); 0.6 g carbo; 9 mg sodium; 0.7 mg chol.

Per tablespoon unflavored regular yogurt cheese: 21 cal. (64 percent from fat); 1.4 g protein; 1.5 g fat (0.1 g sat.); 0.6 g carbo; 6.5 mg sodium; 6 mg chol.

NEAT TRICK
Scraping the surface

An old-fashioned technique that Linda Tebben, one of our recipe retesters, uses when grating foods like lemon peel and chocolate works very well and is so simple. She presses a layer of cooking parchment or the nonstick cooking paper that Reynolds makes for use in the microwave oven onto the grater surface, pushing enough for grates to poke through paper. She grates foods, then lifts off the paper; the grater is unclogged, and

foods that are usually stuck come off with the paper, ready to use.

NEWS NOTE

Changes in Hawaiian food

A t the Ritz-Carlton Big Island Bounty conference on Hawaii last August, I went exploring with chef Sam Choy. As a born and bred Islander (with Hawaiian ancestry on his mother's side), he vividly recalls the cold shoulder that local ingredients once got from *haut* restaurants. Native flavors didn't get a second glance.

No longer. He was literally bursting with pride as we raced from one producer to the next, including a sea vegetable farm and several fish farms. Menus now make much ado about local cheese, lamb, fruit, vegetables, and, of course, fish—just as they once did about foods flown or shipped in from around the world.

Folks line up for a seat at Sam Choy's Restaurant, hidden away in an industrial park at Bay 1, 73-5576 Kauhola Street, in Kailua-Kona; (808) 326-1545. The 20 or so plastic-topped tables (with

seats for 60) are bare for lunch; white cloths dress up the simple room for dinner.

Dishes are a hearty blend of the Pacific Rim sophistications of the moment and foods and techniques Choy remembers from childhood. Laulau-style fish, steamed in ti leaves, is a fine crossbreed. You can use ti leaves from a florist or fold cooking parchment or foil around the fish.

Sam's seafood laulaus. To make 2 servings, put 1 piece (8 to 10 oz.) boned and skinned **swordfish,** mahi mahi, tuna, or halibut in a small bowl. Mix 1 teaspoon minced **fresh ginger,** 1 tablespoon **soy sauce,** and 1 teaspoon **salad oil** with fish. Cover and chill 15 minutes to 2 hours.

Rinse 2 fresh **ti leaves,** cut off stems, and lay leaves flat, crossing in the middle. Lift fish from marinade and set on the cross.

Pour marinade through a fine strainer into an 8- to 10-inch frying pan. Put any ginger in strainer on fish along with 1 tablespoon minced **fresh cilantro.**

To pan, add 1 teaspoon **butter,** about ½ cup small (1 to 1½ in. wide, about ¼ lb.) rinsed **fresh shiitake mushroom caps** (discard stems), and 3 tablespoons **water.** Cook over high heat, stirring often, until liquid evaporates and caps start to brown, about 5 minutes. Stir 3 tablespoons water into pan to release browned bits; when water has almost evaporated, remove

pan from heat.

Arrange mushrooms and juices scraped from pan on fish. Fold the stem end of the top leaf over fish, then fold the tip over fish. Fold the stem end of the remaining leaf over fish, then fold the tip of the leaf over the packet; tie with string.

Steam packet on a rack over 1 to 2 inches boiling water in a covered 4- to 5-quart pan or wok until fish is opaque but still moist-looking in center (reach through crack in leaves and cut to test), 12 to 15 minutes. Fold back leaves and garnish with **cilantro sprigs.**

Per serving: 169 cal. (44 percent from fat); 21 g protein; 8.3 g fat (2.6 g sat.); 1.7 g carbo; 626 mg sodium; 45 mg chol. ■

SAM'S SEAFOOD *laulaus are steamed in fresh ti leaves.*

PETER CHRISTIANSEN

BOB THOMPSON ON WINE

Semillons

C hardonnay's 60,000-acre to 2,500-acre advantage over Semillon in Western vineyards tells the truth about America's wine market but hides the fact that Semillon provides a particularly graceful bridge between lush, rich Chardonnay and lean, crisp Sauvignon Blanc.

Elusive flavors are part of the charm. Even people who dote on Semillon have a hard time pinning down how it tastes. When the wine brings fruit to mind, many say it reminds them of fresh figs. Se-

millons that reveal the grape variety's close botanical kinship to Sauvignon Blanc are often described as haylike rather than herbaceous. Researchers into flavor associations have been driven to describe the wine as having an aroma reminiscent of sun-dried bed sheets as they are being ironed, which sounds crazy but is so fresh and clean a smell that it is not altogether wrong. Your own thoughts are likely to call up other taste memories.

The elusive flavors and silky textures of Semillon make it one of the most versatile of white wines. It rivals Chablis and Champagne as

company for oysters on the half-shell, yet can be equally at home with chicken or veal in a creamy sauce.

Washington state tends to grow the leaner, taste-of-hay examples. Warmer parts of Napa, Sonoma, and Livermore in California deliver richer, figgier wines.

The following well-made, true-to-type examples are all in the $6 to $10 range.

From California: Alderbrook Dry Creek Valley Semillon (pure flavors, richer feeling than most); Benziger Sonoma Mountain Estate Semillon (lightly spiced by oak-aging, rich in texture); Clos du Val Napa Valley

Stags Leap District (clearly marked by oak-aging, firmly textured).

From Washington: Chateau Ste. Michelle Columbia Valley Semillon (clear, fresh, obvious choice with oysters); Columbia Winery Columbia Valley Semillon (clear, fresh); Columbia Winery Columbia Valley Chevrier (the alternative grape name signals a barrel-fermented, oak-aged wine rich enough for creamy sauces); Columbia Crest Columbia Valley Semillon (another crisp candidate for oysters); The Hogue Cellars (clear taste of Semillon, among the richer Washingtonians).

Mexican goes

By Linda Lau Anusasananan

Mexican foods and flavors are so entrenched in what we cook and eat in the West that, intentionally or otherwise, many of our most popular dishes and cooking methods reflect varying degrees of this ethnic heritage. Some of these foods are also surprisingly in step with the times. Salsa, the great low-fat dip and sauce of the '90s, now outsells catsup. Beans, low in fat and rich in nutrients, have surged to newfound popularity as *the* health food of the decade. Cultists promote chilies as the leanest, meanest seasoning of the day.

Yet other favorites—like nachos, enchiladas, chiles rellenos, and fried tortilla chips—are high in fat. In *Sunset*'s new 128-page *Low-Fat Mexican Cook Book* (by the editors of Sunset Books and *Sunset Magazine,* 1994; $9.99), leaner ingredients and fat-trimming techniques render these foods—and others with south-of-the-border spirit—lighter without sacrificing flavor. Here is a seven-recipe sampler from the book, plus these bonuses: authentic-tasting but low-fat tamales and two charts loaded with helpful hints. One describes fat-slashing cooking techniques; the second gives light alternatives to rich ingredients for Mexican foods—and others, too.

Low-fat Chicken Tamales

Traditional masa dough for tamales has an awesome amount of lard. This version has none, yet the masa is tender.

Cornhusks are usually available in supermarkets.

> About 30 large dried cornhusks (about 3 oz. total), at least 8 inches long
>
> Masa dough (recipe follows)

Filling (recipe follows)

Green salsa (recipe follows)

1. Separate husks under running water, discarding silks and other extraneous materials. Large, long husks work best for tamales; smaller or split husks can be spliced or used for ties. Soak husks in warm water until pliable, about 15 minutes. To use, lift out 1 husk at a time and blot dry.

2. For each tamale, you need a husk that makes a rectangle at least 8 by 10 inches. (A large husk may be sufficient, or you can glue narrower husks together with masa dough. To do this, spread husks open and lay side by side, with tips going in opposite directions. Spread a little masa on long edge of 1 husk. Lay another husk onto masa, overlapping edge about ½ in.) Scoop ⅓ cup masa onto husk close to 1 long edge. Evenly spread masa flush to 1 long edge of

PETER CHRISTIANSEN

husk, making a rectangle that is 4½ inches long at husk edge, and 6 inches wide.

3. Mound ⅓ cup filling onto masa-coated husk. Lift husk edge with masa over filling and butt it against opposite masa edge. Wrap plain husk around tamale. Set tamale seam side down; securely tie ends with thin husk strips. Repeat to make remaining tamales.

4. In an 8- to 10-quart pan, position a rack at least 1 inch above 1 inch of water; bring water to boiling on high heat. Stack tamales on rack so air can circulate. Cover pan and adjust heat to keep water gently boiling; occasionally add more boiling water to maintain 1-inch depth. Steam tamales until masa is firm and peels easily from husk, 40 to 50 minutes; to test masa, remove 1 tamale from pan and gently open. If it is undercooked, retie, return to steamer, and continue to cook. Let tamales stand at least 10 minutes (masa firms as it rests); serve

SPREAD MASA dough onto damp cornhusk to make a rectangle.

LIFT HUSK over filling and butt opposite edges of masa. Roll husk around tamale.

TIE ENDS of tamale securely shut with thin strips of husk.

light

Favorite dishes made with lean ingredients and low-fat techniques retain their earthy, authentic vitality

• Low-fat Chicken Tamales •*Made without lard, they have 212 calories each (just 17 percent from fat).*

Mexican goes light

• Black Bean and Fresh Corn Nachos • *Scoop onto tortilla chips that have been oven-crisped, not fried.*

hot. If making ahead, let cool and chill airtight up to 1 day. Freeze tamales to store up to 6 weeks. To reheat tamales (chilled or frozen), steam as directed, preceding, until hot in centers, 15 to 20 minutes. Serve with salsa. Makes 14.

Per tamale: 212 cal. (17 percent from fat); 13 g protein; 4 g fat (0.8 g sat.); 32 g carbo.; 200 mg sodium; 27 mg chol.

Masa dough. Mix 4 cups **masa harina** (dehydrated masa flour), 1¼ teaspoons **baking powder,** ½ teaspoon **salt,** and 3¾ cups warm **water** or regular-strength chicken broth until moistened. Use, or cover airtight and chill up to 2 hours. Makes about 4⅔ cups.

Filling. Place 1½ ounces (about 4 large) **dried ancho** or pasilla **chilies** in a 10- by 15-inch pan. Bake in a 300° oven until fragrant, 3 to 5 minutes; let cool. Discard stems, seeds, and veins. Place chilies in a bowl, cover with boiling water, and let stand until pliable, about 30 minutes.

In a 10- to 12-inch frying pan, combine 2 large (about 1 lb. total) **onions,** chopped; 2 cloves **garlic,** pressed or minced; 1 teaspoon **ground cumin;** 1 teaspoon **dried oregano leaves;** ⅛ teaspoon **ground allspice;** and ¼ cup **regular-strength chicken broth.** Stir occasionally over high heat until onions start to brown, about 6 minutes. Add another ¼ cup broth; stir until liquid boils away and brown film forms in pan. Repeat, adding broth and cooking pan dry until mixture is well browned, about 4 times total.

Drain chilies, discarding liquid. In a blender or food processor, smoothly purée chilies, 1 can (about 14½ oz.) **tomatoes** and their liquid, and 2 teaspoons **sugar.** Add chili mixture to onion mixture; simmer, uncovered, until slightly thickened, about 10 minutes. Mix sauce with 3 cups **shredded cooked chicken** and **salt** to taste. Makes 4⅔ cups.

Green salsa. Husk ¾ pound **tomatillos;** rinse and core. Rinse and stem 2 or 3 **fresh serrano chilies.** In a 10- to 12-inch frying pan, combine tomatillos and chilies. Shake pan often over high heat until vegetables are charred all over, about 8 minutes for chilies, 10 to 15 minutes for tomatillos; remove from pan as charred. Let cool slightly. In a blender or food processor, purée ½ the tomatillos, all the chilies, ½ cup lightly packed chopped **fresh cilantro** (coriander), and 3 cloves **garlic.** Chop the remaining ½ of tomatillos; stir into purée along with ¼ cup chopped **onion** and **salt** to taste. Makes about 1½ cups.

Black Bean and Fresh Corn Nachos

About 1½ cups lime salsa (recipe follows)

Refried black beans (recipe follows)

4 cups cooked yellow or white corn kernels (about 4 large ears); or 2 packages (about 10 oz. each) frozen corn kernels, thawed

1 cup (about 4 oz.) shredded jalapeño-flavor jack cheese

About 12 cups water-crisped corn tortilla chips (recipe follows); or purchased tortilla chips

Fresh cilantro (coriander) leaves

• Fat slashers •

Some of the most beloved Mexican dishes rely on fat-loaded cooking techniques. Yet many other favorites are based on totally lean cooking methods—baking, barbecuing, griddle-roasting, and steaming.

In the recipes in this story, frying and deep-frying have been replaced by leaner, neater methods. Consider these alternative ways to lighten up your own recipes.

Bake instead of deep-frying, as directed for empanadas, page 47.

Barbecue or grill-cook instead of pan-frying pieces of meat, fish, or poultry.

Braise-deglaze chopped vegetables that are usually cooked in fat as the foundation of many dishes, such as fillings for tamales, above center, and empanadas, page 47. Braising-deglazing develops a rich brown color and sweet, intense vegetable flavors.

Broil instead of pan-frying to brown meats, fish, and poultry. Broil to char and cook chilies for roasted chilies with eggs, page 48, and other vegetables; this is an alternative to griddle-roasting, following.

Broth-soften instead of frying. Briefly dip corn tortillas for enchiladas into hot broth to make them limp and flexible. Use broth instead of fat to give a creamy texture to refried bean alternatives, as for black bean and fresh corn nachos, at right.

Griddle-roasting or toasting is a standard Mexican cooking method that intensifies flavors in foods (by dehydrating them). Tortillas are dry-toasted on a griddle.

Fresh ingredients with a fair amount of moisture (such as tomatillos, tomatoes, and fresh chilies) are placed on a griddle over high heat and turned often until surfaces are charred; the green salsa, above right, for tamales starts this way. If food is large and dense (such as ears of corn), reduce heat to medium.

Steaming is integral to making tamales, page 42. It is also a very lean cooking method to use for preparing vegetables, fish, and poultry.

Water-crisp instead of frying to make crisp tortilla chips on page 46.

• Oven-baked Turkey Fajitas • *Lean breast replaces classic choice of fat-streaked beef skirt steak.*

Mexican goes light

• Picadillo-stuffed Empanadas • *Lean wrapper is more like biscuit dough than typical rich pastry.*

1. After making salsa, cover and chill.

2. Spread refried black beans evenly in a large, ovenproof rimmed platter, leaving rim exposed. Sprinkle beans with corn, then cheese. Bake in a 400° oven until hot in center, about 10 minutes.

3. Remove platter from oven. Tuck some chips around edge of beans; garnish with cilantro. Serve remaining chips alongside.

4. Spoon bean mixture onto plates; top with a little salsa. Scoop bean mixture onto chips, adding more salsa to taste. Makes 8 main-dish or 12 appetizer servings.

Per main-dish serving: 423 cal. (24 percent from fat); 18 g protein; 12 g fat (4 g sat.); 67 g carbo.; 668 mg sodium; 22 mg chol.

Lime Salsa

1 large (about 8 oz.) ripe red or yellow tomato, finely diced

8 medium-size (about 8 oz. total) tomatillos, husked, rinsed, and chopped

¼ cup minced red or yellow bell pepper

2 tablespoons minced red onion

1 teaspoon grated lime peel

1 tablespoon lime juice

Mix tomato, tomatillos, pepper, onion, peel, and juice. If making ahead, cover and chill up to 4 hours. Makes about 4 cups.

Per ¼ cup: 7 cal. (9 percent from fat); 0.3 g protein; 0.1 g fat (0 g sat.); 1 g carbo.; 2 mg sodium; 0 mg chol.

Refried Black Beans

4 ounces bacon, coarsely chopped

2 medium-size onions, chopped

2 cloves garlic, minced or pressed

2 cans (about 15 oz. each) black beans; or 4 cups cooked (about 2 cups dried) black beans

About 2 tablespoons distilled white vinegar

Pepper

1. In a wide nonstick frying pan over medium heat, stir bacon often until it begins to brown, about 4 minutes. Discard all but 1 tablespoon of the drippings.

2. Add onions and garlic to pan; stir often until onions are limp and bacon is browned, about 7 minutes.

3. Drain canned beans, reserving ½ cup liquid.

4. To pan, add beans, reserved liquid (with home-cooked beans, use ½ cup low-sodium regular-strength chicken broth), and 2 tablespoons vinegar. With the back of a spoon, coarsely mash beans; season to taste with more vinegar and pepper. If making ahead, cover and chill up to 1 day. Heat, stirring often, until steaming. Makes about 3¼ cups.

Per ½ cup: 199 cal. (22 percent from fat); 11 g protein; 4.8 g fat (1.7 g sat.); 30 g carbo.; 641 mg sodium; 6 mg chol.

Water-crisped Tortilla Chips

6 corn tortillas (6-in. diameter) or flour tortillas (7- to 9-in. diameter)

Salt (optional)

1. Dip each tortilla into hot water, drain, sprinkle with salt, and stack. Cut stack into

---

• Highs and lows: ingredient options •

To modify recipes, here's what you need to know about calories and fat content.

Tortillas
High: 6-inch regular **flour tortillas** (65 cal., 20 percent from fat).
Medium: 6-inch **reduced-fat flour tortillas** (approx. 70 cal., 13 percent from fat).
Low: 6-inch **corn tortillas** (56 cal., 10 percent from fat).

Tortilla chips
High: 1 cup **corn tortilla chips** (142 cal., 47 percent from fat).
Medium: 1 cup **reduced-fat corn tortilla chips** (100 cal., 11 percent from fat).
Low (recipes opposite): 1 cup **water-crisped corn tortilla chips** (83 cal., 10 percent from fat); 1 cup **water-crisped flour tortilla chips** (85 cal., 20 percent from fat).

Sour cream
High: 1 tablespoon **sour cream** (31 cal., 88 percent from fat).
Medium: 1 tablespoon **reduced-fat sour cream** (25 cal., 72 percent from fat).
Low: **unflavored nonfat yogurt** (7.9 cal., 0 percent from fat).

Guacamole
High: 1 tablespoon **avocado** mashed with **lime juice** and **chilies** to taste (approx. 16 cal., 79 percent from fat).
Low: 1 tablespoon of the preceding **avocado mixture** mixed with equal portions *each* **nonfat cottage cheese** and diced **tomatoes** (approx. 9.9 cal., 43 percent from fat).

Refried beans
High: ½ cup **traditional refried beans** (approx. 135 cal., 9 percent from fat).
Low: ½ cup **canned nonfat refried beans** (80 cal., 0 percent from fat).

Cheese
High: 1 ounce (about ¼ cup shredded) **jack** or cheddar **cheese** (approx. 110 cal., 73 percent from fat).
Medium: 1 ounce (about ¼ cup shredded) **reduced-fat jack** or cheddar **cheese** (approx. 90 cal., 50 percent from fat).
Low: 1 ounce (about ¼ cup shredded) **nonfat jack** or cheddar **cheese** (approx. 40 cal., 0 percent from fat).

• Roasted Chilies with Eggs • *There's no frying for these chiles rellenos.*

6 to 8 wedges.

2. Lay tortilla pieces in a single layer on large baking sheets. Bake in a 500° oven for 4 minutes. Turn wedges over with a metal spatula; bake until pieces are browned and crisp, about 2 minutes longer. If making ahead, cool; store airtight at room temperature up to 5 days. Makes about 4 cups corn chips, about 6 cups flour chips.

Per 1 cup corn chips: 83 cal. (10 percent from fat); 2 g protein; 1 g fat (0.1 g sat.); 18 g carbo.; 60 mg sodium; 0 mg chol.

Per 1 cup flour chips: 85 cal. (20 percent from fat); 2 g protein; 2 g fat (0.3 g sat.); 15 g carbo.; 126 mg sodium; 0 mg chol.

Picadillo-stuffed Empanadas

    Empanada pastry (recipe follows)

2 tablespoons slivered almonds

1 teaspoon salad oil

1 large (about ½ lb.) onion, finely chopped

2 cloves garlic, minced or pressed

6 ounces ground turkey or chicken breast

1 can (about 8 oz.) tomato sauce

½ teaspoon ground cinnamon

⅛ teaspoon ground cloves

2 tablespoons raisins

2 teaspoons cider vinegar

    Salt

  1. Set aside prepared pastry.

  2. Toast almonds in a small frying pan over

medium heat until golden, 5 to 7 minutes; stir often. Pour from pan and chop.

  3. In a wide nonstick frying pan over medium heat, stir oil, onion, garlic, and 1 tablespoon water until mixture is deep golden, about 20 minutes; when onion sticks, add water, 1 tablespoon at a time, and stir free. Crumble turkey into pan; stir often over medium-high heat until well browned, about 10 minutes. As pan cooks dry, add more water, 1 tablespoon at a time.

  4. Stir in tomato sauce,

Mexican goes light

cinnamon, cloves, and raisins. Bring mixture to a boil; simmer, uncovered, until most of the liquid is evaporated, about 10 minutes. Remove from heat; stir in almonds, vinegar, and salt to taste.

5. On a floured board, roll pastry ⅛ inch thick. Cut into 3½-inch rounds. Spoon filling equally onto ½ of each round. Moisten pastry edge with water; fold plain pastry over filling and press rims with a fork to seal.

6. Arrange empanadas on a lightly oiled 12- by 15-inch baking sheet. Bake in a 400° oven until lightly browned, about 20 minutes. Makes about 16.

Per empanada: 96 cal. (26 percent from fat); 5 g protein; 3 g fat (1 g sat.); 13 g carbo.; 192 mg sodium; 11 mg chol.

Empanada pastry. In a food processor or a bowl, combine 1 cup **all-purpose flour,** ½ cup **yellow cornmeal,** 1½ teaspoons **baking powder,** ¼ teaspoon **salt,** and 2 tablespoons **butter** or margarine. Whirl or rub with your fingers until mixture resembles coarse crumbs. Add ⅓ cup **milk,** 1 **large egg white,** and ½ teaspoon **cumin seed.** Whirl or stir with a fork until dough holds together; add 1 more tablespoon milk, if needed. With lightly floured hands, pat dough into a ball. Use, or wrap airtight and chill up to 1 hour.

Oven-baked Turkey Fajitas

Lime-vinegar marinade (recipe follows)

1 pound turkey breast tenderloins, rinsed

1 large (about 8 oz.) green bell pepper

1 large red onion

About 1 tablespoon salad oil

4 warm flour tortillas

Lime wedges

1. Pour marinade into a 1-gallon zip-lock plastic freezer bag or large bowl. Add turkey, mix well, and seal bag or cover bowl. Chill at least 20 minutes or up to 1 day; mix often.

2. Stem, seed, and thinly slice bell pepper; thinly slice onion. Combine vegetables in a lightly oiled 10- by 15-inch rimmed pan. Bake in a 400° oven for 10 minutes. Push vegetables to 1 side of pan; lift turkey from marinade and lay in pan; save marinade. Spread vegetables around meat.

3. Frequently baste meat and vegetables with marinade; bake until turkey is no longer pink in thickest part (cut to test), about 20 minutes. Turn vegetables often.

4. Thinly slice turkey and divide equally with vegetables among tor-

tillas. Roll to enclose; eat out of hand, adding lime. Serves 4.

Per serving: 310 cal. (20 percent from fat); 32 g protein; 7 g fat (1 g sat.); 29 g carbo.; 231 mg sodium; 70 mg chol.

Lime-vinegar marinade. Mix together ¼ cup **lime juice,** 1 tablespoon **balsamic** or red wine **vinegar,** 1 clove **garlic** (minced or pressed), ½ teaspoon **honey,** and ¼ teaspoon each **ground coriander** and **ground cumin.**

Roasted Chilies with Eggs

Roasted chilies (directions follow)

1 cup lime salsa (see page 46)

2 large eggs

4 large egg whites

½ cup *each* nonfat cottage cheese and finely chopped spinach leaves

About ⅓ cup thinly sliced green onion

2 teaspoons cornstarch blended with 1 tablespoon cold water

1½ teaspoons fresh or ¼ teaspoon dried thyme leaves

⅛ teaspoon *each* salt and white pepper

1 teaspoon salad oil

Sliced fresh hot red chilies

Thyme sprigs

About ¾ cup unflavored nonfat yogurt

1. After roasting chilies, set aside. After making salsa, cover and chill.

2. In a food processor, smoothly purée eggs, egg whites, cottage cheese, spinach, 1 tablespoon onion, cornstarch mixture, thyme, salt, and pepper.

3. Heat oil in a medium-size nonstick frying pan over medium heat. Add egg mixture to pan; stir often until softly scrambled, 3 to 5 minutes.

4. Spoon mixture equally into chilies. Set on a platter; garnish with red chilies and thyme sprigs. To taste, add yogurt, remaining onion, and salsa. Serves 4.

Per serving: 138 cal. (26 percent from fat); 14 g protein; 4 g fat (1 g sat.); 11 g carbo.; 298 mg sodium; 110 mg chol.

Roasted chilies. Place 4 **fresh green poblano** or Anaheim **chilies** (or other large mild chilies) on a 12- by 15-inch baking sheet. Broil 4 to 6 inches from heat, turning as charred, 5 to 8 minutes. Cover with foil and let cool. Pull off and discard skins. Slit 1 side of each chili almost, but not all the way, to stem end and tip; do not puncture chili elsewhere. Discard seeds and veins. ■

Upgrading gingerbread

J UST A TRIFLE DRESSIER THAN old-fashioned gingerbread, this tender cake is aromatic with fresh ginger. Molasses, which typically sweetens gingerbread, is replaced by sugar, making a lighter-color cake.

Fresh Ginger Cake

¾ cup granulated sugar

¾ cup buttermilk

½ cup salad oil

1 large egg

1 tablespoon grated fresh ginger

1½ cups all-purpose flour

¾ teaspoon *each* baking soda and baking powder

½ teaspoon ground cinnamon

¼ teaspoon ground cloves

Powdered sugar

In a bowl, mix granulated sugar, buttermilk, oil, egg, and ginger. Add flour, soda, baking powder, cinnamon, and cloves; beat to blend well. Pour into an oiled 8-cup tube pan or 9-inch-square pan.

Bake in a 350° oven until cake begins to pull from pan sides, 35 to 40 minutes. Cool 10 minutes; invert onto a plate. Serve warm or cool; when cool, store airtight up to 2 days. Dust with powdered sugar. Serves 8 or 9.

Per serving: 265 cal. (44 percent from fat); 3.5 g protein; 13 g fat (1.8 g sat.); 34 g carbo.; 133 mg sodium; 24 mg chol. ■

By Christine Weber Hale

NORMAN A. PLATE

FRESH GINGER *flavors moist cake.*

CUT TIMBALE *of pasta and eggplant into wedges; serve with marinara sauce.*

Pretty pasta pie

Layers of eggplant keep it organized

SICILIANS PUSH PASTA into shape to make timbales, which are, in effect, merely pies. We encountered this handsome version by Nunzio Alioto at his San Francisco restaurant, Alioto's, in a special series of Sicilian dinners. He served small wedges of the timbale as a first course. But because the pie's flavors are so satisfying—and it can be made ahead—it's a grand main dish, too.

Sicilian Pasta Timbale

2 small (about 1 lb. each) eggplants

About 2 teaspoons salt

4 to 6 tablespoons olive oil

1 pound salad macaroni

3 cups marinara sauce, homemade (recipe follows) or purchased

2 cups (½ lb.) shredded provolone cheese

½ cup grated romano cheese

2 tablespoons fine dry bread crumbs

Fresh basil sprigs (optional)

Trim stems from eggplants, then cut eggplants lengthwise into ¼-inch-thick slices; sprinkle with salt. Let stand 15 minutes. Rinse; pat dry. Coat 2 or 3 pans, each 10 by 15 inches, with 2 tablespoons oil each. Turn slices in oil; arrange in a single layer. Bake in a 425° oven until eggplant is browned and soft when pressed, 15 to 25 minutes; remove as browned.

Meanwhile, bring about 3 quarts water to a boil in a 5- to 6-quart pan. Add macaroni and cook just until barely tender to bite, 5 to 6 minutes. Drain. Mix macaroni with 2 cups marinara sauce, provolone cheese, and 6 tablespoons romano cheese.

Butter sides and bottom of a 9-inch cheesecake pan with removable rim. Dust pan with bread crumbs. Arrange ⅓ of the eggplant slices, overlapping to cover bottom of pan. Cover with ½ of the macaroni mixture. Repeat layers; arrange eggplant to cover top layer. Press down gently to compact layers and make timbale level. Sprinkle with remaining romano cheese. (If

making ahead, cover and chill up to 1 day.)

Bake, uncovered, in a 350° oven until hot in center, about 30 minutes (bake chilled timbale for 30 minutes, then uncover and continue baking until hot in center, about 30 minutes longer). Let stand 5 minutes. In a 1- to 1½-quart pan, stir remaining sauce over medium heat until hot. With a knife, cut around timbale to release; remove pan rim. Garnish timbale with basil. Cut into wedges. Spoon sauce over each piece. Serves 8.

Per serving: 494 cal.; (36 percent from fat), 19 g protein; 20 g fat (6.4 g sat.); 61 g carbo.; 861 mg sodium; 25 g chol.

Marinara sauce. In a 3- to 4-quart pan over medium heat, stir 3 cloves **garlic,** pressed or minced, in 2 tablespoons **olive oil** until garlic is translucent, about 1 minute. Add 1 large can (28 oz.) **tomato purée** and ¼ cup chopped **fresh basil leaves** or 2 tablespoons dried basil leaves. Simmer, uncovered, until reduced to 3 cups, about 20 minutes. Add **salt** to taste. If making ahead, cover and chill up to 1 day. ∎

By Linda Lau Anusasananan

Patrick does St. Patrick's

Follow his plans for a hearty meal to serve 12, 25, or 50 revelers

MIDNIGHT, MARCH 16: *Patrick McEvoy comes home with groceries from the 24-hour supermarket after a planning powwow at the pub.*

CORNED BEEF FEAST *comes with all the trimmings: Irish soda*

8:15 P.M.: PARTYGOER *toasts the meal with a Black and Tan (Irish stout plus lager).*

G ROWING UP WITH A name like Patrick Joseph Peter McEvoy in an Irish American neighborhood in New York, my husband got lots of attention on St. Patrick's Day. And being fond of attention, it was natural that he would host an annual St. Patrick's Day bash when he moved to California. After 10 years, the party has become a bit of a legend among our friends, but not just because it's a great time.

For one thing, everyone agrees that Patrick's corned beef and cabbage is the most delicious they've ever had (is it the not-so-secret Guinness that goes in the pot?). Then there's the scale of the party—50 people is a small crowd, 100 average—and our tiny house is always in chaos.

What's amazing is that Patrick pulls off this feast with no apparent plan and seem-

bread, colcannon (mashed potatoes with butter-steamed cabbage), and vegetables.

ONCE MORE, IN UNISON. *Arm power—or a heavy-duty mixer— mashes spuds for the colcannon.*

PETER CHRISTIANSEN

Patrick's Corned Beef and Cabbage

Ingredients	For 12	For 25	For 50
Onions	1¾ lb.	3½ lb.	7 lb.
Carrots	2½ lb.	5 lb.	10 lb.
Corned beef brisket or round, spiced or unspiced	6 lb.	12 lb.	24 lb.
Malt vinegar	1 c.	2 c.	4 c.
Irish stout	6 oz.	12 oz.	24 oz.
Mustard seed	1 tbsp.	2 tbsp.	4 tbsp.
Coriander seed	1 tbsp.	2 tbsp.	4 tbsp.
Black peppercorns	½ tbsp.	1 tbsp.	2 tbsp.
Dill seed	½ tbsp.	1 tbsp.	2 tbsp.
Whole allspice	½ tbsp.	1 tbsp.	2 tbsp.
Dried bay leaves	2	4	8
Cabbage, rinsed	3 lb.	6 lb.	12 lb.
Small (2 in.) thin-skinned potatoes	2½ lb.	5 lb.	10 lb.
Coarse-grain mustard	⅓ c.	⅔ c.	1⅓ c.
Dijon mustard	⅓ c.	⅔ c.	1⅓ c.

To serve 12, use a 14- to 20-quart pan; for 25, 2 pans (14 to 20 quarts each); for 50, 2 pans (about 35 quarts each).

Coarsely chop enough onions and carrots to make 1 cup *each* (for 12), 2 cups *each* (for 25), or 4 cups *each* (for 50). In one pan or two, as required (dividing equally between two pans), place chopped onions and carrots, corned beef with any liquid (if needed, cut meat to fit pan), vinegar, stout, mustard seed, coriander, peppercorns, dill, allspice, and bay leaves. Add water to barely cover beef. Cover pan and bring to a boil over high heat (20 to 25 minutes). Simmer until meat is tender when pierced, 2½ to 3 hours.

Meanwhile, cut remaining onions into wedges. Cut remaining carrots into 2-inch lengths; halve them lengthwise if large. Cut cabbages in half through cores, then into wedges to make 1 piece per person. Scrub potatoes.

Add onions, carrots, and potatoes to tender corned beef; place cabbage on top. Cover and return to simmering over high heat (8 to 20 minutes); reduce heat and simmer until cabbage is tender when pierced, 15 to 20 minutes.

With a slotted spoon scoop out vegetables onto warm serving dishes. Using tongs and a slotted spoon, remove beef to a cutting board; cut off and discard fat, slice meat across the grain, and place on warm platters. If cooking for 25 or 50, cover vegetables and meat tightly with foil for up to 45 minutes while completing colcannon (keep foil-covered vegetables and meat warm in a 150° oven, or wrap with towels to insulate and keep warm on a counter). Serve vegetables and meat with coarse-grain and Dijon mustards.

Per serving: 599 cal. (48 percent from fat); 35 g protein; 32 g fat (10 g sat.); 43 g carbo.; 2,143 mg sodium; 157 mg chol.

ingly little effort. With our friend Joan and me helping, the preparation and cooking take only 6 hours. (Patrick cooks for 50; when there are larger crowds, he expands the meal with friends' potluck contributions.)

Soda bread and corned beef have always been Patrick's party-day staples. Over time my role has expanded beyond head potato peeler. Now I supply the shortbread and colcannon, a traditional Irish dish of mashed potatoes with butter-steamed cabbage.

Last year, a bold first-time partygoer ventured that the meal seemed heavily tilted toward potatoes. She was quickly set straight. Patrick, the self-proclaimed Spud King, says you can't have too much of a good thing on St. Patrick's Day.

I've adapted Patrick's recipes to serve 12, 25, or 50. For 12 guests, you can cook the colcannon and corned beef on the range at the same time. If you're preparing for 25 or 50, you'll need to cook the colcannon and corned beef in sequence as outlined in the following section. *(The large pots won't all fit on the range at once, and overcrowding could seriously damage the range.)* Follow recipe instructions for reheating foods.

HOW HE DOES IT

Beneath Patrick's off-the-cuff demeanor is the mind of a party general. After years of St. Patrick's celebrations, he has many tips for pulling off this feast.

Overall
• Buy enormous pots to use year after year. Patrick has two 35-quart pans (from a restaurant supply store) to cook corned beef for 50.
• Let friends help. This is not a menu to cook alone. Ask someone to bring appetizers.

One week ahead
• Send out invitations by electronic mail (or phone).
• Buy "cluttery" (disposable cutlery and paper supplies) at a discount store, and beer (Irish stout and lager).
• Make or buy shortbread; freeze.

• Borrow extra vegetable peelers, and coolers for beer.

On the day
2:00 Get organized. Thaw shortbread, if necessary. Ice beer. In obvious spots, set out large, lined trash cans.
2:30 Put on Irish music. Peel potatoes like mad and cook for colcannon. Prepare veg-

Colcannon

Ingredients	For 12	For 25	For 50
Russet potatoes	4 lb.	8 lb.	16 lb.
Cabbage, cut into fine shreds	1 lb.	2 lb.	4 lb.
Butter or margarine	½ c. (¼ lb.)	1 c. (½ lb.)	2 c. (1 lb.)
Milk	1¼ c.	2½ c.	5 c.
Sliced green onions	1 c.	2 c.	4 c.
Salt and pepper			

To serve 12, you'll need a 5- to 6-quart pan; for 25, an 8-quart pan; for 50, a 12-quart pan. Peel potatoes; rinse. Submerge in water until all are peeled. Drain; cut into 2-inch pieces. Place potatoes in pan; cover with water. Bring to a boil, covered, over high heat (10 to 40 minutes). Reduce heat; simmer until tender when pierced, about 15 minutes.

If cooking for 25 or 50, remove pan from range so you can cook beef; let potatoes stand in water, covered, until near serving time, up to 4 hours. To reheat, return to boil, covered, over high heat (15 to 20 minutes).

Drain; mash, part at a time, in a heavy-duty mixer or by hand in a large bowl. As mashed, transfer to a very large bowl; cover.

Place cabbage and butter in pan used for potatoes. Cover; steam cabbage over medium-high heat until well wilted (8 to 15 minutes), stirring often. Meanwhile, stir milk and onions often in a 3- to 4-quart pan over medium heat until simmering, 8 to 10 minutes. Stir milk mixture into potatoes until smooth; stir in cabbage. Season with salt and pepper.

Per serving: 205 cal. (39 percent from fat); 4.1 g protein; 8.8 g fat (5.3 g sat.); 28 g carbo.; 109 mg sodium; 24 mg chol.

Irish Soda Bread

Ingredients	For 12	For 25	For 50
All-purpose flour	3 c.	6 c.	12 c.
Sugar	3 tbsp.	¼ c.	½ c.
Baking soda	1 tsp.	2¼ tsp.	4½ tsp.
Salt	¾ tsp.	1½ tsp.	1 tbsp.
Butter or margarine	9 tbsp.	1⅛ c.	2¼ c.
Caraway seed	1 tbsp.	2 tbsp.	¼ c.
Golden raisins	½ c.	1 c.	2 c.
Dried currants	⅓ c.	¾ c.	1½ c.
Buttermilk for dough	1 c.	2 c.	4 c.
Buttermilk for brushing	1½ tbsp.	3 tbsp.	6 tbsp.

For 50 servings, make half a recipe at a time. In a large bowl, combine flour, sugar, soda, and salt. Cut in butter with a pastry blender or rub with fingers until fine crumbs form. Mix in caraway, raisins, and currants; add buttermilk for dough. Stir until evenly moistened.

Gather dough into a ball and knead about 16 turns on a lightly floured board. Pat into a smooth ball, then into a flat 1-inch-thick round. (For 25 servings, make 3 rounds; for 50, make 6 rounds total.) Evenly space round or rounds on 1 or 2 greased 12- by 15-inch baking sheets.

Slash an X about ¼ inch deep completely across each round; brush with remaining buttermilk. Bake in a 375° oven until deep golden, 30 to 35 minutes; switch pan positions halfway through baking. Serve warm or cool. If making ahead, store airtight up to 1 day, or freeze. Cut into wedges. Makes 1, 3, or 6 loaves.

Per serving: 246 cal. (35 percent from fat); 4.5 g protein; 9.6 g fat (5.6 g sat.); 36 g carbo.; 355 mg sodium; 24 mg chol.

---

etables for corned beef. **4:00** Start corned beef. Make soda bread. Pour a round of Black and Tans (equal parts Irish stout and lager—lager first for less foam).

7:15 When corned beef is tender, add vegetables. Pour more Black and Tans.

7:45 Start dishing up vegetables and carving meat; keep warm. Meanwhile (if for 25 or 50), finish colcannon.

8:15 Clear a path to the table and carry in food to rounds of applause.

CORNED BEEF KNOW-HOW

Corning is a process that cures and flavors beef in a mixture containing salt, sugar, preservatives, and sometimes garlic and pickling spices. Corned beef is available without added spices (sometimes called mild), or with spices (sometimes called old-fashioned), which are either pressed into the meat or included in a separate packet. Patrick prefers corned beef that's spiced, if it's available. You may also see oven-roast style, which has less salt—and would taste a little bland simmered for Patrick's recipe.

Both beef brisket and bottom round are corned. Brisket is fattier and more succulent and flavorful than round, and requires a little carving care to avoid crumbly slices. To carve brisket, cut across the grain at a 45° angle; if meat is crumbly, make thicker slices. Bottom round slices neatly but is drier.

At supermarkets, most corned beef comes sealed in plastic bags in pieces of 1 pound to several pounds. From your butcher, you may be able to special-order a piece that weighs 10 pounds or more (you will need to cut it to fit in the cooking pot). ∎

By Elaine Johnson

Elaine's Shortbread

Ingredients	For 12	For 25	For 50
Butter, softened	1 c. (½ lb.)	2 c. (1 lb.)	4 c. (2 lb.)
Sugar	½ c. + 1 tbsp.	1 c. + 1½ tbsp.	2 c. + 3 tbsp.
All-purpose flour	1½ c.	3 c.	6 c.
White rice flour (or more all-purpose)	½ c.	1 c.	2 c.

Look for rice flour in health food stores. For 50 servings, make half a recipe at a time.

In a food processor or large mixing bowl, whirl or beat butter with the larger amount of sugar until smooth. Gradually add all-purpose and rice flours until well combined (if using a mixer, stir in last half of flour by hand). For 12 servings, spread in a 9- by 13-inch baking dish (for 25 servings, use a rimmed 10- by 15-inch baking pan; for 50 servings, use 2 rimmed 10- by 15-inch baking pans).

Bake shortbread in a 275° oven until pale golden, 55 to 65 minutes, switching pan positions halfway through baking. Place on racks and let cool for 10 minutes. Sprinkle lightly with remaining sugar, then cut into 24, 50, or 100 bars. Let cool completely. Serve, store airtight up to 3 days, or freeze.

Per bar: 126 cal. (56 percent from fat); 1 g protein; 7.8 g fat (4.8 g sat.); 13 g carbo.; 78 mg sodium; 21 mg chol.

HARVEST-SIZE *sturgeon at Sierra AquaFarms in Elverta, California, weighs about 15 pounds. Fish cubes hold together well when threaded onto skewers and grilled.*

PETER CHRISTIANSEN

SIERRA AQUAFARMS

Discovering sturgeon

Farm-raised sturgeon is now showing up in our markets. It's mild, firm, and great for the barbecue

BARBECUED STURGEON STEAK, *served with lentil salad, was marinated in sweet brine to enhance its moistness.*

ONE OF THE NEWER crops on California's fish farms is sturgeon. The state now has a growing sturgeon farming industry, and a good number of the fish are harvested year-round. Restaurants often feature this fish, and now it shows up fairly regularly in well-stocked fish markets, too.

Sturgeon is best known for supplying caviar, but its flesh has a sweet, mild, meatlike flavor and a firm but tender texture. White sturgeon, which is considered one of the best kinds to eat, is the species that's being farmed.

FROM FARM TO MARKET IN 3½ YEARS

Although sturgeon farming has been taking place for more than a decade (mostly near Sacramento), it is still in its early stages. Unlike the case with many other fish, little is known of the sturgeon's biological processes.

Sturgeon was a latecomer to farming because it grows slowly: it takes about 3½ years to reach a practical harvest size of 12 to 19 pounds (and it can take more than 15 years for a fish to mature), whereas a farmed salmon can reach that weight in only 2 to 2½ years. Larger, mature sturgeon are reserved for breeding.

Sturgeon species are found all around the Northern Hemisphere. White sturgeon and the closely related green sturgeon live in some Western rivers as far south as the San Joaquin in Central California, and in the Pacific from Alaska

to Monterey Bay. Restricted numbers of both kinds are harvested wild from the Columbia and Snake rivers.

These bottom-feeding fish can live up to 100 years, and they grow to remarkable sizes—the largest on record was caught in the Caspian Sea and weighed 4,350 pounds. But even at this gigantic size, sturgeon have no bones; their skeletal structure is largely cartilage.

BUYING AND COOKING

Market sturgeon yield steaks similar in size to salmon steaks. You can also buy fillets. Prices range from $6 to $12 per pound. If your market doesn't sell sturgeon, it should be able to order it.

Sturgeon's firm texture means it doesn't fall apart when cooked. And because the fish retains moisture, it tolerates overcooking better than most fish do. Sturgeon contains about 4 percent fat, about the same amount as salmon. Cook sturgeon until it is opaque throughout; it's tough if underdone.

Here are some cooking methods that take advantage of the fish's flavor and texture. In the first, a sugar-salt marinade enhances sturgeon's flavor and moistness; the second dish contrasts the fish's tender-firm texture with crisp jicama. Both dishes include salads for a complete main course.

Grilled Sturgeon with Lentil Tabbouleh

¼ cup sugar

1 tablespoon salt

4 sturgeon steaks (about 2 lb. total), each cut about 1 inch thick

Lentil tabbouleh (recipe follows)

About 1 cup unflavored nonfat yogurt

In a deep bowl, stir sugar and salt with 1½ cups of water until dissolved. Add fish and mix well. Cover and chill 1 hour; turn fish often to expose surfaces equally to the brine. Drain fish, rinse well, and pat dry.

Lay fish on a lightly oiled grill over a solid bed of medium coals (you can hold your hand at grill level only 4 to 5 seconds). Cook 5 minutes; turn steaks over and continue to cook until fish is opaque but still moist-looking in thickest part (cut to test), about 6 minutes longer. Accompany with tabbouleh and yogurt. Serves 4.

Per serving: 542 cal. (28 percent from fat); 44 g protein; 17 g fat (2.8 g sat); 57 g carbo.; 637 mg sodium; estimated 65 mg chol.

Lentil tabbouleh. Sort 1½ cups **decorticated lentils** (hulled and bright orange or yellow) to remove debris. Rinse and drain lentils. In a 2- to 3-quart pan, bring 2 cups **regular-strength chicken broth** to a boil. Stir in lentils. Cover and simmer just until lentils are tender to bite, 4 to 6 minutes. Drain and pour into a bowl. Mix in 2 large (about ½ lb. total) **Roma-type tomatoes,** cored and diced; 1 cup chopped **green onion;** 1 cup minced **fresh** or ¼ cup dried **mint leaves;** ⅓ cup **lemon juice;** 3 tablespoons **olive oil;** and 2 tablespoons minced **fresh ginger.** Add **salt** to taste. Makes about 4½ cups.

Sturgeon and Jicama with Sushi Salad

About 1½ pounds of sturgeon, skin and cartilage cut off

Sichuan marinade (recipe follows)

1½ cups short-grain white (pearl) rice

¼ cup seasoned rice vinegar (or ¼ cup rice vinegar and 1 teaspoon sugar)

1 pound jicama, peeled, rinsed, and cut into ¾-inch cubes

1 medium-size (about 10 oz.) cucumber, peeled and chopped

Cut sturgeon into ¾-inch cubes and place in a bowl with marinade. Mix well, then cover and chill for 1 hour or up to 6 hours; mix fish with the marinade several times.

Meanwhile, in a 1½- to 2-quart pan, combine rice and 1½ cups water. Cover and

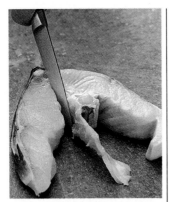

TRIM CARTILAGE *and skin from sturgeon steak, then cut fish into cubes for skewering.*

bring to a boil over high heat. Reduce heat to simmer; do not stir until water is absorbed, 10 to 12 minutes. Stir in vinegar; pour rice into a bowl. Cover and chill.

Thread fish and jicama onto 8 slender 10-inch-long skewers, alternating pieces of fish with jicama. Save the marinade; pour all but 2 tablespoons into an 8- to 10-inch frying pan. Over high heat, boil marinade, uncovered, until reduced to about 2 tablespoons; set aside.

Lay skewers on a lightly greased grill above a solid bed of medium-hot coals (you can hold your hand at grill level only 3 to 4 seconds). Turn fish to cook evenly, basting with the 2 tablespoons reserved (not reduced) marinade. Cook until fish is opaque but still moist-looking in the center (cut to test), about 6 minutes total; jicama will stay crisp. Stir reduced marinade and cucumber into the rice; spoon onto a platter. Arrange skewered fish on platter. Makes 4 servings.

Per serving: 486 cal. (12 percent from fat); 26 g protein; 6.4 g fat (1.3 g sat); 79 g carbo.; 1,041 mg sodium; estimated 65 mg chol.

Sichuan marinade. Stir together ¼ cup *each* **soy sauce** and **seasoned rice vinegar** (or ¼ cup rice vinegar and 1 teaspoon sugar); 1 tablespoon firmly packed **brown sugar;** 1 teaspoon **crushed dried hot red chilies;** 1 teaspoon **Oriental sesame oil;** and 2 cloves **garlic,** minced or pressed. ■

By Betsy Reynolds Bateson

What do those cutting terms mean?

 **C**HOP, DICE, GRATE, mince—what do they really mean? In our test kitchen, we find that common cutting terms are widely interpreted and often misunderstood. *Chop,* for instance, may mean something different to one cook than to another.

Cutting terms generally apply to the shape of pieces—and sometimes to size. The size and shape can affect a dish's texture, volume, cooking rate, and cohesiveness.

Here's how we define the cutting terms we use in *Sunset* recipes.

Chop

Cut food into irregular pieces. (The size is specified if it's critical to the outcome.)

Cube or dice

Cut into small, straight-sided cubes, or into very fine cubes to dice. (The size is specified if it's critical.)

Grate

Rub hard-textured food against a grater (a tool with small, rough, sharp-edged holes) to reduce to fine particles. Grating works best with firm foods; soft foods (such as some cheeses) form clumps.

Julienne

Cut food into fine, matchstick-size strips.

Mince

Chop food into tiny bits.

Shred

Use a knife or a shredder (a cutting tool with round, smooth, sharp-edged holes) to cut the food into long, thin strands.

Slice

Cut food into flat-sided pieces. Some recipes call for food to be cut on the diagonal, which simply means cutting it at an angle. ■

By Linda Lau Anusasananan
Illustrations: Lucy I. Sargeant

Purple asparagus

A NOT-SO-NEW newcomer in many produce stores and supermarkets is eye-catching purple asparagus. These tinted spears join an expanding number of green-purple vegetables, like broccoli, green beans, and bell peppers, which were once quite common but fell out of fashion for many years.

Sightings of purple asparagus in Italy prompted Brian Benson, a West Coast plant scientist, to develop Viola asparagus; Purple Passion, the first variety, is now grown in California's Central Valley. Harvest begins at the end of February and ends in May.

To keep the purple in asparagus, add acid (lemon juice or vinegar) to its cooking water. The acid anchors the red pigment, anthocyanin. If you don't do this, the color fades to green—a bit extravagant, because you pay a premium for the purple. Dishes that maximize purple asparagus's color maximize its value, as in the purple, white, and green asparagus platter and the citrus salad.

How about flavor and texture? Several members of a *Sunset* taste panel rated purple asparagus as slightly sweeter and a little more tender than its green and white counterparts; others found all the asparagus comparable.

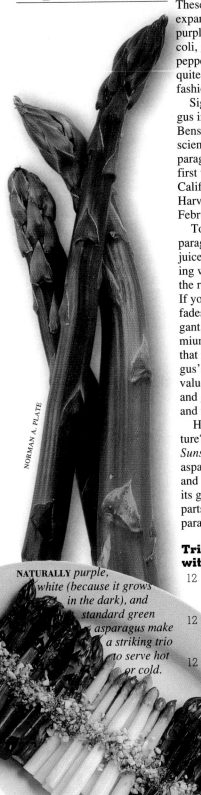

NORMAN A. PLATE

NATURALLY *purple, white (because it grows in the dark), and standard green asparagus make a striking trio to serve hot or cold.*

Tricolor Asparagus with Garlic Streusel

12 thick white asparagus spears (about 1 lb. total), rinsed

12 thick purple asparagus spears (about 1 lb. total), rinsed

12 thick green asparagus spears (about 1 lb. total, or use 2 lb. total purple asparagus)

¼ cup red wine vinegar

Garlic streusel (recipe follows)

Salt and pepper

Remove and discard tough ends of white, purple, and green asparagus; cut spears all the same length (save scraps for soups or salads). For sweetest flavor and tenderest texture, peel white and green spears with a vegetable peeler.

In a 10- to 12-inch frying pan, bring about 1 inch water to a boil over high heat. Add white spears to boiling water. Cook, uncovered, until asparagus is just tender when pierced, about 4 minutes. Transfer with a slotted spoon; immerse in ice water.

In the same pan (add water if needed to maintain a 1-in. depth), cook green asparagus (or ½ the purple spears, if using only purple asparagus; color will turn green) just until tender when pierced, about 4 minutes. Transfer to ice water.

In the same pan (add water if needed to maintain a 1-in. depth), return water to a boil and add vinegar. Cook purple asparagus just until tender when pierced, about 4 minutes. Put in ice water.

Group spears by color on a large platter. Serve cold or hot; if making ahead, chill airtight up to 1 day. To reheat, warm in a microwave oven on full power (100 percent) for 2-minute intervals until hot, or immerse spears in boiling water for about 1 minute, drain, and return to platter. Scatter with streusel and add salt and pepper to taste. Makes 6 to 8 servings.

Per serving: 51 cal. (26 percent from fat); 3.4 g protein; 1.5 g fat (0.2 g sat.); 7.3 g carbo.; 45 mg sodium; 0 mg chol.

Garlic streusel. In a blender or food processor, whirl enough **sourdough bread** chunks to make about 1 cup fine crumbs (you'll need 2 to 3 bread slices or 2 to 3 oz. total). In an 8- to 10-inch frying pan over medium-high heat, stir crumbs, 2 teaspoons **olive oil,** and 2 minced or pressed **garlic cloves** until crumbs are toasted brown, 5 to 7 minutes; set aside. If making ahead, cool and cover airtight up to 2 days. Makes about 1 cup.

Asparagus and Citrus Salad

2 large (about ½ lb. each) oranges

½ cup balsamic or red wine vinegar

3 to 4 teaspoons sugar

¼ teaspoon dried tarragon leaves

12 thick purple asparagus spears (about 1 lb. total), rinsed

Crisped onion slices (recipe follows)

Salt and pepper

Cut peel and white membrane off oranges. Over a bowl, cut between inner membranes and lift out orange sections; place sections in the bowl. Squeeze juice from membranes into bowl. If preparing ahead, cover and chill up to 4 hours.

Drain juice from bowl; put 2 tablespoons in a small bowl and save remainder for other uses. To the small bowl, add ¼ cup vinegar, 3 teaspoons sugar (or more, to taste, depending on sweetness of oranges), and tarragon; mix, then pour into a small pitcher.

In a 10- to 12-inch frying pan, bring about 1 inch water and the remaining ¼ cup vinegar to a boil over high heat. Remove and discard tough ends of the asparagus. Add spears to boiling water. Cook, uncovered, until asparagus is just tender when pierced, about 4 minutes. Drain and immerse spears in ice water until cold; drain.

Divide crisped onion slices evenly among 4 plates. Arrange asparagus spears and orange segments equally on plates. Add dressing, salt, and pepper to taste. Makes 4 servings.

Per serving: 85 cal. (4.2 percent from fat); 3.1 g protein; 0.4 g fat (0.1 g sat.); 20 g carbo.; 5.8 mg sodium; 0 mg chol.

Crisped onion slices. Thinly slice 1 medium-size (about 6 oz.) **red onion.** Put in a bowl with **water** to cover. Squeeze onions to bruise slightly; drain. Add 4 cups **ice cubes,** 2 cups water, and ¼ cup **balsamic** or red wine **vinegar.** Let stand until crisp, 20 to 30 minutes. Drain well and discard ice cubes. ∎

By Karyn I. Lipman

Why?

Why do some favorite cooked foods sometimes behave strangely?

NORMAN A. PLATE

OKRA DEVELOPS *a slippery ooze as long-chain compounds in its tissues swell and lengthen in cooking water. This behavior makes okra a good thickener in gumbo but not very appealing as a cooked vegetable. To minimize, cook okra whole in water; to avoid, cook okra in oil or butter.*

Certain fruits and vegetables can behave strangely when cooked, turning weird colors, developing bizarre textures, and, on occasion, even making you sick. Three often-used foods—blueberries, potato salad, and okra—can have these problems; here's how you keep them under control.

Other color changes in blueberries are much like those in red cabbage in acid or alkaline mixtures (see the May 1992 *Sunset,* page 157). Blueberries turn brighter purple in an acid mixture, such as a lemon-based fruit syrup. If cooked in an alkaline mixture, such as muffins or tea breads with a lot of baking soda, blueberries get bluer.

Why do blueberries in muffins sometimes turn green?

Cooking makes blueberries juicy. If these juices touch cast iron, cold rolled steel, or carbon steel (common materials for kitchen pans and knives), they can turn varying shades of green or even putty yellow.

This may show up when blueberry muffins are baked in pans made of these metals, or when foods containing cooked blueberries are cut with carbon steel knives. The color change, although distracting, is a harmless chemical reaction.

Some people say the discoloration has a slightly metallic taste; others don't notice anything. To avoid this problem when using cast-iron or cold rolled steel pans, bake muffins in paper liners; or you can use aluminum or nonstick pans or glass baking cups.

Why does potato salad often get blamed for food poisoning?

Believe it or not, if the salad does make you sick, it's probably because of the potatoes, not the mayonnaise.

Commercial mayonnaise is a relatively high acid product (as are tart dressings made with vinegar or lemon juice) that inhibits or slows growth of bacteria, even the kinds that make you ill.

Potatoes, however, are full of nutrients that make a fertile ground for the growth of yeast, mold, and bacteria. In fact, scientists have long used potatoes as a growth medium.

If potato salad—or any salad made with eggs, poultry, meat, or fish—has been contaminated by harmful bacteria and sits in a warm place long enough, conditions are ideal for trouble: time, warmth, moisture, and nutrients allow bacteria to flourish.

Next time you serve potato or other susceptible salads, keep them cold, serve them cold or cool, and chill leftover salad immediately after serving to prevent the growth of bacteria.

Why does okra get slimy when cooked?

Okra (and cactus) contain a number of compounds, including sugars and acids, that are linked in long mucilaginous chains. When you cut into okra (or cactus), juices ooze out in stringy, slippery strands. In water, instead of being diluted, these chains swell.

Cooking heat aggravates the leaking and increases the compounds' thickening properties; on standing, they thicken even more.

Okra (or cactus) slime is not harmful, but it is gooey. For least amount, cook okra (or cactus pads) whole in a generous amount of boiling water just until barely tender;

then drain at once. If the vegetable is to be served cold, cool it quickly in ice water, then drain at once.

Or, for no slime, cook whole or cut okra (or cactus) in butter or oil; okra coated with cornmeal and deep-fried is a great traditional Southern favorite.

When okra is cooked in vinegar-water for pickling, the vinegar's acid limits the formation of mucilaginous chains, but it turns the okra drab.

More questions?

If you've encountered other cooking mysteries and would like to know why they happened, send your questions to Why?, *Sunset Magazine,* 80 Willow Rd., Menlo Park, Calif. 94025. With the help of Dr. George K. York, extension food technologist at UC Davis, *Sunset* food editors will find the answers to your questions. ∎

By Linda Lau Anusasananan

Molasses saves the day for pasta sauce

Choice seasonings give asparagus foreign airs

PROUST ATE A MADELEINE and recalled his past in *À la recherche du temps perdu*, a gigantic novel that many have started and few have finished. Kenneth Nesslage reversed the technique: he recalled his past, most notably a spaghetti sauce made by the mother of his childhood sweetheart, and then created the sauce.

Because he did not marry the childhood sweetheart, the recipe did not come to him by inheritance, and it took years for him to achieve the desired flavor. He was aided by one memory in particular: the mother had said that she used molasses because "I don't have to slave over the stove all day, but it will taste like it."

While molasses can help achieve the brownish red look of a long-cooked sauce, and add a hint of caramel flavor, we feel that the rich mélange of meats and herbs deserves some of the credit for the opulent flavor of this sauce.

Pasta Sauce à la Nesslageni

- 1 pound ground lean beef
- 1 pound mild Italian sausages
- 1 package (about 3 oz.) sliced pepperoni
- 1 large (½ lb.) onion, chopped
- 1 small (about ¼ lb.) green bell pepper, stemmed, seeded, and chopped
- ½ pound mushrooms, sliced
- 4 cloves garlic
- 1 tablespoon *each* dried basil leaves, dried oregano leaves, and dried marjoram leaves
- ½ teaspoon dried rosemary leaves
- ¼ teaspoon dried thyme leaves
- ¼ cup molasses
- 2 cans (each 15 oz.) tomato purée
- 1 cup beer
- 1 cup dry red wine
  Hot cooked pasta

In a 5- to 6-quart pan over medium heat, crumble beef with a spoon. Remove sausage casings and crumble sausage in pan. Stir often until meat is well browned, 12 to 15 minutes. Discard drippings. To pan, add pepperoni, onion, green pepper, and mushrooms; stir occasionally until onion is limp, 5 to 8 minutes.

Meanwhile, in a blender or food processor, whirl garlic, basil, oregano, marjoram, rosemary, thyme, molasses, and about ½ cup of the tomato purée until garlic and herbs are finely chopped. Pour mixture into pan; rinse blender with beer and pour into pan along with the rest of the beer and tomato purée, and the wine. Cover and bring to boiling on high heat, then simmer until reduced to about 9 cups, about 1 hour; stir occasionally.

If making ahead, let sauce cool, cover, and chill up to 3 days. To store longer, freeze in easy-to-use portions. Reheat to use. Ladle hot sauce over hot pasta. Makes about 9 cups sauce.

Per cup sauce: 360 cal. (53 percent from fat); 21 g protein; 21 g fat (7.6 g sat.); 22 g carbo.; 946 mg sodium; 67 mg chol.

Kennett Nesslage

Santee, California

WHEN ASPARAGUS IS in season, enthusiasts serve it often. Butter or hollandaise are the preferred sauces, but for a de-lightful change you should try Sandy Szwarc's Asparagus Sauté. Painstaking preparation is what makes this dish a work of genius. Szwarc discards the tough ends of the asparagus, sets aside the tips, and cuts the remaining stalks into 1-inch lengths; these receive 3 minutes more cooking time than the tips.

Asparagus Sauté

- 1½ pounds asparagus
- 1 tablespoon butter or margarine
- ½ pound mushrooms, thinly sliced
- 1 teaspoon minced or pressed garlic
- 3 tablespoons dry white wine
- 1 tablespoon grated orange peel
- ⅛ teaspoon crushed dried hot red chilies
- ¼ teaspoon dried tarragon leaves
- 3 green onions, ends trimmed, cut diagonally into ½-inch lengths
  Salt and pepper

Break off and discard tough ends from asparagus. Rinse asparagus and cut into 1-inch lengths, leaving tips whole. Set tips and stalks aside separately.

Melt butter in a 10- to 12-inch frying pan over medium-high heat; add mushrooms and garlic. Stir often until mushroom liquid evaporates and slices begin to brown, about 10 minutes.

Add asparagus stems; stir for 3 minutes. Add wine, orange peel, chilies, tarragon, and asparagus tips. Cover pan and stir often until all the asparagus is tender-crisp to bite, 2 to 3 minutes longer. Stir in green onions; season vegetables to taste with salt and pepper. Makes 4 or 5 servings.

Per serving: 59 cal. (40 percent from fat); 3.4 g protein; 2.6 g fat (1.5 g sat.); 6.1 g carbo.; 29 mg sodium; 6.2 mg chol.

Sandy Szwarc

Albuquerque

By Joan Griffiths, Richard Dunmire

MALAYSIAN BEEF STEW *is refreshing with pineapple, cucumbers, and rice; chilies and leaves decorate.*

2 tablespoons grated fresh ginger

2 teaspoons ground coriander

½ teaspoon ground turmeric

2 pounds boned and fat-trimmed beef chuck

1 teaspoon sugar

2 cans (14 oz. each) coconut milk

1 tablespoon finely chopped lemon grass (tender part of peeled stem), or ½ teaspoon grated lemon peel

4 fresh lime or lemon leaves, rinsed well and drained (optional)

Salt

In a food processor or blender, combine onions, garlic, chilies (use all 5 for hottest flavor), ginger, coriander, turmeric, and ⅓ cup water; whirl until smoothly puréed.

Cut beef into 2-inch cubes. Mix well with sugar and ½ the onion mixture.

Combine remaining onion mixture with coconut milk, lemon grass, and lime leaves in a 5- to 6-quart pan; bring to boiling over high heat. Reduce heat to medium-high and boil gently, uncovered, until liquid is reduced to about ½, about 15 minutes; stir occasionally.

Add beef mixture and bring to a boil over high heat. Reduce heat, cover, and simmer until meat is well browned and tender enough to shred with a fork but still holds its shape, about 2 hours; stir occasionally to prevent sticking. Remove lime leaves. (If making ahead, cool, cover, and chill up to 4 days. Warm over low heat or in a microwave oven in a microwave-safe container.) Add salt to taste. Serves 6 to 8.

Per serving: 503 cal. (75 percent from fat); 24 g protein; 42 g fat (27 g sat.); 9.3 g carbo.; 82 mg sodium; 77 mg chol. ∎

By Linda Lau Anusasananan, Kaan Gwee

It was a favorite of Malaysian travelers

This stew is not as durable, but it's easier and more succulent

FROM MALAYSIA TO California comes *rendang*, a stew of beef chunks braised tender in coconut milk and spices. Before the days of refrigeration, rendang was preserved by cooking it until the beef was almost as dry as jerky. Its durability made it a favorite of travelers.

Kaan Gwee, a Malaysian living in California, has updated rendang without sacrificing anything but its longevity. His version has authentic flavor, but it is moister, more succulent, less salty, and easier to prepare. Serve rendang with rice, cucumbers, and pineapples.

Beef Rendang

If you use citrus leaves from your garden, be sure they have not been recently sprayed with pesticides.

2 large (about 1 lb. total) onions, chopped

4 cloves garlic, crushed

3 to 5 fresh small hot red chilies (about 3 in. long), stemmed and chopped

PETER CHRISTIANSEN

CHEF LARRY VITO PREPARES LEEKS *to poach; he serves them cool with sweet, caramelized garlic cloves and balsamic vinegar dressing.*

Vito's way with vegetables

These combinations are pretty stunning, and not hard to duplicate

VEGETABLES, CREATIVELY seasoned, ascend to a leading role. Culinary professional Larry Vito uses vegetables, ethnic ingredients, and unlikely flavors to produce stunning combinations.

The results are surprisingly easy to duplicate at home; most ingredients are readily available in supermarkets. You may have to go to a Japanese grocery for aka miso; it imparts hearty body and subtle mellowness to the last dish.

Braised Leeks with Caramelized Garlic

8 large (3½ to 4 lb. total) leeks

1 very large (about 5 oz.) head garlic

1½ cups regular-strength chicken broth

3 tablespoons extra-virgin olive oil

1 tablespoon sugar

¼ cup balsamic vinegar

2 tablespoons chopped shallots

Trim off roots, tough tops, and coarse outer layers of leeks. Split leeks in half lengthwise. Rinse between layers; tie each piece with string to hold it together.

In a 5- to 6-quart pan, bring 2 quarts water to a boil. Add leeks, cover, and simmer until tender when pierced, 5 to 7 minutes; drain. At once, immerse leeks in ice water. When cool, drain. (If making ahead, cover and chill up to 1 day.)

Peel garlic; set aside 1 clove. Put remaining cloves and broth in the 5- to 6-quart pan. Bring to a boil on high heat; cover and simmer until garlic is tender when pierced, 15 to 20 minutes. Lift out garlic; drain until dry.

Boil the broth over high heat, uncovered, until reduced to ⅓ cup, about 5 minutes. Save broth; rinse and dry the pan.

Place pan over high heat. Add 2 tablespoons oil; when hot, add blanched garlic cloves and sugar. On low heat, shake pan often until garlic is golden brown, about 10 minutes. (If making ahead, cover, and chill up to 1 day.)

Meanwhile, mince reserved garlic; mix with broth, remaining oil, vinegar, and shallots. (If making ahead, cover and chill up to 1 day.)

Remove string from leeks and arrange 4 leek halves on each of 4 plates. Top equally with garlic cloves and dressing. Makes 4 first-course servings.—*Larry Vito, Chef-owner, Ariana (opening this month), San Francisco.*

Per first-course serving: 269 cal. (40 percent from fat); 5.5 g protein; 12 g fat (1.7 g sat.); 39 g carbo.; 60 mg sodium; 0 mg chol.

Spaghetti Squash with Mushrooms and Cream

1 medium-size (about 3½ lb.) spaghetti squash

½ to 1 ounce (⅔ to 1⅓ cups) dried morel mushrooms

½ cup walnut pieces

⅔ cup whipping cream

2 tablespoons aka miso (also called red miso) or about 1 tablespoon soy sauce

½ cup diced red bell pepper

2 tablespoons thinly sliced chives

Pierce squash through shell in several places with fork tines, and set squash in an 8- to 10-inch-wide pan. Bake in a 350° oven until soft when pressed, about 1 hour.

Meanwhile, soak morels in 2 cups warm water until soft, about 5 minutes. Cut morels in half lengthwise and rub gently in water to release grit. Swish pieces and lift from water; let drain.

Let sediment settle in soaking water; gently pour 1 cup of the water (avoiding grit) into another bowl; save. Discard gritty water.

About 5 minutes before squash is done, place nuts in an 8- to 10-inch-wide pan. Bake in oven beside squash until nuts are golden under skins, 5 to 8 minutes; set aside. Let squash cool briefly. In a 10- to 12-inch frying pan, combine the reserved 1 cup soaking water, morels, cream, and miso (or 1 tablespoon soy sauce). Boil, uncovered, over high heat until mixture is reduced to about ½ cup, about 8 minutes.

Cut squash open; discard seeds. With a fork, scoop out squash strands and place in 1 large or 8 individual dishes. Spoon cream sauce and morels over squash. Sprinkle with red pepper, chives, walnuts, and add soy to taste. Makes 8 first-course, 4 main-dish servings.

Per first-course serving: 169 cal. (64 percent from fat); 3.1 g protein; 12 g fat (4.5 g sat.); 15 g carbo.; 189 mg sodium; 22 mg chol. ■

By Linda Lau Anusasananan

SUNSET'S KITCHEN CABINET

Creative ways with everyday foods—submitted by *Sunset* readers,
tested in *Sunset* kitchens, approved by *Sunset* taste panels

Warm Granola with Fruit

Katherine J. Shuster, Vancouver, Washington

2 large (about 1 lb. total) tart apples, such as Granny Smith or Newtown Pippin, rinsed

3 cups granola cereal

1½ cups (12-oz. can) frozen peach or apple juice concentrate, thawed

½ cup raisins (optional)

¼ cup water

1½ tablespoons lemon juice

½ teaspoon ground cinnamon

Apple slices (optional)

Milk (optional)

Core and coarsely chop whole apples. In a 4- to 5-quart pan, combine chopped apples, granola, juice concentrate, raisins, water, lemon juice, and cinnamon; mix well.

Stir over high heat until boiling; cover and simmer until apples are just soft to bite, about 5 minutes.

Spoon cereal into bowls, top with apple slices, and offer milk to add to taste. Makes about 5 cups.

Per cup: 516 cal. (24 percent from fat); 8.4 g protein; 14 g fat (7.5 g sat.); 91 g carbo.; 51 mg sodium; 0 mg chol.

APPLE-STUDDED GRANOLA *heated with fruit juice makes a quick breakfast.*

Pasta and Beans with Sausage

Nancy Gonzalez, Millbrae, California

1 pound turkey Italian sausage

1 large (about ½ lb.) onion

4 cloves garlic

1¾ cups regular-strength chicken or beef broth

2 cans (15 oz. each) white kidney beans (cannellini), drained

2 cups (about 6 oz. dried) cooked macaroni or rigatoni

1 can (8 oz.) tomato sauce

¼ cup dry red wine

3 tablespoons minced fresh or 2 teaspoons crumbled dried basil leaves

1 tablespoon minced fresh or 1 teaspoon crumbled dried oregano

About ½ cup grated parmesan cheese

Discard sausage casing and break meat into small chunks, chop onion, and mince or press garlic.

In a 5- to 6-quart pan, combine sausage, onion, garlic, and ¼ cup broth. Stir often over high heat until liquid evaporates and browned bits stick to pan, about 15 minutes. Add another ¼ cup broth, stir browned bits free, and boil again until browned bits stick again.

Add remaining 1¼ cups broth, beans, macaroni, tomato sauce, wine, basil, and oregano. Stir often until mixture is hot, about 5 minutes; mix in ½ cup parmesan. Spoon pasta and beans into bowls and offer additional cheese to add to taste. Serves 4 to 6.

Per serving: 408 cal. (26 percent from fat); 29 g protein; 12 g fat (4.2 g sat.); 45 g carbo.; 1,013 mg sodium; 63 mg chol.

GRATE PARMESAN *onto a lean, robust mix of macaroni, beans, and sausage.*

Asparagus with Currant Sauce

Dawn Dixon, Tucson

1 pound asparagus

½ cup red currant jelly

¼ cup white wine vinegar

2 tablespoons lemon juice

2 tablespoons minced red onion

Salt and pepper

Trim off tough ends of asparagus; if desired, peel stalks with a vegetable peeler. In a 10- to 12-inch frying pan over high heat, bring about 1 inch water to boiling. Add asparagus and cook, uncovered, just until stalks turn bright green and are barely tender

when pierced, about 3 minutes; drain. At once immerse asparagus in ice water; when cold, drain. If making ahead, wrap airtight and chill up to 1 day.

In a 1- to 1½-quart pan over high heat, stir jelly, vinegar, lemon juice, and onion until jelly melts.

Arrange asparagus on a platter; spoon a little of the jelly sauce over the vegetable. Add more sauce, salt, and pepper to add to taste. Serves 4 to 6.

Per serving: 81 cal. (1 percent from fat); 1.4 g protein; 0.1 g fat (0 g sat.); 20 g carbo.; 11 mg sodium; 0 mg chol.

Compiled by Christine Weber Hale

ROSY SAUCE, *based on currant jelly, is tart-sweet; it suits asparagus.*

A grand polenta, rinsing and relishing mushrooms, a rub for ribs, Western ways with Italian reds

By Jerry Anne Di Vecchio

From my vantage point in the kitchen, spring has one delicious advantage over fall. Mild, moist days encourage the earth to send forth some of my favorite wild mushrooms—fat-stemmed porcini (also called *Boletus* or cèpes; they look like the mushrooms that danced in Disney's *Fantasia*) and golden furled chanterelles. But only as the weather grows warmer do crumpled morels pop up, too.

A childhood foray through field and forest with an elderly woman who had been gathering for years and knew the good from the dangerous ended with my first taste of wild mushrooms. But for long after, this new appetite went unappeased, as only foragers had access to these treasures; none were ever in the market.

Even plain old mushrooms, the smooth white or brown cultivated *Agaricus,* were rare when I was learning to cook. Canned or dried mushrooms served me until grocers got wise in the '60s. Regular mushrooms were followed in the '70s by a boom in domestically cultured ones, mostly from Japan: meaty shiitake, all colors of fragile oyster mushrooms (these *Pleurotus* may be white, gray, pink, yellow, blue, or tan), dainty long-stemmed enoki, and white, aptly named pompon blanc. Then, hurrah! Mushrooms harvested in the wild began to appear in markets.

Now, the line between cultivated and wild is wildly confused—and for eating, unimportant. In my mind, all are satisfying.

A mutual passion for earthy foods cemented my friendship with Michael Roberts way back when he was founding chef of the fabled (and now closed) Trumps in Los Angeles. I called him recently to catch up on his new venture, the Twin Palms in Pasadena, and soon conversation gravitated toward mushrooms.

I was delighted to find we are equally devoted to mushrooms in a light sauce that allows their flavor to come through, served with velvety polenta. Michael's secrets for wonderful polenta are simple:

PETER CHRISTIANSEN

Mushroom Ragout with Creamy Polenta

1½ cups polenta

9 cups regular-strength chicken broth

2 tablespoons butter or olive oil

1 cup fresh sage leaves (cut in half if longer than 1¾ in.), rinsed and drained dry (optional)

Mushroom ragout (see recipe below)

In a 4- to 5-quart pan, mix polenta and broth. Stir over high heat until boiling. Reduce heat to maintain a faint simmer. Cook, uncovered, stirring occasionally, until polenta is thick, creamy to taste, and reduced to about 6 cups, about 1 hour.

Meanwhile, in a 10- to 12-inch frying pan, melt 2 tablespoons butter over high heat. Add sage leaves and stir just until they turn a darker green, about 1 minute. With a slotted spoon, transfer leaves to paper towels to drain; discard butter or reserve for other uses.

Pour polenta onto a platter; arrange mushroom pieces from ragout on polenta, scatter with crisp sage leaves. Accompany portions with mushroom ragout. Makes 6 servings.

Per serving: 279 cal. (26 percent from fat); 11 g protein; 8 g fat (3.4 g sat.); 42 g carbo.; 155 mg sodium; 10 mg chol.

slow cooking and plenty of liquid. Polenta made this way doesn't spatter or need constant stirring.

To best show off the mushrooms, our ragout is made in two parts. Choicest pieces and slices are oven-browned to keep their shape. Remnants

are chopped, cooked with shallots, thyme, and butter, then broth is added to make the sauce. Michael uses an elegant homemade broth that is perpetually simmering on his big stove; I have my own brew. But even canned chicken broth or vegetable

broth (should you wish to treat some purely vegetarian guests) is fine because the mushrooms contribute so much character. He thickens his sauce with a fat chunk of butter; I compromise with a light cornstarch finish and, perhaps, a pat of butter. The

choice is yours.

Mushroom ragout. Clean and trim 2 pounds **mushrooms** as directed in Back to Basics (page 64). A mixture of porcini, chanterelle, morel, portabella, shiitake (tough stems discarded), oyster, pompon blanc, and enoki (stem end trimmed off) makes a handsome and tasty blend.

Cut large mushrooms lengthwise in ¼- to ½-inch-thick slices. Leave smaller ones whole. Set aside half the mushrooms, selecting the nicest-looking whole and cut pieces. Coarsely chop the rest.

Put 1 or 2 tablespoons **butter** in a 10- by 15-inch or 12- by 17-inch pan; place in a

450° oven until butter melts. (Or use olive oil and heat.) Place whole mushrooms and slices in buttered pan and turn over to lightly coat, then arrange in a single layer (mushroom pieces can touch but should not overlap much).

Bake mushrooms 10 minutes; turn pieces over. Continue to bake until mushrooms are browned but still moist-looking, 20 to 40 minutes, depending on thickness and moisture content of mushrooms. *As pieces brown, lift out and set aside.*

When mushrooms are cooked, return all pieces to pan and remove the pan from the oven. If making ahead, cover and chill up to 1 day; to serve, return to oven until warm, 5 to 8 minutes.

While pieces bake, put 1 tablespoon **butter** or olive oil in a 10- to 12-inch frying pan over high heat. Add the chopped mushrooms, ½ cup minced **shallots,** and ¾ teaspoon **fresh** or dried **thyme leaves;** stir often until vegetables begin to brown and stick. Add ½ cup **regular-strength chicken broth**; stir to free browned bits. Stir often until vegetables begin to brown again; add ½ cup more broth and repeat step. Add 2 cups more broth; stir browned bits free and bring mixture to a rolling boil. Mix 2 tablespoons **cornstarch** with 3 tablespoons **water** and stir enough of this mixture into boiling ragout to thicken to your taste. If desired, stir in 2 tablespoons butter. Serve or, if making ahead, cover and chill up to 1 day; before serving, stir over medium heat until hot. Present mushrooms and ragout with polenta, on toasted sourdough bread, over hot couscous, or with meats. Makes 6 servings.

BACK TO BASICS

How to bathe a mushroom

Mushrooms grow in the earth or in decaying

TRIM OFF *caked-on soil and brush away loose debris. To thoroughly rinse, place mushrooms in a plastic bag, fill with water, hold closed, and shake briefly.*

matter. If they are good to eat, bugs and such will, logically, find them appetizing, too. Therefore, it is a mystery to me why some say it's a bad idea to wash mushrooms.

Understanding the nature of mushrooms can set matters straight. First, they must be kept dry until you are ready to use them. On the other hand, don't let them dry out. I do not find the standard method of storing them in a paper bag adequate. For best results, loosely wrap mushrooms in an absorbent towel, enclose—but do not seal—the bundle in a plastic bag (or slightly ventilated container), and refrigerate. Even as mushrooms begin to shrink and dry, they remain usable; trim away any soft decay.

You don't need to peel mushrooms. This wasteful habit cropped up when white mushrooms were considered more chic, and someone discovered brown-capped *agaricus* were white just beneath the surface.

You do need to wash mushrooms. Wiping or brushing is not enough to dislodge dirt, grit, and sneaky bugs. Before washing wild mushrooms, you often need to trim or

brush off caked-on soil or to bore out insects. Some of my most disappointing memories are of morels and chanterelles too gritty to eat.

The phobia about putting mushrooms in water does have some basis. Mushrooms should *never* be rinsed and then stored; they'll begin a quick, slimy, smelly decline. Rinsing must be brief and total; most mushrooms are like sponges and extra moisture doesn't improve them. In water, they need gentle swishing because they are fragile and full of crevices. My favorite trick is to fill a plastic food bag with cool water (I use the bag I brought them home from the market in), pinch the bag shut, and shake 2 or 3 seconds, then hold back the mushrooms as I pour out the water. Mushrooms with lots of nooks and crannies (chanterelles and morels in particular) may need more rinsings. After a brief drain on towels, the mushrooms are ready to use.

GREAT TOOL

The wood reamer

What looks like a juggernaut weapon and is useful to every cook? A wood juice reamer. This inexpensive, handy tool is best described as a pointed, grooved lemon-shape on a handle. You'll find it in most cook-

ware stores, priced at $3.50 and up, depending upon the quality and kind of wood. I have two. The one in the bar is made of a smooth fruitwood; the one in the kitchen is a pale, coarser wood. They work equally well.

A wood reamer is most useful when you want just a little citrus juice for a drink or cooking and don't want to dig out the fruit juicer—which is a bit of a chore to clean. The merit of the reamer is that it needs only a swish through water (plain or soapy) before it is returned to the drawer.

The reamer gets used a lot in my house for this ***margarita cooler:*** Cut a **lime** in half and ream juice from 1 or both pieces into a large, wide-bowl glass rimmed with **salt** (rub rim with lime and dip in coarse salt). Add 2 tablespoons **tequila** (or to taste), a few **ice cubes,** and **sparkling water** to fill the glass. Traditionalists can stir in about 1 tablespoon **orange-flavor liqueur,** but I prefer the drink without it.

Per serving: 71 cal. (0 percent from fat); 0 g protein; 0 g fat; 0.5 g carbo.; 0.3 mg sodium; 0 mg chol.

NEWS NOTE

Tortilla trends

If you think your choices of tortillas are limited to flour or corn and various sizes, it's time to look more closely at

TWIST WOODEN REAMER *into citrus half as a quick way to get juice for a drink or a recipe.*

the market shelves and package labels. Here's what you may find:

• Whole-wheat flour tortillas made with sprouted wheat.

• Fat-free white and whole-wheat flour tortillas.

• Yellow corn tortillas frequently joined by blue ones. Traditionally, corn tortillas have no added fat, but now some do.

• Some fresh tortillas are packed uncooked, ready to toast on a griddle.

• Organic corn or flour tortillas.

While browsing in Mrs. Gooch's stylish grocery in Beverly Hills recently, I even unearthed tortillas flavored with chilies and herbs. Look-alike Indian chapatis and naan, stacked with the tortillas, add to the variety. Their ingredients are similar to those of flour tortillas; they are about the same size or thicker; and their seasonings include garlic and the aromatic spice blend masala.

GREAT INGREDIENT
Pork loin ribs

There's an emotional debate afoot that I do not see

ROASTED PORK BACK RIBS *get a good rub of savory seasonings before they bake. They make sumptuous gnawing.*

PETER CHRISTIANSEN

coming to a resolution. In question: Is the meat around the bone the sweetest and most succulent? If, like me, you are of the persuasion that it is, then the advent of more boned pork loin roasts and boned pork chops in the meat case is a good thing, because you get more neat slabs of back loin bones to cook and gnaw.

Personally, I favor pork back ribs over spareribs; they are leaner and easier to cut

apart. I like them roasted crisp, boldly seasoned with a good, dark rub of ground pepper, sage, and fennel.

The following has to be one of the easiest treatments for ribs, one I often pop in the oven when guests are coming. As the ribs bake, there is ample time to set the table, steam potatoes to mash (or bake potatoes in the oven with the ribs), make salad, and compose yourself enough to smile when the doorbell rings.

As for the salad, greens are fine, but tartly dressed cucumbers really complement the rich flavor of the meat.

Rubbed back ribs. Whirl together in a blender or crush to a fine powder with mortar and pestle 2 parts **whole black peppercorns** and 1 part *each* **fennel seed** and **rubbed dried sage leaves** (2 tablespoons peppercorns and 1 tablespoon *each* fennel seed and dried rubbed sage make about ¼ cup, enough for 1½ to 3 lb. of ribs).

Rinse **pork back ribs** (an average slab, about 1½ lb., makes 1½ to 2 servings). Rub ribs to coat all over with the ground herb mixture. Set ribs, cupped side down, on a rack in a pan just long enough to hold meat. Bake in a 450° oven for 30 minutes; turn curved side up and bake 10 minutes more. (When drippings in pan start to smoke, add water to cover pan bottom.) Turn ribs over again and bake until sizzling and well browned (under herb rub), another 10 to 15 minutes. Cut ribs apart and sprinkle with **salt** to taste. Eat hot or cold.

Per serving: 619 cal. (71 percent from fat); 40 g protein; 49 g fat (18 g sat.); 3.1 g carbo.; 168 mg sodium; 193 mg chol. ∎

BOB THOMPSON ON WINE
California reds with an Italian past

Looking for wines to keep comfort food comfortable? Then rejoice, because the Italian wine grapes Sangiovese and Nebbiolo are joining Barbera in California's vineyards and cellars. Whether your starch of choice is pasta or potatoes, all three wines fare well on a dinner table otherwise loaded with burgers, meat loaf, steak, or chicken.

Barbera, in its native Piedmont area of northwest Italy and in California, is a modest-priced, longtime standby. Forthright flavors

and sturdy balance make it an affable companion to an everyday pasta, stew, or meat loaf. It even rivals Zinfandel with a burger.

Rewarding examples ($7–$13): Preston Dry Creek Valley, Sebastiani Sonoma Valley, Monte Volpe Mendocino, Santino Amador County, Louis M. Martini California.

In Italy, *Nebbiolo* is known as Barbera's much richer, incalculably smarter cousin. In California, it is too new to have any reputation at all. Several current ones from Santa Barbara and San Luis Obispo counties put fresh grape flavors foremost, for easy enjoyment. Some aim to match their Italian cousins

with richer, winier flavors. Regardless of aspirations, red meat is proper company for them all—fruity and fresh or rich and complex.

Fruit first ($10–$12): Martin Brothers California, Arciero Paso Robles.
More seriously structured ($12–$20): Il Podere dell' Olivos Santa Barbara, Martin Brothers Paso Robles Nebbiolo Vecchio, Il Podere dell' Olivos Santa Barbara "Parabola."

Sangiovese—the soul of Chianti Classico and the whole being of Brunello di Montalcino—is a much hotter property in California than either Barbera or Nebbiolo.

The delicate, almost floral

taste of Sangiovese, as all true Tuscans know, makes it a satisfying companion to roasted chicken with or without garlic. Yet the wine is sturdy enough to be just as good with steaks, burgers, and other red meats.

Fruit foremost ($9–$16): Noceto Shenandoah Valley, Seghesio Alexander Valley "Vitigno Toscano," Ferrari-Carano Sonoma County, Estancia Alexander Valley, Swanson Napa Valley.
Fuller, with more oak aging ($24–$25): Atlas Peak Napa Valley, Robert Pepi Napa Valley "Colline di Sassi."

None of these are made in large volume, so finding any of them may take extra hunting.

Revolution in your salad bowl

Ready-mix greens have arrived, and Western salads will never be quite the same

By Betsy Reynolds Bateson

Mizuna
Faintly spicy, mildly nutty; tender with substance.

Lollo Rosso
Sweet, mild, lettuce flavor; delicate crunch.

Curly Cress
Snappy, hot flavor; very tender.

Dandelion
Bitter bite; grassy taste and texture.

Anchocress
Lively heat; tender, juicy, and fleshy.

Red Mustard
A little heat; slightly fuzzy, firm texture.

Arugula
Mellow to bold bite, nutty; fleshy and tender.

Tango
Mild, sweet lettuce; tender, soft-crisp.

Frisée
Sweet chicory with faint bitter edge; tender-crisp.

DEBORAH JONES

Perella Red
Sweet, crisp stem; fleshy, smooth, tender leaf lettuce.

Chervil
Cool licorice flavor; delicate, feathery texture.

Radicchio
A little bitter; almost as firm as cabbage.

Romaine
Sweet and juicy; crisp.

Red Oak Leaf
Tender, mild lettuce; velvety texture.

Tatsoi
Mild with faint metallic edge; sturdy, bulky leaf.

A salad mix of many kinds of tender leaves—needing only dressing—is one of the most practical convenience foods to hit the marketplace in recent years. But the idea of a salad mix is not a new one.

It started in and around Nice, in southern France, as *mesclun.* This regional specialty takes its name, meaning *mix,* from the local dialect, and is a combination of tender, early shoots of arugula, dandelion greens, lettuces, watercress, and chervil.

In the West, growing salad mix has long been popular with home gardeners (*Sunset* was telling how in the '50s). In the early '70s, when Alice Waters, a self-proclaimed salad warrior, opened Chez Panisse in Berkeley, she grew ingredients on the premises in order to demonstrate to customers that "the beauty of a salad is the irresistibility of just-picked, tender greens." But demand quickly outstripped her production. One of her

DAVID MAISEL

WARREN WEBER GROWS *baby salad greens near Bolinas and Thermal, California. More than 10 years ago, his first crop went to Berkeley's Chez Panisse, creating an immediate demand from other restaurateurs. Now he grows greens for many restaurants— and markets, too.*

Buy by the pound, with or without flowers

SALAD MIX BY THE POUND *is relatively expensive compared with most salad greens, but just an ounce makes a serving. This mix is from The Farmery in Felton, California.*

frequently, mesclun. Typically, 8 to 16 different kinds of leaves are in mixes that have evolved to meet Western tastes. Some are composed predominantly of sweet, mild, tender greens (of which at least half are lettuces); some have more substance and bitterness (and include more of the chicory, mustard, and cress families); and some (like kale and Swiss chard) do well when lightly cooked, as in stir-frying.

Lettuces commonly used in salad mixes are green and red loose-leaf such as Lollo Rosso, Oak Leaf, and Tango; small romaine such as Little Gem; and butterhead (butter or Bibb) lettuces such as Perella Red. All these have in common delicate, mild flavor; tenderness; and smooth to slightly crunchy texture.

Other leaves or greens (even if they are red) bring to the salad mix more decisive, complex flavors, firmer textures, and even taste temperatures. Arugula is one of the most popular additions. Also typical are dandelion greens, frisée (fine curly endive), inner leaves of Belgian endive, baby Swiss chard and kale (red and green), mizuna, radicchio, red mustard, shiso, tatsoi, watercress (and varieties like anchocress, upland broadleaf cress, and curled cress), and purslane. Chervil is often in salad mixes, as both a green and herb.

Even edible flowers or their petals may be part of the salad mix. These include bachelor's-buttons, calendulas, nasturtiums (and their leaves), and marigolds.

Salad mixes at farmers' markets often reflect the spirit of the producer and usually come with more variety and components than you'll find at the supermarket. Northwesterner Judy Duff, of Duffield Farm, calls the mix she sells at Seattle's Pike Place Farmers Market "an artistic event, cross-cultural and eclectic," with blossoms of borage, lavender, pansies, and violas.

The quality of the mix depends on maturity at harvest, the mixture's variety and freshness, how the mix is maintained at the market, and how quickly you use it. You can expect to find the freshest mixes at farmers' markets.

Another kind of fresh salad mix is multiplying rapidly in the produce section. These are mixes sealed in plastic bags. To preserve freshness, some are vacuum packed, some are nitrogen-flushed (the bags are puffed), and some are in bags that breathe. Brands you'll encounter include Dole, Fresh Express, ReadyPac, and WA Prepack. Some mixes are specific salads like Caesar, spinach, or coleslaw, with a separately packed dressing; or they are combinations of mature lettuces like iceberg, red and green leaf, or romaine, and other greens like spinach, cabbage, escarole, curly endive, and radicchio—even grated carrots. They often have labels like Italian or gourmet. Occasionally, the bags contain baby greens tagged with names such as spring mix.

How much to buy?

About 1 ounce bulk salad mix greens, fluffed up, is about 2 cups. Keep in mind that ½ pound will make 6 to 8 generous servings, or 3 or 4 main-course servings. At the market, salad mix prices range widely, from $5 a pound to as much as $12; packaged salads range from $1 to $3 for 6-ounce to 1-pound bags. This sounds expensive, but as Warren Weber points out, "It's not economical for you to buy all the various head lettuces and greens to make your own mix—let a

first commercial sources was Star Route Farms near Bolinas. Warren Weber grew greens to Waters's specifications. Initially, he delivered them as tiny heads. Soon, for convenience, part of the salad preparation was taken over at the farm, where small leaves were plucked and mixed, then delivered.

Availability of salad mixes expanded with the farmers' market boom of the '80s. In very few years, the mixes moved into supermarkets and are now relatively commonplace. What was once the province of small local farmers is now shared by growers with thousands of acres in production.

Although salad greens sprout quickly—most are harvested in 6 to 12 weeks—and

planting goes on year-round, spring is when they flourish best. April and May, in particular, bring the best in quality, variety, and price. Production is extended by shifting the growing area, or using shelter. Coastal locations are ideal for spring and summer, the deserts of California and Arizona for winter and fall.

What's in the mix?

By French standards, a Western mesclun is a misnomer, as the greens are grown outside of Provence, and—in even greater violation—often go beyond traditional ingredients. You're apt to have several bins of salad mix choices even in supermarkets, with names like spring salad, piquant mix, stir-fry greens, and far less farmer do it for you. You get so many lettuces and greens in one product." Larry Roberts, spokesman for Larry's Markets in Seattle, suggests combining salad mixes "with other less expensive lettuces for a milder flavor and to extend the servings; or serve the mesclun on a bed of Bibb (butter) lettuce leaves."

Tender care for tender leaves

Even though bulk salad mixes are rinsed after picking, rinse the leaves again at home to remove dust and any visiting insects, and to refresh the leaves (especially if they are limp—as happens on warm days at farmers' markets). Immerse leaves in cool water, swish back and forth, lift out, and drain on towels. If you spin greens dry, use at once; tiny bruises cause the leaves to break down on standing.

It's best to use any greens right after purchase, but to crisp or store them, enclose rinsed leaves in towels, seal in a plastic bag, and chill. Crisping may take only 15 minutes, but prime condition greens stored this way may stay fresh looking and tasting up to two weeks.

Packaged salads don't need rinsing. Keep them cool and use before the date limitation.

Greens by mail order or from seed

If salad mixes are difficult to find, you can order them. Or, if you are so inclined, grow your own.

For fresh greens, call Northwest Select, Forgiven & Rejoice Israel, at (800) 622-2693. The mix ($28 per pound, plus $8 for second-day air shipping) includes specialties such as wild chrysanthemum greens, pea tips, mâche (corn salad), edible-leaf amaranth, and anise hyssop. Other mixes include specialty greens ($12 per pound for 10 kinds, plus shipping), available April through October.

For seed or catalogs, write or call *The Cook's Garden*, Box 535, Londonderry, Vt. 05148, (802) 824-3400; or *Shepherd's Garden Seeds*, 6116 Highway 9, Felton, Calif. 95018, (408) 335-6910. ■

Salad greens with prosciutto and shrimp

Golden calendula and lavender bachelor's button petals are part of this salad mix. Add shrimp and sizzled prosciutto to make a main dish for lunch or a light supper. For 4 servings, sliver ¼ pound thinly sliced **prosciutto** and stir with 2 teaspoons **olive oil** in an 8- to 10-inch frying pan over medium-high heat until lightly browned. Pour into a wide salad bowl and add ¾ pound (about 4 qt.) rinsed and crisped **salad mix**, ½ pound rinsed and drained **shelled cooked tiny shrimp**, 2 tablespoons minced **crystallized ginger**, ¼ cup **pear** or rice **vinegar**, 3 tablespoons **salad oil**, and 1 tablespoon **Oriental sesame oil**.

PETER CHRISTIANSEN

Morning feasts in San Francisco's finest dinner settings

Savor the best restaurants even if you're on a budget, or try one of their terrific breakfast entrées in your own kitchen

ESCAPING FROM THE noisy morning hustle of Stockton Street, you retreat into Campton Place's calm, elegant dining room. The friendly staff—and smells of savory-sweet breakfast foods—extends a warm greeting. You relax in soft leather seats—your 2-year-old happily playing with silver spoons and sliced berries—and enjoy the luxury of perfectly prepared breakfast classics delivered with unexpected touches: eggs Benedict served on tender herb biscuits and inch-high pancakes with silver boats of whipped cream and hot maple syrup.

If you've ever wondered how you can experience Campton Place and other top-notch San Francisco restaurants without booking ahead, without the formality that makes bringing the kids out of the question, and without a tab that's more than your budget allows, try breakfast.

Early on weekends or weekday mornings, venture to these restaurants (most in hotels), for a lavish breakfast. Menus offer plenty of kid-friendly foods as well as fancy dishes you may not have time to cook at home. Choices range from eggs Benedict or French toast to a simple espresso and breakfast

RICHARD MORGENSTEIN

ANDY FREEBERG

INDULGE IN THE SHERMAN HOUSE'S *French toast with apples and walnuts.*

REBECCA, *lucky daughter of Postrio chefs Anne and David Gingrass, enjoys hot chocolate and an orange waffle with passion fruit syrup.*

BREAKFAST AT ELKA *offers both a distinctive atmosphere and chef Elka Gilmore's distinctive Asian-American cuisine.*

WILLIAM MERCER McLEOD

pizza or homemade pastries—even yogurt and granola (most made in-house). It's also a good time to indulge in a pot of rich hot chocolate.

Before 10 A.M., there's generally not a problem walking into these restaurants without a reservation. (That's not the case for brunch, which is usually served later, and for which reservations—and often a wait—are required.)

Although you won't find a $3.99 breakfast special at these upscale restaurants, your tab will be considerably less than at dinner. (Fresh-squeezed juice, coffee, hot chocolate, and entrées for two can cost as much as $40.)

GREAT BREAKFASTS IN GREAT SPACES

Here's a guide to some of our favorite breakfasts in choice San Francisco dinner spots. Area code is 415.

The Big Four Restaurant, The Huntington Hotel, Nob Hill, 1075 California Street; 771-1140. From 7 to 10 weekdays, until 11 weekends. Breakfast choices in the elegant dining room include Eggs Huntington (eggs Benedict with smoked salmon) and delicious cinnamon hot chocolate.

Campton Place Restaurant, Kempinski Hotel, 340 Stockton Street; 955-5555.

From 7 to 11 weekdays, 8 to 11:30 Saturdays, 8 to 2:30 Sundays (includes a brunch menu insert). Voted the "Best Breakfast" in the city three times in *San Francisco Focus* magazine. Breakfast classics are done with seasonal flair and excellence.

ELKA, Miyako Hotel, 1611 Post Street; 922-7788. From 6:30 to 11 daily. Enjoy breakfast foods presented in innovative ways, such as poached eggs in chipotle chili broth with flour tortilla, and eggs scrambled with pasta, sausage, and herbs.

The French Room, Four Seasons Clift Hotel, 495 Geary Street; 775-4700. From 6:30 to 11:30 weekdays, 7 to 11:30 weekends; brunch from 10 to 2:30 weekends. Sophisticated entrées, and the famous French Room hot chocolate with cream. An alternative menu features foods lower in calories, cholesterol, sodium, and fat.

The Garden Court, Sheraton Palace Hotel, 2 New Montgomery Street; 392-8600. From 6:30 to 10:30 Mondays through Saturdays; early breakfast not available in the Garden Court on Sundays, when brunch is served from 9:30 to 3. The dining environment in the Garden Court of this historic hotel restored to turn-of-the-century glamour is a bargain in itself. Try the whole-wheat peach crêpes, a house specialty.

Kuleto's, next to Villa Florence Hotel, 221 Powell Street; 397-7720. From 7 to 10:30 weekdays, 8 to 10:30 weekends in the main restaurant. Enjoy a breakfast pizza or a *meini* (an Italian-style scone with cornmeal). Or sample one of the restaurant's classic egg dishes or a cereal. Try the banana-strawberry smoothie or Latte Caldo Cioccolata (hot chocolate).

Postrio, The Prescott Hotel, 545 Post Street; 776-7825. From 7 to 10 weekdays, 9 to 2 weekends. Treat yourself to a quiet morning before tackling the City; follow chefs Anne and David Gingrass's routine

AT THE SHERMAN HOUSE, *morning diners enjoy a meal of special breakfast foods in elegant surroundings.*

and sit in a corner with a cup of cappuccino and freshly baked praline scone while enjoying the dining room.

The Sherman House, 2160 Green Street; 563-3600. From 7 to 11 Mondays through Saturdays (Sunday brunch 8:30 to 2:30). For true indulgence, the French toast with caramelized apples and walnuts wins the award.

Silks, Mandarin Oriental Hotel, 222 Sansome Street; 986-2020. From 6:30 to 10:30 weekdays, 7 to 2 weekends. This jewel of a breakfast stop sits right in the middle of the Financial District. The menu offers a signature granola, and potato pancakes topped with poached eggs, thinly sliced Black Forest ham, and Swiss cheese.

The Terrace, The Ritz-Carlton, 600 Stockton Street; 296-7465. From 7 to 10:30 Mondays through Saturdays (Sunday brunch 11 to 3). One of the few places in the city where you can eat outside—weather permitting—in a beautiful courtyard.

WAKE-UP FAVORITES

If you can't experience these unique breakfasts in person, try these recipes at home.

Postrio's Orange Waffle with Passion Fruit Syrup

1½ cups all-purpose flour
1 tablespoon sugar
1½ teaspoons baking powder
½ teaspoon salt
1 cup buttermilk
½ cup orange juice
3 large eggs, separated
3 tablespoons butter or margarine, melted and cooled
2 tablespoons grated orange peel
About 2 tablespoons salad oil
About 2 cups assorted sliced fruits, such as banana, kiwi fruit, and strawberries
Passion fruit syrup (recipe follows)

Combine flour, sugar, baking powder, and salt; set mixture aside.

In a large bowl, whisk together buttermilk, orange juice, egg yolks, butter, and peel. Gradually whisk in flour mixture until batter is smooth.

With an electric mixer, whip egg whites in a clean bowl until stiff but not dry, about 5 minutes. Gently fold whites into batter.

Heat waffle iron according to manufacturer's directions. Brush grids with oil. Fill ⅔ full with batter, spreading evenly (about 1 cup per 8-in.-square grid). Bake until deep golden, 7 to 8 minutes. Serve, or place directly on racks in a 200° oven to keep warm for up to 30 minutes. Garnish with fruits and syrup. Makes 4 waffles, each 8 inches square.—*Anne and David Gingrass, Postrio*

Per waffle: 680 cal. (28 percent from fat); 13 g protein; 21 g fat (7.8 g sat.); 114 g carbo.; 669 mg sodium; 185 mg chol.

Passion fruit syrup. Slice 2 (about 3 oz. total) **passion fruits** in half; scoop seeds and pulp into a wire sieve over a measuring cup. Using the back of a spoon, press juice from pulp and seeds. Set aside. In a 2-cup microwave-safe glass measure, heat 1 cup **maple syrup,** uncovered, in a microwave oven at full power (100 percent) until hot, about 1 minute. Stir in passion fruit juice.

ELKA's Poached Eggs in Chipotle Broth

1 whole dried chipotle chili
4 cloves garlic, minced or pressed
1 tablespoon olive or salad oil
1 large (10 oz.) yellow onion, thinly sliced
2 large (about 1 lb. total) yellow bell peppers, cored, seeded, and thinly sliced

TREAT YOURSELF *to ELKA's innovative poached eggs.*

2 large (about 1 lb. total) red bell peppers, cored, seeded, and thinly sliced

2 cans (28 oz. each) pear-shaped tomatoes

2 cups regular-strength chicken broth

1 cup thinly sliced red onion

½ cup lime juice

12 medium-size (6 to 8 in.) flour tortillas

12 poached eggs (recipe follows)

About ⅓ cup minced fresh cilantro (coriander) leaves

About ½ cup sour cream

Lime wedges (optional)

Soak chili in ½ cup hot water until soft, about 20 minutes. Remove stem and seeds. Mince remaining chili; set aside.

In a 6- to 8-quart pan over medium-high heat, cook garlic in olive oil until golden. Add yellow onion, and yellow and red bell peppers; cook, stirring often, until soft, about 4 minutes. Stir in tomatoes with juice, broth, and minced chili. Bring to a boil; reduce heat, cover, and simmer about 1 hour.

Meanwhile, combine red onion and lime juice; set aside. Wrap tortillas in 2 layers of foil; heat in a 250° oven until hot, about 30 minutes. Remove from oven; keep covered until ready to use (will hold heat about 15 minutes).

After vegetable mixture has simmered 1 hour, break tomatoes apart with a wooden spoon. Boil mixture, uncovered, until reduced to about 10 cups, about 15 minutes more.

Evenly divide mixture among 6 wide, shallow soup bowls. Lay 2 hot poached eggs over broth in each bowl. Add red onion and cilantro and a dollop of sour cream to each dish. Offer lime wedges to squeeze if desired. Serve immediately with hot flour tortillas. Makes 6 servings.—*Elka Gilmore, ELKA*

Per serving: 476 cal. (40 percent from fat); 22 g protein; 21 g fat (6.6 g sat.); 53 g carbo.; 941 mg sodium; 431 mg chol.

Poached eggs. *To heat-treat eggs for perfect poached eggs.* In a 5- to 6-quart pan, bring about 2 quarts water to a boil. Gently lower **eggs,** one at a time, into constantly boiling water. Begin to time when the first egg is in the water. Cook 8 seconds, then remove eggs in the same order as they were placed in the water. Repeat until you have treated 12 eggs (don't worry if eggs crack). Poach eggs at once, or chill for no more than 2 days.

To poach. In a 5- to 6-quart pan over high heat, bring 2 quarts water and 2 tablespoons **distilled white vinegar** to a gentle boil. Reduce heat, maintaining a temperature that causes bubbles to form on pan bottom (one may pop on top occasionally). Break each egg directly into water (do not crowd; 4 or 5 eggs at a time are manageable), holding it as close to water as possible. Cook until set as you like, about 4 minutes for soft yolks and firm whites (test by poking egg gently with a spoon tip to check firmness).

To store. Lay the poached eggs in a 9- by 13-inch dish, cover with plastic wrap, and chill for up to 2 days.

To reheat. Heat 2 quarts water in a 5- to 6-quart pan until just hot to touch; remove from heat. Add eggs; let stand 5 to 10 minutes, or until eggs feel hot. Lift from water with a slotted spoon, drain, and use.

The Sherman House's French Toast with Apples and Walnuts

Serve the French toast with bacon or ham if desired.

Caramelized apples (recipe follows)

1 cup walnut halves and pieces

1 loaf (about 1 lb., 12 in. long) brioche, challah, or other egg bread

6 large eggs

2½ cups milk or half-and-half

1 tablespoon vanilla

2 teaspoons ground cinnamon

½ teaspoon ground nutmeg

1 cup maple syrup

¼ cup (⅛ lb.) butter or margarine, melted

Prepare caramelized apples; sprinkle with walnuts. Set aside.

Slice ½ inch off each end of the loaf; reserve the ends for other uses. Slice the remaining loaf into 10 slices, each about 1 inch thick.

In a 9- by 13-inch baking dish, whisk together eggs, milk, vanilla, cinnamon, and nutmeg. Lay the bread slices, half at a time, in the batter to saturate 1 side of each slice; turn over to saturate the second side. Repeat, using all of the batter. Arrange the slices in a single layer on a lightly buttered 12- by 15-inch baking sheet.

Bake on the bottom rack in a 450° oven until slices begin to brown, about 15 minutes.

With a wide spatula, turn slices over; continue baking until browned, about 15 minutes longer. Add pan of caramelized apples and walnuts to top rack of oven to warm.

Meanwhile, whisk together syrup and butter.

Heat syrup mixture in a hot water bath or in a microwave oven until hot.

To serve, cut each slice in half diagonally; assemble 4 halves on each dinner plate. Overlap slices to form a V (see photo on page 71). Spoon apples and walnuts over slices; drizzle each serving with 2 tablespoons hot syrup; offer remaining syrup at table. Makes 5 servings.—*Maria Helm, The Sherman House*

Per serving: 954 cal. (41 percent from fat); 22 g protein; 43 g fat (16 g sat.); 124 g carbo.; 678 mg sodium; 351 mg chol.

Caramelized apples. Core 2½ pounds (about 5 large) **apples,** such as Gala, Jonagold, or Fuji. Cut each apple into 8 wedges. In a 10- to 12-inch frying pan over medium heat, melt 2 tablespoons **butter** or margarine, and add apple wedges. Cook, stirring occasionally, until golden and tinged brown, about 20 minutes. Spread on a lightly oiled 10- by 15-inch baking sheet. Set aside. ■

By Betsy Reynolds Bateson

ANDY FREEBERG

HOT CHOCOLATE *is a breakfast specialty at all of these special restaurants.*

BUNS ARE CROSSED with (from left) raspberry jam, lemon curd, raspberry-almond topping, and lemon icing: choose one or all.

Hot cross buns

Homemade candied orange flavors this seasonal favorite

SAN FRANCISCO BAKER Fran Gage, owner of Pâtisserie Française, bakes tender hot cross buns with fresh orange fragrance and spice overtones. Using Gage's recipe, you can bake these delicious buns at home. You'll need to prepare the fresh candied orange a few days before baking.

You can also pick up the buns from the bakery at 4690 18th Street. To order ahead (buns in the case often go fast), call (415) 864-8428.

Hot Cross Buns

¾ cup candied orange (recipe follows)

1 package active dry yeast

¼ cup warm water (about 110°)

3½ to 4 cups all-purpose flour

HOT CROSS TIPS: *1. For fresh candied orange, simply cover orange slices with hot syrup, and chill. 2. To cross buns, firmly squeeze topping through the clipped end of a plastic bag.*

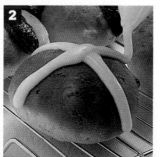

⅓ cup granulated sugar

½ teaspoon salt

¼ teaspoon each ground nutmeg and cloves

¾ cup milk

1 large egg

¼ cup (⅛ lb.) butter or margarine, melted and cooled

⅓ cup dried currants or raisins

Cross toppings

Prepare candied orange 24 hours to 2 weeks ahead according to recipe instructions, following.

In large bowl of an electric mixer with a dough hook attachment, or in another bowl, sprinkle yeast over water; let stand until softened, about 5 minutes.

In another bowl, combine 3½ cups flour, granulated sugar, salt, nutmeg, and cloves; set aside.

To yeast mixture, add milk, egg, and butter. Gradually add 2 cups of the flour mixture. Beat with a mixer until stretchy, or by hand with a heavy spoon until dough is thoroughly moistened and stretchy, about 5 minutes.

To knead with a dough hook. Add 1 more cup of the flour mixture, and mix on low speed until incorporated; then beat on high speed about 5 minutes. Add remaining flour mixture, candied orange, and currants. Mix on low speed until fruits are worked into dough, about 2 minutes (use a rubber spatula to mix fruit into dough if necessary). Remove hook; leave dough in bowl.

To knead by hand. Before kneading, add remaining flour mixture, candied orange, and currants to bowl; stir until dough is evenly moistened. Scrape dough onto a floured board; coat lightly with flour. Knead until smooth and elastic, adding just enough flour to prevent sticking, about 8 minutes. Return dough to bowl.

After kneading, cover with plastic wrap. Let rise in a warm place until doubled, about 2 hours.

Punch down dough; spoon onto a floured board. Add flour as needed to knead dough into a soft rectangle. Cut in half lengthwise, then cut each rectangle into 6 pieces. Roll each piece into a ball, pulling dough to bottom to form a smooth top. Place on 2 lightly oiled baking sheets (each 12- by 15-in.). Loosely cover with plastic wrap; let rise in a warm place until puffy, about 30 minutes.

Bake in a 400° oven until buns are browned and hollow-sounding when tapped on bottom, about 20 minutes (switch pan positions halfway through baking). Cool on a wire rack. When just warm to touch, cross each bun with desired topping (directions follow). Serve warm or cool.

(If making ahead, omit topping. Cool, then wrap airtight and freeze up to 1 month. Reheat frozen buns on a baking sheet in a 400° oven about 10 minutes. Decorate and serve as suggested above.)

Makes 12 buns.

Candied orange. Cut and discard ends from 1 medium-size (8 oz.) **orange;** thinly slice and place in a bowl. In a 1- to 2-quart pan over high heat, bring 1 cup **water** and 1 cup **granulated sugar** to a boil. Pour the syrup over the orange slices; cover and chill for at least 24 hours or up to 2 weeks. Drain slices; chop.

Cross toppings. Spoon desired topping (see choices below) into a plastic sandwich bag (without pleated bottom); push topping to a bottom corner and twist top shut. Clip off about ⅛ inch of filled corner. Squeeze bag to pipe crosses onto bun tops.

Lemon icing. Combine 1 cup **powdered sugar** and 2 to 3 tablespoons **lemon juice.** Stir until smooth and of syrup consistency, adding juice as needed. Top each bun with **lemon peel,** if desired.

Raspberry-almond topping. Stir together ¾ cup **raspberry jelly** and ¼ cup **almond paste** until smooth. Top each bun with **almond slice,** if desired.

Buy *lemon curd* and *raspberry jam* as other choices.

Per bun with lemon icing: 289 cal. (17 percent from fat); 5.3 g protein; 5.3 g fat (3 g sat.); 55 g carbo.; 147 mg sodium; 31 mg chol. ∎

By Betsy Reynolds Bateson

Strawberry snacks

All you need to know to create speedy treats

SWEET, RIPE, AND naked—that's how most people go for strawberries. Their juicy, succulent flesh, curvacious shape, and seductive aroma account for the fact that this fruit is, statistically, mostly consumed as a wholesome snack. A light rinse may be all berries need to make them ready to eat, but with a trifle more effort you can transform these crimson beauties into sophisticated nibbles to fill the roles of breakfast fruit or fruit salad, appetizer, and sweet refreshment.

Right now the flood of strawberries grown in California is beginning. From April through June, the state's peak season, 9.6 million pint-size baskets will be gathered daily by hand from 23,000 acres and rushed to market. And it's only the start—crops from here and other states ripen through summer and into late fall. ■

By Linda Lau Anusasananan

BERRIES WITH PROSCIUTTO TURBANS. *For each appetizer, wrap a stemmed strawberry and a fresh tarragon sprig with a 1-inch-wide strip of paper-thin prosciutto; dip this bundle into a fine balsamic vinegar.*

BERRY TEA CAKES. *Swirl a blend of equal parts lemon curd and unflavored yogurt on buttery shortbread cookies; top each with a strawberry half and mint leaf.*

STRAWBERRY OLÉ. *For breakfast or lunch, set strawberries, stem ends trimmed and tips up, on a plate. Moisten with orange and lime juice and sprinkle to taste with sugar and chili powder.*

PETER CHRISTIANSEN

WHITE FENNEL, with its feathery leaves, makes a mellow partner for fish.

The secret is fennel

Wonderful things happen when it's teamed with fish

THE FRENCH AND Italians have long appreciated the refreshing impact of cool, mild, anise-flavor fennel on fish. Chef Robert Engel of Russian River Vineyards Restaurant in Forestville, California, is also a fan of this duo. His fish stew with fennel and delicate fennel sauce for fish reflect a Western orientation and an imaginative touch.

Fish and Fennel Stew

- 1 large (3 to 4 in. wide) head fennel with feathery green leaves
- 1 large (about ½ lb.) onion, chopped
- 6 cloves garlic, minced or pressed
- 1 tablespoon olive or salad oil
- 6 medium-size (about 1¼ lb. total) Roma-type tomatoes, cored and chopped
- 2 cups regular-strength chicken broth
- 1 bottle (8 oz.) clam juice
- ½ cup dry white wine
- ¼ to ½ teaspoon cayenne

- 1½ pounds skinned and boned firm-texture light-fleshed fish, such as halibut, swordfish, or sea bass, cut into 1½-inch pieces
- 12 mussels, well scrubbed with beards pulled off (optional)

Trim coarse stems, bruises, and root end from fennel. Pull green leaves from stems, mince, and set aside.

Thinly slice fennel head and combine with onion, garlic, and oil in a 5- to 6-quart pan over medium-high heat. Stir often until vegetables are browned and onion tastes sweet, 15 to 20 minutes.

To pan, add tomatoes, broth, clam juice, wine, and cayenne. Bring to a boil over high heat; cover and simmer 10 minutes. Add fish and mussels. Cover and simmer just until fish is opaque but still moist-looking in center (cut to test) and mussels pop open, about 5 minutes. Add minced fennel greens and ladle into wide bowls. Serves 4.

Per serving: 322 cal. (24 percent from fat); 40 g protein; 8.6 g fat (1.3 g sat.); 16 g carbo.; 340 mg sodium; 54 mg chol.

Chilled Fennel Sauce

Serve with hot or cold cooked salmon, halibut, sea bass, or sole.

- 1 large (3 to 4 in. wide) head fennel with feathery green leaves
- 1½ cups regular-strength chicken broth
- ½ cup minced leeks or onions
- ½ cup Riesling (Johannisberg or White) or Gewürztraminer
- ¼ cup whipping cream, softly whipped
- 2 tablespoons anise-flavor liqueur such as Pernod (optional)
  Salt

Trim coarse stems, bruises, and root end from fennel. Pull green leaves from stems, mince, and set aside.

Mince fennel head and combine with broth, leeks, and wine in a 10- to 12-inch pan. Bring to boil over high heat; cover and simmer gently until vegetables mash easily, about 55 minutes. Uncover and boil on high heat, stirring often, until mixture is reduced to about 2 cups; smoothly purée in a blender or food processor. Rub through a fine strainer into a bowl; discard residue. Cover and chill until cold, at least 2 hours or up to 1 day.

Gently fold fennel leaves, whipped cream, and liqueur into purée; add salt to taste. Makes about 2 cups.

Per tablespoon: 11 cal. (49 percent from fat); 0.2 g protein; 0.6 g fat (0.4 g sat.); 0.5 g carbo.; 10 mg sodium; 2.1 mg chol. ■

By Christine Weber Hale

YOLK OF EGG *at left, boiled in the shell for 40 minutes, has an unappetizing gray-green rim. Yolk at right, cooked (not boiled) for much less time, is firm and golden throughout. Light turns potatoes, right, green with solanine under peel. For safety and taste, cut this toxin away with peel.*

Why?

The greening of eggs and potatoes

GREEN SUITS BEANS and broccoli, but on eggs and potatoes this color is not just unappealing; it can even be unpleasant or harmful. Fortunately, a few simple practices in your kitchen can eliminate the color.

"When eggs are hard-boiled, why are some yolks dark around the outside while others remain yellow all the way through?"—*Doris H. Taylor, Santa Barbara*

Boiling is part of the problem. High heat aggravates the color change; long cooking guarantees it. Two elements in an egg are activated as it cooks in the shell—iron in the yolk and sulfur in the white. Iron works its way toward the shell, while sulfur heads for the yolk. If iron and sulfur meet at the edge of the yolk, they turn it an ugly but harmless gray-green. In boiling water, these elements move more quickly than in water below boiling. For an egg that is firm with no discoloration, you need to cook it below boiling, and cool it quickly when done.

The following method for perfect hard-cooked eggs with golden yolks provides easily managed controls that produce consistent results: Place **eggs** in a single layer in a pan with enough cold **water** to cover them by 1 inch. Set pan, uncovered, over highest heat until water reaches 200° and begins to roll (but not actively bubble) at side of pan.

When the first rolling boil breaks the water's surface, immediately reduce heat so only an occasional bubble glides upward from the pan bottom (take pan off heat for minute or two, if needed); hold temperature between 180° and 200° for 12 minutes. At once, immerse eggs in cold water to stop cooking and slow movement of sulfur and iron; with even a few extra minutes of heat, the color change may happen.

"When removing shells from hard-boiled [cooked] eggs, why do some shells peel off the whites easily while others stick and usually pull off some of the white?"—*D. T.*

This question has more than one answer. It may surprise you to know that the most common reason hard-cooked eggs don't peel neatly is because they are too fresh. Egg white is composed of many layers, and in fresh eggs the layer closest to the shell membrane clings to it tightly. As eggs are stored in the refrigerator, their internal acid-alkaline balance becomes more alkaline, and the white gets thinner from the outside in. As the exterior layer thins, it becomes less firmly attached to the membrane, and the egg's shell, to which the membrane is attached, pulls from the egg without tearing the white.

Hard-cooked eggs are also easier to peel if immersed in cold water as soon as they are cooked, and shells are crackled to let the water seep in; peel when cool enough to handle.

A really old (a month or older) refrigerated egg can also be difficult to peel. As the egg sits in the refrigerator, it gradually loses air through the shell. The white shrinks and grows increasingly fragile as a large air cell forms. Sometimes the membrane shrinks snugly with the egg, and this makes peeling difficult. If it doesn't shrink as much, the egg is easy to peel, but the tender white is inclined to tear. (Unrefrigerated eggs deteriorate to this stage very rapidly; for many reasons, it is unsafe and inadvisable to leave eggs out of the refrigerator for more than 4 or 5 hours raw or cooked.)

"Why do potatoes turn green, and what happens to them in the refrigerator?"—*Sadye M. Lawson, Los Angeles*

Potatoes turn green just under their skin when exposed to enough light, and more quickly if they are in a warm place or refrigerated. The color is chlorophyll, and as it forms it indicates the production of solanine, a bitter toxin already present in potato leaves, stems, and eyes. The brighter the color, the higher the concentration of solanine. A bite or so isn't enough to be harmful, but if eaten regularly in quantity, it can be dangerous.

Because solanine concentrates close to the surface, it can usually be cut away as you peel the potatoes. Heat also inactivates some of the toxin; cooking water will leach some of it. However, if a potato is green well below the skin and has started to sprout, it will taste bitter; plant it or discard it.

If you store potatoes in a cool, dark, well-ventilated place, they develop little if any solanine.

However, if you store potatoes (particularly russets) in the refrigerator at or below 42°, not only is it likely some solanine will form, but some of the potato starch will convert to sugar. The potatoes will have an oddly sweet taste, and may get brownish when cooked.

More questions?

If you come across other cooking mysteries and would like to know why they happen, send your questions to Why?, *Sunset Magazine*, 80 Willow Rd., Menlo Park, Calif. 94025. With the help of Dr. George K. York, extension food technologist at UC Davis, *Sunset* food editors will find the solutions. ■

By Linda Lau Anusasananan

PETER CHRISTIANSEN

SERVE WHITE CURRY *and rice with pickled cucumbers topped with fried garlic and ginger.*

Malaysian wedding dish: white curry

It's sweet and mild…with no chili

U NLIKE MOST CURRY dishes, this Malaysian chicken version contains no chilies. A blend of spices—including lemon grass, galangal (an astringent root similar to ginger), and star anise—gives it a sweet, mild pungency.

In Malaysia, this elegant white curry is normally served at weddings or festive dinners. You can serve it to family or guests with rice and crunchy sweet and sour cucumber pickles with chilies.

Look for curry ingredients in Asian markets, or use the supermarket alternatives.

White Chicken Curry
(Ayam Lemak Puteh)

    Spice mixture (recipe
    follows)
 1 can (13½ oz.) coconut
    milk
 2 tablespoons salad oil
12 chicken thighs (3 to 3½
    lb. total), skin removed

 1 stalk fresh lemon grass,
    bruised, or ½ teaspoon
    grated lemon peel
 2 slices fresh galangal
    (optional)
 1 cinnamon stick (3 in.)
 2 star anise (or 1 teaspoon
    anise seed)
    Salt

In a food processor or blender, whirl spice mixture with 3 tablespoons coconut milk to make a paste.

Pour oil into a 5- to 6-quart pan over high heat. When oil is hot, add spice mixture and stir until fragrant, about 1 minute. Add chicken and stir until coated with spice mixture. Add remaining coconut milk, ¾ cup water, lemon grass, galangal, cinnamon, and star anise.

Bring to a boil; cover and simmer over medium heat for 20 minutes, turning chicken once or twice. Uncover and cook until sauce thickens and coats chicken, about 20 minutes; stir often. Reduce heat as sauce thickens. Add salt to

taste. Makes 6 servings.

Per serving: 346 cal. (62 percent from fat); 28 g protein; 24 g fat (14 g sat.); 6.2 g carbo.; 124 mg sodium; 107 mg chol.

Spice mixture. Stir together 1 large (about 8 oz.) **onion,** chopped; 3 cloves **garlic,** crushed; 3 tablespoons **ground coriander;** and 1 tablespoon **ground cumin.**

Cucumber Pickle
(Achar Timun)

1½ pounds pickling
     cucumbers, rinsed
  4 fresh red chilies (each 2
     to 3 in.), stemmed and
     seeded
  1 tablespoon salt
  ¼ cup sesame seed
  ¼ cup salad oil
  4 cloves garlic, sliced
     lengthwise
  ¼ cup thinly sliced fresh
     ginger
  ½ teaspoon ground
     turmeric
  ½ cup distilled white
     vinegar
  2 teaspoons sugar

Cut cucumbers into ½- by 1½-inch strips. Cut chilies into ¼-inch strips. Mix cucumbers and chilies with salt; drain in a colander about 15 minutes. Rinse and drain.

Stir sesame seed in an 8- to 10-inch frying pan over medium-low heat until golden brown, about 10 minutes. Remove from pan; cool and set aside up to 1 day.

Pour oil into frying pan over high heat. When oil is hot, add garlic and ginger; stir until golden brown, about 7 minutes. Remove from pan; set aside. If making ahead, cover and let stand up to 1 day.

In the same pan, combine turmeric, vinegar, ½ cup water, and sugar. Bring to a boil, stirring. Let cool.

In a large bowl, combine cucumbers, chilies, and cool vinegar mixture. Cover and chill for at least 1 hour or up to 1 day.

To serve, top cucumber mixture with ginger mixture and sesame. Serves 6.

Per serving: 151 cal. (72 percent from fat); 2.2 g protein; 12 g fat (1.6 g sat.); 10 g carbo.; 556 mg sodium; 0 mg chol. ∎

By Kaan Gwee

Sashimi from Hawaii

Start with fish used in the Islands

HAWAIIAN FISH suitable for sashimi, the classic Japanese presentation of raw fish, are increasingly available in Western markets. You can also use the same fish caught in other waters.

Sashimi is the ultimate in simplicity and, for the initiated, a refreshing entrée.

Excellent-quality fish is vital; it must smell fresh, clean, and unfishy. Freeze fresh fish to destroy any parasites.

Hawaiian Sashimi

1½ to 2 pounds ahi, mahi mahi, opah, ono, or tombo, or some of several, chilled

1½ tablespoons wasabi powder (green horseradish)

Dipping sauce (recipe follows)

½ cup drained, thinly sliced pickled ginger

If fish is fresh, freeze airtight at least 48 hours at 0° to kill any possible parasites (rarely present in these fish). Thaw, refrigerated. Trim and discard any skin and connective tissue (it looks like gristle). Rinse fish and pat dry. With a very sharp knife, cut across grain into slices ⅛ to ¼ inch thick and about 3 inches long. Arrange on 6 dinner plates; if assembling ahead, cover airtight and chill up to 2 hours.

Stir wasabi with about 2 teaspoons water to make a stiff paste. Use some to season dipping sauce (below) to taste, then form remainder into 6 equal balls. Pour sauce into 6 small cups. If desired, overlap ginger slices to make 6 roselike shapes, or pinch into equal mounds. Place a wasabi ball and ginger rose on each plate.

As you eat, dip fish into sauce and season with ginger and additional wasabi. Serves 6.—*Peter Merriman, Merriman's Restaurant, Kamuela, Hawaii*

Per serving using ahi: 157 cal. (6.3 percent from fat); 28 g protein; 1.1 g fat (0.3 g sat.); 5.8 g carbo.; 890 mg sodium; 51 mg chol.

Dipping sauce. Mix ½ cup **reduced-sodium soy sauce,** 2 tablespoons **mirin** (sweet sake), 2 tablespoons **lime juice,** and **wasabi paste** (preceding) to taste. ■

By Elaine Johnson

PETER CHRISTIANSEN

SIMPLE PRESENTATION, *quality fish are essential for sashimi.*

Ultimate chocolate milk

Start with cocoa beans from a Latino market

THE BEST CHOCOLATE milk we've ever tried." That's the first thing tasters say about Myriam Paiz's special Nicaraguan recipe. Then they ask how she gets the creamy texture and unusually good flavor. Her secret? Cocoa beans, rice, and cinnamon—typical chocolate milk ingredients to Nicaraguans but a little unusual to North Americans.

Rice gives the drink body. Freshly roasted cocoa beans—just chocolate in a more elemental form—add a fresh, complex flavor. The cinnamon gives a subtle spiciness.

Paiz roasts the beans until they crackle, and soaks rice to soften it. Then she pulverizes these ingredients with water in a blender, strains the mixture, and adds milk, sugar, and vanilla.

Many Latino markets sell cocoa beans. Or you can order them by mail from Aliment Research, 751 Laurel St., Suite 434, San Carlos, Calif. 94070. Minimum order is 5 pounds. The cost fluctuates with the market (the current price is $1.92 a pound); shipping is extra.

Nicaraguan Chocolate Milk
(Orchata de cacao)

1½ cups long-grain white rice

2 cups (about ⅔ lb.) cocoa beans

4 cups water

3 cinnamon sticks (each about 3 in.), broken into 1-inch pieces

8 cups whole, low-fat, or nonfat milk

PALE COLOR *of Nicaraguan-style chocolate milk belies its rich taste.*

1½ tablespoons vanilla

1 cup sugar

Ice (optional)

Place rice in a bowl, cover with cool water, and let stand to soften somewhat, 6 to 24 hours; drain.

Place beans in a 9-inch metal baking dish. Bake in 500° oven 5 minutes; shake beans. Continue to bake until beans smoke and some skins have split, 5 to 8 minutes longer.

In a blender, place half the rice, cocoa beans, water, and cinnamon. Whirl until ingredients are very finely puréed. Place a large, fine strainer over a bowl; pour cocoa mixture into strainer and stir to extract liquid. Discard residue. Repeat with remaining rice, cocoa, water, and cinnamon.

Rinse strainer, then line with a double thickness of damp cheesecloth. Pour cocoa liquid through strainer into a bowl, stirring to extract all liquid; discard residue.

To cocoa liquid, add milk, vanilla, and sugar; stir until sugar dissolves. Serve plain or over ice. If making ahead, chill, covered, up to 3 days. Stir to serve. Makes about 10½ cups, 10 servings. —*Myriam Paiz, Los Angeles*

Per serving: 227 cal. (27 percent from fat); 7.3 g protein; 6.9 g fat (4.3 g sat.); 35 g carbo.; 97 mg sodium; 27 mg chol. ■

By Elaine Johnson

Jam surprises beans and rice

Bread gets garlic dimples and classic flavors, and chicken takes a literary turn

BEANS AND GRAINS ARE A great team nutritionally, especially in areas where meat is scarce or when you want to cut back on meat to reduce fat and cholesterol in your diet. Pulses (beans and their relatives) are an excellent source of protein—a protein that is, moreover, rich in lysine, an amino acid found only in small amounts in cereal grains. Consider *dal* (lentils) and rice in India; beans and corn tortillas in Mexico; hummus (garbanzos) and pita in the Middle East; and red beans and rice in New Orleans.

The surprise in Alura Nielsen's Surprising Beans and Rice is a generous dollop of apricot jam, added as the result of inspiration rather than logic. The preserves add an alluring sweet-tart contrast with the mild chili heat.

Surprising Beans and Rice

2 cups dried pinto beans

3 large cloves garlic, minced or pressed

1 teaspoon dried Italian herb seasoning mix (or ½ teaspoon *each* dried basil leaves, dried oregano leaves, and dried thyme leaves)

1 teaspoon crushed dried hot red chilies

1 large (½ lb.) onion, chopped

⅓ to ½ cup apricot jam

3 cups hot cooked rice
   Thinly sliced green onions, including tops
   Salt

Sort beans for debris. Rinse beans and put in a 4- to 5-quart pan; cover with water. Bring to a boil on high heat. Remove from heat, cover, and let stand 1 hour or up to 1 day; drain. To beans, add 2 cups water, garlic, Italian seasoning, chilies, and chopped onion.

Bring to a boil over high heat; cover and simmer until beans are tender to bite, about 1½ hours. Stir occasionally. After 1 hour, mix jam into beans.

If cooked beans are soupier than you like, boil uncovered, stirring often,

until they reach the consistency you want.

Pour beans onto 1 side of a rimmed platter; mound rice opposite and sprinkle both with sliced green onions. Add salt to taste. Makes 5 or 6 servings.

Per serving: 418 cal. (2.4 percent from fat); 17 g protein; 1.1 g fat (0.2 g sat.); 86 g carbo.; 15 mg sodium; 0 mg chol.

Alura Nielsen

Kirkland, Washington

LENORE KLASS IS A champion baker, and she has ribbons from the San Mateo County Fair to prove it. During her 20 years as a contestant, she finished first in the senior baking division several times. Retired now, she divides her time between California and Hawaii, and still enjoys developing new recipes.

She devised this Roasted Garlic–Pepper Flat Bread for a friend who uses olive oil as the only fat in her diet.

With the bread's dimpled surface, pepper topping, and olive oil sheen, this dish is something like a fast focaccia. The garlic is laid on with a generous hand, but its raw strength is tamed by roasting.

Roasted Garlic–Pepper Flat Bread

1 small head roasted garlic (directions follow)

5 to 6 tablespoons olive oil

2 cups all-purpose flour

4 teaspoons baking powder

1½ teaspoons sugar

½ teaspoon finely ground pepper

¼ teaspoon salt

¾ cup milk

1 teaspoon coarsely ground pepper

Squeeze garlic from skins into a small bowl; add 4 tablespoons of the oil and mash garlic with a fork.

In a bowl, mix flour, baking powder, sugar, finely ground pepper, and salt. Add garlic-oil mixture and milk; stir to moisten evenly.

Oil a 9-inch square pan. Scrape dough into pan and knead a few turns. Pat dough evenly over bottom of pan; poke holes liberally in the surface with your fingers. Drizzle with 1 or 2 tablespoons oil and sprinkle with the coarsely ground pepper.

Bake in a 400° oven until a rich brown color, about 20 minutes. Let stand 3 to 5 minutes, cut into squares, and serve hot or warm. Makes 4 or 6 servings.

CHAMPION BAKER *lays on garlic with a generous hand.*

Per serving: 292 cal. (40 percent from fat); 6 g protein; 13 g fat (2.2 g sat.); 39 g carbo.; 433 mg sodium; 4.3 mg chol.

Roasted garlic. Slice ¼ inch off top of 1 head **garlic** (or more, if you want to make extras); rub skin lightly with **olive oil.** Seal garlic (if more than 1 head, in a single layer) in foil. Bake in a 375° oven until garlic is soft when pressed, about 1 hour. Let cool in foil. If making ahead, seal in an airtight container in the refrigerator up to 1 week.

Lenore M. Klass

Koloa, Kauai, Hawaii

WESTERN TABLES have been enriched in recent years by an influx of flavored breads, largely of Italian ancestry. Olive and rosemary are the best known. Parsley and lemon, the classic garnish—with garlic—for osso buco, are used in Carolyn Myers's quick bread.

Parsley-Lemon Quick Bread

2⅓ cups all-purpose flour

½ cup sugar

2 teaspoons baking powder

¼ teaspoon salt

3 large eggs

1 cup milk

¼ cup salad oil

1½ tablespoons grated lemon peel

⅓ cup chopped parsley

In a bowl, mix flour, sugar, baking powder, and salt.

In another bowl, beat eggs to blend with milk, oil, lemon peel, and parsley. Pour into dry ingredients and stir just until moistened.

Pour batter into an oiled 5- by 9-inch loaf pan. Bake in a 325° oven until bread begins to pull from pan and feels firm when gently pressed in center, about 1 hour.

Let bread cool in pan for 10 minutes, then turn out onto a rack and let stand until warm or cool. Serve or, if making ahead, wrap airtight

and hold at room temperature up to 1 day; freeze to store longer. Makes 1 loaf, 1¾ pounds.

Per ounce: 84 cal. (32 percent from fat); 2 g protein; 3 g fat (0.6 g sat.); 12 g carbo.; 66 mg sodium; 24 mg chol.

Carolyn K. Myers

Mill Valley, California

TIGRES CHICKEN, SUSAN Kelso's contribution to the literature of chicken cookery, simmers with an aromatic assortment of spices and goes well with fragrant rice. To complement, garnish with cilantro leaves, yogurt, and chutney.

Tigres Chicken

8 chicken thighs (about 6 oz. each), skin and fat removed

About ½ cup cornstarch

1 to 2 tablespoons olive oil

½ teaspoon each ground cumin, ground coriander, and ground nutmeg

1½ teaspoons chili powder

1½ tablespoons lemon juice

1 teaspoon reduced-sodium soy sauce

1 cup each dry white wine and water

½ cup golden raisins

½ cup chopped, pitted dates

Monsoon rice (recipe follows)

Fresh cilantro (coriander) sprigs

Unflavored nonfat yogurt (optional)

Rinse chicken, pat dry, and coat with cornstarch, shaking off excess.

To a 10- to 12-inch nonstick frying pan over medium-high heat, add 1 tablespoon oil. When oil is hot, add chicken, a portion at a time, and brown well on all sides, about 8 minutes; as pieces brown, remove from pan. Add more oil if needed to prevent sticking.

In the pan, mix cumin, co-

TIGRES CHICKEN *enriches the literature of chicken cookery.*

riander, nutmeg, chili powder, lemon juice, soy sauce, wine, water, raisins, and dates. Return chicken to pan, bring to a boil, cover, and simmer until chicken is no longer pink at bone (cut to test), about 20 minutes. Turn pieces over after 10 minutes.

Spoon rice onto a platter; arrange chicken on rice. Skim and discard fat from sauce; spoon sauce onto chicken. Garnish with cilantro and add yogurt to taste. Makes 6 to 8 servings.

Per serving: 212 cal. (24 percent from fat); 20 g protein; 5.7 g fat (1.2 g sat.); 21 g carbo.; 117 mg sodium; 80 mg chol.

Monsoon rice. Pour 1 tablespoon **olive oil** into a 2½- to 3-quart pan over medium heat; add ½ cup chopped **onion** and 2 cloves **garlic,** minced or pressed. Stir often until vegetables are limp, about 5 minutes. Add ⅛ teaspoon **ground cloves,** ½ teaspoon **ground cardamom,** 1 teaspoon grated **lemon peel,** a 3-inch **cinnamon stick,** and 1 cup **basmati rice.** Stir until rice is opaque, about 5 minutes. Add 2 cups **regular-strength chicken broth.** Bring to a boil on high heat; cover, and simmer until rice is tender to bite, about 15 minutes, stirring several times. Makes 6 to 8 servings.

Per serving: 112 cal. (18 percent from fat); 2.4 g protein; 2.2 g fat (0.4 g sat.); 20 g carbo.; 15 mg sodium; 0 mg chol.

Susan Kelso

Kensington, California

By Joan Griffiths, Richard Dunmire

Sunset's Kitchen Cabinet

Creative ways with everyday foods—submitted by *Sunset* readers,
tested in *Sunset* kitchens, approved by *Sunset* taste panels

Sherried Pork Loin with Onion Blossoms

Mickey Strang, McKinleyville, California

DEEPLY SCORED *onions roast alongside pork basted with sherry and orange.*

⅓ cup dry sherry

2 tablespoons orange marmalade

2 teaspoons grated orange peel

½ teaspoon white pepper

2 cloves garlic, pressed or minced

1 pork loin (3 ½ lb.), fat trimmed and bones cracked

6 small (about 6 oz. each) onions

Salt

Orange wedges

Mix sherry, marmalade, orange peel, pepper, and garlic; rub ½ the mixture all over pork. Peel onions, leaving root ends attached. Starting at stem end, cut each onion into eighths to within 1 inch of root end. Set pork, fat side up, and onions, cut sides up, in a 10- by 15-inch roasting pan. Spoon remaining sherry mixture into cuts in onions.

Roast in a 375° oven until a thermometer inserted in center of the thickest part of pork reaches 155°, 1 to 1¼ hours. Transfer to platter. Add salt to taste; squeeze orange wedges over onions and carved meat. Serves 6.

Per serving: 389 cal. (32 percent from fat); 43 g protein; 14 g fat (5.1 g sat.); 21 g carbo.; 85 mg sodium; 116 mg chol.

Basil Chicken Soup

Elizabeth K. Cooper, Kaneohe, Oahu, Hawaii

ADD SHREDS *of jarlsberg cheese to chicken soup scented with basil.*

1 tablespoon butter or margarine

1 large (about ½ lb.) onion, chopped

1 clove garlic, pressed or minced

1 tablespoon all-purpose flour

3½ cups regular-strength chicken broth

1 large (about ½ lb.) russet potato, peeled and cut into ½-inch cubes

1 cup diced cooked chicken

½ cup chopped fresh basil (or spinach plus 2 tablespoons dried basil leaves)

½ cup shredded light or regular jarlsberg cheese

In a 2- to 3-quart pan, combine butter, onion, and garlic. Stir occasionally over medium heat until onion is limp and slightly tinged with brown, about 10 minutes. Stir in flour to coat onion. Gradually stir in broth, and bring to a boil on high heat.

Add potato; cover and simmer over low heat until potato is tender when pierced, 15 to 20 minutes. Add chicken; cover and simmer just until chicken is hot, 1 to 2 minutes. Stir in basil. Ladle into bowls and offer cheese to add to taste. Serves 4.

Per serving: 237 cal. (35 percent from fat); 19 g protein; 9.1 g fat (4.1 g sat.); 19 g carbo.; 168 mg sodium; 46 mg chol.

Snappy Snapper

JoAnne Wiltz, Santee, California

BAKE FISH FILLETS *with lime; top with tomato sauce spiked with capers.*

About 1 pound skinned and boned rockfish fillets

1 lime

1 small (about 6 oz.) bell pepper

1 small (about 6 oz.) onion

1 teaspoon olive oil

1 clove garlic, pressed or minced

1 can (14½ oz.) Italian-style stewed tomatoes

1 tablespoon drained canned capers

Chopped parsley

Rinse fish; arrange in 1 layer in a shallow 2- to 2½-quart casserole. Squeeze lime juice over fish. Bake, uncovered, in a 350° oven until fish is opaque but still moist-looking in thickest part (cut to test), 15 to 20 minutes.

Stem and seed pepper; slice pepper and onion. In a 10- to 12-inch frying pan, stir oil, onion, pepper, and garlic over high heat until onion is lightly browned, about 5 minutes. Add tomatoes with juice, and capers. Bring to a boil. Simmer, uncovered, over medium heat until liquid evaporates, about 10 minutes. Spoon juice from baked fish into tomato mixture. Boil, uncovered, until liquid evaporates, about 1½ minutes. Spoon over fish. Sprinkle with parsley. Serves 4.

Per serving: 180 cal. (15 percent from fat); 23 g protein; 3 g fat (0.6 g sat.); 15 g carbo.; 485 mg sodium; 40 mg chol.

Thai Pocket Bread Sandwiches

J. Heflin, Kirkland, Washington

- 1 pound ground lean beef
- 2 small (about ¾ lb. total) red bell peppers
- 2 tablespoons minced fresh ginger
- 4 cloves garlic, pressed or minced
- ½ teaspoon crushed dried hot red chilies
- ½ cup chopped fresh cilantro (coriander)
-   Peanut mixture (recipe follows)
- 3 or 4 pocket breads (6 to 7 in.)
- 1 large (about ½ lb.) tomato
- 6 to 8 butter lettuce leaves, rinsed and crisped

In a 10- to 12-inch frying pan, stir beef over medium-high heat until browned and crumbly, 5 to 7 minutes; drain off fat.

Stem, seed, and thinly slice peppers; add to pan along with ginger, garlic, and chilies; stir often until peppers are limp, 3 to 5 minutes. Stir in cilantro and peanut mixture. Set aside.

Cut bread in half crosswise; core and slice tomato. Tuck equally into each half-round the tomato, lettuce, and meat mixture. Makes 6 to 8 pieces.

Per piece: 254 cal. (39 percent from fat); 15 g protein; 11 g fat (3.7 g sat.); 23 g carbo.; 484 mg sodium; 34 mg chol.

Peanut mixture. Combine 3 tablespoons **chunk peanut butter,** 2 tablespoons **soy sauce,** 2 tablespoons **lime juice,** and 1 teaspoon **Oriental sesame oil** (optional).

POCKET BREAD *halves hold ground beef filling spiced with hot Thai flavors.*

Garden Crunch Salad

Karen E. Bosley, Lake Oswego, Oregon

- 1 quart coarsely chopped broccoli flowerets and tender stems
- 1 cup coarsely shredded carrots
- 1 cup ½-inch cubes peeled jicama
- 2 tablespoons minced red onion
-   Dressing (recipe follows)
-   Salt and pepper
-   Thin red onion rings (optional)
-   Crumbled cooked bacon or salted, roasted sunflower seed

In a bowl, combine broccoli, carrots, jicama, onion, and dressing; mix well. Add salt and pepper to taste.

Spoon into a serving dish and garnish with onion rings.

Serve or, if making ahead, cover and chill up to 1 day. Offer bacon to sprinkle over individual portions. Makes 4 to 6 servings.

Per serving: 73 cal. (4.9 percent from fat); 5.6 g protein; 0.4 g fat (0 g sat.); 14 g carbo.; 63 mg sodium; 0.8 mg chol.

Dressing. Mix 1 cup **unflavored nonfat yogurt,** 1 tablespoon **cider vinegar,** 1 tablespoon **sugar,** and ¼ teaspoon **liquid hot pepper seasoning.**

MIX BROCCOLI, *jicama, and carrots with yogurt dressing; top with bacon.*

Glazed Lemon Cake

Jani Buckmaster, Beaverton, Oregon

- 1 cup (½ lb.) butter or margarine
- 2 cups sugar
- 3 large eggs
- 2 cups lemon-flavor nonfat yogurt
- 1 tablespoon grated lemon peel
- 3 tablespoons lemon juice
- 1 tablespoon vanilla
- 3 cups all-purpose flour
- 1 tablespoon baking powder
- 1 teaspoon baking soda
-   Lemon glaze (recipe follows)

Beat butter and sugar until fluffy. Beat in eggs, 1 at a time. Beat in yogurt, peel, juice, and vanilla. Mix flour, baking powder, and soda. Add to butter mixture, beating to blend. Scrape into an oiled and floured 10-inch decorative tube pan, and spread level.

Bake in 350° oven until edges pull from pan and center springs back when lightly pressed, 55 to 60 minutes. Cool 15 minutes. Invert cake to release; tip back into pan. With a long skewer, pierce cake all over. Pour glaze over cake. Cool 1 hour; turn out onto platter. If making ahead, store airtight up to 1 day. Serves 16 to 18.

Per serving: 308 cal. (35 percent from fat); 4.3 g protein; 12 g fat (6.9 g sat.); 46 g carbo.; 287 mg sodium; 65 mg chol.

Lemon glaze. Blend 1 tablespoon grated **lemon peel,** ¾ cup **lemon juice,** and ¾ cup **powdered sugar.**

Compiled by Linda Lau Anusasananan

LEMON GLAZE *soaks deeply into fine-textured yogurt pound cake.*

FOOD GUIDE

A fine rabbit roast, berry fritters, memories of M. F. K. Fisher, and perfect picnic wines

By Jerry Anne Di Vecchio

I'm an old hand at rabbit. When I was 7—at a time when meat was rationed but rabbit wasn't—I became an entrepreneur with my 5-year-old brother. Starting with four prolific bunnies, we eventually earned enough money to buy our first bicycles. The local butcher agreed to use us as his resource, and I helped dress a lot of rabbit. It was obvious, even then, that many parts of the rabbit were very thick, others very thin, and that the bones were hard and sharp. We also ate a lot of rabbit. I found that the pale, lean, fine-textured flesh, if not overcooked, is wonderfully moist and subtly flavored—the perfect white meat. But because of the rabbit's shape, some portions always fell short of expectations.

As I grew wiser in the ways of gastronomy, I returned to the physique of the rabbit determined to resolve the uneven cooking issue. Boning and shaping the meat into a roll that could cook uniformly proved a satisfying solution. It's a handsome one, too, and a dish that I've presented, hot or cold, to many a guest. At this time of year, cold slices of the roast on a bed of greens moistened with lemon-mustard dressing (recipe on page 86) and cold asparagus make a lovely and convenient main course, especially when enjoyed with a dry Sauvignon Blanc.

Concerned that boning a rabbit would make the recipe intimidating, I discussed what I had in mind with the meat cutter at the market where I can buy fresh rabbit. To my surprise, he volunteered to do the job, claiming that anyone who's boned a chicken can handle a rabbit. The rabbit is a trifle more difficult because it doesn't have a skin to hold the pieces together, but you can do some monumental patching as you tie the roast because when it's cooked, no slips show.

Boning specifications. Have front legs cut off; save them and the giblets. Try to keep the rest of the rabbit in 1 piece. Also, have the inside of each back leg slit open the length of the bone. At home, rub your fingers over the rabbit and cut out any tiny bones that have been missed.

To fill out the center of the roll, grind meat cut from the front legs and mix with this filling.

Thyme filling. In an 8- to 10-inch frying pan over medium-high heat, stir 1 tablespoon **butter** or olive oil with ¾ cup minced **shallots** or onions, ¾ cup minced **parsley,** and 2 teaspoons **fresh** minced or dried **thyme leaves** until shallots are limp and lightly browned, 5 to 8 minutes. Remove from heat and stir in ¾ cup **fine dried bread crumbs** and ¼ cup **regular-strength chicken broth.** Let cool slightly, then mix in 1 **large egg.**

(Continued on page 86)

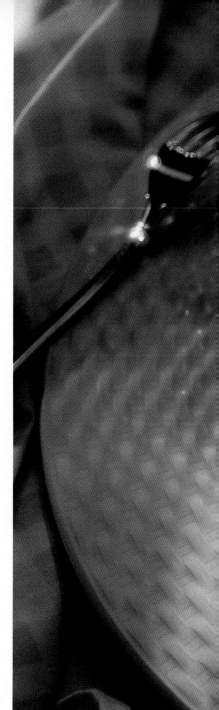

A TASTE OF THE WEST

Boned Double Rabbit Roast with Thyme

2 whole rabbits, about 3 pounds each (including hearts, livers, kidneys), boned to specifications described at left

Thyme filling (directions at left)

2 tablespoons butter or olive oil

Salt

Pull off and discard all fat from rabbit and giblets. Cut meat from front leg bones.

PETER CHRISTIANSEN

Mince this meat with the hearts in a food processor, or grind in food chopper; add thyme filling, and mix.

Cut liver segments apart. In an 8- to 10-inch frying pan, melt 1½ tablespoons butter over high heat until it begins to lightly brown. Add livers and kidneys to pan; cover to control spatters. Brown giblets lightly, 2 or 3 minutes, turning once. Lift from pan and set aside; discard butter.

Lay 1 rabbit out flat with the rather rough, cut side (boned surface) up. Slightly overlap inside edges of the thick thighs. Straighten the two long loins in center, and pat meat with your hand to make it as evenly thick as you can. Also, push any cut gaps together (there will be holes, but pieces seal together as rabbit cooks). Spoon ground mixture evenly down center of rabbit, leaving at least 1½ inches bare around edges. Set liver and kidney pieces down center of filling. Lay the second rabbit, boned side down, on top of the first, with thigh sections placed over shoulder section of bottom rabbit. Overlap rabbit sides and tuck in ends to make a neat log; push together any holes where filling shows.

Slide a long cotton string under the log and wrap around log, tying at about 1-inch intervals. (Pull string firmly enough to hold roll together without squeezing out filling.) Then, with string, tie the log lengthwise and around sides to close any gaps. This is the most bothersome step, but don't rush and don't worry if log looks ragged.

Set roll on a rack in a 10- by 15-inch pan. Bake in a 450° oven until a thermometer inserted in center of the roll reaches 150°; this takes 55 to 65 minutes. After 30 minutes, rub meat with remaining ½ tablespoon butter. Remove rabbit from oven, and let rest at least 20 minutes. Serve hot, or to serve cold, cover roast and chill at least 4 hours or up to 2 days. Snip string, pull off, and discard. Slice roast crosswise; add salt to taste. Makes 10 to 12 servings.

Per serving: 285 cal. (38 percent from fat); 36 g protein; 12 g fat (4 g sat.); 7.2 g carbo.; 137 mg sodium; 107 mg chol.

How to roast and peel peppers and chilies

When peppers and chilies are cooked, the skin becomes annoyingly tough and unpleasant. Getting rid of it is easy: you literally burn it off.

Commercially, peppers and chilies are blackened by a roaring flame as they tumble in a large, rotating bin. At home, the simplest method is to broil the vegetables close enough to the heat to turn the skin black before the flesh turns to mush or dries up.

If you char whole vegetables, you have to turn them as they cook. I use a lazier approach that takes half the time and attention. Just cut each bell or other pepper or large mild chili in half lengthwise, trim out stem and seed, then make a 1- or 2-inch vertical cut through end opposite the stem. Lay vegetables cut side down in a single layer in a foil-lined pan (scorched juices are hard to scrub off). Pieces should have at least ½ inch between them, and can vary as much as 1 inch in height.

PETER CHRISTIANSEN

CLOSE-HEAT CHARRING *roasts peppers and chilies, making them easy to peel.*

Broil 2 or 3 inches below the heat (which looks dangerously close) until the skins are mostly black, anywhere from 10 to 15 minutes. As vegetables soften, press to flatten slightly so edges are exposed to heat. Few broilers brown evenly; you need to juggle the positions of the peppers and chilies to char them well; as vegetables blacken, transfer to a bowl.

The next trick is to let the vegetables steam a bit in their own heat so skins will continue to loosen their hold. Put all the vegetables back in the pan, or leave them in the bowl. Cover with foil or plastic wrap and let stand until lukewarm.

Most cooks rinse the vegetables while pulling off the skins, seeds, and stems. I don't. I like the sweet juices that seep from the peppers and chilies. So I rinse my hands, not the peppers, as I clean them and let their dripping juices collect. When a vegetable is peeled, it gets rinsed only if needed to remove charred bits. If skin at edges sticks, trim it off with a knife.

Roasted peppers or mild chilies, moistened with a dressing of their own juices mixed with **balsamic vinegar** and a few crushed **coriander seed,** are delicious at room temperature.

Macadamia nut oil

The newest monounsaturated oil comes from a most unexpected source, the luxurious macadamia nut. The oil, produced by the Hawaiian Macadamia Nut Oil Company, Waialua, Hawaii (800/ 367-6010), is found in well-stocked specialty and natural food stores in the West. It tastes like the roasted nut, faintly at first, then more distinctly as you savor its flavor.

Macadamia nut oil is most apt to be located among the extra-virgin olive oils and other nut oils like hazelnut, almond, and walnut. It's priced midway ($6 to $7 for 12.7 oz., 375 ml.) between the most costly and least expensive of these oils.

Although the oil is recommended by the maker for high-heat cooking, this utilitarian use drives off the nut taste and aroma. To show off the nut flavor, use the oil in lightly seasoned dressings, like the following one, over fish, poultry, fruit, and greens—especially the greens to go with the cold sliced roasted rabbit roll (page 84).

Lemon-mustard dressing. Combine ½ teaspoon *each* grated **lemon peel** and **fresh** minced or dried **thyme leaves** with 2 teaspoons **Dijon mustard,** 1 tablespoon minced **shallots,** ¼ cup *each* **lemon juice** and **regular-strength chicken broth,** and ½ cup **macadamia nut oil** or other mild salad oil. Makes 1 cup.

Per tablespoon: 63 cal. (99 percent from fat); 0.1 g protein; 6.9 g fat (0.6 g sat.); 0.5 g carbo.; 20 mg sodium; 0 mg chol.

Fabulous fritters

About 9:30 one morning last spring, I stopped at Postrio with a new-to-San-Francisco friend. As we examined the tempting menu choices, her eyebrows shot up. "Berry fritters—never heard of such a thing. I'll have the smoked salmon." But her reaction piqued my curiosity, so, although not much of a fried-food fan, I ordered them.

What a sensual surprise. Each fat, juicy blackberry was lightly cloaked in a thin, tender, golden robe. These little blobs were sitting in a bowl of freshly poached, warm apricots—through which ran a swirl of crème fraîche, that refined crossbreed of sweet and soured cream. As I bit into each fritter, the warm berry popped with the flavor of sun-ripeness. The apricots, by contrast, were tart and more intensely flavored than they ever are raw, and served to make the berries taste sweeter.

I tried duplicating the dish at home. It proved to be less complicated than I had expected, especially because I used a wok for frying. Its curved shape lets a minimum of oil do the job.

To make fritters. Rinse 24 or 30 large **blackberries** and let dry on towels.

In a small bowl, stir together ¼ teaspoon **baking powder,** 2 teaspoons **sugar,** and ¼ cup **all-purpose flour.** Add 1 **large egg white,** 2 tablespoons **water** or milk, and ½ teaspoon **vanilla.**

In a wok (or narrow, deep 1- to 1½-qt. pan), heat about 1 inch **salad oil** to 360° to 370°. Drop berries into fritter batter; turn gently to coat. Lift out 1 at a time with a fork and drop into hot oil. Fill pan but do not crowd. Cook fritters, turning often, until they are golden brown, 1 to 1½ minutes. With a slotted spoon, lay berries in a single layer on paper towels in a wide pan; keep warm in a 150° oven until all the fritters are cooked.

To serve. You need about 6 cups hot, **poached apricots,** sweetened to taste (simmer about 3 lb. sliced fruit with about ¾ cup water and ⅔ cup sugar until fruit falls apart as stirred). Ladle fruit into 6 wide, shallow soup bowls.

Stir about ¼ cup **crème**

BERRY FRITTERS, *resting on warm poached apricots, are a breakfast treat.*

fraîche or sour cream to thin and smooth, then spoon a dollop onto apricots in each bowl. To make swirls, draw the tip of a knife through the cream. Set an equal number of berry fritters onto fruit in each bowl. Dust with **powdered sugar** to taste. Makes 6 servings.

Per serving: 289 cal. (23 percent from fat); 4.5 g protein; 7.5 g fat (1.9 g sat.); 55 g carbo.; 37 mg sodium; 4.2 mg chol.

MEMORABLE MOMENTS
Picnicking with an icon

Mary Frances Kennedy Fisher always said she wasn't a food writer. But that's how most of us know her. She died about two years ago, escaping a body that had all but trapped her exceptional wit and humor. However, her last book, *Stay Me, Oh Comfort Me: Journals and Stories, 1933–1941* (Pantheon Books, New York, 1993; $23), is a sensitive, personal examination of love and death that she completed despite physical limitations.

It was Mary Frances's evocative ways with words in *The Art of Eating* (now in paperback, Collier Books, New York, 1990; $16) that first drew me, many summers ago,

to the old yellow Victorian on Oak Street in St. Helena, California.

I had been elected to ask her to speak at a staff gathering, and someone casually mentioned that she lived in the wine country.

"She's in the phone book, you know, under her married name." I looked. She was.

A sweet, little-girl whispery voice said, "Hello. Yes, I know your magazine. Yes, I'd be happy to discuss your project. Would you like to come up to the valley to talk?

"Oh, you'll bring a picnic. That will be lovely. I know a nice spot north of town." And she hung up.

What had I done? Had I really volunteered to prepare a meal for a living icon, my idol?

Several nightmares later, I settled on the menu. A tiny cold roast fillet, cold Italian green beans, Dijon mustard (a novelty then), a rice salad, some good sourdough bread, and ripe peaches.

For starters, I splurged on a jar of real foie gras (none was available fresh).

The wine was a red that was good cool. And there was champagne. Both were from California because I knew she had nice things to say about California wines.

She answered the door herself. She'd been folding laun-

dry (my goddess?) and she was hungry. Truthfully, in my memory, the day passed in a blurry tumble.

I remember it was hot. She was wearing a Chinese cotton jacket, her rosebud lips were painted a vivid red, her remarkable blue eyes were accented by matching shadow.

The eyebrows that arched so well—and frequently—were carefully accented. Altogether, a delicately sensuous, feminine creature.

Wonder of wonders, she enjoyed the meal. Miffed when yellow jackets took after her foie gras, she beat them off with seaworthy remarks, followed by a slightly defiant smile.

She was real. She was funny. Although she had the advantage of several decades, she didn't act it.

The warm sun and wine mellowed us quickly. When we opened the champagne, the cork blew.

A geyser of foam spewed down my hand and speckled her. We got the giggles, grabbed our glasses, and salvaged what was left.

It was a glorious afternoon. And from that day, now more than 30 years ago, M. F. K. Fisher ceased to be an icon. She became something more wonderful. A true and lasting friend, who is sorely missed. ■

BOB THOMPSON ON WINE
Breezy days and picnics

Gewürztraminer and Grenache are ideal wines for spring picnics because they have fruit aromas strong enough to notice even when flags stand straight out from their poles and sand gets into sandwiches faster than anybody can eat them.

Gewürztraminers that will hang onto their perfumes smell something like carnation blossoms, or smell and taste rather like the canned litchis familiar in Cantonese

cookery. Occasionally a Gewürztraminer will be outright spicy, as the translation of its German name promises. Vineyards in the Anderson and Russian River valleys are especially good sources of such wines, but they are not the only ones.

Grenache has aromas harder to pin down in words, but the perfumiest of its wines also have a spiciness bold enough to battle stiff breezes. Odd as it may seem, the perfumes seem richer in rosés than reds. Lamentably few wineries make Grenache as a rosé.

Both Gewürztraminer and

Grenache are well adapted to fried chicken, sausages, lunch meats, cheeses, and other traditional contents of the picnic basket.

Some producers in the following list are small and hard to find. However, representative samplings are widely available. Prices range from $12 a bottle downward. Choices run from dry (no perceptible sugar) to frankly sweet (unmistakable residual sugar).

Dry Gewürztraminer: Navarro Vineyards Anderson Valley, Hop Kiln Russian River Valley, Louis M. Martini Russian River Valley,

Davis Bynum Russian River Valley. *Off-dry Gewürztraminer:* Husch Anderson Valley, De Loach Russian River Valley, Thomas Fogarty Monterey, Buena Vista Carneros, Joseph Phelps Vineyards California (Anderson, Sonoma, and Napa valleys), Firestone Vineyard Santa Ynez Valley. *Frankly sweet Gewürztraminer:* Geyser Peak Sonoma County, Fetzer California.

Dry Grenache rosé: Vin du Mistral California (from Joseph Phelps Vineyards). *Off-dry Grenache rosé:* Chateau Ste. Michelle Columbia Valley.

¡Viva! ¡Viva! ¡Cinco de Mayo!

Celebrate Mexico's Independence Day with a fajitas fiesta

IN THE WEST, CINCO de Mayo is celebrated with more of a Fourth-of-July kind of hoopla than it is in Mexico. There, solemn parades and thoughtful speeches commemorate a battle on May 5, 1862, in the city of Puebla, when Mexican patriots forced troops of France's Napoleon III to retreat. Without this victory, it's possible that our southern neighbors would be conversing in French.

In the United States, Cinco de Mayo has become an occasion to eat and party. Agustín Gaytán, a chef, cooking instructor, and consultant in Berkeley, California, honors the independence of his native land with a barbecue inspired by the red, white, and green colors of the Mexican flag. The menu is centered on *carne asada*, meat grilled at the table by the host and the guests, to wrap with all the trimmings in tortillas as fajitas. The preparation is simple,

the display colorful, the flavors fresh and straightforward, and the dining pace relaxed.

Use a tabletop barbecue (such as a hibachi), or place a grill alongside the table. Set a gas grill on high heat or keep coals hot with regularly added briquets (every 30 minutes, sprinkle coals with one or two handfuls of briquets—enough to sparsely dot the surface). Guests can lay slices of tequila-marinated beef on the grill and flip once or twice to brown the meat lightly. They can also warm tortillas on the grill. To make fajitas, pile meat onto a tortilla, embellish with spoonfuls of red salsa, green guacamole, and beans or salad, and roll up to eat. Accompany with more salad, beans, roasted onions, and hot sausages.

Serve the meal buffet-style, with comfortable seating at another table.

As beverages, offer watermelon punch and iced beer.

For dessert, try Mexican-style snow cones, with homemade strawberry syrup poured over crushed or shaved ice.

Day-before steps you can complete to help this party flow smoothly include slicing meat and making marinade and salad, cooking beans, roasting onions, partially cooking sausages, and making the strawberry sauce and watermelon punch. Up to 4 hours before serving, make salsa and guacamole. Just before the party, marinate the meat, warm the tortillas, and crush the ice.

Carne Asada

- 2 pounds beef skirt or flank steak, fat trimmed
- ½ cup tequila
- ½ cup orange juice
- 3 tablespoons lemon juice
- 3 cloves garlic, pressed or minced
- 1 medium-size (5 to 6 oz.) onion, coarsely chopped
- ½ teaspoon freshly ground pepper
  Salt

Cut beef diagonally across the grain in ¼-inch-thick slices 4 to 6 inches long. In a large bowl, mix tequila, orange juice, lemon juice, garlic, onion, and pepper. If making ahead, cover and chill meat and sauce separately up to 1 day.

About 15 minutes before putting foods on the table, mix beef with marinade. Lift meat from marinade and overlap slices on a small platter. To cook, lay slices flat on a grill above a solid bed of hot coals (you can hold your hand at grill level only 2 to 3 seconds). Turn slices as

they brown lightly, about 3 minutes total for medium-rare. Serves 6 to 8.

Per serving: 141 cal. (40 percent from fat); 17 g protein; 6.2 g fat (2.7 g sat.); 1.1 g carbo.; 51 mg sodium; 41 mg chol.

Warm Tortillas

- 16 flour tortillas (7 in. wide) or 24 very fresh corn tortillas (6 in. wide)

CINCO DE MAYO CON FAJITAS DE RES
(Fifth of May with Beef Fajitas)

Carne Asada *(Grilled Skirt Steak)*

Warm Tortillas

Salsa Bandera *(Flag Salsa)*

Guacamole

Ensalada de Col y Zanahoria
(Cabbage and Carrot Salad)

Frijoles Charros *(Cowboy-style Pinto Beans)*

Cebolla Morada Asada *(Roasted Red Onions)*

Chorizo Asado *(Grilled Sashed Sausages)*

Raspados con Jalea de Fresa
(Shredded Ice with Strawberry Sauce)

Cerveza Mexicana *(Mexican Beer)*

Agua Fresca de Sandía *(Watermelon Punch)*

GRILL-WARMED *tortilla holds cook-your-own fajita beef filling along with beans and sauces.*

To *heat on grill,* lay tortillas, as needed, in a single layer on the grill over hot coals (you can hold your hand at grill level only 2 to 3 seconds), turning frequently until limp and warm, 2 to 3 minutes total. Use at once.

To *heat in a microwave* oven, stack tortillas in a towel, or loosely enclose in a heat-resistant plastic bag. Heat at full power (100 percent) until hot, 2 to 3 minutes.

To *heat in the oven,* stack tortillas, seal in foil, and bake at 350° until hot in center, about 20 minutes.

Wrap stack of heated tortillas in a thick cloth towel to keep warm as served. Makes 6 to 8 servings.

Per flour tortilla: 90 cal. (20 percent from fat); 2.4 g protein; 2 g fat (0.3 g sat.); 16 g carbo.; 132 mg sodium; 0 mg chol.

Salsa Bandera

1½ pounds (about 3 large) firm-ripe tomatoes, cored and chopped

1 tablespoon chopped fresh cilantro (coriander)

2 tablespoons lemon juice

½ cup chopped onion

2 or 3 fresh jalapeño chilies

Salt

Mix tomatoes, cilantro, lemon juice, and onion. Stem and mince chilies and add to tomato mixture with salt to taste.

Use, or cover and let stand up to 4 hours; stir well before using. Makes about 3½ cups, 6 to 8 servings.

Per serving: 22 cal. (12 percent from fat); 0.9 g protein; 0.3 g fat (0 g sat.); 5.1 g carbo.; 8.4 mg sodium; 0 mg chol.

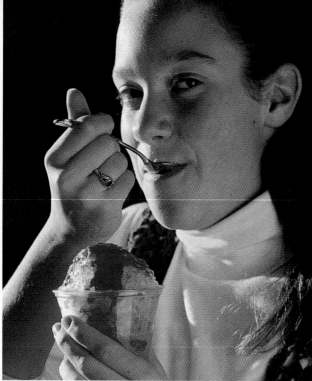

MEXICAN VERSION *of a snow cone is fresh strawberry syrup poured over shaved ice.*

Guacamole

3 large (about 1½ lb. total) firm-ripe to ripe avocados

⅓ cup salsa bandera (recipe precedes)

2 tablespoons lemon juice

Salt

Cut avocados in half, remove pits, and scoop flesh from peels. Coarsely mash avocado flesh. Mix in salsa and lemon juice; add salt to taste. Use or, if making ahead, cover tightly with plastic wrap and chill up to 4 hours. Makes about 3 cups, 6 to 8 servings.

Per serving: 104 cal. (84 percent from fat); 1.3 g protein; 9.7 g fat (1.5 g sat.); 5.4 g carbo.; 7.9 mg sodium; 0 mg chol.

Ensalada de Col y Zanahoría

4 cups finely shredded purple cabbage

4 cups finely shredded green cabbage

2 large (about ½ lb. total) carrots, peeled and shredded

½ cup lemon juice

½ teaspoon pepper

Salt

In a bowl, mix purple and green cabbage, carrots,

lemon juice, pepper, and salt to taste. Use or, if making ahead, cover and chill up to 1 day. Serves 6 to 8.

Per serving: 32 cal. (5.6 percent from fat); 1.2 g protein; 0.2 g fat (0 g sat.); 7.7 g carbo.; 22 mg sodium; 0 mg chol.

Frijoles Charros

1½ pounds (about 3½ cups) dried pinto beans

1 large (about ½ lb.) onion, quartered

6 cloves garlic, pressed or minced

Salt

Sort and discard debris from beans. Rinse beans, drain, and place in a 5- to 6-quart pan. Add 3 quarts water and cover pan. To soak beans for faster cooking, let stand overnight. To speed process, bring water to boiling over high heat, boil 3 minutes; remove from heat and let stand 1 to 4 hours. Drain and rinse beans.

In pan, combine beans with onion, garlic, and 1½ quarts water. Bring to a boil on high heat; cover and simmer until beans are tender to bite, 45 minutes to 1 hour. Add salt to taste. If beans are soupier than you like, boil uncovered, until liquid is reduced to desired amount. Pour beans into a bowl;

serve hot or at room temperature. Serves 6 to 8.

Per serving: 304 cal. (3 percent from fat); 18 g protein; 1 g fat (0.2 g sat.); 57 g carbo.; 9.7 mg sodium; 0 mg chol.

Cebolla Morada Asada

4 medium-size (5 to 6 oz. each) red onions

¼ cup red wine vinegar

2½ tablespoons firmly packed brown sugar

1 tablespoon olive oil

Salt

Cut unpeeled onions in half lengthwise, leaving root end attached. In a 9- by 13-inch baking dish, mix vinegar, sugar, and oil. Lay onions, cut side down, in dish. Bake, uncovered, in a 350° oven until tender when pierced, 30 to 40 minutes. Serve at room temperature; if making ahead, let stand up to 4 hours or cover and chill up to 1 day. Or reheat cooked onions on a grill over hot coals (you can hold your hand at grill level only 2 to 3 seconds), turning often until slightly warm, 8 to 10 minutes. Serves 6 to 8.

Per serving: 67 cal. (24 percent from fat); 1.4 g protein; 1.8 g fat (0.2 g sat.); 12 g carbo.; 11 mg sodium; 0 mg chol.

Chorizo Asado

2 dried cornhusks, soaked in water until soft

8 (about 1 lb. total) pork link sausages

Tear husks lengthwise into about ¼-inch-wide strips. Snugly tie cornhusk strips around sausages, to divide each piece in half or in thirds. Trim ties to about 1-inch long.

In a 10- to 12-inch frying pan, cover sausages with water and bring to a boil on high heat; reduce heat and simmer, covered, for 10 minutes. Lift out; if making ahead, cool, cover, and chill up to 1 day.

To brown sausages, turn often on a grill over hot coals (you can hold your hand at grill level only 2 to 3 seconds) for 3 to 5 minutes. Don't be alarmed if ties burn and char. Serves 6 to 8.

Per serving: 98 cal. (76 percent from fat); 5.2 g protein; 8.3 g fat

(2.9 g sat.); 0.3 g carbo.; 345 mg sodium; 22 mg chol.

Raspados con Jalea de Fresa

If you lack the equipment to shave or crush ice, serve the strawberry syrup over vanilla ice cream.

4 cups strawberries, rinsed and hulled

¼ to ⅓ cup sugar

2 tablespoons lemon juice

3 to 4 pounds (8 to 10 cups) ice cubes

Fresh mint sprigs (optional)

In a blender or food processor, purée strawberries. Pour purée into a 2½- to 3-quart pan; add sugar to taste. Stir occasionally over medium heat until mixture comes to a boil. Stir in lemon juice; let mixture cool, then cover and chill at least 2 hours or up to 1 day.

Shortly before serving, finely crush or shave ice in an ice crusher or shaved ice machine. Or drop cubes into a spinning food processor to crush fine. Spoon ice into paper cones or chilled small cups or bowls. Pour strawberry sauce over ice. Garnish with mint. Serve at once. Serves 6 to 8.

Per serving: 48 cal. (5.6 percent from fat); 0.5 g protein; 0.3 g fat (0 g sat.); 12 g carbo.; 1.6 mg sodium; 0 mg chol.

Agua Fresca de Sandía

1 watermelon (10 lb.), or a 10-pound piece

¼ to ⅓ cup sugar

2 cups cold water

Ice cubes

Cut off watermelon rind and discard. Cut flesh into about 1-inch cubes. Purée melon, a portion at a time, in a blender or food processor. Pour through a strainer into a bowl to remove seeds. Mix melon purée with sugar and water to taste. If making ahead, cover and chill up to 1 day. Pour into glasses over ice cubes. Makes 3 quarts, 6 to 8 servings.

Per serving: 119 cal. (9.8 percent from fat); 1.8 g protein; 1.3 g fat (0 g sat.); 27 g carbo.; 6 mg sodium; 0 mg chol. ■

By Linda Lau Anusasananan

ENGLISH PEAS, *plump sugar snaps, flat Chinese pea pods, and tender pea greens all taste as fresh as the spring season.*

The peas (and greens) of spring

A trio of choices: shelled, edible-pods, and tendrils with leaves

GOOD COOKS AND gardeners know that spring's mild, cool weather brings out the best in most peas.

Standard English peas in the pod, which are climate tolerant, produce well throughout the summer, but primarily along foggy coasts. For pure pleasure, pop these peas from the pod to munch raw, or cook them briefly.

The two edible-pod peas, sugar snaps and Chinese pea pods, are available most months. Raw sugar snaps make grand nibbling. Both kinds, quickly cooked, turn brighter green as they become tender-crisp.

Making a bid to go mainstream are pea greens, the fragile leaves and tender stems and shoots of pea plants. These greens enjoy epicurean status in fine Chinese restaurants and are increasingly available in Asian grocery stores and at farmers' markets. Use the smallest, most tender greens raw in salads, or lightly wilt more mature pieces in stir-fry dishes and soups.

Triple Pea Stir-steam

1 tablespoon sesame seed

1 pound English (regular) peas, shelled (about 1 cup)

½ pound edible-pod peas, ends and strings removed

½ pound tender pea greens, rinsed, drained, and cut into about 2-inch pieces

1 tablespoon Oriental sesame oil

Salt

In a wok or 10- to 12-inch frying pan over medium heat, frequently shake sesame seed until golden, about 5 minutes. Pour from pan and save. Turn heat to high; add shelled peas, edible-pod peas, and 3 tablespoons water to pan; cover and stir occasionally until peas are tender to bite, about 3 minutes. Add pea greens; stir until wilted, 1 to 2 minutes. Add sesame seed and sesame oil; pour into a bowl. Add salt to taste. Serves 6.

Per serving: 69 cal. (42 percent from fat); 3.6 g protein; 3.2 g fat (0.5 g sat.); 7.4 g carbo.; 18 mg sodium; 0 mg chol.

May Wine Peas

Acid in the wine makes the green color of cooked peas fade quickly.

1 pound edible-pod peas, or English (regular) peas in the pod

1 tablespoon butter or margarine (optional)

2 tablespoons regular-strength chicken broth or water

¼ cup Johannisberg or White Riesling, or other slightly sweet white wine

Salt

Remove ends and strings from peas; rinse peas. In a 5- to 6-quart pan, melt butter over medium-high heat. Add peas and broth. Stir, cover, and cook for 2 minutes. Add wine, stir, cover, and cook until peas are tender-crisp to bite, about 2 minutes. Pour into a dish.

Just eat the edible-pod peas. But to eat peas from the English pea pods, pull the warm pods, 1 at a time, between your teeth, and peas will pop into your mouth; discard the pods. Sprinkle both kinds of pea pods with salt to taste. Edible-pod peas serve 4; English peas serve 2.

Per serving edible-pod peas: 58 cal. (4.7 percent from fat); 3.2 g protein; 0.3 g fat (0.1 g sat.); 8.6 g carbo.; 6.8 mg sodium; 0 mg chol. ∎

By Linda Lau Anusasananan

SEASON BROTH-SIMMERED MEAT *and vegetables with chili sauce (top left), avocado, and lime; sip broth from a cup. Stew includes beef and pork, cabbage, plantains, potatoes, corn, cassava, and fresh tomato sauce.*

Colombia gives us a hearty dinner stew

With vegetables, meats, broth, and ají, it's a whole meal

IN THE HIGH-elevation city of Bogotá, where nights are often chilly, hearty, warming stews are popular. One of the best known is *puchero*, and the version Colombian transplant Lucy Cabieles makes is equally satisfying on a cool spring evening in the West. She simmers meat and earthy vegetables, then lifts them from the broth to serve with a warm, fresh tomato sauce and avocado slices; the broth is ladled into mugs.

Like most Colombian dishes, puchero is simply seasoned. For zip, *ají*, a chili-herb sauce, is added to taste.

Many supermarkets carry the banana-shape plantains to use in the stew. Look for them both unripe (green and starchy like potatoes) and ripe (with yellow to black skin); ripe plantains are sweeter and creamier in texture. If you find plantains, you'll likely find fresh or frozen *yuca*, too. Yuca (also called cassava) is a starchy root with barklike skin; frozen yuca is peeled. If you can't find these ingredients in a supermarket, look for them in a Latino market.

Puchero

1 *each* medium-size (about ½ lb. total) green and yellow plantains (or use all of 1 kind)

2 quarts regular-strength beef broth or water

⅔ pound boned beef chuck (fat trimmed), cut into 4 equal pieces

⅔ pound boned pork shoulder or butt (fat trimmed), cut into 4 equal pieces (or use more beef chuck)

1 teaspoon ground cumin

3 tablespoons chopped fresh cilantro (coriander)

5 green onions (ends trimmed), cut into 1-inch lengths

1 pound yuca, fresh or frozen

1 large (about 12 in.) ear of corn, husk and silk removed, cut crosswise into 4 equal pieces

4 small (about ½ lb. total) red thin-skinned potatoes, scrubbed

About ¾ pound green cabbage, cut into 4 equal wedges (don't core)

1 medium-size (5 to 6 oz.) onion, cut into large slivers

1 tablespoon butter or margarine

2 medium-size (about 1 lb. total) firm-ripe tomatoes, cored, peeled, and chopped

1 medium-size (about ½ lb.) avocado, pitted, peeled, and quartered

Fresh cilantro sprigs

Salt and pepper

Lime wedges

Ají (recipe follows)

Cut ends off plantains. Score peel lengthwise, then pull off and discard peel. Cut plantains into 1½-inch chunks, keeping green and yellow pieces separate; set aside.

In a 5- to 6-quart pan over high heat, bring broth, beef, pork, cumin, 2 tablespoons chopped cilantro, and half the green onions to a boil. Cover and simmer for 45 minutes. Add green plantain; simmer 15 minutes longer.

Meanwhile, if using fresh yuca, cut crosswise into 1½-inch chunks. Cut off all peel, pink underskin, and any dark spots; halve chunks lengthwise and remove the fibrous core. (Frozen yuca needs no preparation; discard core when eating.)

Push yuca, corn, and potatoes into the broth. Cover, return to a boil over high heat, then simmer for 15 minutes. Push yellow plantain into broth and lay cabbage on top of the mixture. Simmer, covered, until plantains are tender when pierced, about 15 minutes longer.

Meanwhile, in a 1½- to 2-quart pan over medium heat, stir slivered onion often in butter until onion is limp, about 10 minutes. Add remaining green onions, remaining chopped cilantro, and tomatoes. Cover and simmer over medium heat, stirring occasionally, until tomato pieces begin to break apart, 3 to 5 minutes.

To serve, use a slotted spoon to transfer meat and vegetables to warm dinner plates. Garnish each portion with 1 avocado quarter and cilantro sprigs. Serve broth in small cups to sip. Top portions equally with tomato mixture and season to taste with salt, pepper, juice from lime wedges, and ají. Makes 4 servings.

Per serving: 744 cal. (28 percent from fat); 43 g protein; 23 g fat (7.2 g sat.); 98 g carbo.; 209 mg sodium; 108 mg chol.

Ají. In a small bowl, mix together ¾ cup chopped **green onions,** 3 tablespoons minced **fresh cilantro,** 1½ tablespoons minced **fresh jalapeño chili,** and ½ cup **hot broth** from **puchero** (recipe precedes). Makes about ¾ cup.

Per tablespoon: 2.6 cal.; 0.2 g protein; 0 g fat; 0.5 g carbo.; 0.6 mg sodium; 0 mg chol. ■

By Elaine Johnson

SPICY, SWEET SHRIMP *are a favorite in Malaysia; the chili level can be mild to outrageous.*

Malaysia's shrimp dishes can sizzle

Simple seasonings, distinctive results

THREE CULTURES— Malay, Chinese, and Indian—coexist in Malaysia, and many dishes reflect influences from each group.

Even though these shrimp dishes have a number of ingredients in common, cultural styling makes each distinctive. Chili shrimp has a Chinese touch—a light, sour-sweet, hot glaze. In the second, Indian design shows in the sweet coconut-curry sauce. The last—with pan-toasted bits of crunchy coconut—is Malay.

Chili Shrimp

1 pound large (31 to 35 per lb.) shrimp

1 tablespoon salad oil

1 tablespoon minced fresh ginger

3 cloves garlic, minced or pressed

3 tablespoons catsup

1 tablespoon each cider vinegar, soy sauce, and sugar

½ to 1 teaspoon crushed dried hot red chilies

½ teaspoon Oriental sesame oil

About 3 cups hot cooked rice

Sliced green onions

Peel shrimp, leaving last section of shell on tail; devein and rinse. Place a wok or 10- to 12-inch frying pan over high heat. Add salad oil; when oil is hot, add shrimp. Stir-fry until shrimp are pink and opaque in center (cut to test), about 3 minutes.

With a slotted spoon, lift out shrimp, drain briefly, and set aside.

To pan, add ginger and garlic; stir-fry until garlic is tinged with gold, about 30 seconds. Add catsup, vinegar, soy sauce, sugar, and chilies to taste; stir until boiling. Add shrimp, any accumulated juices, and sesame oil; mix well. Mound rice on a platter; top with shrimp mixture and onions. Serves 4.

Per serving: 363 cal. (15 percent from fat); 23 g protein; 6.1 g fat (1 g sat.); 52 g carbo.; 530 mg sodium; 140 mg chol.

Curry Shrimp

1 pound large (31 to 35 per lb.) shrimp

1 tablespoon salad oil

4 medium-size (about ¼ lb. total) shallots, minced

1 tablespoon minced fresh ginger

2 cloves garlic, minced or pressed

1 tablespoon curry powder

½ teaspoon ground turmeric

1 large (½ lb.) onion, thinly sliced

1 cup (part of a 15-oz. can) canned coconut milk

⅛ to ¼ teaspoon cayenne

About 3 cups hot cooked rice

Fresh cilantro (coriander) sprigs

Peel shrimp, leaving last section of shell on tail; devein and rinse. Place a wok or 10- to 12-inch frying pan over high heat. Add salad oil; when oil is hot, add shallots, ginger, and garlic. Stir-fry until shallots are limp, about 3 minutes.

Add curry powder and turmeric to shallot mixture; stir-fry 30 seconds.

Add onion and coconut milk; stir until onion is limp, about 5 minutes. Season to taste with cayenne. Add shrimp and stir until pink and opaque in center (cut to test), about 3 minutes.

Mound rice onto a platter and top with shrimp mixture and cilantro. Serves 4.

Per serving: 489 cal. (33 percent from fat); 26 g protein; 18 g fat (12 g sat.); 57 g carbo.; 153 mg sodium; 140 mg chol.

Shrimp with Pan-toasted Coconut

1 pound large (31 to 35 per lb.) shrimp

2 tablespoons butter or margarine

½ cup unsweetened shredded dried coconut

2 teaspoons sugar

Seasoned noodles (recipe follows)

Peel shrimp, leaving last section of shell on tail; devein and rinse. Place a wok or 10- to 12-inch frying pan over high heat. When pan is hot, swirl butter until melted, then all at once add shrimp and coconut.

Stir-fry until shrimp are pink and opaque in center (cut to test), about 3 minutes. Sprinkle with sugar and stir-fry for about 30 seconds. Spoon shrimp over seasoned noodles on plates. Makes 4 servings.

Per serving: 563 cal. (24 percent from fat); 33 g protein; 15 g fat (8.8 g sat.); 73 g carbo.; 1,223 mg sodium; 238 mg chol.

Seasoned noodles. In a covered 5- to 6-quart pan over high heat, bring about 3 quarts **water** to a boil. Add 1 pound **fresh Chinese noodles** (spaghetti-size; found in refrigerated section of Asian markets and some supermarkets) or fresh spaghetti or linguine. Cook, uncovered, until tender to bite, about 5 minutes. Drain.

Mix noodles with 1 medium-size (about ¾ lb.) thinly sliced **cucumber** and 3 tablespoons each **soy sauce** and **seasoned rice vinegar** (or rice vinegar mixed with 1½ teaspoons sugar). ■

By Betsy Reynolds Bateson

LEAFY GREEN *perpetual spinach produces all summer when picked regularly. Swiss chard grows behind it. Below, lettuce varieties supposedly good for growing in summer turned bitter when allowed to mature.*

Salads from your summer garden

These are greens that thrive in hot weather

SUCCULENT LEAFY greens needn't vanish from the vegetable garden with the onset of warm summer weather. Many thrive in heat.

When picked young, all of the greens shown on these pages make delicious additions to summer salads (for recipes, see page 97). Mature leaves of amaranth, orach, perpetual spinach, and chard taste best when cooked. (Avoid old leaves; they're usually tough, and sometimes bitter.) Unless you garden in a fog belt, harvest summer lettuce as described on page 96.

Flavors and textures of the different greens vary substantially, and not all of them appeal to every taste. Certain greens (particularly Malabar climbing spinach) win rave reviews from some cooks, thumbs-down from others. Experiment using different greens—in different ways—until you find the ones that you like.

Look for seeds at nurseries or order by mail as soon as possible, so you can plant early this month.

SPINACH SUBSTITUTES
THAT TAKE THE HEAT

The toughest, most heat-tolerant of the group are amaranth, Malabar climbing spinach, and New Zealand spinach. Often sold in catalogs as warm-season substitutes for spinach, they can be used as wilted greens, to replace other greens in recipes, in stir-fries, or fresh in salads.

Orach is grown in spring and fall in France and Asia, but in the West you can harvest all summer if you keep the seed heads pinched off.

Amaranth may be familiar to some gardeners as a 3-foot-tall ornamental plant, but it is also a tasty green. Leaves may be brilliant scarlet, plain green, or mottled red, green, and yellow. Choose leaf varieties, not grain-producing types. Harvest leaves before plants flower.

Cooked amaranth is less watery and more flavorful than spinach, although not as smooth. Tender, young leaves add a colorful touch to salads.

Malabar climbing spinach is a fast-growing vine that can be trained on a trellis or fence. When eaten fresh, leaves are succulent and mild. As wilted greens, they are somewhat slippery like okra, but they'll give good flavor

GLENN CHRISTIANSEN

and body to soups.

New Zealand spinach is a spreading plant that grows 6 to 8 inches high. In mild-winter climates, it's perennial. Pluck off the top 3 inches of tender stems and leaves. Served raw, leaves are mild, slightly salty, succulent, and fleshy. Cooked, they taste like spinach.

Orach (also sold as mountain spinach; often mistaken

DRESS A SALAD *of tender New Zealand spinach (right) or of mixed summer greens with a mustard-tarragon vinaigrette or oil and vinegar to taste. Sprinkle nasturtium flowers over the mixed greens as a colorful, flavorful accent.*

PETER CHRISTIANSEN

DARROW M. WATT

BRIGHT PURPLE STEMS *of Malabar climbing spinach contrast handsomely with its flavorful, dark green leaves. Left, lettuce seedlings are thinned out for use in salad.*

for lamb's quarters) grows 3 feet tall if leaves are pinched off regularly; otherwise, it can reach up to 9 feet. Red- or green-leaf types are available. Leaves are smaller when orach is grown in summer rather than in spring and fall. The young, tender leaves can be eaten raw in salads. Cooked orach tastes like spinach.

GREENS YOU CAN GROW ALMOST ALL YEAR LONG

Chard and perpetual spinach are commonly thought of as cool-season greens, but they thrive during the summer in most areas (except the desert). Because they're biennial, they are less likely than regular spinach to bolt and go to seed. Harvest outer leaves; new leaves grow from the center. 'Rhubarb' ('Ruby Red') chard is red stemmed; perpetual spinach, a type of chard, has smaller ribs than other types of chard. Use in soups, stir-fries, lasagna, or as bundle wrappers (see recipe on page 97).

Mâche is a small-leafed green that's popular in France for its mild nutty flavor in salads. It's often grown in the cool season but does well in summer if seeds are sown before soil temperatures go above 65°. Choose either 'À Grosse Graine' or 'Piedmont', large-seeded types that tolerate heat better than the small-seeded kinds. Harvest individual leaves or cut the head 1 inch above ground (it will resprout).

Nasturtium is often grown just for its flowers, but both the leaves and flowers can be used in flavorful appetizers, as shown at left, and make tasty additions to summer salads. (Mix the peppery leaves and flowers with mild greens for interesting flavor con-

trasts.) You can buy seeds of mixed flower colors, of individual colors (apricot, cherry, mahogany, gold, yellow, and red), and of one with variegated leaves ('Alaska').

Summer lettuce is best grown by broadcasting seeds and then harvesting at the baby stage (see far left photo), unless you live on the coast or cover plants with shadecloth. When kept evenly moist and harvested very early, lettuce won't turn bitter—as it is likely to do if left to mature. Mix seed with sand so you can broadcast it evenly and not too thickly. As the plants grow, thin some of the seedlings and use them in salads. Harvest when leaves are 3 to 4 inches long.

PLANT IN WELL-AMENDED SOIL AND KEEP MOIST

Start seeds of all but the lettuce and nasturtiums in containers, or sow all seeds directly in the ground. Once they're planted in the ground and at the seedling stage, mulch the soil to conserve water. Water regularly to keep the soil moist, and fertilize once every week or so with fish emulsion (if you use another fertilizer, follow package directions).

Train Malabar climbing spinach on a trellis.

Begin harvesting summer greens when plants can yield enough for a meal. Pick amaranth and orach regularly to control growth. Mix all types together or use individually.

WHERE TO ORDER SEEDS

The Cook's Garden, Box 535, Londonderry, Vt. 05148; (802) 824-3400. Catalog $1. Sells all but Malabar climbing and New Zealand spinach.

Ornamental Edibles, 3622 Weedin Court, San Jose, Calif. 95132. Catalog free. Sells most types.

Seeds Blüm, Idaho City Stage, Boise, Idaho 83706; fax (208) 338-5658. Catalog $3. Sells every type listed.

By Lauren Bonar Swezey

PETER CHRISTIANSEN

NASTURTIUM LEAVES HOLD *tiny shrimp and dollops of sour cream for a quick fresh appetizer.*

DARROW M. WATT

AFTER BLANCHING, *fill chard leaves with chopped stems and fold into bundles. Drizzle with a piquant caper dressing before serving.*

PETER CHRISTIANSEN

Young summer greens make delicious salads; mix several varieties for interesting flavor and texture. Dress lightly with olive oil and vinegar (or lemon juice) to taste or with your favorite dressing. Some mature greens taste best cooked. To wilt lightly, cook in oil and garlic.

Summer Greens Salad

3 quarts (¾ to 1 lb.) bite-size pieces baby leaf lettuce, New Zealand spinach, Malabar climbing spinach, nasturtium leaves, small tender orach, perpetual spinach, or Rhubarb chard leaves (use 1 kind or a mixture), rinsed and crisped

    Mustard-tarragon vinaigrette (recipe follows)

    Salt and pepper

    Nasturtium flowers (optional)

In a large bowl, combine greens and vinaigrette; mix and add salt and pepper to taste. Garnish with flowers. Makes 6 to 8 servings.

Per serving: 73 cal. (88 percent from fat); 0.6 g protein; 7.1 g fat (0.9 g sat.); 2.3 g carbo.; 88 mg sodium; 0 mg chol.

Mustard-tarragon vinaigrette. Mix ¼ cup **olive oil,** ¼ cup **white wine vinegar,** 1½ tablespoons **Dijon mustard,** 1 teaspoon **dried tarragon leaves,** and 1 clove **garlic,** pressed or minced.

Nasturtium Leaf and Shrimp Appetizers

12 nasturtium leaves (each 2 to 2½ in. wide), stems trimmed, rinsed and patted dry

2 tablespoons sour cream

12 to 24 (½ to 1 oz.) shelled cooked tiny shrimp

    Nasturtium flowers (optional)

Place leaves in a single layer on a serving platter. Spoon about ½ teaspoon sour cream in center of each leaf; top with 1 or 2 shrimp. Garnish platter with flowers, if desired. To eat, pick up and roll leaf around shrimp. Makes 12 appetizers.

Per serving: 7.7 cal. (58 percent from fat); 0.4 g protein; 0.5 g fat (0.3 g sat.); 0.4 g carbo.; 4.6 mg sodium; 3.4 mg chol.

Chard Packets with Caper Vinaigrette

1½ pounds chard or perpetual spinach with leaves at least 6 by 8 inches

    Caper vinaigrette (recipe follows)

    Salt and pepper

Wash chard well; discard bruised leaves. Trim off discolored stem ends; discard. Cut stems off leaves; keep leaves and stems separate.

In a 5- to 6-quart pan, bring about 3 quarts water to a boil over high heat. Push chard stems into water. Cook, uncovered, until stems are limp, 6 to 12 minutes. Lift out; drain well.

Push leaves gently down into boiling water; cook until limp, 1 to 2 minutes. Lift out carefully; immerse in ice water. When cool, drain well.

Select 6 of the largest, prettiest leaves; if leaves are longer than 8 inches, trim to this length. Set leaves aside. Chop remaining leaves, trimmings, and stems together; drain well.

Lay reserved leaves flat in a single layer; mound onto each an equal portion of chopped chard about 3 inches from base of leaf. Fold sides and ends of leaf over filling to enclose; lay seam down on a serving dish. If making ahead, cover and chill up until next day. Bring to room temperature to serve. Offer caper vinaigrette to pour over bundles; add salt and pepper to taste. Makes 6 bundles, 3 to 6 servings.

Per serving with 1 tablespoon vinaigrette: 63 cal. (69 percent from fat); 1.9 g protein; 4.8 g fat (0.6 g sat.); 4.5 g carbo.; 284 mg sodium; 0 mg chol.

Caper vinaigrette. Mix ¼ cup **olive oil,** ¼ cup **white wine vinegar,** 2 teaspoons **Dijon mustard,** 2 tablespoons minced **shallots,** and 2 tablespoons drained **capers.** If making ahead, cover and chill up until the next day. Makes ¾ cup. ∎

By Linda Lau Anusasananan

GAME HENS, VEGETABLES, and cherry pie all cook at the same time in a convection oven. Circulating hot air quickly seals in juices, so smells and flavors don't transfer.

Making the most of convection cooking

Sunset's tests show the advantages of cooking with hot air

PROFESSIONAL CHEFS HAVE long favored convection ovens for baking and roasting. The main reasons: speed and even cooking and browning. Now these ovens are becoming widely available to home cooks, and they are particularly worth exploring if you cook a lot, or are looking for a more versatile oven.

TWO BASIC SYSTEMS

In a convection oven, moving air conveys the heat. A fan continuously circulates the air, maintaining a constant temperature throughout the oven; the hot air surrounds the food, quickly penetrating and cooking all surfaces evenly.

The result is consistent browning—without the need to move pans, or turn or stir the food—even during multi-rack cooking. Cooking times can be faster as well, depending upon what's being cooked (see "What testing found," on facing page).

There are two basic convection systems. One has heating elements on the top and bottom just like a conventional oven. With this design, air heats inside the oven cavity as the fan circulates it over the heating elements.

In the rear-element convection oven, often touted as the "true" convection oven, a concealed heating element surrounding the fan—outside the oven cavity—warms the air, then blows it back inside. (Some ovens have variations on this theme, such as heating elements embedded in the oven floor.)

Does one system work better than the other? We didn't find much difference when we conducted tests in seven major manufacturers' built-in convection ovens. Both systems produced good results most of the time.

Yet Michael Heintz of University Electric in Santa Clara, California, suggests that a rear-element convection system may perform better in some circumstances. With an oversize pan on the bottom rack, you'll get better air circulation. And when there's no hot element under the pan, there's less chance of burning when using the lowest rack position. Also, prolonged multilevel cooking may be more even when heat comes from the back rather than from top and bottom.

SHOPPING CONSIDERATIONS

Convection options are most often offered in top-of-the-line ranges and wall ovens. A few portable countertop ovens and small microwave-convection combinations are also available.

Prices range from $200 for countertop models to $2,500 for some built-ins. A convection oven usually costs $200 to $300 more than a similar conventional oven. A 27-inch

CROSS-SECTION *drawing shows fan circulating air from heating elements on top, bottom, and back of oven.*

Top heating element

Fan

Air flow

Heating element

Bottom heating element

thermal wall oven without convection, for instance, might cost about $650; with the convection feature, it could be about $950.

What's the $300 advantage? Most of these ovens are two ovens in one. With a turn of a dial or push of a button, you can switch between convection and conventional heating systems.

If your kitchen has room for only one oven, this combination may be a good choice because of its versatility, convenience, and performance. You get standard bake and broil, as well as at least one convection setting. (Settings are defined differently by each manufacturer.) Additional convection cooking modes aren't essential, but they may decrease guesswork, shorten the cooking times of some foods, and improve browning over the basic convection setting.

If you're shopping for a convection oven, be sure to check an oven's inside measurements. Pans or foods with broad dimensions may not fit in some smaller European models. The capacity of many of these imports, however, is similar to wider ovens because they can cook four or five levels of food at a time—and many manufacturers provide pans with the ovens.

WHAT TESTING FOUND

For best results, manufacturers suggest following their cooking recommendations to take advantage of the design and features of their particular oven. This is good advice if you find the suggestions work fairly consistently, and if you like the results.

Sometimes, a manufacturer's literature contradicts itself, is confusing, or doesn't include what you want to cook. If results aren't to your liking, manipulate the temperature to get the results you want.

In our tests, we roasted a chicken and baked—one at a time—a pound cake, a yeast bread, and three pans of cookies.

General guidelines

Air circulation is important. Don't cover racks with foil. Allow 1 to 1½ inches around pans (also above and below pans for multirack baking).

For maximum browning, use pans with low sides, and rimless cookie sheets. Many ovens come with special pans and racks that lift roasts so air flows all around. If possible, place the long sides of the pan parallel to the oven door.

Cakes, cookies, muffins, quick breads, yeast breads

A convection oven produces more even browning, slightly greater volume, and, sometimes, a lighter texture.

Reduce oven temperature 25° from conventional recipes. Preheat oven. Cooking time may be the same or 10 to 25 percent less than in conventional baking.

For most baked goods, temperature adjustment is critical to the texture: the moving hot air cooks the outside first and could solidify the structure before it has a chance to rise, producing a heavy, dense result.

Convection-baked cookies are superb. We baked three pans of sugar cookies at a time in preheated ovens, reducing the temperature 25°. Unlike a standard oven, which requires switching pans midway to achieve consistent results, the circulating hot air baked all the cookies evenly without changing pan positions, and in a slightly shorter time. Some ovens accommodate four or five pans.

For really dense or large cakes, you may need to reduce the temperature slightly more. At lower baking temperatures, you may not save any time; in fact, it may take longer than in a regular oven. With loaf-size cakes and quick breads, especially, there is little time saved. Yeast breads may bake faster.

If the surface is well browned but hard and dry, and rising is uneven, reduce the oven temperature slightly

more, and check earlier for doneness.

For pale color and low volume, increase temperature slightly. Check the manual; some ovens provide a setting that gives extra top or bottom browning suitable for some baked goods.

Roast meats and poultry

Preheating is not necessary. Place meats on a rack in the roasting pan for better browning. Roasting time may be 20 to 30 percent less than in a conventional oven if temperatures aren't reduced. Some ovens offer a special roasting mode that provides top and/or bottom browning or an initial surge in heat in addition to the fan. These modes make it easy to get optimum results in a shorter time.

Do not reduce oven temperatures for small pieces, skinny roasts, or unstuffed poultry. In our tests, we roasted a 3½-pound chicken at 375°. In about an hour, about 20 percent less time than for conventional cooking, it was beautifully browned, with succulent flesh.

In more limited testing, we found smaller, slender beef roasts also browned handsomely, maintaining an even doneness throughout.

For large, dense roasts and big stuffed turkeys, you may need to reduce the temperature 25° during part or all of the roasting time. When you lower the temperature, the meat may be juicier and shrink less, but it will take longer to cook. ∎

By Linda Lau Anusasananan

PETER CHRISTIANSEN

SUGAR COOKIES BAKED *on three racks at a time in a standard thermal oven (top row) browned unevenly. The evenly browned cookies in the bottom row were baked in a convection oven.*

PETER CHRISTIANSEN

SERVE CHOCOLATE BISCOTTI *tipped with white chocolate (foreground), delicate poofs (left), and country-style florentines with champagne for a more festive occasion.*

Pure Italian sweets

Tradition and olive oil enrich these cookies

MEAL IN GEMMA Sciabica's Modesto home isn't complete without a homemade cookie. Sciabica bakes daily, and it's only natural that she adds olive oil for rich, full flavor—the Sciabica family has been producing the oil in California's Central Valley for more than 50 years.

Most often, Sciabica serves cookies with seasonal fruits and a cup of coffee—milk for the grandchildren. But on special occasions, and after dinner, she pairs them with a sparkling wine or sweet dessert wine.

Chocolate Biscotti

    3   cups all-purpose flour
    ¾   cup granulated sugar
    ½   cup firmly packed
        brown sugar
    1   tablespoon baking
        powder
    ¾   teaspoon salt
    3   ounces unsweetened
        baking chocolate,
        melted and cooled
    3   large eggs
    ⅓   cup olive oil
    2   tablespoons *each*
        orange juice and rum
    1   tablespoon grated
        orange peel
    1   teaspoon vanilla
    1   cup semisweet
        chocolate baking chips
    1   cup chopped pecans,
        walnuts, or almonds
   12   ounces white chocolate
    1   tablespoon vegetable
        shortening

In a large bowl, combine flour, granulated and brown sugars, baking powder, and salt. Add melted unsweetened chocolate, eggs, oil, juice, rum, peel, and vanilla; stir to combine. Add baking chips and nuts; mix until dough is well blended.

Quarter dough; shape into 4 logs, each about 2½ inches wide by 14 inches long. Place 2 logs on each of 2 lightly oiled (10 by 15 inch) baking pans. Bake logs in a 350° oven until just firm to touch, about 20 minutes. Cool logs slightly in pans; using a serrated knife, cut diagonally into ½-inch-wide slices. Place slices cut side down on pans; bake until crisp, about 15 minutes more. Cool cookies.

Meanwhile, in a double boiler melt white chocolate and shortening over hot water, stirring until smooth (or heat in a nonmetal bowl in a microwave oven on 100 percent power for 15 seconds at a time, stirring after each interval, until soft and smooth, about 1½ minutes total). Dip 1 end of each cookie about 1 inch into white chocolate to coat. Lay cookies on wire racks until firm; chill to speed process. Serve, or wrap airtight to store up to 2 days; freeze for longer storage. Makes about 6 dozen cookies.

Per cookie: 100 cal. (46 percent from fat); 1.4 g protein; 5.1 g fat (1.9 g sat.); 13 g carbo.; 51 mg sodium; 8.9 mg chol.

Poofs

        About 2 cups sifted
        powdered sugar
    1   cup all-purpose flour
    1   teaspoon baking
        powder
    ¼   teaspoon ground
        cinnamon
    1   tablespoon olive oil
    1   large egg, beaten
    2   tablespoons anisette
        liqueur, or 1 teaspoon
        anise extract and 1½
        tablespoons water
    1   teaspoon vanilla

In a large bowl, combine 2 cups sifted powdered sugar, flour, baking powder, and cinnamon. Add oil, egg, anisette liqueur, and vanilla; stir to blend. Turn out onto a board lightly dusted with powdered sugar; knead until smooth, about 4 turns.

Cut dough into 6 pieces. Roll each piece into a ½-inch-wide rope that is 20 inches long. Cut each rope into 2-inch pieces. Place pieces about 1½ inches apart on 3 lightly oiled (about 12 by 15 inch) cookie sheets. Let cookies stand, uncovered, 8 to 24 hours.

Bake in a 325° oven until pale golden, about 8 minutes. Immediately transfer cookies carefully to racks to cool. Serve, or wrap airtight up to 2 days; freeze for longer storage. Makes about 5 dozen cookies.

Per cookie: 25 cal. (11 percent from fat); 0.3 g protein; 0.3 g fat (0.1 g sat.); 5.1 g carbo.; 9.3 mg sodium; 3.5 mg chol.

Florentines

    2½ cups ground almonds
    1   cup sliced almonds
    1   cup sugar
    ⅓   cup all-purpose flour
    ¾   cup whipping cream
    2   tablespoons olive oil
    1   large egg
    ½   cup diced candied
        orange peel
    ½   cup diced candied
        pineapple
    1   teaspoon almond extract
    ½   cup semisweet
        chocolate baking chips

In a large bowl, combine ground and sliced almonds, sugar, flour, cream, oil, egg, candied orange peel and pineapple, and almond extract; mix until well blended. With a 1¼-inch ice cream scoop, spoon dough 2 inches apart on oiled and floured 12-by 15-inch baking sheets. Flatten balls with a moistened fork into 2½-inch rounds.

Bake cookies in a 325° oven until golden, about 20 minutes. Immediately transfer cookies to cooling racks. (If cookies become too brittle to remove from pans, return pans to oven for 30 seconds and remove cookies quickly.)

Place chocolate chips in a plastic sandwich bag (not pleated). In a microwave oven on 100 percent power, heat chips for 15-second intervals, squeezing between intervals to see if chocolate is soft, about 45 seconds total. (Or place bag in a double boiler over simmering water about 5 minutes, squeezing chips occasionally to check softness.)

Clip off about ⅛ inch of filled corner. Squeeze chocolate over tops of cool cookies in a zigzag pattern. Let cool. Serve, or wrap airtight to store up to 2 days; freeze for longer storage. Makes about 3 dozen cookies.

Per cookie: 130 cal. (55 percent from fat); 2.3 g protein; 7.9 g fat (1.9 g sat.); 14 g carbo.; 4.7 mg sodium; 11 mg chol. ∎

By Betsy Reynolds Bateson

Potatoes and eggs reach new heights

The corned beef's secret is honey

IDAHO IS A LAND WITH snowcapped peaks, fertile plains, and yawning chasms. It is also a land of potatoes—big, brown, mealy russets. For those mornings when your stomach is a yawning chasm, turn to these russets for succor. Sheila Mills shows you how with her Oh, Idaho! Breakfast Potatoes, in essence a potato-egg scramble with a decidedly Mexican flavor. As an accompaniment, Mills suggests tortillas, which you could wrap around the scramble to form tacos.

This recipe splits a mere tablespoon of oil among six hungry people. To further cut fat, you can replace the eggs with 1½ cups liquid egg substitute.

Oh, Idaho! Breakfast Potatoes

2 large (about 1 lb. total) russet potatoes, peeled and cut into ½-inch cubes

1 tablespoon Oriental sesame oil

3 medium-size (5 to 6 oz. each) onions, chopped

6 cloves garlic, minced or pressed

3 fresh jalapeño chilies, stemmed, seeded, and finely chopped

⅔ cup chopped fresh cilantro (coriander)

2 teaspoons ground cumin

3 tablespoons lime juice

8 large eggs, beaten to blend

Salt and pepper

Homemade or prepared salsa

Warm flour or corn tortillas (optional)

Pour 1 inch water into a 2- to 3-quart pan. Add potatoes, cover, and bring to a boil over high heat; simmer until potatoes are tender when pierced, 10 to 12 minutes. Drain well.

Meanwhile, pour oil into a 10- to 12-inch nonstick frying pan over medium heat. When oil is hot, add onions and garlic. Stir often until onions are limp, about 10 minutes. Add chilies, cilantro, and cumin; stir often for 1 to 2 minutes. Mix potatoes and lime juice with ingredients in pan, then spread out to make rather level. Pour eggs over potatoes; as they cook, use a wide spatula to scrape and lift firm portions from pan bottom, so uncooked egg can flow beneath. Cook until eggs are set as firmly as you like. Scoop onto plates and season portions to taste with salt, pepper, and salsa, and accompany with tortillas. Makes 6 servings.

Per serving: 213 cal. (40 percent from fat); 11 g protein; 9.4 g fat (2.4 g sat.); 22 g carbo.; 95 mg sodium; 283 mg chol.

Sheila Mills

Eagle, Idaho

A LACK OF MODESTY, when justified, is as fresh as the blossoms of spring. And when Frank Doherty wrote, "This is one of the best ways to prepare corn beef," he was not overstating facts. His secret is remarkably simple: honey.

He starts by soaking the corned beef overnight to reduce its saltiness (unfortunately, the available USDA nutridata do not make allowances for this step; hence the sodium disclaimer that follows the recipe). After simmering the corned beef to tenderness, he bakes it, basting with honey. The shiny glaze the honey forms on the succulent meat is just downright good.

Frank's Honey-baked Corned Beef

1 piece, about 4 pounds, corned beef brisket or round

2 dried bay leaves

2 cinnamon sticks (each about 3 in. long)

2 large (about 1 lb. total) onions, chopped

3 cloves garlic, quartered

½ cup cider vinegar

⅓ cup honey

Place corned beef in a 5- to 6-quart pan. Rinse well with cool water, rubbing meat gently to help desalt it. Drain and fill pan almost to brim with water. Cover pan and place in the refrigerator for at least 12 hours.

Drain and discard water. To pan, add bay, cinnamon, onions, garlic, and vinegar. Add enough water to cover meat by at least 1 inch. Bring to a boil over high heat; reduce heat, cover, and simmer until meat is very tender when pierced, about 3 hours.

Transfer meat to a 9- by 13-inch pan; brush top of meat with honey. Bake, uncovered, in a 350° oven until meat is lightly browned and glazed, about 30 minutes; baste several times with drippings. Serve hot or cold, thinly sliced. Makes 6 to 7 servings.

Per serving: 364 cal. (54 percent from fat); 22 g protein; 22 g fat (7.2 g sat.); 21 g carbo.; approximately 1,290 mg sodium (less if soaked overnight); 111 mg chol.

Frank Doherty

Las Vegas

By Joan Griffiths, Richard Dunmire

SUNSET'S KITCHEN CABINET

Creative ways with everyday foods—submitted by *Sunset* readers,
tested in *Sunset* kitchens, approved by *Sunset* taste panels

Yogurt-Rice Salad

Laxmi Hiremath, El Sobrante, California

TANGY RICE SALAD *is seasoned with ginger, cumin, and jalapeño.*

About 2 cups regular-strength vegetable broth

1 cup long-grain white rice

2 tablespoons minced fresh ginger

1 teaspoon cumin seed

1 cup unflavored nonfat yogurt

1 medium-size (about ¾ lb.) cucumber, chopped

½ cup golden raisins

3 tablespoons minced fresh cilantro (coriander) leaves

1 small jalapeño chili, stemmed, seeded, and minced

1 tablespoon lemon juice

Lettuce leaves, rinsed and crisped

Lemon peel and fresh cilantro (coriander) sprigs (optional)

In a 1½- to 2-quart pan over high heat, bring 1¾ cups broth to a boil. Stir in rice, ginger, and cumin. Cover and simmer until rice is tender, about 18 minutes. Spoon rice mixture into a bowl and fluff with a fork; cool.

When cool, fold in yogurt, cucumber, raisins, cilantro, chili, and lemon juice. If mixture is too thick, add broth, 1 tablespoon at a time, until you like the consistency. Serve on lettuce. Garnish with peel and cilantro sprigs. Serves 8.

Per serving: 142 cal. (3.8 percent from fat); 3.9 g protein; 0.6 g fat (0.1 g sat.); 31 g carbo.; 279 mg sodium; 0.6 mg chol.

Pork Chili Verde

Susan S. Bouchard, Scottsdale, Arizona

PORK CHILI VERDE *simmers until tender and succulent.*

2½ pounds pork kebabs, or pork shoulder trimmed of excess fat and cut into 1-inch cubes

1 cup regular-strength chicken broth

6 cloves garlic, minced or pressed

2 cans (14½ oz. each) Mexican-style or Italian stewed tomatoes

2 cans (7 oz. each) diced green chilies

1 medium-size (½ lb.) onion, chopped

2 teaspoons minced fresh oregano leaves, or 1 teaspoon dried oregano leaves

Warm flour tortillas and lime wedges (optional)

In a 5- to 6-quart pan over medium heat, combine pork, ½ cup broth, and garlic. Cover; cook 30 minutes. Remove lid; cook, stirring often, until liquid caramelizes and meat browns, about 20 minutes. Add remaining broth; scrape brown bits from bottom of pan.

Add tomatoes with juice, green chilies, onion, and oregano. Cover and simmer gently, stirring occasionally, until meat pulls apart easily, about 1½ hours. Serve with warm flour tortillas or over rice, with lime wedges to squeeze over meat mixture, if desired. Makes about 10 cups; 6 to 8 servings.

Per serving: 284 cal. (35 percent from fat); 30 g protein; 11 g fat (3.9 g sat.); 86 g carbo.; 779 mg sodium; 95 mg chol.

Cashew–Bell Pepper Stir-fry

Maureen Ward Valentine, Seattle

PEPPERS AND ONION *team up in a coconut-curry stir-fry; serve over couscous.*

2 teaspoons olive or salad oil

2 medium-size (each about 6 oz.) bell peppers, 1 red, 1 green, stemmed, seeded, and thinly sliced

1 medium-size (about ½ lb.) onion, cut into wedges

2 cloves garlic, minced or pressed

2 teaspoons curry powder

About ⅓ cup regular-strength chicken broth

1 cup coconut milk

Hot couscous (recipe follows)

½ cup roasted and salted cashews

To a 12-inch frying pan or wok over medium-high heat, add oil; when oil is hot, stir in peppers, onion, and garlic.

Cook vegetables until edges are tinged a golden brown, about 5 minutes. Stir in curry powder, and cook for about 30 seconds. Immediately add broth; cover, and continue to cook until peppers are tender to bite, about 4 minutes longer. Add coconut milk and heat until bubbling, about 30 seconds. Spoon over hot couscous and sprinkle with cashews. Makes 5 or 6 servings.

Hot couscous. In a 2- to 3-quart pan, bring 1½ cups **water** or regular-strength chicken broth to a boil. Add 1 cup **couscous;** stir. Cover; simmer 5 minutes. Remove from heat; keep covered until served, up to 20 minutes.

Per serving: 298 cal. (45 percent from fat); 7.5 g protein; 15 g fat (8.4 g sat.); 35 g carbo.; 81 mg sodium; 0 mg chol.

Greek-style Chicken and Potato Salad

Ellen Nishimura, Fair Oaks, California

1½ pounds small (1½-in. diameter) thin-skinned potatoes, scrubbed

3 cups bite-size pieces cooked chicken

1 jar (6 oz.) marinated artichoke hearts

1 jar (4 oz.) sliced pimientos, drained

1 can (2¼ oz.) sliced black olives, drained

½ cup thinly sliced green onions

¼ cup lemon juice

Lettuce leaves, rinsed and crisped

½ cup (about 3 oz.) feta cheese, crumbled

Freshly ground pepper

In a 3- to 4-quart pan, bring about 2 quarts water to a boil. Add potatoes; reduce heat. Cover; simmer until potatoes are tender when pierced, about 25 minutes. Cool; cut into quarters.

In a large bowl, combine potatoes, chicken, artichoke hearts with marinade, pimientos, olives, green onions, and lemon juice. Gently fold to mix seasonings; chill at least 15 minutes, or up to 4 hours.

On 4 dinner plates, arrange lettuce leaves; divide chicken-potato mixture equally among plates. Sprinkle with feta; add pepper as desired. Serves 4.

Per serving: 466 cal. (35 percent from fat); 38 g protein; 18 g fat (6 g sat.); 39 g carbo.; 708 mg sodium; 112 mg chol.

QUICK CHICKEN AND POTATO SALAD *is topped with feta cheese.*

Eggplant-Zucchini Lasagna

Linda Strader, Amado, Arizona

2 medium-size (about 2½ lb. total) eggplants, ends trimmed

4 medium-size (about 1 lb. total) zucchini, ends trimmed

About 1 tablespoon olive or salad oil

1 package (1 lb. 3 oz.) firm tofu

1 container (1 lb.) nonfat cottage cheese

8 ounces (about 2 cups) mozzarella, shredded

1 cup cooked brown rice

½ teaspoon fennel seed, crushed

½ to 1 teaspoon crushed dried hot red chilies

2½ cups purchased (26-oz. jar) or homemade spaghetti sauce

About 3 tablespoons grated parmesan cheese

Cut eggplants crosswise into ½-inch slices; cut zucchini lengthwise into ¼-inch slices. Lay in single layer in 3 oiled pans, each 10 by 15 inches (or bake in sequence). Bake in a 400° oven until soft and golden brown, 30 to 40 minutes (turn after 15).

Meanwhile, slice tofu; lay between paper towels. Press to release excess liquid. Mash tofu in a bowl; add cottage cheese, mozzarella, rice, fennel, and chilies. Spoon ½ cup spaghetti sauce into oiled 9- by 13-inch baking dish. Layer ½ of the eggplants, zucchini, and tofu mixture, and 1 cup spaghetti sauce; repeat layers. Sprinkle with parmesan. Bake in a 400° oven until hot, about 45 minutes. Let rest 15 minutes before serving. Serves 8.

Per serving: 410 cal. (42 percent from fat); 28 g protein; 19 g fat (5.5 g sat.); 38 g carbo.; 782 mg sodium; 27 mg chol.

EGGPLANTS AND ZUCCHINI *replace noodles in a vegetable lasagna.*

Fresh Strawberry Pie

Ruth Mitchell, Eugene, Oregon

5 cups strawberries

⅓ cup lemon juice

½ cup sugar

2 tablespoons cornstarch

1 envelope gelatin

¾ cup low-fat vanilla-flavor yogurt

½ cup whipping cream

½ teaspoon vanilla

1 baked 9-inch pastry shell

Rinse strawberries and drain on towels; hull fruit. Thickly slice 3 cups of the prettiest berries and set aside. Reserve 1 whole berry for garnish. In a blender or food processor, whirl remaining berries with lemon juice until puréed.

In a 2-quart pan, mix sugar, cornstarch, gelatin, and puréed berries. Cook, stirring often, over medium heat until mixture comes to a full boil, about 6 minutes. Stir in yogurt; chill until slightly thickened, about 1 hour.

Meanwhile, with an electric mixer, beat cream and vanilla until soft peaks form. Gently fold cream and sliced berries into cool berry mixture. Pour into pastry shell; chill until firm, at least 3 hours or until next day. Serves 8.

Per serving: 271 cal. (43 percent from fat); 4.2 g protein; 13 g fat (5 g sat.); 36 g carbo.; 146 mg sodium; 18 mg chol.

Compiled by Betsy Reynolds Bateson

STRAWBERRIES, YOGURT, *and whipped cream combine in a chiffonlike filling.*

FOOD GUIDE

Barbecued salmon, tomatillo salsa, making lettuce last, and defining "sweet" wine

By Jerry Anne Di Vecchio

Pietro Parravano is a commercial fisherman. He jumped ship from a teaching career about 12 years ago, opting for a more precarious but freer livelihood from the sea. He fishes off the Central California coast on the *Anne B,* a sturdy, weathered craft built in Seattle in 1947. Pietro's catch includes Dungeness crab and rockfish. But his face lights up when he talks about his favorite trophy, line-caught king (chinook) salmon. During the season, he sells the salmon at the Menlo Park and Palo Alto farmers' markets.

Pietro and I met through an environmental group dedicated to preserving a balanced relationship between land and sea, in part by promoting the restoration of river habitat for salmon spawning. In Pietro's eyes, the most magnificent salmon are wild, and he's politically, actively committed to their survival and well-being. But he also likes to cook and eat them, delivering, concurrently, sage advice on how to do both.

PARRAVANO *shares his appreciation for fresh salmon with Di Vecchio. His cooking philosophy: the larger the piece of fish, the better.*
DAVID MAISEL

One of his favorite ways to prepare a salmon fillet is this month's Taste of the West recipe. Not only is it very simple, but it enriches without concealing salmon's fine flavor and character. Pietro's first piece of advice: cook salmon in as large a piece as possible. Bigger hunks stay moister. And since salmon is as good cold as it is hot, you can get more than one meal from a single effort. Barbecu-ing salmon with moderate indirect heat is the cooking technique he likes best, so the surface of the salmon will stay moist as heat penetrates and firms the center.

Judging doneness is a little intimidating if you don't cook much fish, but guidelines are easy to observe. As the fish cooks, the layers of flesh become less firmly attached and push apart easily. In recipe terms, the fish flakes when prodded. However, this separation starts on the surface and works inward. You need to know what the fish looks like in the center of the thickest part to know how done it is, so slide the tip of the fork or a knife down farther along this natural flake separation and take a look. Salmon gets lighter in color and less translucent as it cooks; when perfectly done (to most tastes), the interior will be

E. K. WALLER

Pietro's Barbecued Salmon

- 1 tablespoon butter or margarine
- 1 tablespoon *each* honey and firmly packed brown sugar
- 2 tablespoons soy sauce
- 3 tablespoons Dijon mustard
- 1 tablespoon olive oil
- 1 teaspoon minced fresh ginger or minced garlic
- 1 salmon fillet with skin (3½ to 4½ lb.; a 12-lb. whole salmon yields 2 about this size)
- Lime slices and wedges
- Whole chives (optional)

In a 6- to 8-inch frying pan over medium heat, stir butter with honey and sugar until butter melts. Remove from heat; add to pan the soy, mustard, oil, and ginger; mix well. Let sauce cool slightly.

Meanwhile, rinse fish and pat dry. To make fish easier to handle when cooked, set it, skin down, on a large piece of foil; trim foil (or fold under) to fit outline of fish. Set fish and foil in a rimmed pan large enough to hold fish. Stir sauce and spoon evenly over fish; let stand 15 minutes to 1 hour; frequently spoon sauce over fish.

Put salmon with foil on a grill over indirect heat (see Back to Basics, below). Cover barbecue with lid, open any vents, and cook until fish is opaque but still moist-looking in thickest part (cut to test), 20 to 30 minutes. To move fish onto a platter, support with 2 large spatulas, or slip a rimless baking sheet under fish. Set, or slide, fish onto a platter. Serve salmon hot or cold; if making ahead, cover and chill up to 1 day. Squeeze juice from lime wedges onto portions. Makes 10 to 12 servings.

Per serving: 209 cal. (43 percent from fat); 25 g protein; 10 g fat (1.9 g sat.); 3.3 g carbo.; 348 mg sodium; 70 mg chol.

---

paler than raw fish, but a little darker than the surface. The center should look moist and juicy but not wet and squishy. Heat equalizes for a few minutes after the fish comes off the grill, so the interior will cook a bit more.

Moving a large piece of salmon on and off the grill is a challenge, especially when it is cooked. Pietro describes the salmon skin as a natural layer of foil, and he is adept at moving the fish with two wide spatulas (the skin usually sticks to the grill, even if oiled) from the barbecue onto a platter.

Frankly, this is more than I can manage for a typical 4- to 5-pound fillet. So I take the easy way out and fit the skin side of the fish with a piece of foil; the fish sits on the foil on the grill, and I can get under the foil to move the fish without breaking it apart. I push a baking sheet without sides beneath the foil, scooping up the fish. Then I slide the whole works onto a platter.

BACK TO BASICS

Barbecuing with indirect heat

There are two basic ways to barbecue. One is with heat right under the food— direct-heat cooking. The other—indirect-heat cooking—has heat balanced around the food but not beneath it. The arrangement you choose is determined by how fast you want the food to cook, and how fatty it is.

Small or relatively thin pieces that develop the most flavor when the surface is well browned—chops, steaks, chicken pieces, quail, even eggplant slices—generally do best over direct heat. However, if a food is fatty and drips onto the heat, flare-ups are a constant problem. Also, big "hunk" foods—turkey, chicken, roasts—overcook on the bottom. For such foods, and more delicate ones like fish, indirect heat is ideal, and comes with a bonus: foods that brown do so without having to be turned over.

Direct-heat cooking on a charcoal-fueled barbecue is generally done uncovered. Gas barbecues lose heat quickly, and cook best with the lid down.

But to cook with indirect heat, always cover the grill, whether charcoal or gas.

The way the heating element of a gas burner is designed determines how effectively indirect heat is delivered. If your barbecue is designed so you can control heat in front and back (or on opposite sides of the food) and you can turn off the heat beneath it, it will do the job. If the burners on each side of the barbecue ignite independently, and the food is either over heat or has heat on only one side, then indirect cooking isn't possible.

To cook indirectly with charcoal briquets, stack and ignite 60 briquets on the firegrate in a barbecue with a lid. When briquets are covered with ash, in about 30 minutes, push half the coals to opposite sides of firegrate. Place grill 4 to 6 inches above coals and set food on grill but not over coals. Cover barbecue with lid and open the vents. Temperature will be about 350°; to maintain heat, add 5 briquets every 30 minutes to coals on each side of firegrate (10 briquets, total).

NORMAN A. PLATE

To cook indirectly with gas, adjust for indirect cooking (ignite burners parallel to foods but not beneath) and turn heat to high; close lid. When barbecue is heated, quickly put food on grill, but not over heating elements; cover with lid. Adjust heat to medium-high; temperature should be 325° to 350°.

GREAT INGREDIENT

Tangy tomatillos

From their quiet, specialty-vegetable post in most supermarkets, tomatillos look much more exotic than they should. Under their Chinese paper lantern husk, they are firm, green, and waxy smooth—rather like primitive tomatoes. Raw, their tart, somewhat floral flavor—in thin slices for salad or laid onto cooked fish or hamburg-

ers—is a taste I love. Cooked tomatillos get juicy, soft, mellow, and fruity. They add a delicious dimension when simmered with pork for stew, with beans, or in chili.

In Mexico long ago, I watched a good cook char whole tomatillos on a dry *comal* (sort of half griddle, half frying pan) until they turned soft and pale yellow green. She also charred some onions and chilies, then smashed the vegetables into a chunky sauce that she seasoned freely with chopped cilantro and lime juice. This roasted salsa is superb with grilled meat and poultry, and it makes a refreshing dip to scoop with tortilla chips.

To enhance the color and texture of the sauce, I often mix in some chopped raw tomatillo.

While making a batch of salsa the other day, I asked my friend Eligio Hernandez

GREEN TOMATILLOS, pan-roasted with chilies and onions, make a tart salsa. Cilantro and lime season the mix. Mash some salsa with avocado for a quick guacamole.

how his mother—back home in Veracruz, Mexico—used tomatillos, and he chuckled. Seems tomatillos grow wild there, and she spends more time weeding them than cooking them.

Roasted Tomatillo Salsa

¾ pound tomatillos

¼ pound small (about 1 in. wide) onions

1 or 2 (about ¼ lb. total) mild fresh green chilies such as poblano or Anaheim

½ cup packed fresh cilantro (coriander)

2 to 4 tablespoons lime juice

Salt

Pull off and discard tomatillo hulls. Rinse tomatillos and set aside 1 tomatillo that is about 1½ inches wide. Place remaining tomatillos, onions (don't peel onions if you want sauce to have a mild roasted flavor), and chili in a 10- to 12-inch frying pan over high heat (use an old pan; the process tends to discolor the surface). Shake pan or turn vegetables frequently until they are charred all over, about 15 minutes. Tomatillos should be soft when pressed. Let vegetables cool. Peel onions if roasted in their skins. Pull loose skin from chili and discard; also cut out and discard stem and seed. In a food processor or with a knife, mince uncooked tomatillo; roasted tomatillos, onions, and chili; and cilantro. Season mixture to taste with lime juice and salt. Serve or, if making ahead, cover and chill up to 4 days. Makes about 2 cups.

Per tablespoon: 5.2 cal. (17 percent from fat); 0.2 g protein; 0.1 g fat (0 g sat.); 1 g carbo.; 0.5 mg sodium; 0 mg chol.

For a first-rate *guacamole,* peel, pit, and mash a ripe avocado. Stir in a big spoonful or two of roasted tomatillo salsa, and add more lime juice and salt to taste.

GREAT IDEA

Cool move

When food writer Christine Weber Hale gave a party recently, she served margaritas whirled to a slush with ice, and also accidentally reinvented the wheel. She whirled up a big batch of the tequila-based drink, filled glasses for guests, and had some left over. She stuck the blender in the freezer, planning to pull it out shortly for refills. But the steak came off the grill early and the balance of the margaritas was forgotten—until she spotted it at cleanup time. To her surprise, the drink was still nice and slushy. The alcohol in the tequila (and some of the sweetness in the Cointreau, too) kept the margarita from freezing hard.

So next time you serve frozen daiquiris, margaritas, or similar concoctions using high-alcohol spirits, and want to be ready early, just pop a pitcher of the mix in the

RINSED SALAD GREENS, *wrapped in towels to drain, will stay fresh and crisp enclosed in a plastic bag.*

NORMAN A. PLATE

freezer several hours before pouring time.

SEASONAL NOTE

Keeping greens crisp

I had just returned from the market with bags of groceries when my pal Sally dropped by for a cup of coffee and a good chat. While we sipped and talked, I unpacked the bags and, as usual, dumped the lettuce into a sinkful of water, broke off the leaves, swished them thoroughly to remove field grit, shook off the water, and laid the leaves to drain on towels. The whole process took 3 to 4

minutes. As I was loosely rolling the mound of greens into the towel and putting the bundle in a large plastic bag, Sally stopped midsentence and said, "Why are you doing that? I just wash lettuce when I'm ready to use it and dry it in my salad spinner."

I was caught a little short. Then the answer poured out, suspiciously like a confession. First, I'm not a salad spinner fan (heresy?). Second, I like crisp, perky lettuce ready to use when I'm running late (which is almost always), and third, I don't like to waste food. Calculating how much salad the family will consume is impossible, so I keep a supply on hand all the time.

If I leave the lettuce in the store bag and put it in the refrigerator, in hours the leaves begin to droop and wilt. A day or so later, there's some slime between the leaves as well as where moisture and leaves touch the plastic; before the week is gone, any remaining lettuce is over the hill and gets tossed. If I rinse, drain, wrap, and store the leaves airtight and chill them as soon as I get home, they're crisp, clean, dry, and ready to use for an indecent period— up to two weeks. Stem ends usually get rusty after several days, but I just snap them off.

The spinner is great if you're going to make salad right away. But if you store those leaves—even overnight—fine, spidery bruises from the spinning show up, and the leaves are in decline.

I also rinse and store other leafy greens, especially herbs, the same way. Ordinarily, tender herbs like basil or greens like watercress don't do well after a day or two. Rinsed, drained, wrapped, and stored like the lettuce, they stay usable for 5 or 6 days. Cilantro is salvageable for 7 to 10, and arugula outlives lettuce.

"Hmmmm," said Sally. ∎

BOB THOMPSON ON WINE

How sweet is sweet?

No words in insider wine talk bewilder the general public more than "dry," "sweet," and "fruity," because what is dry to one is sour to another, while what is fruity to some is just plain sweet to their neighbors.

The confusions revolve around residual sugar—r.s. for short. Residual sugar itself is simple. It is unfermented sugar from grapes, and wineries routinely measure it down to a 10th of a percent. Some even go to a 100th.

Technically, dry wine has 0.2 percent or less r.s. In the

real world, dry wine doesn't have enough r.s. to notice. Here, among the 10ths and 100ths, is where wine talk and everyday English start to slip apart. Under test conditions, some people notice sugar, and thus sweetness, at 0.3 percent, others at 0.7, some not until 1.0.

This gets more complicated because people who notice r.s. at the same level do not always agree on how much it takes to make a wine sweet, any more than coffee drinkers agree on one lump or three. Some of the people who taste sugar at 0.3 think 0.5 is outlandishly sweet, while others don't mind 0.7 calling itself dry. My uncle Lee thinks wine is still sour

at 4.0 percent.

"Fruity" only deepens the muddle. In winespeak, fruity means the wine smells like a fruit, any fruit from bananas to apples to grapes. In this definition, a dry wine can be fruitier than a sweet one. In regular English, fruity is a common synonym for sweet, on the reasonable grounds that most fruit not only tastes but is sweet.

So as not to tax you with a headful of numbers, I regularly describe wines from 0 to 0.5 percent r.s. as dry, those from 0.8 to 1.5 as off-dry, and anything with 2.0 and up as frankly sweet. The gaps help take care of wines that could fall into the camp on either side, depending on tart-

ness (tart wines can hide sugar just like green apples can), tannin (similar effect), and fruitiness.

To help you do a little self-calibration: spicy, faintly bitter Gewürztraminer can hide sweetness; try Obester Anderson Valley (0.3), De Loach Russian River Valley (1.4), and Geyser Peak Northcoast (2.3).

Blandly berrylike White Zinfandel and Zinfandel Rosé tend to show r.s. readily, moving most winemakers to treat sweetness as a virtue; you might try J. Pedroncelli Sonoma County Zinfandel Rosé (0.8), Seghesio California White Zinfandel (1.6), and Beringer California White Zinfandel (3.4).

The Farmers' Market *frenzy*

*The West is blazing new trails from the farm to you. Here's **where** to shop, **how** to shop, and **what** to buy if you want really ripe, really fresh, often organic produce*

*By Linda Anusasananan
with Lynn Ocone and Jena MacPherson*

CHAD SLATTERY

ANN SUMMA

IN SANTA MONICA, *California grower Clive Hinckley (left) shows off pink pearly seeds of pomegranates, shoppers (center) select willow branches and sunflowers, and Linda Nakamura (right) tempts customers with vine-ripe strawberries.*

AT PIKE PLACE PUBLIC MARKET *in Seattle, Katherine Lewis artfully displays her organic produce. Lettuces, squash blossoms, haricots verts, fresh herbs, and golden beets tempt a wide range of customers, from professional chefs to home cooks.*

I t's 7 A.M. As the gray fog shrouding Santa Monica's Arizona Avenue business district begins to quickly dissipate, the Wednesday morning silence is broken by the growl of trucks maneuvering into parking spaces. In a few hours, four blocks of the avenue will be lined with temporary stalls bursting with freshness as the Santa Monica Farmers' Market swings into its weekly day of business.

Patti Scott and her assistant, John, pull into their regular slot opposite McGoo's restaurant. They've been up since 3. At the ranch, they loaded just-picked white nectarines, Asian pears, and Red Flame grapes onto their truck; the 200-mile drive from Dinuba has roused their appetites. Heading for a quick breakfast, they wave greetings to other growers.

Snippets of news and gossip fill the air at McGoo's: "Just when you think you've got it right, you have to change." "Not all produce is created equal—people sample and buy from the best." "The health department has put a stop to sampling cut pieces of fruit." "He was kicked out of the market for selling out-of-state produce."

With a few last sips of coffee, the growers move out. Laura Avery, market manager, is on hand as farmers move to their assigned spots. With only so much space allocated by the city for the market, farmers must keep quality high if they want to maintain their positions. Avery has a long list of other growers who'd love to fill in for any laggards and enjoy the profitable returns.

At 8:30, traffic barricades are pulled into the street, blocking off the market. Immediately, farmers and their crews speed into well-rehearsed action. Tables unfold, chairs bang, crates drag. It's a race to be ready when the 9:30 horn signals selling time.

Out of the corner of her eye, Patti Scott spots a regular

ON WEDNESDAYS *in Santa Monica, more than 8,000 people shop for produce once the opening horn sounds at 9:30.*

WHERE TO FIND THE BEST MARKETS IN THE WEST
Each has its own flavor and way of doing business

Informally, we queried growers and managers who serve more than one market (often three or more) and customers throughout the West who've shopped at a number of markets. The following list is a consensus of their favorites; times and dates change occasionally, so call ahead to check.

CALIFORNIA

DAVIS. Central Park, Fourth and C streets; (916) 756-1695; 8 to noon Saturdays year-round; Wednesdays 2 to 6 November through April and 4:30 to 8:30 May through October. This is *the* place to be on Saturday morning. Strong community and social atmosphere; park setting. True farmers' market bazaar, diverse produce, some processed food, bread, and crafts; live entertainment. Gardening and canning experts often present.

SAN FRANCISCO. Ferry Plaza, in front of Ferry Building at foot of Market Street on the Embarcadero; (415) 981-3004; 9 to 2 Saturdays year-round. Produce (about 50 percent organic), supplemented by locally raised meat, game, fish, organic dairy products, breads, sausages, and pasta. Special seasonal events include great street food from the city's top restaurants. Programs feature Shop with the Chef and Market Cooking for Kids (a biology and cooking lesson). Good metered parking adjacent.

SANTA BARBARA. Corner of Cota and Santa Barbara Street; (805) 962-5354; 8:30 to noon Saturdays year-round. Wonderful mix, from backyard gardeners to big growers. Beautiful flowers, many subtropical fruits, good variety in produce. Sea farms sell mussels, abalone, and shrimp. Spontaneous entertainment and massage chairs keep atmosphere relaxed; a feel-good market for the entire family. Kids available to help carry food to cars.

SANTA MONICA. Arizona Avenue and Second Street; (310) 458-8900; 9:30 to 3 Wednesdays year-round. On the day of the market, this is

customer, Inez Olson of Venice, in the waiting crowd. Scott automatically sets aside some of their popular white nectarines for her.

Meanwhile, since advance sales are prohibited, Olson takes advantage of the lull to survey the market and plan her shopping strategy. She strides rapidly through aisles piled high with Brown Turkey figs, aromatic basils, Morello cherries, ice cream bananas, and much, much more. It's already crowded and noisy. Voices of all ages mingle in dozens of languages.

Promptly at 9:30, the selling horn sounds and the rush is on. Olson goes into action. First stop: a flower stand for a splashy bouquet of sunflowers; the prettiest go first. As she waits her turn, apple vendors on either side

chant, "Taste this apple, you'll love it," and hand out little Braeburn apples for sampling.

Flowers in hand, Olson heads for the vegetables. As she makes her selection, another customer, standing alongside, is placing an order. "Can you bring me three dozen zucchini blossoms for stuffing next week? I need them for a party." With a nod of assent and a smile, the agreement is sealed.

Across the street, Olson spies some newcomers. In a glass tank, farm-raised catfish stare idly as someone asks the vendor, "How do you sell them?" Comes the reply: "Live for $3 a pound . . . you clean them."

On Olson's list are Asian pears from Patti Scott. As she strolls up, Scott pulls out the reserved nectarines—

they've been going fast. "My all-time favorites, a piece of heaven!" exclaims Olson. "In L.A. it's so nice to have someone know who you are!" She hands over three of the dollar bills she brought so making change would be easier for the farmers.

The market will be in full swing until 3, but by 10, Olson's bags are stuffed. She heads home to stow her trophies.

As the closing hour nears, some growers shout out reduced prices. Waiting shoppers move in for the bargains, and inventory declines rapidly. When the market closes, the street quickly empties as stands are dismantled and loaded trucks pull away. Cleanup is in motion, and by 4:30, Arizona Avenue is as it was.

the largest produce outlet in the state, serving 8,000 people in 5½ hours. Eccentric to tony farmers and shoppers, plus occasional Hollywood celebrities, provide eye-opening social entertainment. Quality produce, lots of ethnic choices, tremendous variety. Crowded and fast-paced; watch your belongings—pickpockets are a problem. Buy flowers first, since lines for them are longest. Bring quarters for metered parking.

SAN RAFAEL. Marin Civic Center, N. San Pedro Road just off U.S. Highway 101; (800) 897-3276; 8 to 1 Thursdays and Sundays year-round. Food sets the stage for the festival atmosphere. Outstanding collection of mainstream and specialty produce; 50 percent organic. Baked goods, crafts, cheese, honey, flowers, fish, meat products. Pony rides, tastings of peak season produce, lots of activities.

COLORADO

BOULDER. Thirteenth Street between Arapahoe Street and Canyon Boulevard; (303) 494-4997; 8 to 2 Saturdays, April 16 through October 29; 2 to 6 Wednesdays, June 1 through September 28. Colorful canopies mark site on tree-lined street in city park. About 60 vendors every week; 70 percent organic. Produce and farm-related crafts. Lots of festivals.

NEW MEXICO

SANTA FE. Sanbusco Market Center, 500 Montezuma Street; (505) 983-4098; 7 to 11:30 Saturdays and Tuesdays, June to early November. About 90 vendors from Rio Grande area; primarily produce and a few craft vendors. Native chilies include the prized Chimayo, fresh and dried. Many varieties of Southwest beans.

OREGON

BEAVERTON. On Hall Boulevard between Third and Fifth streets; (503) 643-5345; 8 to 1:30 Saturdays, June 4 to October 29. Produce (20 percent organic), cut flowers, potted plants, lamb, fish from Astoria, and some prepared foods. A master gardener, a recycler, and a preserver (all extension agents) give advice. Live country music. It's a real social event.

GRANTS PASS. F Street between Fourth and Fifth streets; (503) 476-5375; 9 to 1 Tuesdays, June through September; 9 to 1 Saturdays, March 19 through November 19. Five-county area is source for a remarkably wide range of agricultural products. Produce, some processed food, crafts, musicians.

WASHINGTON

OLYMPIA. 401 N. Capitol Way at Percival Landing Waterfront Park; (206) 352-9096;

10 to 3 weekends, April, November, December; 10 to 3 Thursdays through Sundays, May through September; 10 to 3 Fridays through Sundays, October. Located on the waterfront with sweeping views on clear days of the Olympic Mountains and Budd Inlet. Produce, crafts, street entertainers, seafood, international fast food. Lots of festivals. Often a human gridlock in the summer.

PASCO. Fourth Avenue and Lewis Street; (509) 545-0738; 8 to noon Wednesdays and Saturdays, 4 P.M. to sellout Thursdays, May through November. Located in the center of an agricultural belt, it offers a tremendous selection of produce; specialty foods and crafts also sold. About 90 vendors.

SEATTLE. Pike Place Public Market, corner of First Avenue and Pike Street; (206) 682-7453; 9 to 6 Monday through Saturday, 11 to 5 Sundays year-round. World-renowned public market includes a large farmers' market of 50 to 100 growers at low metal tables (day or low stalls) in the North and Main Arcades; don't confuse them with the permanent high stalls, some stocked with farmers' produce, some by wholesalers. Handcrafts are also sold in the day stalls.

Market is very crowded at lunch and on Saturdays. Parking is tough; try the Public Market Parking Garage on Western Avenue behind the market. An information booth is at First Avenue and Pike Street.

HOW TO FIND A MARKET NEAR YOU

Check with the state agricultural department, county agricultural commission, or local cooperative extension office for the farmers' markets nearest you. Or write to the following organizations, and include a stamped, self-addressed envelope; they will send you a list.

CALIFORNIA. California Federation of Certified Farmers' Markets, Box 1533, Sacramento 95812-1533. Southland Farmers' Market Association, Marion Kalb, Director, 1010 S. Flower St., Room 402, Los Angeles 90015.

COLORADO. Colorado Farmers' Market Association, 212 Pikes Peak Place, Longmont 80501.

OREGON. Oregon Department of Agriculture, Agricultural Development and Marketing Division, 121 S.W. Salmon St., Suite 240, Portland 97204.

WASHINGTON. Washington State Farmers' Market Association, 11910 C Meridian St. E., Suite 29, Puyallup 98373.

Colorful market scenes much like this one are played out at least once or twice a week in communities all over the West. The personalities of markets vary, but the mechanics that make them function are similar.

"Urban dwellers are panting for the farmers' produce," says market manager Laura Avery. Demand is so great, markets can't keep up.

THE PUSH IS ON FOR FARM PRODUCE

Today's farmers' market is a far cry from those of the past, and from the wholesale produce markets that are still commonplace.

As cities grew, so did regulations about how farmers could sell foods. Sometimes these rules aided the con-

sumer, but far too often they served the needs of the handlers and grocery stores and supermarkets.

Crave a ripe peach? Chances are it's not firm enough for a commercial packer. Want some little apples for the kids to munch? Commercial grading excludes many sizes. Starving for just-harvested sweet corn? It may take up to a week to reach a supermarket shelf.

Until California blazed a trail of change, such foods rarely reached the marketplace. The state department of agriculture, with grassroots support, established guidelines for farmers' markets in 1977. The basic rule: you have to grow it or produce it to sell it. The

KATHERINE LEWIS SHARES *her recipe for white-stemmed Treviso radicchio.*

REX RYSTEDT

Farmers' Market Treasures:
Regional specialties to seek out

YELLOW ZUCCHINI

ANN SUMMA

CUSTOMERS BUY *barhi dates at the Santa Monica market; they're hard to find elsewhere.*

The foods you'll find at a farmers' market are a mix of locally grown specialties. Noncommercial varieties abound—pale, unusually sweet carrots, extremely fragile peaches with wonderful flavor, yellow peppers with exceptional taste, big crisp grapes with seeds. Many foods qualify as exotic; some overlap supermarket selections but are fresher.

Following are some of the special items you're likely to find at markets in these areas. Don't be intimidated by an unfamiliar variety of produce or food. Most producers are more than happy to tell you what it is and how to eat it or how to cook it.

NORTHWEST
Dairy: goat milk, goat cheese. **Apples:** Criterion, Chehalis, Gala, Idared, King. **Berries:** Tay, Marion, Logan, Boysen, huckle, goose, red currants. **Cherries:** Van, Rainier, Royal Anne, Lambert, sour, dried. **Fruit:** Pinot Noir grapes. **Seafood and meat:** Olympia and Willapa Bay oysters, lamb. **Vegetables:** candystripe beets, edible flowers, Treviso radicchio, Romanesco broccoli, mizuna, ground cherries (*poha*), purple potatoes.

NORTHERN CALIFORNIA CENTRAL COAST
Dairy: sheep milk, sheep cheese, organic eggs. **Fruit:** Northern Spy, Black Twig,

Anna apples; Charentais melons; Ambrosia cantaloupes; Star-Moon watermelons; cherimoyas; Snow Queen nectarines; Last Chance peaches; Blenheim apricots; Wickson and Mariposa plums; salmon and thimble berries. **Tomatoes:** Sweet 100's on the branch, Brandywine, Radiator Charlie, Mortgage Lifter, Green Zebra. **Miscellaneous:** almond sprouts, fresh macadamia nuts in the shell. **Meats, fish:** pheasant, game birds, rock crab. **Vegetables:** haricots verts, bitter melon, bitter melon greens, Chinese long beans, pea tendrils, mature miniature corn on the cob, Dragon Tongue beans, Thai basil, wild mushrooms—including morels.

CALIFORNIA CENTRAL VALLEY
Fruit: white peaches, Pinkerton and Gwen avocados, Concord grapes, Juneau pears. **Berries:** Olallie, Boysen, Young, Sylvan, Tay, and Boughton raspberries. **Cherries:** Black Oregon, Royal Anne, Brooks. **Melons:** Charentais, musk, Magnum 45, Emerald Jewel, Spanish Ananas. **Tomatoes:** Green Grape, Park's Whoppers, Marvel Striped. **Miscellaneous:** Crimson Flame raisins, dried persimmons, pistachio butter. **Vegetables:** Maui onions, Sunburst and Rondenice squash, Mediterranean cucumbers, Corno di Toro peppers, Rosa Bianca and Farmers Long-lavender

eggplants, Rose Gold and Yellow Finn potatoes.

SOUTHERN CALIFORNIA
Fruit: fresh Medjool and barhi dates, feijoas, sapotes, Brown Turkey figs, Morello cherries, passion fruit, White Champagne Babcock and Arkansas Red Indian peaches. **Bananas:** Brazilian, Manzano, Mysore (ladyfinger), ice cream. **Herbs:** fenugreek, *tareh* (kind of a leek or chive). **Meat, fish:** live rabbits and chickens for pets or slaughter, muscovy duck, Santa Barbara spot prawns, ridgeback shrimp, farm-raised mussels, farmed catfish. **Miscellaneous:** jojoba oil, sproutnut spread, kitty grass. **Vegetables:** black radishes, *nopales* (cactus pads), Persian cucumbers, black trumpet and coral mushrooms.

INLAND, ROCKY MOUNTAINS
Dairy: goat milk. **Fruit:** Ambrosia cantaloupes, O'Henry peaches. **Meat, fish:** Animals on the hoof to slaughter—rabbits, chicken, sheep, cows; live farmed trout. **Miscellaneous:** fresh milled flours. **Vegetables:** Sandia and Pasilla chilies, arugula, mâche, sweet corn.

SOUTHWEST
Fruit: Champagne apples. **Miscellaneous:** fresh and dried chili ristras and wreaths, Chimayo chili powder, red and blue corn posole. **Vegetables:** Chimayo and Española Improved chilies, Mexibell peppers, fingerling potatoes, squash blossoms, and dried Anasazi, Yin Yang, and tepary beans.

FEMALE ZUCCHINI WITH BLOSSOMS

BITTER MELON

KITTY GRASS

LIVE CHICKENS AND ORGANIC EGGS

MAGNUM 45 CANTALOUPE

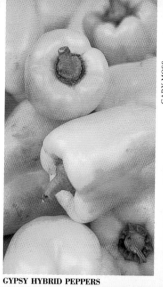
GYPSY HYBRID PEPPERS

Boughton Hybrid Raspberry 2.00 Bsk. 3 for 5.50

GARY MOSS

BOUGHTON HYBRID RASPBERRIES

GOLD NUGGET CHERRY TOMATOES

ROSA BIANCA EGGPLANT

CHAD SLATTERY

'SWEETIE 82' CORN

FRESH SUNFLOWER SEED HEADS

Red Globe grape with seeds $1 a lb

RED GLOBE GRAPES

AMSTERDAM MINI-CORE CARROTS

standards for grading and packing were also relaxed.

But beyond this, all products at a farmers' market—the obvious ones like fruits, vegetables, and flowers, plus any other harvested food that clucks, moos, baas, or squeals (even fish, if caught or grown by the seller) and by-products like eggs, cheese, or honey—must meet the same quality and health standards as those of any other food producer. Farmers' markets are subject to inspection, too. It's who's selling (growers), not size or volume of production, that's restricted. Goods can come from a backyard garden or a multi-acre ranch.

California's regulations are the most stringent; they're administered by county agricultural commissioners. Other states have followed California's you-sell-it, you-grow-it pattern, but rules are enforced by the markets instead of a state agency.

California now has more than 250 widely scattered markets. In the last five years, Washington's markets have doubled, to about 45. Colorado boasts 30,

FAMILIES AND THEIR FARMS: *Some are old-timers, some are opting for a new life*

THE PERRY CLAN

Farming courses through the Perry family's veins. "We all grew up on the farm. My dad came from Portugal when he was 13 or 14 years old, my mom when she was about 26. They started farming here in the 1920s," says John Perry. Four brothers and one sister manage more than 1,000 acres in California's rich Central Valley, 150 of which are devoted to fresh produce for farmers' markets—corn, red and green tomatoes, cantaloupes, peaches, peppers, summer and winter squash. "Every year is better than last year. We always overplant rather than not have enough to sell."

The bachelor brothers, Frank and Joe, farm full-time. John and Joaquin have outside jobs but help on weekends. Joe handles the commercial production; Frank runs the Perrys' roadside stand in Sacramento and the stalls at farmers' markets—14 of them a week in season.

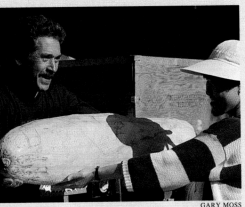
GARY MOSS
FRANK PERRY *was born to farm.*

How do they do it? Hard work, good organization, dedicated employees, and helpful families. "Saturday is family day. This is the day you contribute to the family," John tells his kids. That day they have four markets to attend. Son Jim, age 23, understands; he started at the Davis market when he was 10. "People watched me grow up there."

THE SCOTT FAMILY

Jay Scott was raised in a farming family. His grandfather, a dry-land farmer near Roseville, California, grew grapes and nuts. As a youngster, Jay sold newspapers and put away money for his first farm. After serving in Vietnam, he studied pomology at California State University Chico and viticulture at Cal State Fresno.

ANN SUMMA
PATTI SCOTT *married a farmer.*

In 1975, he and wife Patti bought their first farm. Now they are on their third, 35 acres in the Central Valley town of Dinuba. In addition to Asian pears, Red Flame grapes, and white nectarines, they also grow Thompson seedless grapes, Angeleno plums, Hayward kiwi fruit, and peaches. "If we had any more than that," says Patti, "Jay couldn't have a day job." He is a field manager with a packing company; they depend on his job for health insurance and funds to invest in the farm.

Patti, a registered nurse, left that career three years ago. "I decided it wasn't worth the stress so I'm doing this." She devotes herself full-time to the farm and has two assistants. The three Scott children, ages 23, 15, and 11, also lend a hand. Although most of the fruit goes to packing houses, Patti reserves enough to supply the three farmers' markets she attends, and three more where assistants run the stands.

The Scotts, who were at the Santa Monica market on opening day in 1981, say they make more selling directly, and they think customers buy more when they're able to meet the grower. "Trust is important. We have regular customers. Good sales could be the produce, or it could be the farmers." And for her, answering questions is "an educational mission."

LEWIS AND LOSPALLUTO

This is the eighth year Katherine Lewis and Steven Lospalluto have sold produce at Pike Place Public Market in Seattle. Neither came to farming through family. She was raised in the suburbs of the Santa Clara Valley, he in Cincinnati. They first leased a total of 15 acres near Puyallup, and have just purchased 18 acres near Mount Vernon in Washington's Skagit Valley to start a new farm; Lombrici's, which means "earthworms" in Italian, is the

and there are at least 20 to 25 each in Oregon and New Mexico.

Despite their temporary nature, farmers' markets don't just happen; they come together with a plan. Typically, a hired or elected manager with a board of directors (usually community members and farmers) determines where the market is located, how big it is, when it takes place, who can sell, what can be sold, and what other kinds of activities, if any, there will be.

Markets compete for the best producers, and many producers wait months, even years, to get a stand in a popular market because direct sales are so strong.

WHY THE BOOM?

Reason number one is flavor," says Randall Guzzardo of the Seattle restaurant Two Dagos from Texas. He shops regularly at Pike Place Public Market's day stalls. Value and quality come next on his list as he assesses a fragile head of lettuce at Katherine Lewis's stall. "Her stuff was cut this morning or yesterday. It may cost more, but with every leaf usable, it's good value."

In Davis, California, university student Linda Kaczmarek loads her bike with Summerset peaches, Red Globe grapes, and Sun-glo tomatoes. "I love

it here. You can't beat the quality. This fits into how I eat—fresh and raw."

Even if these varieties were to turn up in the supermarket, they wouldn't be as ripe or as fresh. Most farmers harvest produce the night before or on market morning. All, or a good portion, is sold within 24 hours. Fruit can be picked ripe and full of sugar—but it won't keep a week in the refrigerator. Corn that journeys only a few hours, not days, is sweet and juicy and should be eaten as soon as you get it home. Apples and cucumbers right from the garden don't need wax to preserve their moisture.

With all this wonderful freshness,

IT'S A NEW LIFE for Steven Lospalluto and Katherine Lewis; they chose to live off the land and just bought their first farm.

name they gave to both these enterprises.

They are part of a new breed that has chosen farming as a way of life. Lewis stresses that it is a lifestyle, not just a job. While it's a risky business and the work is hard, the returns fueled their desire to own their own farm.

Today, Lospalluto picks corn and has the truck loaded by 5 A.M. Then Lewis makes two restaurant deliveries and arrives at the market by 7. She's assigned to a spot she's had often in the day stalls.

With some help, Lewis lays out a display of squash blossoms, beans, celeriac, candystripe beets, zucchini, and other vegetables and herbs—about 20 kinds, from parsley to lemon verbena. Everything is organically grown.

Lewis and Lospalluto have sold at weekend markets in Sequim and Puyallup, but prefer Pike Place, which has a week-long schedule (they're there four times weekly, in season) and a clientele very interested in food. "Seattle is a food town," says Lewis. "There's a synergy to being in the market. . . . This is my social life, these are the people that I spend the most time with. . . . They are my livelihood, but they're also my friends, and that's real important."

taste memories explode and new expectations are born. Ever eat a Northern Spy apple from an heirloom tree? That delicious memory might be triggered by a Northern Spy revived and revered by a local grower who brings a few to market. If your family hails from as far away as Thailand or Eastern Europe or as close as Mexico, it's here at market you're most apt to find the lemon grass and scented purple basil or tiny golden beets and glossy Hungarian peppers and many other foods that have the flavor of home.

It's the unusual, the long-forgotten, the rare, and even the new that turn up regularly at farmers' markets. Experi-menting is economically feasible on a small scale, and for farmers, it often opens lucrative doors. Jerry Rutiz of Rutiz Farms in Arroyo Grande, California, noted considerable demand for his Persian cucumbers and *tareh* (a kind of leek or chive) from Middle Eastern families in Los Angeles, so he planted more. Now he sells these items in large quantities at the Santa Monica market.

As a testing ground for new tastes and a vehicle for changing the foods we eat, farmers' markets have a glowing track record. Notable among many examples are fresh-cut herbs, mesclun (mixed baby salad greens), and Fuji ap-ples. All made their debut in farmers' markets and are now found in mainstream supermarkets.

Variety is a solid dimension of farmers' markets, and surprises are always popping up, like cherimoyas in Marin County, bananas in Southern California, or Romanesco broccoli in Seattle. One gem at the Davis farmers' market is the Boughton hybrid raspberry. At his berry stand, Timothy Boughton, from Amber Oaks in Auburn, describes its origin: "I started this berry hybrid when I was 8 years old. I started with a wild raspberry and crossed it with a cutting a lady gave me. . . . It has more flavor and a longer growing season, from May through September."

A listening shopper interjects, "Do you spray them?"

Boughton replies: "We use no pesticides. Praying mantises and spiders control pests; turkey manure is our fertilizer. You don't even need to wash them."

An adolescent, waiting with his mom to buy some berries, stage-whispers, "You better wash them if he covers them with turkey manure."

Like Boughton, growers at the market are more than happy to fill you in on any details of their farming practices and pest controls. You can find out whether chemicals are used, what they are, what they're for, and when they were last applied.

All of which raises the tangled issue: What's organic?

For an operation to be identified as a California Certified Organic Farm (CCOF), the grower's statements regarding organic practices are verified. To be registered as organic, you have to do some paperwork and pay a fee, but no verification is involved. Washington and Colorado have state certification seals for organic. Other certification seals include the acronyms TILTH, FVO, OCIA, and OGBA.

Confused? Ask a grower to explain.

On the other side of the organic fence from Boughton—and just across the street at the Davis farmers' market—is Perry's Garden Highway Garden stand. Their famous 'Sweetie 82' corn has an enhanced gene that keeps its sugar from converting to starch. Experience has taught John Perry that pesticides aren't unacceptable to many of his customers. "More people would rather have some pesticide than worms," he says. "With the cost of pesticides, we certainly wouldn't use them unless we needed to."

The proof of his corn's popularity is sales. On a Saturday, 400 dozen ears go home with customers. Another 70 to 80 dozen are sold at their roadside stand in Sacramento—even more at the three other farmers' markets family members attend on the same day.

A TASTY EDUCATION

Want to know what something tastes like before you buy it? Or which variety of melons you'll like best—musk, Emerald Jewel, Spanish Ananas? Maybe you're just curious. Consumer sampling is extremely popular at farmers' markets for three reasons: it attracts buyers, helps them make satisfying decisions, and educates them. Unfortunately, this practice is restricted in some counties. Some local health departments require approved settings in which to cut fruit, although they remain amenable to whole fruit given away for sampling. This is fine if you're selling cherry tomatoes, but not so practical for larger items. Farmers and shoppers agree that the opportunity to taste is an invaluable feature of farmers' markets, and that a more effective solution than the one now proposed by health departments is needed.

With so many unfamiliar items at market, growers wisely and happily field even the most outlandish or naive questions. Wonder why one pepper is green and the other red? Don't know how to store tomatoes? Want to know if you can eat corn silk? How to cook radicchio? Just ask. It's the inquisitive who go home with answers.

Often there are experts on hand. At San Francisco's Ferry Plaza Farmers' Market, star chefs lead market tours. As they fill their baskets, they explain how to cook their selections. At many markets, agricultural extension agents or other qualified individuals are regularly present to answer questions on such diverse subjects as freezer jams and diagnosing an ailing plant.

SHOW BUSINESS IS GOOD BUSINESS

Entertainment is part of market fun. "I go there for the theater," says Lyra Halprin of Davis.

Live music—country, Andean, a French chanteuse, a steel band—swirls through most markets. Magicians, face painters, jugglers, or even petting zoos give reason to pause, enjoy, and socialize. Special events like Pig Out at the Davis Farmers' Market Day, Boulder's Old-Time Farm Day, and Olympia's Strawberry Festival bring the whole town out to party.

Market crowds spill into the community, often reviving commercial vitality. In Pasco, Washington, the farmers' market has been an economic incubator for the town's growing crafts industry. In appreciation, the city built a permanent structure for the market.

In Boulder, Colorado, interest in supporting local agriculture spurred development of the farmers' market. The market proved successful, and pumped an unexpected bounty of funds into the city's economy.

Other towns where business wasn't booming echo this theme. "A live downtown is a healthy downtown, and that is good for business," declares Virginia Thigpen, past president of the Davis Downtown Business Association. The Davis market's summer fest drew a crowd of about 3,000.

Madeleine Kenefick, a 13-year veteran customer of the Davis market, sums it up: "The market is like a microcosm of life—you watch [as] kids grow up, babies [are] born, friends die. The market is like an extended family." ∎

SHOP-SMART TIPS

• **GO EARLY** for best selection, a convenient parking space, and crisper salad greens.

• **ARRIVE LATE** for best bargains; farmers don't want to carry their goods home.

• **DON'T BUY AT THE FIRST STAND.** Walk the entire market first to check prices and selection; they vary more than you'd suppose.

• **BRING LOTS OF SMALL BILLS** and change. Charge cards usually aren't accepted; some vendors take checks and food stamps.

• **KEEP MONEY IN YOUR POCKET** or fanny pack; a big purse is just extra baggage. Pickpockets like crowded urban markets.

• **BUY LIGHTEST FOODS FIRST;** some growers will let you leave heavy purchases with them until you're ready to leave.

• **ALWAYS BARGAIN** for large quantities. Don't haggle over small purchases, except at closing time.

• **BRING RIGID CONTAINERS** to protect delicate berries, peaches, and tomatoes from being crushed.

• **RETURN PLASTIC BERRY BASKETS** and orange bags to farmers for recycling.

• **BRING LARGE HEAVY-DUTY SHOPPING BAGS;** canvas ones work well. Old collapsible baby carriages make great shopping carts.

• **ON A HOT DAY BRING AN ICE CHEST** to keep greens fresh, cool down berries, and keep fish, meat, dairy products, and other perishable items cold.

• **BRING A CAN OF WATER** to keep flowers fresh.

• **DON'T BUY MORE** than you can eat or preserve in a few days. Most fully ripe produce has a short life.

• **GET TO KNOW THE GROWERS** and producers. Place special orders, ask questions. They can tell you how to prepare and store foods they sell, identify varieties, and explain how their products are grown.

PETER CHRISTIANSEN

BRIGHT BROCCOLI *and bell pepper add crunch, freshness to an open-faced omelet.*

These are super supper omelets

They're fast, easy, in just one pan

USUALLY RELEGATED to breakfast or brunch, omelets can also become quick, nutritious, and inexpensive main dishes for hurried—or relaxed—suppers, especially when teamed generously with colorful vegetables that also cook in the same pan.

If the trick of rolling an omelet, French-style, out of the pan intimidates you, put this concern aside. These omelets are flat and open-faced, like frittatas. The last step is a touch of heat from the broiler to melt the cheese topping. Serve omelets right from the pan, accompanied by a green salad and whole-wheat toast or a hearty, multi-grain bread.

Controlling your egg in-take? Make the omelet with a liquid egg substitute; use 1½ cups of the mixture instead of the 8 large eggs.

Broccoli and Cheddar Omelet

1 large (about 10 oz.) red bell pepper

½ pound broccoli

2 teaspoons butter or margarine

Basic omelet (recipe follows)

¾ cup shredded cheddar cheese

2 Roma-type tomatoes (about 6 oz. total), cored and chopped

Salt

Crushed dried hot red chilies (optional)

Stem and seed bell pepper; cut into ¼-inch strips. Cut off broccoli flowerets; slice flowerets lengthwise. Thinly slice stems crosswise.

In a 9- to 10-inch oven-proof, nonstick frying pan, melt butter over medium-high heat. Add bell pepper, broccoli stems, and 1 table-spoon water. Stir often until stems are tender when pierced and liquid has evap-orated, about 3 minutes. Add flowerets and 1 tablespoon water; stir just until flowerets turn bright green but are still crisp, 3 to 5 minutes. Pour vegetables into a bowl and keep warm.

Make basic omelet; when eggs are softly set, cover with ½ the cheese. Add vegetable mixture and tomatoes; sprin-kle with remaining cheese. Broil omelet 6 inches from heat until cheese melts, about 3 minutes. Add salt and chilies to taste. Cut in wedges or scoop from pan. Serves 4 or 5.

Per serving: 234 cal. (62 percent from fat); 16 g protein; 16 g fat (7 g sat.); 8.1 g carbo.; 238 mg sodium; 362 mg chol.

Basic omelet. In a bowl, beat to blend 8 **large eggs.** Pour into frying pan (used to cook vegetable mixture). Cook on medium-low heat until eggs on bottom begin to set; push aside or lift cooked egg to let liquid egg flow to pan bottom. Repeat until eggs are set but still creamy looking on top, about 7 min-utes total.

French Country Omelet

4 slices (about 2½ oz. total) bacon, finely chopped

2 small (about ½ lb. total) thin-skinned potatoes, scrubbed and cut into ¼-inch cubes

1 small (3 or 4 oz.) onion, chopped

1 clove garlic

Basic omelet (recipe precedes)

¾ cup shredded jack cheese

2 tablespoons minced parsley

Sour cream or nonfat sour cream (optional)

In a 9- to 10-inch oven-proof, nonstick frying pan, combine bacon, potatoes, onion, and garlic. Stir often over medium heat until ba-con is crisp and potatoes are browned, 20 to 25 minutes. Spoon mixture into a bowl; keep warm.

Make basic omelet. When eggs are softly set, sprinkle with ½ the cheese. Top with potato mixture and sprinkle with remaining cheese. Broil 6 inches from heat until cheese is melted, about 2 minutes. Sprinkle with pars-ley; top portions with sour cream to taste. Cut into wedges or scoop portions from pan. Serves 4 or 5.

Per serving: 312 cal. (61 percent from fat); 17 g protein; 21 g fat (5.5 g sat.); 12 g carbo.; 294 mg sodium; 364 mg chol. ∎

By Christine Weber Hale

NANCY GAFFNEY *and her baby Alpines are part of the new movement in Western cheesemaking.*

What's new with Western goat cheese?

Many more cheesemakers, greater availability, and new choices—from flavored soft to hard grating types

I N THE SUNNY CHEESE room at Sea Stars Goat Cheese in Santa Cruz, California, the air smells sweet and tangy. As owner Nancy Gaffney scoops white curds from a stainless steel tank into cheesecloth bags, the only sound is the steady drip of the yellow whey as it drains from the hanging bags. A vase of blue and fuchsia bachelor's buttons decorates the windowsill; after Gaffney salts and shapes the curds, she will sprinkle them with petals to make her Monet cheese. Outside, all that separates Gaffney from the bright Pacific are goats with names like Champagne and Artemis, more flowers, and a field of emerald green brussels sprouts. "Just another day in paradise!" she laughs.

Twenty years ago, you would have had to go to Europe to find a scene like this. Handcrafted goat cheeses were an imported novelty. Now, the West's goat cheese-

makers number more than 20, and their cheeses encompass a wide range of styles. Seasonal production is reaching its peak, making this a great time to check out the new options.

Most Western goat cheesemakers started out making mild, soft fresh logs. These still dominate the market, but there's an enormous variety of other types: soft cheeses flavored with everything from jalapeños to cranberries; layered tortes like dried tomato–basil; and varieties usually associated with cow's milk, such as cheddar, jack, and mozzarella. There are even aged goat cheeses in the parmesan style that develop nuttier, stronger flavors, and surface-ripened cheeses reminiscent of brie.

Some adventurous styles— such as Sea Stars's Monet, or aged goat cheese wrapped in grape leaves by Sally Jackson in Oroville, Washington—are unique to the cheesemaker and may be available only locally. While a few tiny com-

panies sell just at regional farmers' markets, larger operations sell throughout the West in upscale grocery and specialty stores and health food stores. Some sell by mail (see list, page 121).

Expect to pay about $3.50 for a 4-ounce fresh goat cheese log and up to $20 per pound for specialty cheeses. Limited production brings up the price; also, goats give less milk than cows, and produce it seasonally, drying up in the winter before they kid.

What about nutrition? Softer cheeses have the fewest calories, about 76 an ounce; as cheeses get firmer (and water content decreases), calories, fat, protein, and cholesterol are concentrated.

Mary Keehn, owner of Cypress Grove Chèvre in McKinleyville, California, gives the best reason to enjoy Western goat cheeses: "You're not going to get this variety or flavorful excitement in factory-made cheeses. It's like looking at a print

Goat cheese guide

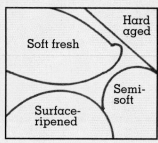

Goat cheeses come in a host of styles, with a roster of names from foreign to fanciful. (There are no official identification standards.) Yet nearly all goat cheeses fall into one of four main types. Within these categories, depending on the cheese and the cheesemaker's style, tastes range from very mild to pungent, and plain to fla-vored. Goat cheese textures can be soft to hard, depending on age and style.

- **Soft fresh** (the bulk of the market). The huge range of available styles includes spreadable, soft to firmer *fromage blanc* (shown here in bowls); cylinders of cheese marinated in oil (in jar); flower-covered disk; plain log; rounds with chives and with spices; and layered tomato-basil torte. Textures range from spreadable to sliceable. Cheeses may be called *chèvre, chabis, fromage de chèvre, montrachet*-style, and other names.

- **Semisoft** (fresh or aged). Typical styles include feta (here, with dried vegetables), block of *queso fresco* (similar to feta, but less salty), and mozzarella ball.

- **Hard aged.** Two examples are white cheddar and a hard grating cheese.

- **Surface-ripened.** Like cow's milk brie, these have an edible, velvety surface mold. They can be semisoft or firmer; in rounds, pyramids, or wedges; and plain or with an ash coating or blue vein, as shown.

versus an original work of art—there's no comparison."

SHOPPING, USING, AND STORING

• At the store, *soft fresh* goat cheese should look moist. Reject if air-bloated, moldy, or leaking whey. *Semisoft* and *hard* cheeses shouldn't be dry or cracked. Minor mold can be trimmed, but it indicates a lack of freshness. *Surface-ripened* cheeses should have a very white bloom (unless a blue style) with no cracks; odor can be mild to pungent, but not ammonia-like.

• Enjoy goat cheeses on their own, served at room temperature for fullest flavor. Or use them in cooking; some styles melt better than others.

• In the refrigerator, protect cheeses from air with original wrappings, plastic wrap, or waxed paper. Keep blue types in separate containers. Discard cheeses that develop an off-odor, strange colors, or more than a touch of mold.

10 WAYS TO ENJOY SOFT GOAT CHEESE

• Spread on toast or bagels, and add jam or lox.

• Substitute for cream cheese in dips.

• Swirl or layer with pesto to spread on crackers.

• Sandwich with sliced smoked turkey and arugula on black bread.

• Top green salads with crumbled cheese, or with slices briefly warmed in the oven.

• Dab over pizza.

• Stuff into seeded mild fresh chilies; broil until golden.

• Stir into hot bean or vegetable soups.

• Layer into lasagne.

• Sweeten with powdered sugar, honey, or jam. Add a little amaretto or brandy, and lemon peel. Spoon onto blintzes or nut breads, or serve with fruit.

Fresh Herbs–Cheese Plate

Try this after-dinner cheese plate with contrast-

DINNER CONCLUDES *elegantly with cheeses and feathery herbs.*

PETER CHRISTIANSEN

ing cheeses, such as soft fresh, semisoft, and surface-ripened.

This presentation was a collaboration by San Francisco chefs Elka Gilmore of ELKA and Traci des Jardins of Rubicon with cheesemaker Laura Chenel, for an International Association of Women Chefs and Restaurateurs event.

1 cup Italian parsley leaves

1 cup fresh chervil sprigs (or more parsley)

¼ cup small (1 to 2 in.) fresh basil leaves

¼ cup 1½-inch pieces chives

2 tablespoons thinly sliced shallots

1 tablespoon walnut oil

2 teaspoons champagne or white wine vinegar

Salt and pepper

½ to ¾ pound (total of 3 different types at room temperature) goat cheeses

Thinly sliced dense bread such as walnut, date, or sourdough

Rinse, dry, and chill parsley, chervil, basil, and chives to crisp. In a bowl, combine shallots, oil, and vinegar. Add herb leaves, mix gently, and season to taste with salt and pepper.

Scatter about 1⅓ cups of the leaves around 4 salad plates. Cut each cheese into

4 portions; divide among plates. Offer with bread and additional herb leaves. Makes 4 servings.

Per serving: 249 cal. (72 percent from fat); 14 g protein; 20 g fat (12 g sat.); 4.7 g carbo.; 242 mg sodium; 43 mg chol.

Goat Cheese–Spinach Pasta

You can use any unsweetened, flavored, soft fresh goat cheese (such as herb, pepper, garlic, or chili) or a drained, oil-marinated type; the cheese melts to form a flavorful sauce.

SPINACH FETTUCCINE *and leaves, lightly cloaked with flavored cheese, make a quick supper.*

12 ounces dried spinach fettuccine

3 quarts lightly packed, rinsed, drained fresh spinach leaves, in 2-inch pieces

⅔ cup regular-strength chicken broth

½ pound (1 cup) unsweetened, flavored, soft fresh goat cheese, broken into chunks if possible

2 cups room-temperature ripe cherry tomatoes, cut into ⅓-inch slices

Salt and pepper

Fill a 6- to 8-quart pan ⅔ full with water; bring to a boil over high heat. Add fettuccine and boil until barely tender to bite, 5 to 6 minutes. Add spinach and boil until wilted, 30 to 45 seconds. Drain fettuccine and spinach and return to pan.

Meanwhile, in a 1- to 2-quart pan over high heat, bring chicken broth to boiling. Stir in goat cheese until melted, and remove from heat. Add cheese mixture to fettuccine and spinach; mix to coat. Spoon pasta mixture onto a platter and scatter tomatoes over top. Season to taste with salt and pepper. Makes 4 servings.

Per serving: 539 cal. (28 percent from fat); 30 g protein; 17 g fat (9.4 g sat.); 70 g carbo.; 449 mg sodium; 107 mg chol.

PEACH-CROWNED *ginger tart has a mild goat cheese taste.*

Gingered Peach and Goat Cheese Tart

1 large egg

½ pound (1cup) unflavored soft fresh goat cheese

3 tablespoons sugar

3 tablespoons chopped crystallized ginger

1 teaspoon grated lemon peel

Press-in crust (recipe follows)

2 teaspoons lemon juice

1¼ cups ⅓-inch-thick slices peeled, firm-ripe peaches

1 tablespoon melted peach jam

In a bowl of an electric mixer, beat egg, cheese, sugar, 2 tablespoons of the ginger, and lemon peel until smooth. Spread mixture in crust.

Combine lemon juice and peaches; arrange peach slices, slightly overlapping, over cheese. Brush fruit with jam; sprinkle with remaining ginger.

Bake in a 325° oven until edge of filling is set and slightly firm when lightly touched, 35 to 40 minutes. Let cool on a rack until room temperature. Serve, or chill airtight up to 6 hours. Carefully push up bottom of pan from rim; transfer tart on pan to a platter. Makes 8 servings.

Per serving: 222 cal. (49 percent from fat); 7.4 g protein; 12 g fat (7.2 g sat.); 22 g carbo.; 162 mg sodium; 78 mg chol.

Press-in crust. In a food processor or a bowl, combine ½ cup **all-purpose flour** and 1 tablespoon **sugar.** Add 3 tablespoons **butter** or margarine, cut into small pieces; whirl, or rub with fingers, until fine crumbs form. Add 1 **large egg yolk;** whirl, or mix with a fork, until dough holds together. Press dough evenly over bottom and sides of a 7½-inch tart pan with a removable rim. Bake tart in a 325° oven until pale gold, 20 to 22 minutes. Use warm.

FINDING WESTERN GOAT CHEESES

For a complete list of Western goat cheese companies, send a self-addressed, stamped envelope to Goat Cheese, *Sunset,* 80 Willow Road, Menlo Park, Calif. 94025. The following sell all or some of their cheeses by mail; expect to pay extra for shipping.

CALIFORNIA. *Alpine Chèvre,* Lakeport; (707) 263-8131, or (800) 499-8131 within California. Four flavors soft fresh. Semisoft Chevito: plain or dried vegetable. Hard aged Shepherd's cheese.

Bodega Goat Cheese, Bodega; (707) 876-3483. Peruvian-style cheeses. Very soft, plain *queso crema.* Six flavors ricotta-style *queso ranchero.* Unripened semisoft *queso fresco.*

Laura Chenel Chèvre, Sonoma; (707) 996-4477. *Fromage blanc:* plain. Other soft fresh: five flavors plus herb oil–marinated. Surface-ripened: *crottin* and *taupinière* (white surface bloom over ash-coated cheese).

Corralitos Cheese Company, Watsonville; (408) 722-1821. Soft fresh: plain, herb-garlic, fresh pinwheel with basil and tomato pestos. Feta.

Cypress Grove Chèvre, McKinleyville; (707) 839-3168. Four flavors *fromage blanc.* Other soft fresh: five flavors. *Fromage à trois* with layers of basil, tomatoes, and pine nuts. Cheddar. Surface-ripened: log, pyramid, and 1-pound loaf.

Rachel's Goat Cheese, Sebastopol; (707) 823-1322. *Fromage blanc:* plain, and dried tomato–garlic and smoked salmon–chive flavors. Other soft fresh: four flavors.

Redwood Hill Farm, Sebastopol; (707) 823-8250. Three flavors soft fresh, feta, mozzarella, cheddar.

HAWAII. *Orchid Island Chèvre,* Kurtistown; (808) 966-7792. Soft fresh: plain, herb oil–marinated.

IDAHO. *Rollingstone Chèvre,* Parma; (208) 722-6460. Widest selection, including flavors of *fromage blanc,* other soft fresh, tiny soft *crottin,* layered tortes, oil-marinated, soft fresh to hard aged pyramids. Semisoft jalapeño. Three kinds hard aged. Surface-ripened *blue âge.*

NEW MEXICO. *Coon Ridge Goat Cheese,* Pie Town; (505) 293-9150. Herb *fromage blanc.* Oil-marinated herb or chili-garlic.

Sweetwoods Dairy, Peña Blanca; (505) 465-2608. Soft fresh: 11 flavors.

OREGON. *Willamette Valley Chèvre,* Canby; (503) 266-1644 or (800) 343-4628. Five flavors *fromage blanc.* Other soft fresh: five flavors plus oil-marinated. Plain or dried tomato–basil feta. Plain or jalapeño jack. *Queso fresco.*

WASHINGTON. *Quillisascut Cheese,* Rice; (509) 738-2011. Aged semisoft or hard Spanish-style *curado* in five flavors, plain smoked, or chipotle chili smoked. ■

By Elaine Johnson

A midsummer night's turkey

Barbecued, it's no fuss. The price is right, and it certainly looks grand

T URN THE TABLES ON the season with a big turkey dinner designed for warm weather. It's a natural twist, because turkey, one of today's great values, practically cooks itself on a grill. And when other parts of the meal share the same heat, cooking becomes almost recreation.

This party menu for 8 to 10 is exceptionally flexible. The turkey is delicious hot or cold. Its companions are a trio of wilt-resistant salads. A cool, lavish berry dessert ends the meal—which is most likely to be followed another day with snacks of leftover turkey.

The barbecue is the center of action, and for starters, you brown corn and onions to mix with barley and seasonings for one salad.

Then you organize the grill for indirect cooking of the turkey, and surround the bird with potatoes to roast over direct heat. The roasted potatoes, with a dressing, make a second salad. A baste of dried tomatoes gives the turkey a piquant finish.

As a third salad, compose a colorful platter of cold cooked green beans and sliced ripe tomatoes; scatter with bits of feta cheese and moisten with an oil and vinegar dressing.

Make the dessert hours beforehand.

Giblet gravy is a delicious addition to this menu, to ladle over the turkey and even onto some of the salads. But you need to start it before you cook the turkey—even the day before. A simple but effective preparation begins by combining neck and giblets (except liver) with a couple of coarsely chopped onions and carrots in a pan. Cover giblets generously with chicken broth and simmer until meat is very tender when pierced, about 1½ hours. Add the liver and simmer until firm, about 15 minutes. Pour mixture through a strainer into a bowl; return broth to pan. Chop the neck meat and the giblets and add to broth; discard the vegetables. Bring gravy to a boil,

E. K. WALLER

RICH BROWN TURKEY *is dinner party centerpiece. In support: potatoes dressed with lemon and basil, barley salad with grilled corn and onions, and sliced tomatoes with cold green beans.*

and thicken to taste with a paste of cornstarch and water.

Barley Salad with Grilled Corn and Onions

Ignite coals or turn on a gas barbecue and use the first heat to cook the corn and onions. Then adjust heat for turkey and potatoes.

If you want to make just the salad, omit drip pan.

4½ cups regular-strength chicken broth

1½ cups pearl barley

1 tablespoon grated lemon peel

4 large ears (10 to 12 in. long) yellow corn, husks and silk removed

2 large (about 1 lb. total) red onions, halved

2 cups (about 2 oz.) lightly packed fresh mint leaves, minced

½ cup minced fresh cilantro (coriander)

½ cup rice vinegar

½ teaspoon pepper

Mint and cilantro sprigs (optional)

Salt

Combine broth, barley, and lemon peel in a 3- to 4-quart pan. Cover and bring to a boil over high heat; simmer until barley is tender to bite, about 30 minutes. Drain barley, reserving broth. If making ahead, cover and chill barley and broth separately up to 1 day.

In a charcoal-fueled barbecue with a lid, ignite 60 mounded charcoal briquets on firegrate. Let burn until briquets are so hot you can hold your hand at grill level only 1 to 2 seconds, about 15 minutes. Push coals equally to opposite sides of firegrate. Place a drip pan between coals. Set grill 4 to 6 inches above coals.

On a gas barbecue, adjust controls for indirect heat, and set a drip pan between heat sources (if manufacturer recommends). Turn heat to high and close lid; allow 5 to 10 minutes to reach temperature. Keep lid down as much as possible to keep grill hot.

Position corn and onions on grill directly over coals or gas heat. Cover with lid; if lid

GLAZED RASPBERRIES *make a sparkling red crown for cream cheese and yogurt mousse.*

has vents, open them. Turn vegetables often until slightly charred, 12 to 15 minutes; set aside until cool.

To maintain heat for additional cooking, add 5 briquets to each mound of coals every 30 minutes; turn gas heat to medium. Cover grill with lid.

Cut corn from cob and chop onions. In a bowl, mix vegetables with barley, minced mint and cilantro, vinegar, pepper, and enough of the reserved broth to give salad the moistness you like. Garnish with mint and cilantro sprigs, and add salt to taste. Serves 8 to 10.

Per serving: 178 cal. (8 percent from fat); 6.2 g protein; 1.6 g fat (0.3 g sat.); 37 g carbo.; 40 mg sodium; 0 mg chol.

Barbecued Turkey with Tomato Glaze

Prepare barbecue for indirect cooking, and maintain heat as instructed for the barley salad.

1 turkey, 14 to 16 pounds

2 ounces (about 1 cup) dried tomatoes (not oil-packed)

⅓ cup dry red wine

⅓ cup regular-strength chicken broth

3 tablespoons lime juice

2 cloves garlic, minced or pressed

2 teaspoons minced fresh or 1 teaspoon crumbled dried rosemary

Discard leg truss; pull tail, if necessary, out of body cavity so it can brown. Rinse turkey and pat dry; pull off

and discard any fat lumps. Set turkey, breast up, on a grill (charcoal or gas) over drip pan. Cover grill with lid, and open vents. Cook turkey until a thermometer inserted through the thickest part of the breast to the bone registers 160°; allow 2 to 2½ hours. Start checking doneness after 1½ hours, as cooking times vary with shape of bird and barbecues. If parts of the turkey darken excessively before the bird is done, drape dark areas with foil.

Meanwhile, combine tomatoes, wine, broth, lime juice, garlic, and rosemary in a 3- to 4-quart pan. Cover and bring to a boil over high heat; simmer until tomatoes are easy to mash, 20 to 25 minutes. Whirl mixture until smooth in a blender or food processor.

When the breast reaches 145°, about 20 minutes before cooking is complete, begin brushing frequently with tomato mixture, using it all. Let turkey stand at least 15 minutes, then carve. Makes 14 to 16 servings, or 8 to 10 servings with leftovers.

Per serving: 471 cal. (40 percent from fat); 64 g protein; 21 g fat 6 g sat.); 3.1 g carbo.; 170 mg sodium; 186 mg chol.

Grilled Roasted Potatoes with Basil

16 small (about 1½ in. wide, about 2¼ lb. total) red thin-skinned potatoes, scrubbed

¼ cup extra-virgin olive oil

2 tablespoons lemon juice

2 tablespoons grated

lemon peel

½ cup finely shredded fresh basil leaves

Basil sprigs (optional)

Salt and pepper

Cut potatoes in half crosswise and rub lightly with oil. Lay cut side down on grill over hot coals (you can hold your hand at grill level only 1 to 2 seconds). Cover grill with lid; open vents. Turn potatoes occasionally until browned and tender when pierced, 30 to 40 minutes. In a bowl, mix potatoes with remaining oil, lemon juice, and lemon peel. Let stand until room temperature. Just before serving, stir in shredded basil and garnish with basil sprigs. Season to taste with salt and pepper. Serves 8 to 10.

Per serving: 134 cal. (39 percent from fat); 2.1 g protein; 5.8 g fat (0.8 g sat.); 19 g carbo.; 8.9 mg sodium; 0 mg chol.

Raspberry Cream Mousse

1 large package (8 oz.) neufchâtel (light cream) cheese

1 cup whipping cream

1 cup low-fat vanilla-flavor yogurt

½ cup sugar

2 tablespoons cornstarch

5 cups raspberries, rinsed and drained

2 tablespoons raspberry liqueur or orange juice

In a deep, chilled bowl, beat cheese with a mixer on high speed, slowly adding cream so mixture stays thick enough to hold soft peaks. Stir in yogurt. Scrape mixture into a wide 8- to 9-cup bowl. Cover and chill.

In a blender or food processor, whirl sugar with cornstarch; add 1 cup raspberries, and purée until smooth. Pour into a 1- to 1½-quart pan; stir over high heat until boiling. Remove from heat; gently stir in liqueur and remaining berries. Spoon mixture over cheese filling. Serve, or cover and chill up to 8 hours. Scoop into individual bowls. Serves 8 to 10.

Per serving: 231 cal. (51 percent from fat); 4.4 g protein; 13 g fat (8.2 g sat.); 24 g carbo.; 114 mg sodium; 45 mg chol. ∎

By Christine Weber Hale

hold your hand at grill level only 4 to 5 seconds). Baste frequently with peach sauce and turn ribs as needed to develop a rich brown glaze, about 20 minutes. Pour remaining sauce into a bowl. Cut ribs between bones and accompany ribs with more sauce added to taste. Makes 6 to 8 servings.

Per serving: 601 cal. (63 percent from fat); 35 g protein; 42 g fat (15 g sat.); 20 g carbo.; 662 mg sodium; 161 mg chol.

Marina, California

A THOUSAND POETS HAVE sung the praises of the rose, but so far as we know only Robert Louis Stevenson has eulogized the onion in verse. In "To a Gardener," he writes:

First let the onion flourish there,
Rose among roots, the maiden-fair
Wine-scented and poetic soul
Of the capacious salad bowl.

Don Lavoy, obviously moved by the same sentiments, created this onion salad.

The Midas touch for ribs

And an onion salad that's pure poetry

MEDIEVAL ALCHEMISTS tried to transmute lead into gold. Every chef who barbecues ribs is engaging in a similar endeavor, attempting to transform a base material—visually the least promising portion of the carcass—into gustatory gold. The difference is that many chefs, like Chris Osserman, succeed.

Killer Ribs

About 5 pounds pork loin back ribs
1 large (10 oz.) onion, coarsely chopped
2 teaspoons ground cinnamon
1 tablespoon dried basil leaves
1½ teaspoons ground allspice
1½ teaspoons ground ginger
1 or 2 teaspoons crushed dried hot red chilies

3 dried bay leaves
3 cloves garlic, minced or pressed
1 can (about 1 lb.) sliced peaches, drained
1 bottle (18 oz.) prepared barbecue sauce

Trim and discard excess fat from ribs. Place ribs in an 8- to 10-quart pan; add onion, cinnamon, basil, allspice, ginger, 1 teaspoon of the chilies, bay leaves, and garlic.

Fill pan with just enough water to cover ribs. Put lid on pan and bring water to boiling over high heat. Reduce heat to simmer and cook until meat is tender when pierced, about 50 minutes.

Meanwhile, in a blender or food processor, purée peaches. Stir peaches to mix with barbecue sauce and remaining 1 teaspoon chilies.

Drain ribs; lay on a grill 4 to 6 inches above a solid bed of medium-hot coals (you can

Walla Walla Salad

1 large (about 1¼ lb.) head romaine lettuce
½ medium-size (6 oz.) Walla Walla, Maui, or other sweet onion
½ cup diced red or yellow bell pepper
⅓ cup crumbled blue cheese
2 tablespoons balsamic vinegar
1 can (2 oz.) anchovy fillets
1 to 3 cloves garlic, minced

Rinse, drain, and crisp romaine leaves. Cut leaves into 1-inch-wide strips. Coarsely chop onion. In a salad bowl, combine lettuce, onion, bell pepper, blue cheese, vinegar, and oil from anchovies. Chop anchovies and add to salad along with garlic to taste; mix well. Serves 8 to 10.

Honolulu

RANDALL RICHARDSON'S NOT Pecan Praline Bars, to paraphrase Samuel Johnson on second marriages, represent the triumph of hope over experience. They also show the power of Yankee ingenuity. (The element of luck should not be ruled out, either.)

One night, Richardson began to make pecan praline bars by greasing a pan and preheating the oven. Then, and only then, did he begin to assemble his ingredients.

There was no shortening, so he substituted margarine. When the brown sugar box yielded only ¼ cup, he added ¾ cup white sugar. And on it went. Even though the finished product did not look like pecan praline bars, his family paid him the ultimate compliment: they ate them all before Richardson could save one for lunch.

Not Pecan Praline Bars

About ¼ cup (⅛ lb.) butter or margarine, melted

¾ cup granulated sugar

¼ cup firmly packed brown sugar

¼ cup vanilla-flavor yogurt

¾ cup all-purpose flour

¼ cup rolled oats

1 teaspoon baking soda

1 cup chopped walnuts

In a bowl, stir together ¼ cup butter, granulated sugar, brown sugar, and yogurt.

Mix flour, oats, and baking soda; add to butter mixture along with walnuts. Stir to blend thoroughly.

Spread batter in a buttered 8-inch square pan. Bake in a 325° oven until center feels firm when gently pressed, about 35 minutes.

Cool in pan, then cut into 16 squares. Serve, or if making ahead, package airtight up to 1 day; freeze to store longer. Makes 16.

Camarillo, California

By Joan Griffiths, Richard Dunmire

A PLATTER FULL *of polenta and vegetables is a wholesome dish for family and friends.*

A broccoli lover's repast

Polenta is its foundation

POLENTA AND BROCCOLI MAKE strong partners for a vegetable entrée with plenty of make-ahead steps. If you are really in a rush, skip the cooling and cutting step for the polenta, mound the hot mixture onto a platter, top with the herb-seasoned vegetables, sprinkle with the cheese, and slip under the broiler to finish as directed.

Toasted Polenta with Broccoli and Fontina

7 cups regular-strength vegetable or chicken broth

2 cups polenta or yellow cornmeal

2 to 2½ pounds broccoli, rinsed

2 large (about 10 oz.) red bell peppers (or 1 red, 1 yellow), stemmed, seeded, and cut into 1-inch chunks

1 large (about ½ lb.) onion, thinly sliced

1 tablespoon minced fresh or 1 teaspoon crumbled dried rosemary leaves

2 teaspoons minced fresh or ½ teaspoon crumbled dried thyme leaves

1 tablespoon dry marsala or dry sherry

2 teaspoons cornstarch

About ⅓ pound fontina or jarlsberg cheese, shredded

Combine 6 cups broth and polenta in a 5- to 6-quart pan. Over high heat, stir often until boiling; reduce heat and stir often (mixture spatters) until polenta is thick enough to hold its shape when mounded, 10 to 15 minutes. Spread polenta evenly in a 9- by 13-inch pan; cover and chill until firm, at least 2 hours or up to 2 days.

Cut flowerets from broccoli. Trim off tough stem ends and discard; thinly slice stems. Rinse the 5- to 6-quart pan and half-fill with water. Bring to boiling on high heat. Add flowerets and stems; cook uncovered until broccoli is barely tender when pierced, about 3 minutes. Drain and, at once, immerse in ice water until cold; drain. If making ahead, cover and chill up to 1 day.

In the pan used for broccoli, combine peppers, ¼ cup broth, onion, rosemary, and thyme. Stir often over high heat until liquid evaporates and vegetables stick to pan, about 10 minutes. Add ¼ cup broth and stir to free browned bits. Stir often until liquid evaporates; remove from heat. Mix remaining ½ cup broth with marsala and cornstarch.

Meanwhile, invert polenta from pan onto a flat surface and cut into 6 squares, then cut each square in ½ diagonally to make 12 triangles. Arrange triangles in a single layer on a heatproof platter or a 10- by 15-inch pan. Broil about 4 inches from heat until polenta is toasted lightly, about 15 minutes. If on a pan, transfer polenta to a warm, heat-resistant platter; keep warm.

Return vegetable mixture to high heat, add broth mixture, and stir until boiling. Add broccoli and stir until hot, 1 to 2 minutes. Pour broccoli mixture onto center of polenta and sprinkle vegetables with fontina cheese. Broil about 6 inches from heat until cheese melts, about 2 minutes. Makes 6 to 8 servings.

By Christine Weber Hale

GRANITA PAIRS *crab salad with a green wasabi sauce.*

An adventure with soft-shell crab

Cook it tempura-style and serve over greens

FIRST, THE TROPHY: the golden, crunchy, edible shells and delicate flavor of soft-shell crabs, served over salad greens with spicy wasabi cream. It's a remarkably good combination of flavors and textures.

Now, the adventure. Dealing with live crabs is not for the squeamish, and frankly, cooking them in hot oil makes a mess. (To head off spatters, line the work area with newspapers and cover the pan with a mesh screen.)

That said, this is a special entrée, one to enjoy during summer, when the Atlantic blue crab sheds its hard shell. Reliable air freight is making this East Coast delicacy more available in Western seafood markets and in restaurants like Granita, in Malibu, California, where this recipe originates.

Live soft-shell crabs are quite perishable. Try to cook them the day of purchase. Or chill up to a day if necessary, covered with a damp towel in a container with air holes.

You'll find wasabi powder in many supermarkets. Buy *nanami togarashi*, a Japanese mix of chilies and other seasonings, at an Asian market, or use cayenne.

Ready for the wilds of your kitchen? Line up some appreciative guests, and pull out your safari hat.

Granita's Soft-Shell Crabs with Wasabi Cream

12 live (about 3 oz. each) soft-shell crabs

2 cups all-purpose flour

½ teaspoon *each* pepper and paprika

¼ teaspoon *each* salt and cayenne

2 cups club soda

4 to 8 cups salad oil (depending on pan size)

4½ quarts (1 lb.) lightly packed salad mix, rinsed and crisped

Radish sprouts (optional)

Wasabi cream (recipe follows)

Nanami togarashi (optional)

Hold each crab with claws away from you; cut crosswise with scissors completely through shell ¼ inch behind eyes to kill crab instantly. (It may move a little after snip-

ping.) To clean each crab, lift up sides of flexible top shell; pull off and discard fan-shaped gills. Pull off and discard triangular flap of shell on crab bottom. Rinse crabs; pat dry.

Place ⅔ cup flour in a bag and gently shake 2 crabs at a time to coat; shake off excess. In a bowl, combine remaining 1⅓ cups flour, pepper, paprika, salt, and cayenne. Add club soda; whisk until batter is smooth.

Line floor beneath range-top and counters next to range with newspapers. In a wok or 5- to 6-quart pan, heat 1½ inches oil to 400°. Using long-handled tongs and oven mitts, dip a crab in batter, then lower into hot oil; oil may spatter. Repeat with a second crab. Cover with wire mesh spatter screen, if available, and cook crabs until deep golden, 3 to 4 minutes.

Lift crabs to paper towels to drain. Keep warm on a large, towel-lined platter in a 200° oven up to 1 hour. For each remaining batch, skim bits of batter from oil and return oil to 400° before adding the crabs.

On 6 plates, mound greens and sprouts; spoon some of the wasabi cream onto the plates. Place 2 crabs on top of each. Sprinkle with nanami togarashi, and offer with remaining cream. Serves 6.

Per serving: 645 cal. (53 percent from fat); 35 g protein; 38 g fat (8.9 g sat.); 40 g carbo.; 859 mg sodium; 153 mg chol.

Wasabi cream. In a blender, whirl 1¼ cups lightly packed **Italian parsley** sprigs, 1 cup **crème fraîche** or sour cream, ¼ cup **seasoned rice vinegar,** 1 tablespoon **lemon juice,** and 4 teaspoons **wasabi powder** (green horseradish) until a smooth purée. Season to taste with **nanami togarashi** (½ to ¾ teaspoon; or use ¼ to ½ teaspoon cayenne) and **salt.** Makes 1½ cups. ∎

By Elaine Johnson

SUNSET'S KITCHEN CABINET

Creative ways with everyday foods—submitted by *Sunset* readers,
tested in *Sunset* kitchens, approved by *Sunset* taste panels

Strawberry Cheesecake French Toast

Jerry Robbins, Flagstaff, Arizona

- 1 cup (8-oz. carton) part-skim ricotta cheese
- 3 tablespoons powdered sugar
- 1 teaspoon vanilla
- 16 diagonal slices (each ⅓ in. thick and 5 to 6 in. long) French bread
- 2 large eggs
- 1 cup low-fat milk
- 1½ tablespoons butter or margarine
- 2 cups hulled, sliced strawberries
  Berry syrup

In a bowl, stir ricotta, powdered sugar, and vanilla until smooth. Spread 1 side of half of bread slices with ricotta; top with remaining bread. In a bowl, beat eggs and milk to blend.

Place 1 or 2 nonstick frying pans (each 10 to 12 in. in diameter) over medium heat. Add ½ tablespoon butter to each. Dip ricotta sandwiches in egg mixture; place slightly apart in pans. Cook, turning, until deep golden and firm to touch, about 5 minutes per side. Keep warm while cooking remaining toast with remaining butter. Offer with strawberries and syrup. Serves 4.

Per serving: 347 cal. (36 percent from fat); 16 g protein; 14 g fat (7.2 g sat.); 39 g carbo.; 433 mg sodium; 140 mg chol.

SWEETENED RICOTTA *filling between French toast slices tastes like cheesecake.*

Sausage, Basil, and Port Fettuccine

Thomas Shook, Tempe, Arizona

- 1¼ pounds mild or hot Italian sausages, casings removed
- 2 cloves garlic, minced or pressed
- 1½ cups sliced green onions
- 3 cups thinly sliced red onions
- 1½ cups port
- 3 cups chopped ripe tomatoes
- 2 tablespoons balsamic vinegar
- ¾ cup chopped fresh basil leaves
- 12 ounces dried fettuccine, cooked according to package directions
  Salt and pepper
  Fresh basil sprigs

In a 10- to 12-inch frying pan over medium-high heat, break sausages into 1-inch chunks and stir often until brown, 8 to 10 minutes; lift from pan and set aside.

Discard all but 2 tablespoons fat from pan. Over medium heat, add garlic and green and red onions. Stir often until onions are very limp, 12 to 15 minutes. Add port, bring to a boil over high heat, and boil until reduced by half, about 5 minutes.

Add tomatoes, sausages, and vinegar; stir often until bubbling, about 2 minutes. Stir in chopped basil. On a platter, spoon sausage mixture over fettuccine. Season to taste with salt and pepper. Garnish with basil sprigs. Serves 6.

Per serving: 629 cal. (34 percent from fat); 25 g protein; 24 g fat (7.8 g sat.); 64 g carbo.; 698 mg sodium; 111 mg chol.

BOLD SAUCE *for pasta has Italian sausages, green and red onions, tomatoes, fresh basil, and port.*

Gazpacho Sorbet

J. Hill, Sacramento

- 2 cups seasoned tomato juice
- 1 envelope unflavored gelatin
- ¼ cup fresh lime juice
- ¼ teaspoon ground cumin
- ¼ teaspoon liquid hot pepper seasoning
- ⅓ cup finely chopped, peeled, and seeded cucumber
- 1 tablespoon chopped fresh cilantro (coriander)
  Fresh cilantro sprigs and lime twists

In a 1- to 2-quart pan, stir tomato juice and gelatin; let stand for 5 minutes. Stir often over medium-high heat until steaming, about 4 minutes; let cool. Stir in lime juice, cumin, and hot pepper seasoning. Pour mixture into ice cube trays and freeze until almost firm to touch, about 2½ hours. If making ahead, freeze airtight up to 1 month.

About 30 minutes before serving (45 minutes if frozen solid), let tomato cubes soften at room temperature. In a food processor or bowl of an electric mixer, whirl or beat cubes until smooth. Stir in cucumber and chopped cilantro. Spoon into goblets; garnish with cilantro sprigs and lime. Serves 4.

Per serving: 33 cal. (2.7 percent from fat); 2.6 g protein; 0.1 g fat (0 g sat.); 7 g carbo.; 453 mg sodium; 0 mg chol.

Compiled by Elaine Johnson

A NEW LOOK *for gazpacho: purée frozen, spicy tomato juice, then stir in chopped cucumber.*

Soup for dessert, skewer savvy, Western barbecue sauces, and burger wines

By Jerry Anne Di Vecchio

A true artist uses many media, but Elka Gilmore's favorite is food. Her approach to design focuses on the plate as a canvas, but it is also reflected in the imaginative, eclectic detail of her San Francisco restaurant, ELKA. When I first saw her version of fruit soup, thoughts of Swiss expressionist Paul Klee popped into my head. Thin squiggles of nectarines, squares and dots of kiwi fruit and plum, bumpy rounds of berries, and other colorful bits were floating with modern flair in the pale, tea-color broth.

But this dish has more than superficial beauty. It's simply delicious and looks more complex than it is. The soup base is nonseasonal—sweet water intensely infused with a complex blend of fresh ginger, citrus peel, aromatic seasonings, and fresh herbs. Once made, it keeps for weeks in the refrigerator.

The seasonality of the soup depends on what's ripe. Practical Elka points out that you can use the soup base in fall with persimmons, pomegranates, apples, and pears, and in winter with citrus and tropical fruit.

Serve fruit soup for a party, using the full recipe, or make by the bowl with any summer fruit you have on hand. The zingy flavor comes from the pulpy, edible seed of ripe, wrinkled passion fruit. Occasionally, I've come across canned or frozen passion fruit pulp; 2 tablespoons of either equals 1 whole fruit.

BACK TO BASICS

Doing skewers right

Skewers make some foods much easier to handle on the barbecue grill. With them you can:

• Control small bits of food. Threaded onto skewers, the pieces become a single unit to lift and turn—no more rescuing your dinner from the coals.

• Keep foods flat. Whole birds—chicken, pheasant, quail—that have been split and pressed open have less tendency to pull back when a skewer is threaded through the bird from shoulder to shoulder. A skewer through split lamb or veal kidneys keeps them from curling as they cook. Parallel skewers through floppy pieces of meat, like boned leg of lamb, make them easier to manage.

• Weave foods together. Ripple a long skirt steak onto a skewer and secure sprigs of herbs against the meat. Weave bacon strips between pieces of food for self-basting.

When loading skewers, keep in mind that meat, poultry, firm-texture fish like swordfish, and shellfish shrink as they cook, tightening their hold on the skewer. Most everything else gets softer or more fragile.

Vegetables and fruit, in particular, tend to

WITH BOLD STROKES, *Gilmore creates a masterpiece dessert for Di Vecchio.*

A TASTE OF THE WEST

Summer Fruit Soup

- 4 or 5 ripe passion fruit
- 1 ripe to firm-ripe small (4 to 5 oz.) nectarine or small (5 to 6 oz.) peeled peach
- 1 small (4 to 5 oz.) red-skin plum
- 1 medium-size (4 to 5 oz.) kiwi fruit
- 6 to 8 strawberries, rinsed and hulled

  About 2 dozen

blackberries, boysenberries, or olallieberries

About 2 dozen raspberries or other berries

About 1 cup total other in-season fruits (such as mango, papaya, melon, pineapple) in small dice, thin slices, or julienne strips (optional)

Mint sprigs

Soup base (directions follow)

Cut passion fruit in half. Cut nectarine, plum, and kiwi fruit into thin slices; use slices whole or cut them into geometric shapes: thin strips, squares, triangles, or cubes. Thinly slice strawberries; cut other berries (except raspberries) in half.

Into each wide, shallow soup bowl or deeply rimmed dessert plate, scoop pulp and seed from a passion fruit half. Divide remaining fruit and berries equally among bowls. Garnish fruit with mint sprigs and set bowls at serving places.

From a pitcher, pour or ladle about 1 cup soup base into each bowl. Makes 8 to 10 servings.

Per serving: 172 cal. (2 percent from fat); 0.9 g protein; 0.4 g fat (0 g sat.); 43 g carbo.; 4.1 mg sodium; 0 mg chol.

Soup base. In a 4- to 5-quart pan, combine 10 cups **water**, 1½ cups **sugar**, 1 cup chopped **fresh ginger**, ¼ cup **coriander seed**, 2 cups coarsely chopped **fresh cilantro** (coriander), 1 cup coarsely chopped **fresh spearmint leaves** (or regular mint), 1 **vanilla bean** (slit open lengthwise), and pared peel (colored part only) from 2 **lemons**, 2 **oranges**, and 3 **limes.**

Bring mixture to a boil over high heat. Remove from heat, cover, and chill at least 4 hours or up to 12. Pour liquid through a fine strainer into a bowl. Rinse vanilla bean and let dry to use another time; discard remaining seasonings. Cover and chill until cold, at least 3 hours or up to 3 weeks. Makes 9 to 10 cups.

soften as they cook and lose their grip. Parallel skewers in these foods give them support and keep them from spinning or flopping. You get maximum control by pushing 2 skewers perpendicularly through foods, each about ⅓ of the distance in from opposite ends of the food.

Crisp or firm vegetables and fruit tend to split when pushed onto thick skewers; slender, sharply pointed metal or bamboo skewers work best for these foods (to keep bamboo skewers from charring, soak a few minutes in water before using).

Foods that fall apart when cooked (such as sole or other flaky fish) are not suitable for skewer cooking.

GREAT TOOL
Poultry shears

My poultry shears probably work just as hard at the dinner table as they do in the kitchen. There is no faster way to reduce a whole duck, chicken, or any similar-size or smaller bird into pieces than snipping it apart. The same is true for pork or lamb ribs, rabbit, and any other meats with bony parts—and not much meat to carve—that are tough to cut with a knife. Poultry shears look like scis-

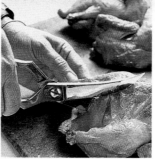

POWERFUL BITE *of poultry shears snips right through roast game hen.*

sors, but their design makes them more powerful. The power is multiplied if the hinge has a mechanical advantage—such as a built-in tension spring—like mine do. Typically, the tips of the long blades are curved slightly upward so they can be poked into difficult-to-reach crevices.

Like any cutting tool, shears' quality and design vary widely. Prices start around $10; a serviceable pair will be $40 to $50, but can be much more if materials are costly and detailing elaborate (bone or fine wood handles, engraving, inlays).

Try on shears before buying; the handle should feel comfortable, the grip easy to manage, the design sturdy, the material suited for the uses you anticipate (fancier for table, utilitarian for kitchen). I bought my stainless steel pair years ago at cook's heaven, E. Dehillerin

in Paris, and they're still good as new. But anywhere good knives are sold—cutlery shops, cookware stores, department stores—you will find poultry shears.

MARKET REPORT
Comparing barbecue sauces

While wandering down a grocery aisle recently, I was struck by the staggering number of barbecue sauces. I wondered how different they could be. A tasting seemed in order, but some practical editing was needed. So I gathered everything that was made in the West and had "barbecue sauce" written (not just implied) on the label. If a brand had flavor variations, I picked the original. I also imposed on friends in Southern California and the Northwest to send me what they could find in their supermarkets. In the *Sunset* kitchen, we tasted each sauce on beef patties; the meat was turned in the sauce before grilling, and then served with more of it.

The panelists rated the sauces, noting what they liked best about the taste and texture, how well the flavors sank in, and how the sauce coated the meat. Among the six sauces that got the most

votes, there was considerable ingredient variation and an intriguing mix of geographic influences.

Cinnabar CinnaBar-B-Que Sauce (Prescott, Arizona) was the most unusual and controversial of the lot. Most tasters commented that lamb, pork, or chicken would benefit more than beef from the sauce's aromatic, India-influenced spices.

Ebara Korean Barbecue Sauce (Santa Fe Springs, California). Comments: soy-sauce salty, lively ginger bite, thin, more sour than sweet.

Firehouse Bar-B-Que Sauce (Auburn, California). Comments: thick, sweet but not too much so, light smoky flavor. Said one taster: "What a Westerner thinks a Southern sauce should be."

Jackie's Oklahoma Style Barbecue Sauce (Greenbrae, California). Comments: thick and spicy, good sweet-sour balance; ingredients include raisins and orange peel.

Matheny's B-B-Q Sauce (Moreno Valley, California). Comments: powerful, tart, hot, sweet, lively, clings well; tastes of Asian influence.

Mrs. Renfro's Barbecue Sauce (Fort Worth, Texas). Comments: nice smooth balance, mellow tomato flavor, chili overtones, not sweet, clings well. ∎

BOB THOMPSON ON WINE
Burger wines

Could there be such a thing as a perfect burger wine? Bet your grandmother's secret recipe for pickle relish on it.

Before we can settle on a wine, though, we have to agree on the burger. A classic burger must have fresh ground beef, traditional bun, tomato, lettuce, pickle relish, mustard, and mayo. Together, they have to be juicy enough to drip a little, and have a certain sly sweetness. Onions, catsup, and barbecue sauces are optional adjustments, okay only as long as

they do not foul up the sweet, classic juiciness of the burger.

Now, think of a perfect burger wine as one more option, even though you take it on the side. That is, it cannot foul up the sweet juiciness, so it cannot have much drying tannin but must have a generous amount of fruit in its flavors.

Two basic choices are Barbera and Gamay (also called Gamay Beaujolais). Not many Zinfandels temper their tannins and avoid oak well enough for this job, but the ones that do count among the best burger wines on the continent. And Washington State

Lembergers can be described the same way. But Gamays are probably the safest choice when you do not know the winemaker's style. The following wines range from $9 down to $4.

With the classic, no onions, try: Louis M. Martini California Barbera, J. Lohr Estates "Wildflower" Monterey Gamay, or The Hogue Cellars Yakima Valley Lemberger. E. & J. Gallo Hearty Burgundy can stand in for the Gamay.

With the classic, plus sweet onions, try: Seghesio Sonoma County Zinfandel, Sutter Home California Zinfandel, or Fetzer Gamay

Beaujolais. (If it is not a season for sweet onions, sauté pungent ones until they are mellow and mild; raw, they take too much juiciness out of wine. Lembergers are a little too tart for any onions.)

While we're at it, here are wines for a few variations on the classic burger.

Traditional cheeseburger with cheddar: the Lemberger.

Untraditional cheeseburger with Oregon blue and no tomato: the Barbera, Zinfandels, or Gamay Beaujolais.

Southwest cheeseburger using jack plus chopped green chilies: the Gamay Beaujolais, Barbera, or Zinfandels.

PETER CHRISTIANSEN

On the trail of Western honey

Check out the West's regional honeys next time you're exploring

CALIFORNIA WILDFLOWER *honey flows from a honey swizzle to a toasted English muffin. (Above) Honeycomb is totally edible; cut and spread it on warm rolls, or chew it like candy.*

D O YOU TRAVEL TO collect honey? It's not as strange as it might seem. Searching out the West's specialty honeys is a sweetly rewarding pursuit—and great fun when you're on vacation or traveling around the West. All 13 Western states produce honey; California is the top honey-producer in the nation. Distinctive Western plants and climates support many different-tasting honeys.

FOLLOWING THE BEES

What bees eat makes a difference. The nectars they collect from flowers within a 1-mile radius of the hive determine the honey's aroma, flavor, body, and color. A great variety of flower nectars accounts for the diverse flavors of Western honeys. Alfalfa, clover, dandelion, star thistle plants, and sunflower are the most common nectar sources. Other plants valued for the flavors they impart to honeys are buckwheat, eucalyptus, mesquite, sage, and thyme. Avocado, blueberry, lavender, orange blossom, raspberry, and a blend of wildflower nectars also flavor Western honeys.

Western climates affect the honeys as well. Drier climates have plants with drier nectars, resulting in lower-moisture, thicker honeys.

LOOKING FOR REGIONAL HONEYS

Point your car toward the desert states of New Mexico and Arizona to locate mesquite honey, a light-colored honey with a mild flavor.

If you get to the mountain states of Colorado, Idaho, and Montana, check out the classic clover honey. (Clover honeys do not all taste the same.)

In Washington and Alaska, search for fireweed honey. The farther north it's produced, the paler and milder the honey will be—some is almost clear.

Tropical Hawaii produces two special honeys, macadamia nut and lehua (made from nectar of the lehua tree). Lehua has a pronounced flavor with a slightly salty aftertaste. It's frequently sold as creamed honey because it tends to crystallize. Macadamia nut honey, on the other hand, is very slow to crystallize. It has a nutty flavor and aroma.

Specialty regional honeys are frequently packaged by small honey producers. You'll find them in specialty food shops, farmers' markets, and health food stores. State and county fairs also feature honey, and sometimes sell honeycomb-on-a-stick.

If you want to dive into a serious honey search, call the local beekeepers or honey producers' associations of the state in which you're interested. In Alaska, call the Department of Natural Resources, (907) 745-7200; in Arizona, contact the USDA Research Service, (602) 670-6380.

ABOUT CRYSTALLIZATION

Once you get home with your honey, don't be alarmed if it crystallizes. Many honeys naturally become opaque and hard within days of being harvested; some never do. Honey producers can't control crystallization; it depends on the honey's components. Honeys high in glucose tend to crystallize more readily than those higher in fructose.

If honey crystallizes, make it liquid again by heating the jar (without the lid) in hot water or in a microwave oven at full power, checking at 20-second intervals.

COOKING WITH HONEY

The unique chemical structure of honey makes it ideal for baking. It's hygroscopic, which means it holds moisture in baked products.

You can substitute honey for sugar in muffins, cornbread, and breads, but be sure to reduce another liquid proportionally to take into account honey's liquid and its hygroscopic qualities. ■

by Betsy Reynolds Bateson

A SAMPLING OF WESTERN *regional honeys: (1) macadamia nut (Hawaii), (2) mesquite (Arizona), (3) fireweed (Alaska), (4) alfalfa (California), (5) huckleberry (Oregon). Flavors range from mild-sweet to spicy to floral.*

ROTISSERIE REVIVAL

All you need to know to spit-roast meats with professional flair

By Linda Lau Anusasananan

RESTAURANTS HAVE TURNED SPIT roasting into theater. Meats rotate slowly, grow browner, promise more succulence with each turn, and flood the air with rich aromas. Inside the turning meat, flavorful juices fight gravity. Instead of rapidly draining down and out of the meat, they flow through it, lubricating the interior and basting the surface automatically. It's a show that wakes up appetites in-house and has patrons wanting more of the same at home. And it's as easy as it looks.

"Far and away, it's the best way to cook large pieces of meat; [it's] more flavorful.... Our customers are highly enthusiastic," claims Reed Hearon of Restaurant LuLu in San Francisco. "Rotisserie cooking has the things people want these days—no added fat, crisp skin, moist meat, and lots of flavor," adds Michael Roberts of Twin Palms in Pasadena.

Spit roasting is one of the hottest trends on the restaurant scene. Rotisseries are ensconced in some of the glitziest kitchens in the West: Twin Palms in Pasadena, Restaurant LuLu and Bistro Roti in San Francisco, Wolfgang Puck Cafe in Universal City near Los Angeles and in Las Vegas, and Il Fornaios up and down California.

Some chains, such as Grand Roaster & Ale House in Washington, and San Francisco's California Roastery and Gira Polli, serve spit-roasted meats almost exclusively.

Even KFC has supplemented its buckets of Kentucky fried with—you guessed it.

SCIENCE AND HISTORY OF SPIT ROASTING

Spit-roasting and rotisserie cooking gear is hardly new. Giant fireplaces in kitchens of many historical houses and European castles have hand-turned or spring-wound spit-roasting gear. *Sunset,* in the late 1930s and early '40s, often reported on rotisseries in lavishly equipped outdoor kitchens. And now both the rotisserie and outdoor kitchens are popular again.

The spit—a metal rod with flattened sides (probably a smooth stick in the beginning)—is pushed through the meat and balanced so the rod will turn with little effort. Spit forks, poked into each end of the meat, are tightened onto the spit to keep the meat from slipping as it rotates. The heat is parallel to but never directly beneath the cooking foods. Many deli rotisseries have a wall of heat. Similar vertical gas burners are available on outdoor grills made by Dynamic Cooking Systems, Ducane, Pacific Gas Specialties, Onward Multi-Corp (Broil King), and Circle W Manufacturing Company (The Cooking Machine).

You can buy spit-roasting gear for many models of gas and some charcoal-fueled home barbecues. If you can't find equipment that matches your model, contact the manufacturer or ask your local dealer to order it for you. Or adapt your barbecue with a universal spit-roasting kit, from about $30.

SETTING UP TO SPIT-ROAST

You can control the heat and cooking time in several ways. First, decide what level of heat you need. If the diameter of the meat is 4 inches or less, use high heat so it will be well browned when cooked.

For larger cuts, such as a turkey or thick roasts, use medium heat so meat will be cooked through by the time it is well browned. Also, be sure the turning meat will clear the heat source by 1 to 4 inches, as the manufacturer suggests.

To start, remove barbecue grill. If rotisserie

SPICED CHICKENS *and lamb revolve on multiple spits over a wood fire at Restaurant LuLu in San Francisco. Each day, customers consume 80 to 100 chickens and 50 orders of lamb.*

PAUL HAMMOND

ANDY FREEBERG

LOADING THE SPIT

Push a spit fork onto the spit with sharp ends pointed toward the oncoming meat. Push the spit through the approximate center of the longest dimension of the meat. Center meat on spit. Slip another spit fork onto spit; push pointed ends of forks into the meat and secure forks against the spit. With cotton string, tie any loose sections such as flaps of meat, skin, drumsticks, or wings firmly against the meat. Snip off string close to knots.

Boned, rolled, and tied roasts are very easy to balance on a spit; so is poultry. Just run spit through the center of the meat or through the neck and body opening of a bird. You can rotisserie cook a pair of chickens or a quar-

tet of squab or game hens together; for best browning, place them end to end, securing each with spit forks on both ends. The length of the barbecue and spit capacity determine the number. Most spits can manage up to 12 pounds of meat at a time.

To test the balance of a loaded spit, support the ends of the spit in your palms and roll it. The meats should turn all the way over with relative smoothness. The real test is when the motor runs: properly balanced, it turns the spit without straining; improperly balanced, the meat sort of flops over with each rotation and the motor whines.

Irregularly shaped bone-in cuts like leg of lamb are a real challenge. Attach a counterweight to the spit; several types are available from about $10. Adjust according to design and test with several turns of the spit.

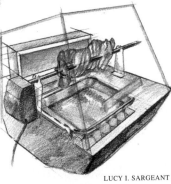

SPIT-ROASTED *foods cook with indirect heat. A drip pan beneath catches juices. Heat can be parallel to but not directly beneath food on gas or charcoal barbecues* (above). *Some gas models* (right) *have a vertical rear burner for rotisserie cooking. To cook boned roasts, run spit through center. To cook ribs, weave spit in and out between bones. Spit forks at each end secure meats.*

LUCY I. SARGEANT

LEG OF LAMB: *The bone makes balancing on the spit difficult; for smooth rotation, use an attachable metal counterweight, which is slid onto the spit.*   PAUL HAMMOND

is a separate unit, position spit supports and motor.

To cook with hot coals. For a standard 22-inch-diameter round, covered barbecue, mound and ignite on firegrate 50 to 60 charcoal briquets (use minimum for medium heat, maximum for high heat). For a rectangular barbecue with lid, measure out enough briquets to make 2 rows, each 2 briquets wide, that extend the length of firegrate; mound and ignite.

Let briquets burn until dotted with gray ash, about 30 minutes. Then, in a round barbecue, bank coals equally on opposite sides of firegrate. Add 5 or 6 briquets to each side now and at 30-minute intervals during cooking.

In a rectangular barbecue, bank coals equally on opposite sides of the spit down the length of the firegrate. Space the beds of coals (with spit in center) 6 to 8 inches apart. Set 1 briquet on hot coals every 3 to 4 inches now and at 30-minute intervals during cooking.

Place a metal or foil drip pan between coals. Fit loaded spit into motor and spit support; turn motor on. Move drip pan so it is directly beneath the meat. If you can adjust firegrate, position it 4 to 6 inches from surface of meat. Cover barbecue, open vents, and cook until meat is done to your taste. Maintain heat by adding briquets as specified. To reduce heat, add fewer briquets, partially close vents, or drop firegrate a few inches from the food.

To cook with gas. On barbecues with heat source below spit, turn burners on high and cover with lid. Preheat as manufacturer recommends (usually 10 minutes). Turn off center burner. If there is no control for heat in center of barbecue, set a foil drip pan with about ½ inch water in center of burners. Fit loaded spit into motor and spit support; turn motor on. Move drip pan so it is directly beneath the meat. Maintain high heat, or reduce to medium, as food requires. Cover barbecue.

On barbecues with vertical wall heat, turn burner on high; do not use bottom burners at the same time. Cook as directed with gas (preceding).

HOW LONG TO COOK

Monitor roasting meats frequently. You can judge the rate of cooking by how quickly the meat browns; if it's getting too dark or browning too fast, reduce the heat. Generally, spit-roasted meats cooked on high heat in a barbecue take about the same amount of time as in a 375° to 400° oven; on medium heat they cook about as fast as in a 350° oven. The diameter of the meat, not its weight, determines cooking time. A 3-inch-diameter boned pork loin roast cooks just as fast whether it weighs 2 or 4 pounds. For best results, use a meat thermometer in the center of the thickest part; pork is done at 155°, beef and lamb at 140° for rare. Turkey is done when 160° at the bone in thickest part of breast, chicken and game hen when 185° at bone in thickest part of thigh; smaller birds, such as quail or squab, are done when well browned.

FLAVORS, INCLUDING SMOKE

If you marinate meats in mixtures with honey and sugar, they tend to brown faster. Start with high heat until browning begins, then reduce heat to medium or medium-low.

If you add thick barbecue sauces and sweet glazes, brush them on during the last third or quarter of cooking.

For smoky flavor, soak wood chips at least 30 minutes. Sprinkle drained chips over coals about ½ cup at a time. When smoldering stops, add more chips, but remember that a little smoke goes a long way.

To smoke on gas grills, put chips in a metal box or tray designed for smoking, or cup chips in heavy-duty foil and set on burners.

NORMAN A. PLATE

SEASONED RICOTTA CHEESE *peeks out from under breast skin of spit-roasted chicken.*

SEASONING SECRETS FROM PROS

We asked some master spit-roasting chefs how they season foods, especially chicken.

CARLO MIDDIONE, VIVANDE, SAN FRANCISCO.

For chicken and other small birds: under breast skin, stuff a blend of ricotta and parmesan cheeses, parsley, garlic, and dried hot red chili flakes. For leg of lamb: bone, lightly pound into meat a mix of fresh rosemary, pepper, and salt, then roll snugly into a roast.

MICHAEL ROBERTS, TWIN PALMS, PASADENA.

"I like to put a huge tray of garlic cloves under the meat in the rotisserie. As the fat drips on the garlic, the cloves also roast," he says.

For chicken: soak bird in salt brine for half an hour, then tuck herbs between the skin and flesh and pat more all over the skin. His favorite blend is *herbes de Provence* (thyme, rosemary, and fennel) with added savory, lavender, pepper, and garlic. For pork loin: spread the flat sides of two equal-size boned pork loins with grainy mustard and top mustard with a solid layer of fresh sage leaves; sandwich filling between the roasts, then tie

snugly to make a roll. Roll roast in dried crumbled sage, salt, and pepper.

TIM FIRNSTAHL, GRAND ROASTER & ALE HOUSE, SEATTLE.

For chicken: brush inside and out with mixture of lemon juice, olive oil, basil, thyme, brown sugar, salt, and pepper. Stuff with a lemon half and chill, covered, 24 hours. Cool smoke (almost no heat) for 4 or 5 hours over cherry wood, then spit-roast.

CINDY PAWLCYN AND NELSON COGNAC, BISTRO ROTI, SAN FRANCISCO.

For poultry in general: put moist seasonings inside, dry ones outside. Moisture on skin keeps it from crisping.

For chicken: rub inside with salt, pepper, and a purée of onion, garlic, and lemon. Rub skin with salt, sugar, and fresh thyme. For duck: steam for 10 minutes to render fat, then marinate in rice vinegar, lemon grass, soy sauce, and orange juice for 30 minutes. Hang for a day in refrigerator to dry skin, then spit-roast.

BRADLEY OGDEN, ONE MARKET RESTAURANT, SAN FRANCISCO.

For chicken and other meats: accent with chipotle chili–flavor barbecue sauce,

and garlic-and-herb-infused olive oil.

CLAUDE ALRIVY, LE CHARDONNAY, LOS ANGELES.

For chicken: rub inside with chopped fresh thyme and rosemary; rub outside with salt and pepper. For duck: roast plain; serve with a honey and ginger sauce. For pork loin rack: roast with salt and pepper; serve with a green peppercorn sauce.

JOSHUA GILBERT, CALIFORNIA ROASTERY, SAN FRANCISCO.

For chicken: to merge seasonings with juices, tuck various seasonings, such as chopped garlic, fresh sage leaves, fresh tarragon sprigs, and crushed dried hot red chilies, under the skin. For a lean but juicy alternative, try

skinning the chicken and rubbing it well with salt and pepper before spit roasting.

EDMONDO SARTI, IL FORNAIO, BEVERLY HILLS.

For chicken and rabbit: stuff with sprigs of fresh rosemary and sage, garlic; sprinkle with salt and pepper.

ROBERT COWEN, ROTISSERIA ON MAIN, WALNUT CREEK, CALIFORNIA.

Season meats a few hours ahead of cooking time for maximum flavor. For pork loin rack: marinate in a thin mixture of honey, mustard, and orange juice. For beef tri-tip roast: dust with a mix of salt, pepper, garlic, fresh oregano, parsley, and bay leaf. For duck: pierce skin, and soak in a blend of soy, ginger, and honey.

REED HEARON, RESTAURANT LuLu, SAN FRANCISCO.

"Since all the seasoning is on the outside, you need to overseason big pieces of meat. During the resting time [as juices settle for carving], 20 to 30 minutes, the seasonings permeate the meat," he says.

For chicken: a paste of thyme, garlic, lemon peel, and aromatic spices. For leg of lamb: stud gashes in meat with garlic slivers, fresh rosemary sprigs, and chopped anchovy, then generously salt and pepper. For pork loin: soak overnight in a salt-sugar solution, then rub meat with a paste of garlic and fennel seed. ■

TWO PORK LOINS, *sandwiched, hold fresh sage and mustard.*

PETER CHRISTIANSEN

TOP FISHERWOMAN *Angela Hildebrand (above) wins the pool for the largest catch with her 25-pound king. Audrey (left) shows off her salmon, with cucumbers.*

The great salmon chase... and feast

Family and friends spend weekend fishing and eating

FISH ON!" ARE THE magic words. Eric Beneken, deckhand on the *Wacky Jacky,* promises, "If they're here, it will happen."

This is my first time on the Pacific Ocean fishing for salmon. I'm here as the guest of Ron Hildebrand, an avid salmon fisherman and equally enthusiastic salmon cook, who for seven years has organized this annual share-the-costs fishing trip for family and friends. Rousted at 4:30 A.M., I'm on board and ready for action by 6. We've cruised rapidly from San Francisco's Fisherman's Wharf on a gray sea, under gray skies, to this gray spot where the electronic screen of the fish finder indicates signs of salmon below. Captain Jacky Douglas maneuvers us into position. The fog is cold and thick, and the boat rolls increasingly as we slow to a halt.

"Let 'er rip!" the captain roars. We drop our lines. "Fish on! Fish on!" shouts Ron, letting everyone know there's a fish on the line. His 10-year-old granddaughter, Audrey, has hooked a salmon. "Follow him," commands deckhand Eric, rushing to her aid. The fish is a big one, a fighter, and it pulls hard. Audrey grips the quivering rod, following the line as it races from bow to stern. Everyone in her path ducks or darts out of the way. She pulls and reels, then pulls and reels some more. Finally,

TWO WHOLE SALMON, *baked and poached, are stars of this lavish cooperative buffet held the day after the fishing trip. Guests chip in with salads, breads, desserts.*

136

JULY

Eric swings a big net into the water and scoops up a gleaming 18-pound silver—a keeper for sure.

Audrey beams, says she's tired, then proceeds to reel in another big one. A little later, her aunt Angela gets the trophy fish of the day—a 25-pound king. My 5-pounder looks dinky alongside, but it's mine. Empty-handed Ron jokes that he can "go fishing at the store."

The Hildebrands fish with a purpose, and the next day our party regroups at home to feast on Audrey's catch. One fish is poached and served cold, the other is stuffed and baked. The recipes they use are purposely simple, to show off the freshness of the fish, and flexible, to accommodate the vagaries of size in the catch the day before.

WANT TO PLAN YOUR OWN FISHING TRIP?

You can charter day boats with crew and fishing gear all along the West Coast. Look in the yellow pages under Fishing Parties or Fishing Trips. If salmon is your objective, be sure to check its sport-season dates with your state department of fish and game. Currently, salmon fishing is permitted off the coasts of Alaska, western Canada, and much of California. In Oregon and parts of Washington, salmon fishing is very limited; conservation efforts have restricted the number of fish that can be taken.

Cost for a day of fishing varies, but the prices for our San Francisco outing are pretty much the average: $50 per angler, $20 per rider, $11 for a rented rod and tackle, $5.50 for a one-day fishing license—and the crew cleans the fish.

Ron sends invitations with date, time, and costs two to three months ahead. Guests reserve their spot with a check. Most boats have fee minimums. If Hildebrand's party doesn't meet the minimum, the captain can fill in

with other customers—or cancel the trip.

Ron's Cold Poached Salmon

1 whole salmon (5 to 7 lb. with head and tail), cleaned

1 cup dry sherry or dry white wine

2 green onions, ends trimmed, chopped

2 teaspoons whole peppercorns

4 to 6 dried bay leaves

1 large (about ½ lb.) slender cucumber

1 green or black ripe olive (optional)

Parsley sprigs

Lemon wedges

Mustard sauce (recipe follows)

Salt and pepper

In a fish poacher at least as long as the salmon, combine 5 quarts water with wine, onions, peppercorns, and bay leaves. (If your salmon is too big, cut it in half crosswise at its midsection. Cook pieces separately, in sequence, using the same liquid.) Bring liquid to a boil over high heat; you may need to set the pan on 2 burners.

Meanwhile, rinse salmon and set on fish poacher rack. Measure fish at thickest point. Holding rack, set fish into boiling liquid. If needed, add more hot water to cover fish. Put lid on pan. Return liquid to a boil, then reduce heat and simmer very gently until a thermometer inserted in center of thickest part reaches 135°, or fish is opaque but still moist-looking in thickest part (cut to test), 10 to 12 minutes for each inch of thickness.

Lift fish from pan on rack; save liquid for other uses or discard. While still warm, cut just through skin behind the gills and head and at the base of the tail on the top side of fish; gently pull off and discard skin. If desired, scrape off the gray fat on side of fish.

Transfer fish, skinned side up, to a serving platter (butt cut ends together if fish is in 2 pieces), cover, and chill until cold, at least 4

hours or up to 1 day.

Up to 4 hours before serving, peel cucumber and cut into paper-thin rounds. Overlap slices on fish, covering like scales. Use the smallest cucumber slices at tail end.

Cut a round slice from olive center; use it to cover the fish's eye. Garnish platter with parsley and lemon.

To serve, cut fish into portions and season to taste with mustard sauce, salt, and pepper. Allow ½ pound fish for each serving.

Per serving: 219 cal. (39 percent from fat); 30 g protein; 9.4 g fat (1.4 g sat.); 2.1 g carbo.; 67 mg sodium; 81 mg chol.

To oven-poach. Use ingredients in preceding recipe, modifying the amounts as follows. Lay rinsed fish in foil-lined 12- by 17-inch roasting pan. Cup foil upward and pour sherry onto salmon. Add 1 cup water, onions, peppercorns, and bay leaves. (If fish is too big for pan, cut in half crosswise at its midsection and cook in 2 pans, putting 1 recipe's worth of cooking liquid in each.) Seal fish in foil.

Bake in a 425° oven until a thermometer inserted in center of thickest part reaches 135°, or fish is opaque but still moist-looking in thickest part (cut to test). Allow 10 to 12 minutes for each inch of thickness. Cool and chill.

Mustard sauce. Mix ¾ cup **reduced-fat** or regular **mayonnaise,** ¾ cup **coarse grain** or Dijon **mustard,** 2 tablespoons minced **onion,** and 1 tablespoon **lemon juice.** Makes 1½ cups.

Per tablespoon: 28 cal. (80 percent from fat); 0.6 g protein; 2.5 g fat (0.5 g sat.); 1.1 g carbo.; 116 mg sodium; 2.5 mg chol.

Ron's Baked Stuffed Salmon

1 whole salmon (5 to 7 lb. with head and tail), cleaned

1 lemon, cut in half crosswise

1 tablespoon butter or margarine at room temperature

1 teaspoon pepper

Salmon stuffing (recipe follows)

Parsley sprigs

If fish is longer than 17 inches, cut in half crosswise at midsection. Rinse fish, pat dry, then rub inside and out with cut side of ½ lemon and all the butter. Sprinkle fish with pepper.

About 1½ inches apart, lay 12-inch lengths of cotton string under body and perpendicular to it (if fish is cut in half, cap cut ends with foil and tie foil against fish). Prop fish so open cavity is on top. Fill fish with stuffing and tie to secure in cavity.

Measure and note thickest point of fish. Pour 1½ cups hot water into 12- by 17-inch roasting pan. Lay fish on its side in pan (diagonally, or in 2 pans, as needed for fit) and cover loosely with foil. Bake in 425° oven just until fish is opaque but still moist-looking in thickest part (cut to test), or a thermometer inserted in thickest part reads 135°; allow 12 to 15 minutes for each inch of thickness.

Supporting salmon with 2 wide spatulas, carefully transfer fish to a warm platter (butt cut ends together, gently pulling off foil). Remove strings.

Cut remaining lemon half into wedges; garnish the salmon with lemon and parsley (conceal seam if fish is in 2 pieces).

To serve, cut fish into portions; spoon stuffing onto plates with salmon. Allow ½ pound fish for each serving.

Per serving: 274 cal. (43 percent from fat); 30 g protein; 13 g fat (2.5 g sat.); 7 g carbo.; 161 mg sodium; 84 mg chol.

Stuffing. In a 6- to 8-inch frying pan over medium-high heat, stir 2 tablespoons **olive oil,** ¼ cup chopped **onion,** 2 cloves minced or pressed **garlic** until onion is tinged lightly with brown, about 5 minutes.

Combine onion mixture with 1 cup chopped **celery,** 1 cup coarsely crushed dried **sourdough bread** or croutons, ½ cup **cooked wild rice,** 2 tablespoons chopped **parsley,** 1½ tablespoons **dry sherry,** and ½ teaspoon **Cajun spice blend** (or ¼ teaspoon *each* cayenne and dried thyme leaves). If making ahead, cover and chill, up to 1 day. Makes 3 cups. ■

By Linda Lau Anusasananan

Fresher, lighter jams

They're less sweet and less complicated—really goof-proof

Raspberry

OMEMADE JAM HAS always enticed and intimidated me—simultaneously. For years I wanted to reproduce the just-picked summer fruit flavor of my grandmother's jams. Yet memories of all that canning equipment and the huge amount each recipe yielded quickly drained my enthusiasm. Even more off-putting was the volume of sugar traditional recipes use—equal to, if not more than, the amount of fruit! With a background in nutrition, I automatically balked.

But curiosity and tempting mountains of ripe fruit finally got the better of me. However, I was determined to end up with a jam that suited inexperienced, nutrition-minded cooks like me.

I dug out a recipe for dehydrator-made jam that appeared in the July 1986 issue of *Sunset* (page 78); I remembered it didn't use much sugar. I had heard that its flavor was exceptionally fresh, not cloyingly sweet. The recipe also made a small, manageable amount, and—best of all—required only one pan. It took longer to make than a traditional jam, but you didn't have to pay much attention as it cooked.

I liked those pluses. But lacking a dehydrator, I took another tack, and baked my jam, which is faster. And I ended up with a delicious, softly thickened jam that uses about an eighth of the usual amount of sugar. Encouraged, I tried sweetening the fruit with apple juice concentrate for a no-sugar variation. This,

too, has wonderfully fresh flavor. But like commercial no-sugar jams, it isn't as brightly colored as jams with sugar.

As a novice jam maker, I find my new method virtually foolproof and uncomplicated. The only tricky part is deciding when the jam is done. When hot, the mixture is very syrupy, and it's hard to tell how thick the cold jam will be. Cooking time isn't much of a guide because it varies with the ripeness and juiciness of the fruit.

But an old-fashioned method my grandmother used turned out to be just the test I needed. When you spoon a little of the hot syrup onto a very cold plate, the syrup cools quickly, and resembles, more or less, the finished jam. If the cooled syrup retains a clear path as a spoon is drawn through it, the jam is ready. Even if you're wrong, don't worry. If the cooled jam is too runny, just put it back in the oven. If it's too thick, simply rewarm it and stir in a little bit of water.

Low-sugar Baked Berry Jam

8   cups raspberries, blackberries, boysenberries, blueberries, or hulled strawberries

    About 1¼ cups sugar

3   tablespoons lemon juice

    Rinse berries, drain dry, and put in a 10- by 15-inch

Plum

Blackberry

Blueberry

Peach

Nectarine

Strawberry

spooned onto the chilled saucer, doesn't immediately flow together when you pull the tip of a spoon or your fingertip through it (as you lift your finger, the liquid holds on, forming a small droplet), about 1 hour for blueberries, 1 to 1½ hours for the other berries. Let jam cool; if necessary, reheat and adjust consistency (see following directions).

Spoon into a bowl or small jars. Serve, or cover airtight and chill up to 2 weeks; freeze to store longer.

Makes about 1½ cups raspberry, blackberry, boysenberry, or strawberry jam or about 2½ cups blueberry jam.

Per tablespoon raspberry jam: 61 cal. (3 percent from fat); 0.4 g protein; 0.2 g fat (0 g sat.); 15 g carbo.; 0.5 mg sodium; 0 mg chol.

To adjust jam consistency, let jam cool completely in baking pan. If too runny, return to oven; stir and test every 20 minutes un-

til jam reaches desired thickness. If jam is too thick, warm it in the oven, then stir in water, 1 teaspoon at a time, until it is the desired consistency.

Low-sugar Baked Stone Fruit Jam

2 pounds ripe peaches, nectarines, plums, or apricots

About ⅔ cup sugar

3 tablespoons lemon juice

If using peaches, immerse in boiling water to cover for 30 seconds. Drain; let stand

until cool enough to touch, then peel. Cut fruit from pits and coarsely chop. In a 10- by 15-inch baking pan, mix fruit, sugar to taste, and lemon juice.

Bake, uncovered, in a 375° oven until fruit releases juices, about 10 minutes. Meanwhile, put a ceramic

baking pan. If using strawberries, slice them. Mix fruit, sugar to taste, and lemon juice. Bake, uncovered, in a 375° oven until berries release juice, about 10 minutes. Meanwhile, put a ceramic saucer in the freezer.

Reduce oven temperature to 325°. Every 20 minutes or so, gently stir berries to moisten well with juices. Bake until a little berry liquid,

MIX BERRIES *with sugar and lemon juice in a wide, shallow pan. As the fruit bakes, the mixture becomes quite syrupy; stir often to keep the fruit moist.*

PETER CHRISTIANSEN

saucer in the freezer.

Reduce oven temperature to 325°. Every 20 minutes or so, gently stir fruit to moisten well with juices. Bake fruit until a little of its liquid, spooned onto the chilled saucer, doesn't immediately flow together when you pull the tip of a spoon or your fingertip through it (as you lift your finger, the liquid holds on, forming a small droplet), 45 to 55 minutes. Let jam cool; if necessary, adjust consistency (see preceding recipe). Spoon into bowl or small jars. Serve, or cover airtight and chill up to 2 weeks; freeze to store longer. Makes about 2 cups.

Per tablespoon: 26 cal. (0 percent from fat); 0.2 g protein; 0 g fat; 6.7 g carbo.; 0.3 mg sodium; 0 mg chol.

No-sugar Jams

Follow the preceding directions for making the berry or stone fruit jam, omitting lemon; instead of sugar, use an equal measure (to taste) of **reduced apple juice con-**

centrate. To reduce the concentrate, pour 1 large container (16 oz. or 2 cups) thawed **frozen apple juice concentrate** into a 5- to 6-quart pan. Boil rapidly, uncovered, until reduced to 1¼ cups, 4 to 8 minutes. Use, or cover and chill up to 1 week.

Per tablespoon raspberry jam: 35 cal. (5.1 percent from fat); 0.3 g protein; 0.2 g fat (0 g sat.); 8.6 g carbo.; 3.5 mg sodium; 0 mg chol. ∎

By Christine Weber Hale

JAM IS DONE *when a dab of hot syrup on a chilled plate holds a clear track as a spoon is drawn through it.*

Italian and Chinese ways with fresh favas

EVER WONDER IF shelling those big, oversize fava beans now in the market is worthwhile? The best indicator is the popularity the tender beans enjoy with cooks around the world. Here are two simple, appealing dishes that show off shelled favas' creamy, sweet texture and green color. The first is a pasta combination from Italy, the second a stir-fry with shrimp from China.

When you buy favas, it's helpful to know that you need at least 1 pound of beans in pods to yield 1 cup of shelled beans. Choose pods that are firm and green, or trim off discolored portions; if you shell the beans ahead, cover and chill airtight up to 1 day.

One caution: a few people (usually of Mediterranean descent) lack a specific enzyme and have a serious allergic reaction to fava beans; if favas are new to you, check your family history before you try them.

Linguine with Favas and Basil

¼ pound pancetta or bacon, chopped

¼ cup minced shallots

2 cups (about 2 lb. in the pod) shelled fava beans

About 9 ounces fresh linguine

1 cup regular-strength chicken broth

¼ cup lightly packed fresh basil leaves, cut into thin slivers

¾ cup freshly grated parmesan cheese

Freshly ground pepper

In a 10- to 12-inch frying pan over medium-high heat, cook pancetta, stirring often, until crisp, about 5 minutes. Discard all but 2 tablespoons of the fat from the pan. Add shallots and beans to pan; cook, stirring, until membranes on beans begin to blister and to brown lightly, 4 to 6 minutes.

Meanwhile, in a 5- to 6-quart pan, bring 2 quarts water to a boil on high heat. Add linguine and cook, uncovered, until pasta is just tender to bite, 6 to 8 minutes. Drain well; return pasta to pan on low heat.

Add broth, bean mixture, basil, and ½ cup cheese to pasta; mix well, lifting with 2 forks. Pour onto a warm platter. Add remaining cheese and pepper to taste. Makes 4 or 5 servings.

Per serving: 330 cal. (35 percent from fat); 17 g protein; 13 g fat (5.2 g sat.); 36 g carbo.; 437 mg sodium; 81 mg chol.

Shrimp and Fava Stir-fry

1 pound large (31 to 35 per lb.) shrimp, shelled and deveined

1 tablespoon rice wine or dry sherry

1 tablespoon soy sauce

1 tablespoon *each* salad and Oriental sesame oil

1½ cups (about 1½ lb. in the pod) shelled fava beans

¼ cup diagonally sliced green onions

Mix shelled shrimp with wine and soy sauce; let stand 10 minutes.

Set a wok or 10- to 12-inch frying pan over high heat. When pan is hot, add salad oil and sesame oil and swirl over pan bottom. Add fava beans and stir-fry until their membranes begin to blister and to brown lightly, 2 to 5 minutes.

Add shrimp with marinade and stir-fry 2 to 3 minutes. Add onions and stir-fry until shrimp are opaque in thickest part (cut to test), about 1 minute longer. Serves 4.

Per serving: 197 cal. (39 percent from fat); 21 g protein; 8.6 g fat (1.3 g sat.); 6.8 g carbo.; 414 mg sodium; 140 mg chol. ∎

By Paula Smith Freschet

NORMAN A. PLATE

CHILLED, *oils that are predominantly monounsaturated slowly firm, thicken, and turn opaque in salad dressing (right), while oils that are mostly polyunsaturated stay clear and liquid (left).*

Why?

Why do oil and vinegar dressings separate, stay blended, get thicker, get hard?

As days heat up, salads become a daily ritual—and so do questions about the curious behavior of oil and vinegar dressings. The answers have a lot to do with the way oil reacts to various conditions.

"Why does my olive oil and vinegar salad dressing sometimes turn very thick after mixing it [in a blender]?"—*Franklyn W. Meyer, Honolulu*

When you shake oil and vinegar in a jar or mix the two with a fork or whisk, you separate the oil into small drops that are dispersed throughout the vinegar, making a short-lived, opaque blend called an

EVEN THOUGH *oil feels thicker, it's lighter than vinegar and floats on top of it; after stirring, oil and vinegar begin to separate at once. Whirled in a blender, dressing stays creamy longer, but not permanently.*

emulsion. On standing, the lighter oil quickly floats to the top of the vinegar, the oil drops rejoin, and the mixture separates.

If you whirl oil and vinegar in a blender, the power and speed of mixing make the oil drops very tiny and the vinegar can keep them apart longer, creating a thicker dressing that clings more readily to salad. But even with mechanical help, this marriage slowly comes apart.

Binders that help give additional body to salad dressings and slow down separation include mustard (dry or prepared), mayonnaise, and whipping cream.

"Why does oil and vinegar dressing turn white and solid when refrigerated?"—*Anita Shank, Somers, New York*

Fats and oils are made of a combination of three kinds of fatty acids: saturated, mono-unsaturated, and polyunsaturated. If there are enough saturated fatty acids, the fat is solid at room temperature or colder; heated, it usually melts. If a monounsaturated (single) fatty acid dominates, the fat is a liquid or an oil at room temperature or warmer, but it will partially solidify when it is chilled. When polyunsaturated (two) fatty acids dominate, the fat is a liquid and inclined to stay so even when it is chilled, because it has a more mobile molecular structure.

Refrigeration gradually slows the molecular activity of monounsaturated oils—olive, peanut, avocado, and macadamia—and they will become firm (although not as hard as butter), and turn cloudy or opaque. Returned to room temperature or heated, they quickly liquefy.

If your salad dressing is made with a monounsaturated oil and stored for a week or more in the refrigerator, chances are the oil will turn paler in color and get lumpy or solidify; but at room tem-

perature it returns to liquid and is fine to use.

Why does oil get rancid?

It's oxygen that does the dirty deed. Fat's flavor deteriorates when oxygen hooks onto the bonds (especially the double bonds) that link together oil's basic elements: carbon and hydrogen. Oxygen then begins to break apart the fatty acids. A by-product of this decomposition is rancidity, a nasty taste and smell.

Because polyunsaturated oils have the most double bonds, they are the easiest for oxygen to attack and become rancid much more quickly than monounsaturated oils. Safflower oil and sunflower oil, for example, are high in polyunsaturated fatty acids and more prone to spoilage than extra-virgin olive oil, which is high in monounsaturated fatty acids—and which, if stored well, remains fresh for many months.

Heat and light make it easier for oxygen to get at an oil; so does salt (as in a dressing) and metal (most metal cans for oil have a protective coating). To protect oils, store them airtight in a cool, dark place. Once an oil container has been opened for use, the oil will keep best if tightly covered. If you buy oil in large containers, you can extend the oil's longevity by pouring the balance of the opened oil into smaller glass or lined metal containers and keeping them tightly closed.

More questions?

We would like to know what kitchen mysteries you're curious about. Send your questions to Why?, *Sunset Magazine,* 80 Willow Rd., Menlo Park, Calif. 94025. With the help of Dr. George K. York, extension food technologist at UC Davis, *Sunset* food editors will try to find solutions. We'll answer the questions in the magazine. ■

By Linda Lau Anusasananan

Lamb carries apple butter well

PAIRINGS OF MEAT AND FRUIT ARE popular these days, even though some (especially those using blueberries) seem more trendy than judicious. Mike Roddy has hit on a successful partnership with his Glazed Lamb Burgers. They contain familiar lamb seasonings such as garlic and mint, as well as some highly unconventional ingredients—grated orange peel and lemon peel, and most surprising of all, apple butter. This dark, spicy jamlike mixture appears on every Pennsylvania Dutch table as one of the seven sweets and seven sours—a must for a proper country meal. The apple butter sauce forms a glaze on the burgers as they simmer.

Glazed Lamb Burgers

1 pound ground lean lamb

1 teaspoon minced or pressed garlic

⅛ teaspoon liquid smoke

⅛ teaspoon pepper

1 tablespoon chopped parsley

½ cup apple butter

2 tablespoons rice vinegar

1 tablespoon minced fresh or crumbled dried mint leaves

1 tablespoon minced fresh ginger

1 teaspoon *each* grated orange peel and grated lemon peel

4 English muffins, split and toasted

   Thinly sliced green onions, including tops

   Salt

In a bowl, mix lamb, garlic, liquid smoke, pepper, and parsley. Divide mixture into 4 equal portions and shape each into a ¾-inch-thick patty.

In a 10- to 12-inch frying pan over medium-high heat, brown patties well on both sides, about 8 minutes. Lift meat from pan and discard drippings. To pan, add apple butter, vinegar, mint, ginger, orange peel, and lemon peel. Bring to boiling over high heat; return meat to pan. Reduce heat and simmer, uncovered, until patties are no longer pink in center (cut to taste), about 4 minutes. As meat cooks, turn pieces over 2 or 3 times and stir sauce occasionally. Set each patty on a muffin half and spoon sauce equally over portions. Sprinkle with green onions and accompany with remaining muffins. Add salt to taste. Makes 4 servings.

Per serving: 362 cal. (18 percent from fat); 28 g protein; 7.4 g fat (2.4 g sat.); 44 g carbo.; 331 mg sodium; 77 mg chol.

Anchorage

THE TAMARILLO PLANT, A NATIVE of Peru, can be started from seed by devoted gardeners who shelter it in a greenhouse over winter or guarantee it a frost-free site outdoors. A *Sunset* staff member grew a tamarillo several years ago and found the fruit showy but too acid to eat with any degree of pleasure. What he didn't know is that it needs to be stewed with sugar or some other seasoning.

Rick Eastes, who travels the world buying and selling produce, shares his recipe for Tamarillo and Berry Compote, which is as delicious as it is beautiful.

Tamarillo and Berry Compote

4 ripe tamarillos (about ½ lb. total; they give to slight pressure)

1 tablespoon lime juice

3 tablespoons honey

1 cup raspberries

1 cup blackberries

2 large (about ½ lb. total) kiwi fruit

   Sugar

Cut tamarillos in ½ and scoop seeds and pulp into a 1½- to 2-quart pan. Add lime juice and honey. Stir often over medium heat until mixture boils. Let cool.

Rinse raspberries and blackberries; drain well. Peel kiwi and cut crosswise into thin slices. Combine berries and kiwi and spoon into individual bowls. Evenly spoon tamarillo sauce over fruit, adding sugar to taste. Makes 4 servings.

Per serving: 186 cal. (5.3 percent from fat); 2.9 g protein; 1.1 g fat (0 g sat.); 46 g carbo.; 3.8 mg sodium; 0 mg chol.

Visalia, California

NOT EVERYONE SPEAKS ILL OF excess. John Keats observed that "poetry should surprise by a fine excess," and Blake wrote that "the road of excess leads to the palace of wisdom." It would almost seem that these generous sentiments guided Peter Rock as he assembled this appetizer spread. (Actually he was just trying to please a visiting sister from the East who loves avocado and caviar.) This spectacular combination of three fine elements, each a delight in itself, has but one drawback: it's so attractive that you hate to mar it to eat it.

Layered Avocado and Caviar Spread

2 medium-size (about 1 lb. total) ripe avocados

¼ cup lime juice

¼ to ½ teaspoon liquid hot pepper seasoning

1 clove garlic, minced or mashed (optional)

Salt

4 large hard-cooked eggs

3 tablespoons reduced-fat or regular mayonnaise

2 tablespoons thinly sliced green onion, including tops

1 jar (2 oz.) black or red caviar (such as lumpfish)

2 lemons, cut into thin wedges

Melba toast or crackers

Peel and pit avocados. Coarsely mash avocados with lime juice, liquid hot pepper, and garlic; season to taste with salt.

Shell and finely mash eggs with mayonnaise; mix in onion and add salt to taste.

On a rimmed platter, spread avocado about ½ inch thick. Top evenly with egg mixture, leaving a rim of avocado exposed. If making ahead, cover and chill up to 1 day.

Pour caviar into a fine strainer and rinse gently under cold running water until water runs clear; drain well. Spoon caviar onto egg mixture. Garnish platter with lemon wedges. To eat, spoon portions of the avocado mixture onto toast; add lemon juice to taste. Makes 8 to 10 servings.

Per serving: 118 cal. (73 percent from fat); 4.9 g protein; 9.6 g fat (1.8 g sat.); 6 g carbo.; 143 mg sodium; 120 mg chol.

Martinez, California

By Joan Griffiths, Richard Dunmire

Savor fresh oregano

Its flavor can range from pungent to mild

FRESH OREGANO IS A SAVORY treat—especially when you grow it yourself. Depending on the type of oregano, flavors vary intensely.

Cretan, Greek, and Syrian varieties offer the strongest flavors. Kirghizstan, Sicilian, and Italian types are mild and herbaceous, sometimes with a minty quality. The following recipes were created using stronger oregano. If you use a milder type (Italian is the type most commonly sold in markets), consider doubling oregano amounts.

DISTINCTIVE FLAVOR *in a refreshing cold soup comes from oregano.*

Cucumber-Yogurt Soup

2 cups unflavored low-fat yogurt

1 medium-size (about ¾ lb.) cucumber, peeled and chopped

1 cup regular-strength chicken broth

2 tablespoons *each* lemon juice and orange juice

2 to 4 teaspoons minced fresh oregano leaves

Salt and pepper (optional)

Fresh oregano sprigs

In a bowl, stir together yogurt, cucumber, broth, lemon and orange juice, and minced oregano to taste. Add salt and pepper to taste. Chill at least 1 hour or up until next day. Garnish each serving with an oregano sprig. Serves 4.

Per serving: 95 cal. (21 percent from fat); 7.1 g protein; 2.2 g fat (1.2 g sat.); 12 g carbo.; 99 mg sodium; 6.8 mg chol.

PETER CHRISTIANSEN

OREGANO LENDS *a delightful accent to a lamb meatball salad.*

Lamb Meatball Salad

1 pound ground lamb

½ cup fine dry bread crumbs

2 tablespoons minced fresh oregano leaves

½ cup water

1 large egg

1 tablespoon Dijon mustard

¼ teaspoon *each* salt and pepper

8 cups shredded napa cabbage

Warm oregano dressing (recipe follows)

¼ cup thinly sliced green onion

8 lemon wedges (optional)

Fresh oregano sprigs

Mix together lamb, bread crumbs, and minced oregano leaves; set aside. Whisk together water, egg, mustard, salt, and pepper; stir into lamb mixture.

Divide lamb mixture into 24 equal portions; form balls with hands and place 1 inch apart in a 10- by 15-inch baking pan. Bake in a 425° oven until well browned, about 20 minutes; turn balls after 10 minutes.

On 4 dinner plates, evenly divide cabbage and meatballs. Drizzle salads with warm dressing and garnish with green onion, lemon wedges, and oregano sprigs. Serves 4.

Per serving: 442 cal. (61 percent from fat); 25 g protein; 30 g fat (12 g sat.); 19 g carbo.; 479 mg sodium; 136 mg chol.

Warm oregano dressing. In a 1- to 2-quart pan, stir together 1 cup regular-strength **chicken broth,** ¼ cup **rice vinegar,** 2 tablespoons **lemon juice,** 2 teaspoons minced **fresh oregano leaves,** 2 teaspoons **cornstarch,** and 1 teaspoon grated **lemon peel.** Over medium-high heat, bring mixture to a boil while stirring frequently. Let cool until just warm to touch, about 10 minutes. ∎

By Betsy Reynolds Bateson

PETER CHRISTIANSEN

BLACK BEAN *and chicken filling overflows gorditas' pockets. Serve with plenty of napkins.*

Better than burritos?

These generously filled homemade masa cakes could be the burrito's next rival

LITTLE PLUMP ONE. That's the rough English translation of *gordita*—and the name is very appropriate. The Mexican treat starts with a thick corn tortilla, or masa cake, which is split and plumply filled with beans, meat, lettuce, and salsa.

This chicken-chili version was inspired by a trip to Grand Central Market in Los Angeles. At the covered food hall, gorditas are a popular choice with the international clientele.

Our gorditas are grilled rather than fried, and the chicken's cooking liquid is boiled down to form a flavorful, and not quite so drippy, sauce. Nevertheless, have napkins ready; gorditas still make a delicious mess.

Chicken-Chili Gorditas

Prepare masa cakes and filling before heating beans and assembling gorditas.

2 cans (15 oz. each) black or pinto beans

Masa cakes (recipe follows)

3 cups shredded lettuce or spinach, or a combination

Chicken-chili filling (recipe follows)

¾ cup mild to hot green salsa, with chopped cilantro and onion to taste (optional)

In a 2- to 3-quart pan over medium-high heat, bring beans and their liquid to simmering, stirring often, about 10 minutes; drain and keep hot. For each gordita, fill a masa cake with about ¼ cup lettuce, then with about 3 tablespoons *each* beans and chicken filling. Serve with salsa. Makes 12 gorditas, 4 to 6 servings.

Per gordita: 273 cal. (23 percent from fat); 14 g protein; 7.1 g fat (2.1 g sat.); 40 g carbo.; 458 mg sodium; 21 mg chol.

Masa cakes. In a bowl, rub with your fingers until fine crumbs form: 3½ cups **dehy-drated masa flour,** ¾ teaspoon **salt,** and ¼ cup **lard** or solid shortening. Add 1¾ cups **water,** and mix with hands until dough is smooth and evenly moistened.

In bowl, divide dough into 12 equal portions; cover with a damp towel. With wet hands, shape 1 portion into a smooth ball. Then pat back and forth between palms into an evenly thick, flat, very smooth circle, 4¼ to 4½ inches wide. With fingers, pat smooth any cracks (pay special attention to edges). Place on plastic wrap, cover with a damp towel, and repeat to make remaining cakes; arrange in a single layer.

In a 10- to 12-inch nonstick frying pan over medium heat, cook 3 cakes at a time until golden and speckled dark brown, turning once, 3 to 6 minutes per side. Move from pan to cutting surface.

Let cakes cool slightly. With a small serrated knife, slit each cake ⅛ of the way around edge, then slide in knife to within ½ inch of opposite edge, cutting to form a wide pocket. Place cakes in a single layer in a greased, rimmed 10- by 15-inch baking pan. Cover with a damp towel, then with foil; keep warm in a 250° oven until used, up to 1 hour.

Chicken-chili filling. In a 3- to 4-quart pan over medium heat, frequently stir ¾ cup chopped **onion** and 2 teaspoons **salad oil** until onion is limp, about 12 minutes. Stir in 1½ teaspoons **ground cumin;** cook 30 seconds. Add 1 cup **regular-strength chicken broth,** ¾ pound **boned, skinned chicken breast halves,** and 2 tablespoons **canned diced jalapeño chilies.** Bring to a simmer over high heat; reduce heat and simmer, covered, 5 minutes. Turn chicken over; simmer until no longer pink in thickest part (cut to test), 3 to 5 minutes more.

Lift chicken from sauce and let stand until cool enough to handle; tear into shreds. Meanwhile, boil sauce over high heat, stirring often, until reduced to 1 cup, 4 to 5 minutes. Return chicken to sauce and stir over medium heat until simmering; use warm. ∎

By Elaine Johnson

SUNSET'S KITCHEN CABINET

Creative ways with everyday foods—submitted by *Sunset* readers,
tested in *Sunset* kitchens, approved by *Sunset* taste panels

Thai Basil Chicken

J. Hill, Sacramento

- 2 tablespoons minced garlic
- 1 tablespoon salad oil
- 4 boned and skinned chicken breast halves (about 1¼ lb. total)
- 1 cup lightly packed fresh basil leaves
- 3 tablespoons *each* lemon juice and water
- 1 tablespoon soy sauce
- 1 tablespoon sugar
- ½ teaspoon pepper

Combine garlic and oil in a 10- to 12-inch frying pan. Stir often over medium-high heat until garlic is golden, 3 to 4 minutes. With a slotted spoon, transfer garlic to a small bowl.

Add chicken to pan. Cook, turning to lightly brown, about 5 minutes. Thinly slice basil. Add ½ cup basil to pan with garlic, lemon juice, water, soy, sugar, and pepper. Cover and simmer until chicken is white in thickest part (cut to test), 6 to 7 minutes; spoon juices over chicken often. Put chicken on a platter; keep warm. Boil pan juices, uncovered, over high heat until reduced to ¼ cup. Stir in remaining sliced basil; pour over chicken. Serves 4.

Per serving: 226 cal. (22 percent from fat); 34 g protein; 5.4 g fat (0.9 g sat.); 9.7 g carbo.; 355 mg sodium; 82 mg chol.

PAN-BROWN *chicken breasts, then top with a tart-sweet basil and garlic sauce.*

Caribbean Baked Beans

Amanda Bohm, Huntington Beach, California

- 2 cans (about 15 oz. each) black beans
- 1 can (8 oz.) crushed pineapple in unsweetened juice
- ½ cup tomato-based barbecue sauce
- ½ cup chopped green onions
- ⅓ cup firmly packed brown sugar
- ¼ pound finely chopped cooked ham
- 2 tablespoons lime juice
- 1 tablespoon minced fresh ginger
- 2 teaspoons dry mustard
- Whole green onions

Rinse and drain beans; drain pineapple. In a 1- to 1½-quart shallow casserole, mix beans, pineapple, barbecue sauce, chopped onions, sugar, ham, lime juice, ginger, and mustard. If making ahead, cover and chill up to 2 days.

Bake bean mixture, uncovered, in a 375° oven until bubbling in center, about 25 minutes; stir occasionally. Trim ends of whole onions; use onions to garnish beans. Serves 6.

Per serving: 203 cal. (13 percent from fat); 10 g protein; 3 g fat (0.7 g sat.); 35 g carbo.; 690 mg sodium; 11 mg chol.

SPICED BLACK BEANS *baked with ham and pineapple use shortcut ingredients.*

Blackberry Pie

Jennifer Stein, Canyon City, Oregon

- 1 cup sugar
- 3 tablespoons quick-cooking tapioca
- 6 cups blackberries, rinsed and drained dry
- ½ teaspoon almond extract
- ⅛ teaspoon ground nutmeg
- Pastry for a double-crust 9-inch pie

In a bowl, mix sugar and tapioca. Add berries, almond extract, and nutmeg; stir gently.

On a lightly floured board, roll ½ the pastry into a 12-inch-wide round; ease into a 9-inch pie pan. Fill with berry mixture.

On floured board, roll remaining pastry into an 11-inch-wide round; lay pastry over fruit. Fold pastry edges under, and pinch rim to crimp and seal. Cut several long slits in top pastry.

Set pie in a foil-lined 10- by 15-inch pan (to catch boilover juice). Bake on lowest rack in a 400° oven until filling bubbles in center and crust is well browned, about 1 hour and 10 minutes. If rim begins to get dark brown, drape lightly with foil. Let pie cool; if making ahead, cover at room temperature up to 1 day. Cut in wedges. Serves 8.

Per serving: 395 cal. (34 percent from fat); 3.5 g protein; 15 g fat (3.7 g sat.); 63 g carbo.; 251 mg sodium; 0 mg chol.

Compiled by Christine Weber Hale

OLD-FASHIONED *berry pie is flavored subtly by a hint of almond and nutmeg.*

Steak flavored with olives, the art of corn, and wine with water the French way

By Jerry Anne Di Vecchio

Beef was once the safest—and least controversial—menu choice, especially if it was steak. You could serve it hot, you could serve it cold. Salt and pepper were accepted as sufficient seasoning. Now I find that my guests have much more diverse tastes, and steak, when it appears, needs a bit of window dressing to get due respect.

My favorite is steak grilled over hot coals, but it's more practical, from my perspective, to barbecue one large slab instead of tending a lot of individual pieces. The pluses include flexible portions because the meat is sliced for serving. And those who like well-done beef can get slices from the edges, while those who want rare meat get center pieces.

An exceptionally flavorful cut is the beef rib-eye, the long, round muscle in the center of a rib roast. Instead of buying it in steaks, I order a boned roast, by length. After trimming off all surface fat, I butterfly the roast. Laid open, the meat makes a generously scaled rectangular steak about 1½ inches thick.

When I was in Los Angeles recently, a discerning food critic recommended that I try the grilled rib-eye steak at Campanile. When my order arrived, I was captivated by the aroma and the rich, dark color of the meat; the beef taste was enhanced and enriched, not masked. Chef Mark Peel's secret is a coating of well-peppered tapenade, the seasoned olive paste that is ubiquitous in southern France.

I tried making the dish myself, using a recipe for tapenade from a good cooking friend in Provence. Then Mark and his wife,

baker-chef Nancy Silverton, presented an interesting variation in their new book, *Mark Peel & Nancy Silverton at Home* (Warner Books, New York, 1994; $24.95). In it, lemon peel replaces the more typical capers, so I merged their recipe with mine. Slathered over my butterflied rib-eye, the team-effort tapenade puts salt and pepper to shame.

BACK TO BASICS

Cooking corn: It's easy to do it right

I'm sure you're not surprised to learn that my daughter considers me the fount of food knowledge, but occasionally she does refer to cookbooks. She did so the other night—then my phone rang. "How long am I supposed to cook corn? Nobody agrees!" My answer: just until it's plenty hot. Corn kernels are tender enough to eat raw, but heat emphasizes their sweet taste.

Freshly harvested sweet corn is at its peak when it's just picked, but most market varieties retain their sugar up to several days. The best way to deal with corn on the cob is simply, whether it's boiled, grilled, baked, or even microwaved.

In water. Choose a pan (or pans) large enough to hold the amount of corn you want to cook, with room for water to cover the corn. Cover the pan and bring water to boil on high heat; I purposely add no salt, preferring to salt the ears to taste. Add husked corn ears and continue to cook on high heat (covered or not) until kernels are very hot, 3 or 4 minutes.

Drain and serve hot or tepid, or, if you're

A TASTE OF THE WEST

Butterflied Rib-eye Steak with Tapenade

1   boned beef rib-eye roast, 4 to 6 inches long (2½ to 3¾ lb.)

Tapenade (directions follow)

Trim and discard fat from surface of beef. Make a lengthwise cut through the center of the meat, leaving about 1 inch uncut, and lay meat open to create a butterfly shape. With your

PETER CHRISTIANSEN

palms, press meat to flatten evenly. So meat will be easier to manage on the grill, thread 2 metal skewers through the flattened butterfly, about 3 inches apart and parallel. Rub 2 or 3 tablespoons tapenade on all sides of meat.

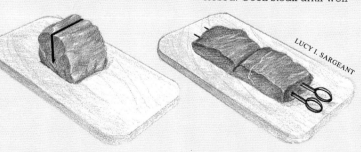

LUCY I. SARGEANT

Lay steak on grill over a solid bed of hot coals (you can hold your hand at grill level for only 1 or 2 seconds); do not cover barbecue. Or cook over high heat in a gas barbecue (allow 10 minutes for grill to heat) with lid closed. Cook steak until well browned, 8 to 10 minutes on each side for rare (to test, cut to center of thickest part). For meat cooked beyond rare, turn occasionally.

Transfer steak to a board. Serve hot or cool, thinly sliced. Accompany with remaining tapenade. Makes 8 to 12 servings.

Per 3-ounce cooked portion (4 oz. raw): 198 cal. (45 percent from fat); 24 g protein; 10 g fat (4.1 g sat.); 0.4 g carbo.; 106 mg sodium; 68 mg chol.

Tapenade. Pinch or cut pits from 1¼ cups **calamata olives** (brine-cured, or replace up to ½ the calamatas with oil-cured olives). Put pitted olives in a food processor; add 2 cloves **garlic,** 1½ teaspoons **freshly ground pepper,** ¾ teaspoon **grated lemon peel,** 1 tablespoon **lemon juice,** and 2 drained **canned anchovy fillets.** Purée coarsely (or mince with a knife). Use, or if making ahead, cover and chill up to 1 week. Makes about 1 cup.

Per tablespoon: 14 cal. (77 percent from fat); 0.3 g protein; 1.2 g fat (0.2 g sat.); 1 g carbo.; 111 mg sodium; 0.3 mg chol.

having a party, borrow this trick from markets in Mexico: vendors selling ears of corn for snacks keep them ready and waiting for several hours in tubs of warm-to-touch water. Instead of butter, the ears are rubbed with lime wedges and sprinkled with salt. This nonfat alternative is very good.

In the husk—barbecued or baked. Corn cooked this way is steamed and doesn't taste very different from boiled corn. But it's fun to serve in the husk because you can season or butter the corn before you cook it. I also like corn cooked in the husk for two other reasons: It's decorative, and the hot husks give off a fresh, grassy aroma or, when charred, a nice smoky smell.

To prepare, pull husk back from each ear of corn, but leave attached at base of cob. Pull off and discard silk; trim off any insect damage, and rinse ears. If you want to butter them, pat ears dry and rub with soft butter. Pull husks back up around corn.

If you want the husk to stay snugly against the ear, pull off 1 or 2 of the outer husk layers, tear lengthwise into thin strips, and tie them around ear in several places. Just before cooking, immerse the ears in cool water and lift out.

To barbecue over gas or hot coals, place corn on a grill over medium heat (you can hold your hand at grill level for only 2 or 3 seconds) and turn occasionally. The corn kernels will be very hot in about 15 minutes.

To bake, prepare corn as directed for grilling, but put ears in a single layer, separating them slightly, directly on the oven rack or in a pan. Bake in a 375° oven until corn is very hot, about 10 minutes.

Shucked ears—on the grill. Use the same heat suggested for barbecuing corn in the husk. Lay shucked ears on the grill and turn often to heat evenly, about 10 minutes. I love the bonus of a little browning—dark spots get chewy and extra sweet.

Microwaving. High-tech is perfect for cooking just 1 ear of corn. Husk corn and discard silk. Rinse corn and wrap loosely in a microwave-safe towel (cloth or unrecycled paper). Cook on full power (100 percent) until ear is very hot to touch, 1 to 2 minutes.

One ear of corn, about 8 inches long, unseasoned: 99 cal. (13 percent from fat); 3.7 g protein; 1.4 g fat (0.2 g sat.); 22 g carbo.; 18 mg sodium; 0 mg chol.

PETER CHRISTIANSEN

DESSERTS ARE EASY *with these cylinder freezers.*

GREAT TOOL

Fabulous freezer

I had almost talked myself into a major investment—a self-refrigerated ice cream maker—when the ingenious cylinder ice cream freezer came on the market.

Not only did this alternative save me a bundle, but it is remarkably simple to operate and very tidy—no ice and salt mess. The cylinder is the freezing element; it's a straight-sided, double-walled aluminum bowl with coolant sealed inside. Frozen at least 8 hours at 0° or below, it's cold enough to freeze chilled liquids—a quart in 15 to 30 minutes, sometimes less. The liquid freezes as it touches the cylinder, and a hand-turned or electric plastic paddle keeps everything moving inside. Freezers come in 1-cup to 1-quart sizes; prices run from $10 to $60, often less at summer sales. I keep two quart-size units and a 1-cup model in the freezer all the time.

Fruit or vegetable juices make refreshing ices ready to eat as soon as they are frozen (liquids frozen without sugar get rock hard if left standing). Plain orange juice is delicious, and a friend raves about a mix he discovered in a little country store—equal parts apple juice and carrot juice with fresh ginger. Strong coffee makes a cooling slush. And of course you can make regular ice cream.

My family has dubbed one of their favorites *frozen berry:* Rinse and hull 6 to 8 cups **strawberries.** Purée fruit in blender or food processor with 1 can (6 oz.) partially thawed **frozen orange juice concentrate.** Add **sugar** to taste; 2 or 3 tablespoons suits me. Chill the purée until cold, at least 1 hour. Pour into 1-quart frozen cylinder and position paddle and lid. Rotate paddle 5 or 6 turns every 3 or 4 minutes until mixture is softly frozen, about 15 minutes. Spoon into dishes or onto ice cream cones. Makes 3 to 4 cups.

Per ½ cup: 100 cal. (5.4 percent from fat); 1.6 g protein; 0.6 g fat (0 g sat.); 24 g carbo.; 2.3 mg sodium; 0 mg chol. ∎

BOB THOMPSON ON WINE

When water works

People who have read one or two wine books feel guilty about pouring water into wine and view ice cubes with the same qualms. Not to worry: even the French do it.

A virtuoso performance in a modest restaurant in Bordeaux one September evening will illustrate. A Frenchman came in, took his accustomed table, and got a carafe of local red wine without having to ask for it.

He poured his glass about two-thirds full, then topped it off with water. He drank a little more than half of it while he waited for his first course, which turned out to be a fillet of sole. When that dish arrived, he topped his glass to the brim with water. This pale mixture he drained while eating the fish. As his steak arrived, he poured a full glass of red. Another glass of full-blooded red with the cheese course, and the carafe was empty and he was full. Out he went into the balmy night, whistling a contented tune.

If this practical demonstration doesn't convince you that wine and water are socially acceptable in the same glass, take heart from several other perfectly good reasons for watering your wine.

Four hard sets of tennis are dehydrating. Mix about four parts water to one part white wine for a restorative tonic. It refreshes because of the wine's acidity, and tastes more interesting than lemonade, especially if the wine is a pretty good one. Serve the rest of the wine for dinner. The recipe, not incidentally, comes from Clos Du Val winemaker Bernard Portet, a bred-in-the-bone Bordelais.

Another instance: at a hastily organized picnic, the white wine is a little too warm and tastes too sweet as a result. Toss some ice cubes into it.

Or the backyard is baking hot when the hamburgers come off the grill, and the Beaujolais is at room temperature. Slip some ice cubes into it.

Then there's the Cabernet Sauvignon that tastes thicker than the sauce on your meat at dinner, and feels harder than nails. Thin it out with water, starting slowly and working up to what feels right. If the wine costs a lot of money and you cannot shake your sense of having betrayed its lofty pedigree, use a little Sauvignon Blanc instead of water. But blending wines is the beginning of another story.

SWEET-SOUR GLAZE *coats spareribs; serve surrounded by thinly shredded cucumbers.*

Shanghai ribs: an honorable secret

E ATING MEATY BONES is like a treasure hunt. As you chew around the knobby protrusions and along the smooth sides, you discover prizes: sweet, tender morsels of flavorful meat, bits of chewy gristle, and crunchy cartilage. It's a dining experience that the Chinese, in particular, fully appreciate.

Bruce Cost, founder of Berkeley's Ginger Island and San Francisco's late Monsoon Restaurant, isn't Chinese, but he cooks as if he were. Taught by a superb teacher, the late Virginia Lee, he absorbed the spirit of Chinese food. Under her tutelage he learned, as Asians do, to value some of the humbler foods, bones among them.

Here he presents Shanghai-style pork spareribs. Chinese black vinegar, dark soy sauce, and sugar contribute their essence to the lavish glaze. You'll find these ingredients in Chinese markets, or use readily available alternatives.

Shanghai-style Sweet-Sour Ribs

At the market, have ribs sawed crosswise into 1½-inch lengths. Ribs are typically fried, then glazed, but it's less messy to bake them first.

3 pounds pork spareribs, cut across bone into 1½-inch lengths

½ cup sugar

⅓ cup Chinese black vinegar or balsamic vinegar

1 tablespoon dark soy sauce (or 2½ teaspoons soy sauce and ½ teaspoon dark molasses)

Salt

Rinse ribs. Cut between bones to separate. Place in a 10- by 15-inch pan. Bake, uncovered, in a 450° oven, stirring often until well browned, about 30 minutes. Drain ribs on paper towels; keep warm, or if making ahead, let cool and chill airtight up to 2 days. If chilled, cover meat (in the same pan), heat 20 minutes in a 350° oven, then continue.

In a wok or 10- to 12-inch frying pan, mix sugar, vinegar, and soy. Bring to a boil on high heat. Reduce heat to medium; stir often until mixture is reduced to about ½ cup, 8 to 10 minutes. Mix ribs with sauce. Scrape onto a platter; serve warm or at room temperature. Salt to taste. Makes 8 appetizer or 3 or 4 main-dish servings.

Per appetizer serving: 314 cal. (57 percent from fat); 19 g protein; 20 g fat (7.8 g sat.); 13 g carbo.; 190 mg sodium; 80 mg chol. ∎

By Linda Lau Anusasananan

Fresh *from the* West

Cooks from Los Angeles to Seattle celebrate the West's summer bounty with outstanding regional salads

I

T TAKES OUTSTANDING INGREDIENTS TO create outstanding salads—and the West has plenty of both.

To put it simply, the West's emphasis on using fresh, local produce—and our abundant supply of it—is unique. In fact, the West can claim honors as the country's largest producer of salad greens, tomatoes, lemons, and berries. And it's a major producer of shellfish and wild and medium-grain rice.

What's more, Western salad ingredients reflect the region's rich and diverse culinary cultures. Salsas of chilies and fresh herbs come by way of Latin America, for instance, while rice vinegar, sesame oil, and soy sauce emigrated with settlers from Asia.

Then there's the Westerner's adventuresome spirit—a major force behind the West's creative new wave of salads. Here, five innovative Westerners share their favorites, featuring diverse components such as crayfish, corn relish, and fresh berry salsa. Recipes begin on page 156.

An Alfresco Feast

A

ndrea Bell's Pacific Palisades hillside is a place of harmonious convergence—a garden retreat where she relaxes, entertains, and grows food and flowers. In this urban oasis near Los Angeles, Bell harvests fresh ingredients for food she prepares for friends and clients of her catering business, L.A. Celebrations! Her small, terraced garden supplies only a portion of what she needs, but, Bell says, "the homegrown ingredients are better quality because of their freshness and care." She also grows ingredients she can't readily buy, like lemon verbena, Meyer lemons, and curry plant.

When produce is ready for harvest, there's no better place to prepare and serve her creations, like the sumptuous grilled salad shown here, than the garden itself.

Salads are a popular element of Bell's repertoire. "People are looking for lighter ways of eating," she says, "and a salad like this one becomes an entrée or a full meal." Flavor and presentation are all-important. Bell aims for contrast by combining nutty-textured rice with soft grilled eggplant, red peppers with yellow, and sweet balsamic vinegar with zippy chives.

Her culinary endeavors determine much of what she grows. "I choose flowers based on how much I love looking at them, and whether or not they're edible. At times my garden may appear to some to be overgrown with nasturtiums, but they're great on salads. Combined with Johnny-jump-ups, calendula, borage flowers, pansies, English roses, and chive blossoms, I can create a salad of beauty and delicious taste." Bell recalls one black-tie dinner when guests ended up discussing the unusual assortment of flowers in their salads.

In addition to what you'd expect to find in a chef's garden—a cornucopia of herbs, garnishes, and succulent produce—Bell's is full of surprises. She's not afraid to bend rules when going for impact. She lets her zucchini grow to bat-size and uses them, along with corn stalks, to decorate buffets. And she allows cucumbers to grow into giants, then stuffs them with a refreshing mixture of peeled, seeded cucumber, yogurt, lemon balm, peppermint, lemon verbena, pepper, a little salt, and sugar.

Bell is as concerned about growing techniques as she is about cooking. To avoid pesticides, Bell depends on hungry helpers like frogs, turtles, and ladybugs to help control pests like slugs and aphids. She's willing to accept a few holes in her mint to maintain a wholesome cycle from planting to harvest to table.

By Betsy Reynolds Bateson & Lynn Ocone with Linda Lau Anusasananan

Grilled Garden Bounty
Vegetable and Rice Platter

CHEF AND GARDENER *Andrea Bell (left) shares her wonderful ways with vegetables in a delectable grilled salad dinner. Purple potatoes, red peppers, yellow pear-shaped tomatoes, green zucchini, purple eggplant, and earthy brown mushrooms combine in a kaleidoscope of colors. Corn, rice, and peppers tossed with herb dressing accompany the sliced vegetables. Garden-fresh variegated basil garnishes the platter. (Recipe on page 156.)*

RUSS A. WIDSTRAND

Sacramento Valley Salads

Three salads from Sacramento Valley cooks showcase the season's—and valley's—finest. Taste-tested at a salad party last summer, the salads make the most of the region's best assets: crayfish from delta rivers, rice from some of the country's largest rice producers, tomatoes from the tomato capital of the West, and fresh berries from local farmers' markets.

For salad inspiration, Annette Davis, creator of the Spicy Delta Salad, need only step out into her yard in Walnut Grove. Here she grows several varieties of tomatoes, herbs, bell peppers, chilies, and cucumbers. Farther out at the yard's edge, Davis harvests crayfish from the bank of the Sacramento River. In fact, she and her husband often get their parties going with a pile of freshly boiled crayfish. Friends get to stand around the kitchen butcher block popping open crayfish and dipping the succulent tail meat into hot chili sauce.

Davis lives close to Locke, a historic river town built by Chinese immigrants. She infuses her crayfish salad with bold Chinese seasonings: Oriental sesame oil and hot chili oil. And when she cooks crayfish for her crayfish parties, she seasons the cooking liquid with hot chili oil and dried hot red chilies.

Tomatoes are Davis's favorite summer vegetable. She likes to serve them juicy-ripe and unadorned save for a few other ingredients, as in her simple Summer Harvest Tomato Salad. Davis has a degree from the Culinary Institute of America in New York, but she credits much of her initial interest in cooking to her German grandmother, and to a summer spent working in a German pastry kitchen. Cooking with fresh produce is her top priority.

Fresh produce is also important to Julie Coyle, of Granite Bay near Sacramento. To her, a summer salad means fresh fruit. On their ritual Friday stroll to a local farmers' market, Coyle and her daughter, Brooke, look for beautiful berries from the "berry man."

A member of the Cookbook Committee of the Junior League of Sacramento, Coyle brought a salad she made from the league's cookbook, *Celebrate!*, to the salad party.

Spicy Delta Salad

IN EARLY EVENING, *Annette Davis checks the crayfish catch in her backyard on the bank of the Sacramento River. She combines cooked crayfish with garden vegetables, rice, and a piquant chili-lime vinaigrette in her Spicy Delta Salad (left). (Recipe on page 156.)*

ANNE HAMERSKY

152

Summer Harvest Tomato Salad

GOLDEN AND RED *sliced tomatoes, juicy yellow pear-shaped tomatoes, cucumber crescents, and a mint vinaigrette unite in Annette Davis's appealing salad still life. (Recipe on page 157.)*

PETER CHRISTIANSEN

Garden Greens with Berry Salsa is a creation of Sacramento chef Mitch Miller. When he owned Mitchell's Terrace, Miller put the salad on the menu as a special. But it soon became a regular menu item during berry season.

He stresses that the combi-

Garden Greens with Berry Salsa

SACRAMENTO CHEF *Mitch Miller combines a festive salsa of raspberries, blueberries, strawberries, and tomato with crumbled goat cheese over crisp salad greens. (Recipe on page 157.)*

nation of sweet, fresh summer berries and citrus dressing is key to the recipe's success. It's derived from a time when his family had a second home in northern Mexico. There his grandmother learned to mix three citrus juices for salsas. Miller explains that the fresh orange juice offers sweetness, the lemon juice "heartiness," and the lime juice a tart zing. He adds goat cheese and jalapeño chilies, he says, "to stir things up and make the salad come alive."

This fall, Miller will take his cooking expertise to the new Granite Bay Golf Club, northeast of Roseville, California.

153

Northwest Salads

Brian Poor, executive chef at Chandler's Crabhouse and Fresh Fish Market in Seattle, is passionate about Northwest cuisine in general and seafood in particular. Poor grew up fishing, and he has never lost his fascination for Northwest seafood. As a result, he insists on superior quality. "Nothing less than the best," he states.

This philosophy carries over to all aspects of restaurant operations, and Poor feels that customer satisfaction is the key to his success at Chandler's. "What you want is what you will get—guaranteed," he says.

When it comes to salads, freshness is his first priority. Greens must be perfect, seafood handled impeccably, and the presentation beyond customers' expectations. Poor keeps presentations simple. "Make the food bigger than life," he says, "and let the food do the work."

The top-selling salad at Chandler's is a grilled salmon salad with mixed wild greens, vine-ripened tomatoes, and fresh basil vinaigrette. It originated three years ago when Poor and Ted Furst, a corporate chef, were experimenting with new menu ideas, particularly the "hot-cold" concept so prominent in Asian cuisine—a strong influence in the Northwest.

Grilled salmon and corn are an obvious pairing for the summer months, he says, but his seasonings—chili paste, lots of fresh basil, olives, and bell peppers—are a delicious surprise.

According to Poor, salads are the restaurant's most popular dishes in summer. Although the Summer Salmon and Corn Relish with Basil Vinaigrette is the top seller, a seafood Caesar featuring crab, prawns, and smoked salmon is close behind.

Chandler's Crabhouse and Fresh Fish Market is at 901 Fairview Avenue N., Seattle; (206) 223-2722. Lunch from 11:30 to 2 Mondays through Fridays, 10:30 to 3 weekends; dinner from 5 to 10 Mondays through Thursdays, 5 to 11 Fridays and Saturdays, and from 4:30 to 10 Sundays.

Jacqueline Roberts, owner of The Pink Door Ristorante, at Pike's Place Market in Seattle, says salads are in great demand by health-conscious customers.

Roberts, who loves the fragrance of fresh fruits and vegetables, describes herself as a salad fiend. She grew up with an avid—or as she laughingly explains it, "crazy"—Italian gardener, her father. Her dad not only planted a large garden at home, but also borrowed the yards of friends. Roberts reaped the benefits, she says, with fresh foods on the dinner table each day.

Salads have always been more than lettuce and dressing for Roberts. Because of her family's abundant produce supply, she was lucky to experience unique salads early on—wild dandelion greens, grilled beets and fennel, endive and onion—all seasoned with her dad's homemade vinegar. Restaurants near Florence, Italy, were her culinary training grounds, and were where she discovered arugula and extra-virgin olive oil in the late '70s.

Roberts's seafood salad, Insalata di Mare, was inspired by the produce grown at Penn Cove Farms on Whidbey Island, and by a salad she enjoyed in Italy. Its plump fresh mussels, shrimp, clams, and calamari illustrate her desire to present dishes with fresh flavors and bold visual appeal. She uses only the freshest seafood and highest-quality olive oil, along with fresh lemon juice, cracked pepper, and parsley.

Other favorite salads at The Pink Door Ristorante are a giant Caesar salad with shrimp; spicy greens with grilled chicken; a summer spinach salad with pine nuts, goat cheese, and prosciutto; and a salad of mixed greens with roasted hazelnuts, parmesan, and fennel with a balsamic vinaigrette.

The Pink Door Ristorante is at 1919 Post Alley (Pike Place Market), Seattle; (206) 443-3241. Lunch from 11:30 to 2:30, dinner from 5:30 to 10 Tuesdays through Saturdays. Closed Sundays and Mondays. ■

Summer Salmon and Corn Relish with Basil Vinaigrette

AS A BOY, BRIAN POOR *enjoyed fishing with his dad in Pullman, Washington. Today, as chef at Chandler's Crabhouse in Seattle, his enthusiasm for seafood is expressed in innovative salads. Below, grilled salmon and corn relish share a basil marinade. (Recipe on page 157.)*

Insalata di Mare

MICHAEL SKOTT

JACQUELINE ROBERTS, *owner of The Pink Door Ristorante in Seattle, acquired her love of unique salads from her restaurateur-gardener dad. Above, her Insalata di Mare is composed of plump fresh shellfish and calamari nestled in a bowl of greens. (Recipe on page 157.)*

Six great salad recipes

Innovative Western cooks showcase regional ingredients

T HE WESTERN COOKS we profiled on pages 150 through 155 combine regional produce and other top-quality ingredients in six salads you can try at home.

Grilled Garden Bounty Vegetable and Rice Platter

¾ cup *each* wild rice and long-grain brown rice

4 medium-size (about 1¼ lb. total) zucchini, ends trimmed, cut diagonally into ½-inch-thick slices

6 large (about 3¼ lb. total) ears corn

4 medium-size (about 2 lb. total) unpeeled red onions, halved lengthwise

4 large (about ¾ lb. total) Asian eggplant, halved lengthwise

8 large (about 10 oz. total) fresh shiitake or large common mushrooms

8 boiled 2-inch-diameter (about 2 lb. total) red or purple thin-skinned potatoes, halved

5 large (about 2½ lb. total) red or yellow bell peppers

Herb dressing (recipe follows)

Salt and pepper

2 cups (about ¾ lb.) yellow or red pear-shaped or cherry tomatoes

Fresh fennel or basil sprigs (optional)

Pour wild rice into a fine strainer; rinse well. In a 5- to 6-quart pan, bring 2 quarts water to a boil. Add wild and brown rice; cover and simmer until both rices are ten-der to bite, 40 to 45 minutes. Drain well.

Scatter 10 briquets over a solid bed of about 70 hot coals (you can hold your hand at grill level only 2 to 3 seconds). Place grill 4 to 6 inches above coals. If desired, run thin wooden skewers through zucchini slices to hold flat. Place zucchini, corn, and onions on grill. Cook, turning vegetables often. After corn cooks about 5 minutes, pull down husks and remove silk. Continue grilling corn until lightly browned, about 10 minutes more. Cook zucchini until lightly browned on both sides, about 10 minutes.

As you remove zucchini and corn, add eggplant, mushrooms, potatoes, and 4 of the peppers. Cook and turn vegetables until mushrooms and potatoes are lightly browned, about 15 minutes total; peppers are browned and soft when pressed, 15 to 20 minutes; eggplant are darkly browned and very soft when pressed, 15 to 25 minutes; and onions are somewhat soft, about 30 minutes. As vegetables are done, remove from grill; set aside. Halve and seed grilled peppers.

Cut kernels off 5 ears of corn; add to rice. Stem, seed, and dice remaining raw bell pepper. To rice, add 1½ cups herb dressing, diced pepper, and salt and pepper to taste; mix well. (If making ahead, cover and let stand at room temperature up to 2 hours or chill up to 1 day, stirring occasionally.)

Mound rice salad on a large platter. Surround with grilled vegetables and drizzle with any remaining dressing. Garnish with remaining ear of corn, tomatoes, and fennel or basil sprigs, if desired. Serves 8.
—*Andrea Bell, Pacific Palisades, California*

Per serving: 489 cal. (29 percent from fat); 12 g protein; 16 g fat (2.1 g sat.); 82 g carbo.; 38 mg sodium; 0 mg chol.

Herb dressing. Mix 1⅓ cups **balsamic vinegar,** ½ cup **olive oil,** ½ cup thinly sliced **garlic chives** (or plain chives plus 1 clove garlic, pressed), ⅓ cup chopped **shallots,** ⅓ cup chopped **fresh basil** or 3 tablespoons dried basil leaves, 1½ tablespoons **fresh lemon** (or regular) **thyme leaves** or 1 teaspoon dried thyme leaves, 1 tablespoon chopped **fresh oregano leaves** or 1 teaspoon dried oregano, and 1 teaspoon chopped **fresh rosemary leaves** or ½ teaspoon crumbled dried rosemary. Makes about 2 cups.

Spicy Delta Salad

You will need about 7 pounds of live crayfish to get 1½ pounds peeled, cooked tails for this recipe (directions follow). Or order 1½ pounds fresh or frozen crayfish tails. Another option is to substitute shelled cooked tiny shrimp.

1½ pounds (about 4 cups) peeled, cooked crayfish tails, thawed (if frozen), or shelled cooked tiny shrimp

Chili-lime vinaigrette (recipe follows)

2 cups long-grain rice, cooked and cooled

2 medium-size (about 6 oz. total) carrots, thinly sliced

2 medium-size (about ½ lb. each) bell peppers, 1 red and 1 yellow, cored, seeded, and sliced into ¼- by 1½-inch pieces

1 cup thinly sliced green onions

⅓ cup minced fresh mint leaves

¼ cup minced fresh cilantro (coriander) leaves

About a dozen lettuce leaves, rinsed and crisped

8 whole crayfish (optional)

Mix crayfish meat with chili-lime vinaigrette; chill 20 minutes. Meanwhile, combine rice, carrots, peppers, onions, mint, and cilantro. Stir in crayfish mixture. Cover; chill at least 2 hours or up until next day.

Line a large salad bowl with lettuce; fill with crayfish-rice mixture. Garnish with whole crayfish, if desired. Serve in smaller bowls. Serves 8.—*Annette Davis, Walnut Grove, California*

Per serving: 385 cal. (23 percent from fat); 25 g protein; 10 g fat (1.4 g sat.); 47 g carbo.; 665 mg sodium; 152 mg chol.

Chili-lime vinaigrette. Mix together ⅓ cup *each* **seasoned rice vinegar** (or rice vinegar with 2 teaspoons sugar) and **reduced-sodium soy sauce;** 3 tablespoons *each* **lime juice** and **Oriental sesame oil;** and 2 to 3 tablespoons **hot chili oil.**

To cook crayfish. In a 10- to 12-quart pan over high heat, bring about 1½ gallons water to boiling. Drop half of **7 pounds live crayfish** into water. Cover and cook on high (boil may not resume) until tail meat is firm and opaque in center (pull off a tail to test), 7 to 8 minutes. Remove crayfish with slotted spoon. Bring water back to boil; repeat to cook remaining crayfish. Drain and cool. If desired, reserve 8 whole crayfish for garnish.

To remove meat. Twist tail and body in opposite directions and pull apart. Pinch in tail sides to crack ridges along inside of tail. Pull sides of tail back to crack shell and loosen meat. Pull tail meat from cracked shell. Twist off big claws (little claws are too time-consuming) and crack shells to dig out meat. Repeat with remaining crayfish.

Crayfish sources. Your local fish market is the best place to start. Some markets require a minimum order and a week's notice. If you don't have a local source, you can mail-order from *Jake's Famous Crawfish & Seafood,* Box 97, Clackamas, Ore. 97015; (503) 657-1892. Live crayfish are available from April through October; frozen cooked whole crayfish and frozen peeled cooked tails are available all year. No minimum; freight costs vary depending on where you live.

In the San Francisco area, you can pick up crayfish at *California Crayfish/San Francisco Seafood,* Pier 45, Building D, San Francisco; (415) 474-8678. No mail order; must reserve orders three days in advance. Pickup 10:30 to 2 Mondays through Saturdays; minimum order is 5 pounds live crayfish, 1 pound crayfish tails.

Garden Greens with Berry Salsa

2 cups *each* raspberries and blueberries

1 cup *each* strawberries and diced firm-ripe tomato

¼ cup *each* minced fresh cilantro and minced red onion

2 medium-size fresh jalapeño chilies, stemmed, seeded, and minced

Citrus dressing (recipe follows)

8 cups (about ⅓ lb.) lightly packed salad mix, rinsed and crisped

4 ounces (about ¾ cup) soft fresh goat cheese, crumbled (optional)

Rinse all berries; drain on towels. Hull and halve strawberries. In a large bowl, combine berries, tomato, cilantro, onion, jalapeños, and all but ¼ cup dressing. Chill 1 to 4 hours.

Combine salad mix with remaining dressing; arrange on 4 dinner plates. Equally distribute salsa over greens; sprinkle with goat cheese, if desired. Serves 4.—*Mitch Miller, Loomis, California*

Per serving: 214 cal. (46 percent from fat); 2.6 g protein; 11 g fat (1.3 g sat.); 30 g carbo.; 292 mg sodium; 0 mg chol.

Citrus dressing. Mix together 2 teaspoons **sugar,** ½ teaspoon **salt,** and 3 tablespoons *each* **orange juice, lemon juice, lime juice,** and **salad oil.**

Summer Harvest Tomato Salad

3 medium-size (about 1½ lb. total) firm-ripe red tomatoes

3 medium-size (about 1½ lb. total) firm-ripe golden (orange) tomatoes

1 small (about ¾ lb.) European cucumber

2 cups halved yellow pear-shaped tomatoes

Fresh mint dressing (recipe follows)

Fresh mint sprigs (optional)

Salt and pepper

Core red and golden tomatoes. Slice tomatoes crosswise into ⅜-inch-thick slices. Divide tomato slices equally among 8 plates, arranging in alternating colors along one side of each plate. Peel cucumber, halve lengthwise, and remove seeds if necessary; thinly slice crosswise into crescents. Mound next to tomatoes on each plate. Mound halved pear-shaped tomatoes beside sliced tomatoes and cucumber on plates. Drizzle equal amounts of dressing over vegetables. Garnish with mint sprigs; add salt and pepper to taste. Chill 1

to 4 hours. Serves 8.—*Annette Davis, Walnut Grove, California*

Per serving: 117 cal. (60 percent from fat); 2.2 g protein; 7.8 g fat (1.1 g sat.); 13 g carbo.; 20 mg sodium; 0 mg chol.

Fresh mint dressing. Finely chop ¾ cup loosely packed **fresh mint leaves.** Combine with ¼ cup **extra-virgin olive oil,** ½ cup **red wine vinegar,** 1 teaspoon **sugar,** and 2 cloves **garlic,** minced or pressed.

Summer Salmon and Corn Relish with Basil Vinaigrette

4 baby salmon fillets, each 6 to 7 ounces

Basil vinaigrette (recipe follows)

Corn relish (recipe follows)

8 to 10 cups (about ½ lb.) salad mix, rinsed and crisped

2 large (1¼ lb. total) firm-ripe tomatoes, cored and thickly sliced

Rinse fillets; pat dry. Place in a 9-by 13-inch baking dish. Pour ¾ cup basil vinaigrette over fillets. Chill about 1 hour (turn fillets every 15 minutes), or up until next day (turn every couple of hours when possible). Meanwhile, make relish. Chill about 1 hour or up until next day.

Ignite a pile of charcoal briquets (about 60) on a firegrate. When coals are completely covered with gray ash, about 30 minutes, arrange in a single layer. Spray the grill with non-stick cooking spray; set grill about 6 inches above firegrate. Coals are ready when you can hold your hand at grill level for only 3 to 4 seconds.

Lift fillets from vinaigrette; lay on grill. Cook until moist-looking but opaque in thickest part (cut to test), 8 to 10 minutes, turning fillets after 4 minutes. Remove from grill; cover with foil to keep warm.

Mix greens with remaining vinaigrette; evenly divide among 4 dinner plates. Spoon relish and tomato slices next to greens. Lay warm fillets over greens. Makes 4 servings.—*Brian Poor, Chandler's Crabhouse and Fresh Fish Market, Seattle*

Per serving: 662 cal. (56 percent from fat); 40 g protein; 41 g fat (5.8 g sat.); 38 g carbo.; 206 mg sodium; 94 mg chol.

Basil vinaigrette. In a blender or food processor, combine ⅓ cup *each* **balsamic vinegar** and **red wine vinegar;** ½ cup chopped, packed **fresh basil leaves;** 1 tablespoon *each* minced **garlic** and **fresh tarragon leaves;** and 2 to 4 teaspoons **Asian red chili paste with garlic.** With blender or food processor on, slowly add ½ cup **olive oil.** Chill until ready to use or up to 2 days.

Corn relish. In a bowl, combine 3 cups **corn kernels** (cut from about 4

ears of cooked corn), ⅓ cup *each* diced **green** and **red bell peppers,** ¼ cup diced **black olives,** and ½ cup diced **red onion.** Stir in ⅓ cup **basil vinaigrette;** add **salt** and **pepper** to taste. Chill until ready to serve or up to 4 hours.

Insalata di Mare

First, run cool water over clams and mussels to see if they are alive and healthy; they should close tightly. Discard any that stay open.

½ pound squid

1½ cups *each* dry white wine and water

12 extra-large (26 to 30 per lb.) shrimp, peeled (leaving tail pieces) and deveined

2 pounds *each* small clams and mussels, rinsed and scrubbed

1 cup thinly sliced celery

½ cup *each* chopped green onion and parsley

½ cup lemon juice

¼ cup *each* extra-virgin olive oil and regular-strength chicken broth

Salt and pepper

8 to 12 green lettuce leaves, washed and crisped

Lemon wedges (optional)

4 green onions, ends trimmed

Rinse squid tubes and tentacles. Check for inner clear cartilage in tubes; remove. Slice tubes into ¼-inch rings. Remove pointy beak from center of tentacles.

In a 10- to 12-inch frying pan, bring wine and water to a boil over high heat. Add squid; cook just until opaque, about 45 seconds. With a slotted spoon, lift squid from cooking liquid; set aside. Add shrimp and cook just until opaque (cut to test), 1 to 2 minutes. Remove with a slotted spoon; set aside with squid. Add clams and cook until fully open, 3 to 8 minutes, removing from pan as they pop open (discard those that fail to open). Drain and add to other fish. Repeat process with mussels, cooking 1 to 3 minutes.

Stir together celery, onion, parsley, lemon juice, oil, and broth; pour over seafood and chill 1 to 4 hours. Add salt and pepper to taste.

Line 4 shallow soup bowls with lettuce leaves; mound seafood mixture in bowls. Garnish each with lemon and a green onion. Serves 4. —*Jacqueline Roberts, The Pink Door Ristorante, Pike Place Market, Seattle*

Per serving: 384 cal. (42 percent from fat); 30 g protein; 18 g fat (2.7 g sat.); 12 g carbo.; 340 mg sodium; 223 mg chol. ∎

By Betsy Reynolds Bateson

Portland's fresh and filling food

Try these places for breakfast, seafood, and brewpub grub

With sources of fresh and varied seafood and produce close at hand, Portland restaurants have never had to go far for fine ingredients. And the reverse sides of dinner menus are increasingly devoted to Willamette Valley wines and in-town microbrews.

Still, sophisticated dining on a par with other major Western cities is a fairly recent phenomenon here. Chefs will tell you that's because Portlanders are more appreciative and less fickle than diners in other large cities, and that they hold good berry pancakes in equal esteem with fancy French pastries.

Several of our readers' top restaurant choices reflect their loyalty to places with well-established track records for high-quality fare. Here are favorites in three categories in which Portland particularly ~~ticularly~~ ~~nes.~~

AT HEATHMAN PUB, *try the Northwest pizza and Widmer's Hefeweizen, an unfiltered wheat beer.*

Big breakfasts

Portlanders take breakfast seriously. Sure, you can find dainty croissants, but restaurants here have built their reputations on rib-sticking fare such as salmon hash, breads studded with seasonal fruit, and plenty of good coffee to chase it all down.

Leave any foolish ideas about dieting at the door of the **Original Pancake House** (8601 S.W. 24th Avenue, at Barbur Boulevard; 503/246-9007). This local institution deserves unchecked enthusiasm for the hearty portions and just-as-they-oughta-be flavors. The puffy apple pancake with cinnamon glaze, the restaurant's most popular dish, is more than enough for two. Sourdough flapjacks come eight to the order. The fluffy, five-egg ham and cheese omelet is stuffed full of cheddar and smoked ham.

In business since 1953, this is Portland at its old-fashioned best: knotty-pine walls, waitresses in pink aprons, coffee cups refilled as fast as they're emptied, and nary an untoward glance when your kid plays musical spoons on the high-chair tray. Come prepared for a long wait, though.

Two other restaurants received readers' kudos for their excellent breakfasts: **Zell's: An American Cafe** (1300 S.E. Morrison Street; 239-0196), and **Bijou Cafe** (132 S.W. Third Street; 222-3187). (Both were featured in the June 1993 *Sunset,* page 136.)

Seafood, classic and twisted

With Portland's location at the confluence of the Willamette and Columbia rivers and its proximity to the coast, the popularity and abundance of seafood come as no surprise. Local waters yield numerous choices: salmon and Dungeness crab, certainly, as well as steel-

JOHN RIZZO

KIJAFA SOUR CHERRY CREPES *overflowing with fruit nearly escape their dinner-size plate at the Original Pancake House.*

head, sturgeon, halibut, cod, oysters, shrimp, and smelt, to name several.

For a taste of the sea and a slice of old Portland, head to **Jake's Famous Crawfish Restaurant** (401 S.W. 12th Avenue; 226-1419). Though its lineage goes back 102 years, Jake's began serving crawfish in the 1920s, when Jacob Freiman raised the crustaceans in ponds in the basement.

Simply cooked items from the extensive list of fresh seafood are the best bets: crawfish in a spicy boil, oysters on the half-shell with an excellent horseradish cocktail sauce, and the chilled seafood platter. Jake's appeal goes beyond the food, though, to wood-paneled walls, 19th-century oil paintings depict-

C. BRUCE FORSTER

ing Oregon landmarks, a lively bar, and an accommodating staff.

McCormick & Schmick's Seafood Restaurant (235 S.W. First Avenue; 224-7522) is operated by the same owners as Jake's and has much in common with its older brother. Both are housed in buildings on the National Register of Historic Places (McCormick's site is actually older) that have a convivial, clubby feel. Both focus on high-quality seafood from the Northwest and around the world, and offer some of the same menu items. McCormick and Schmick's departs from Jake's by offering classics with a twist. A couple of our favorites: the perfectly cooked alder-smoked salmon fillet, served with red pepper polenta triangles, and the creamy Northwest seafood stew, with shiitake mushrooms and dried cranberries over hazelnut shortcake.

Brewpub mania

Why does Portland have more microbreweries than any other city in the United States? In a rainy climate, pubs are a natural place to socialize; a full-bodied ale warms you up on a damp day. Then, too, the ingredients are right here: soft water, and hops grown in the Willamette and Yakima valleys.

The McMenamin brothers have the beer-and-burger idea down so well that their mini-empire now encompasses 22 Portland-area sites. One of the most popular is the historic **Cornelius Pass Roadhouse and Brewery** (4045 N.W. Cornelius Pass Road; 503/640-6174) in Hillsboro, west of Portland off U.S. Highway 26. On a hot day, you can't ask for a

better spot than a picnic table on the lawn or front porch of the roadhouse, built in 1866 as the Imbrie Farmstead. And you can't ask for a more refreshing drink than a pint of Ruby (a mild raspberry ale), Hammerhead (a highly hopped chestnut-colored ale), or toasty Terminator Stout. The burgers, such as Mel's Communication Breakdown (with cheddar, grilled onions and bell peppers, and mushrooms), are great, too. Fries with the skins on are cut to order and really taste like potatoes.

For inventive beer food, try **Heathman Bakery & Pub** (901 S.W. Salmon Street; 227-5700). The grilled, grape leaf–wrapped goat cheese comes with dried tomatoes, capers, roasted garlic, and bread from the wood-burning hearth oven. The smoked lamb sandwich is complemented by a smoky chipotle chili mayonnaise.

Of the pizzas, our vote goes to the Northwest, with shrimp, smoked salmon, roasted red peppers, feta, and

JOHN RIZZO

PACESETTER FOR THE '90s, *Zefiro's stylish interior catches eyes of passersby on N.W. 21st Avenue. Equally eyecatching is this salad, below, from Higgins, with pickled fiddlehead ferns, Oregon bay shrimp, and salmon mousseline.*

calamata olive paste, all on a crisp crust. To go with the food, the pub has 13 brews on draft, including five German varieties from Widmer Brewing, located just on the other side of a glass wall.

At **BridgePort BrewPub** (1313 N.W. Marshall Street; 241-7179), in an 1886 brick building in Portland's Pearl District, the staff is happy to explain the differences among their four British-style ales; the rotating Brewer's Select Series (with names

like Broadway Best Bitter, Ross Island Red, or other Portland bridge derivatives); and their special cask-conditioned ales (what Brits call "real ale"). Food choices, simple but very good, include focaccia bread or pizza from a sourdough that contains wort (a beer-making derivative), with toppings of your choice; check out the Walla Walla sweet onions and Italian sausage by Portland's Salumeria di Carlo.

—*Elaine Johnson*

THE NEW WAVE—CRITICS' CHOICE

Where would we take out-of-towners for a taste of the new Portland? Three stylishly casual restaurants are changing the city's dining scene, with skill and an attention to flavor that elevate even a simple stew above the ordinary. Much of their cooking starts with Mediterranean country fare and adds a strong, seasonal overlay of the Northwest.

For deceptively straightforward, utterly delicious food, *Zefiro* (500 N.W. 21st Avenue; 226-3394) has set the standard that other Portland restaurants aspire to. Key to its success since opening in 1990 is chef and co-owner Christopher Israel's attention to details,

from the artisan-style bread made in-house to the perfectly cooked vegetables. You really can't go wrong, but sure bets are the Caesar salad, appetizers like grilled spot prawns and squid with a garlicky *romesco* sauce, tender braised meats such as rabbit, and grilled fish in a tamarind marinade. On the dessert front, look for sorbet that's the essence of summer fruits, and knockout pastries. Zefiro's success is no secret; expect a long wait, even with reservations.

Cory Schreiber, a fifth-generation Portlander whose family owns the venerable Dan & Louis Oyster Bar, honed his cooking skills in San Francisco and else-

where before returning last spring to open *Wildwood* (1221 N.W. 21st Avenue; 248-9663). Early interest has swamped the restaurant; give them a little time to smooth out some rough edges. The name refers to Portland's popular hiking trail, portrayed in the mural behind the bar, and to the wood-fired brick and tandoori ovens. The menu includes inventive starters like roasted mussels in saffron vinaigrette, and entrées such as grilled salmon with stuffed oyster.

Food and service can be a little uneven at *Higgins* (1239 S.W. Broadway; 222-9070), chef and co-owner Greg Higgins's new

venture, but many dishes are so creative and spot-on that it's easy to feel indulgent, as the diners packing the place seem inclined to be. Higgins has been a strong proponent of Northwest cuisine since his days at the Heathman Hotel. Excellent dishes include braised escarole with Oregon hazelnuts, dried cherries, and duck confit; and saffron-scented Oregon mussel and scallop *bourride* (a French-style stew). Save room for desserts such as lavender-honey ice cream, and profiteroles—warm, crisp cream puffs filled with soft Oregon goat cheese, in a pool of raspberry sauce.

—*E. J.*

Lemon Ginger Tea Sparkler

Cranberry Cherry Tea Sparkler

Cinnamon Citrus Tea Sparkler

PAUL HAMMOND

Apricot Tea Sparkler

Honey Vanilla Peach Tea Sparkler

Raspberry Mint Tea Cooler

Spiced & Iced

With fruit and bubbles, tea hits its stride as the smoother cooler

I CED TEA, DRESSED UP, IS THE SOFT drink of the '90s. Skyrocketing sales of prepared teas and tea-juice blends are pushing carbonated beverages aside on market shelves.

The concept of these tea drinks is simple

enough to take home. Iced tea fans can easily create an exotic array of tea-juice blends. The starting point is extra-strong tea concentrate that keeps in the refrigerator for a couple of weeks. You can use the concentrate alone, diluted with water, or flavor it further with spices and other seasonings. To make a drink, dilute the concentrate by the pitcher or the glass.

You can use any tea as the concentrate base, but to emphasize a juice companion, pick a tea that has the same or a complementary flavor. For example, to intensify the overall fruit flavor of Apricot Tea Sparkler (at right), start with a concentrate made with apricot-flavor tea.

A tremendous array of varietal or flavored teas is available, even in supermarkets and especially in tea and coffee stores. Pairing them compatibly with the ever-increasing kinds and blends of fruit juices—refrigerated, canned, or made from concentrates—holds promise for many refreshing hours. Adding sparkling water gives the flavored teas a tingling effervescence.

Try our recipes, then let them guide you to more adventures. Keep in mind that the ratio we found strong enough to retain plenty of flavor when poured into an ice-filled glass is 1 part tea concentrate to 2 parts water or juice.

Not only do these teas look cool and refreshing, but some of them will make layered drinks. When tea is poured onto some kinds of sweet fruit juice, the tea floats, making ribbons of color until you stir and sip.

Apricot Tea Sparkler

For the most emphatic fruit taste, make the concentrate with apricot-flavor tea.

1⅓ cups tea concentrate (see box, top left)

1⅓ cups chilled canned apricot nectar

1⅓ cups chilled sparkling water

Ice cubes

Combine concentrate, nectar, and sparkling water. Pour into tall ice-filled glasses. Makes 4 servings.

Per serving: 49 cal. (1.8 percent from fat); 0.3 g protein; 0.1 g fat (0 g sat.); 13 g carbo.; 9.6 mg sodium; 0 mg chol.

Honey Vanilla Peach Tea Sparkler

1⅓ cups tea concentrate (see box, top left)

1 piece vanilla bean, about 3 inches long

2 tablespoons honey

1⅓ cups chilled canned peach nectar or juice

1⅓ cups chilled sparkling water

Ice cubes

In a 1- to 1½-quart pan, combine concentrate, vanilla, and honey; heat to boiling. Cover and chill until cold, 1 hour or up to 2 days. Remove vanilla bean and reserve for other uses (let dry and store airtight with sugar). Combine concentrate with nectar and sparkling water. Pour into tall ice-filled glasses. Makes 4 servings.

Per serving: 81 cal. (0 percent from fat); 0.3 g protein; 0 g fat; 21 g carbo.; 13 mg sodium; 0 mg chol.

Lemon Ginger Tea Sparkler

1⅓ cups tea concentrate (see box, top left)

1 lemon, thinly sliced

¼ cup finely chopped crystallized ginger

2⅔ cups chilled ginger ale

Ice cubes

In a 1- to 1½-quart pan, combine tea concentrate, ½ the lemon slices, and ginger; bring to boiling. Cover and chill until cold, at least 1 hour or up to 2 days. Pour through a fine strainer into a pitcher and add ginger ale; discard used lemon slices and ginger. Pour tea into tall ice-filled glasses. Drop remaining lemon slices into tea, or use to garnish glasses. Makes 4 servings.

Per serving: 118 cal. (0.8 percent from fat); 0.4 g protein; 0.1 g fat (0 g sat.); 32 g carbo.; 29 mg sodium; 0 mg chol.

Cranberry Cherry Tea Sparkler

1⅓ cups tea concentrate (see box, top left)

⅓ cup dried cranberries

1⅓ cups chilled canned cherry cider or juice

1⅓ cups chilled sparkling water

Ice cubes

In a 1- to 1½-quart pan, combine tea concentrate and cranberries; bring to boiling. Cover and chill until cold, at least 1 hour or 2 days. Pour mixture through a fine strainer into a large pitcher; discard cranberries. To pitcher, add cider and sparkling water; mix. Pour into 4 tall ice-filled glasses. Makes 4 servings.

Per serving: 69 cal. (1.3 percent from fat); 0.1 g protein; 0.1 g fat (0 g sat.); 18 g carbo.; 10 mg sodium; 0 mg chol.

Cinnamon Citrus Tea Sparkler

One liquid floats on another in this fascinating beverage. Ideal swizzle sticks for mixing it are very long cinnamon sticks—the kind that are used more for decoration than seasoning.

1⅓ cups tea concentrate (see box, top left)

Thinly pared peel (colored part only) of 1 small orange

1 cinnamon stick, about 2 inches long

2⅔ cups chilled sparkling water

Ice cubes

¼ to ½ cup thawed frozen orange juice concentrate or tangerine juice concentrate

In a 1- to 1½-quart pan, combine tea concentrate, orange peel, and cinnamon stick; bring to boiling. Cover and chill until cold, at least 1 hour or up to 2 days. Discard orange peel and cinnamon stick. Combine concentrate with sparkling water.

Fill 4 tall glasses (at least 12-oz. size) with ice cubes. To make liquid layers, pour thawed orange juice concentrate equally into each glass, then gently pour tea mixture into glasses. Stir before sipping. Makes 4 servings.

Per serving: 32 cal. (0 percent from fat); 0.4 g protein; 0 g fat; 8 g carbo.; 7.7 mg sodium; 0 mg chol.

Raspberry Mint Tea Cooler

This drink stays in three layers until you stir it to sip. Whipping cream is the more stable choice for the middle layer, but it's also richer.

1⅓ cups tea concentrate (see box, top left)

1 cup firmly packed (about 1 oz.) fresh mint leaves

2⅓ cups chilled sparkling water

Ice cubes

½ cup thawed frozen raspberry juice concentrate or cranberry-raspberry juice concentrate

½ cup half-and-half (light cream) or whipping cream

In a 1- to 1½-quart pan, combine tea concentrate and mint; bring to boiling. Cover; chill until cold, at least 1 hour or up to 2 days. Pour concentrate through a fine strainer into a pitcher; add sparkling water. Discard mint.

Fill 4 tall glasses (at least 12-oz. size) with ice cubes. To make liquid layers, pour raspberry concentrate equally into each glass. Next, gently pour an equal amount of cream into each glass, and then gently fill glasses with the tea mixture. Stir beverage with drinking straws to mix as you sip. Makes 4 servings.

Per serving: 117 cal. (28 percent from fat); 1.2 g protein; 3.7 g fat (2.1 g sat.); 21 g carbo.; 23 mg sodium; 11 mg chol. ■

By Christine Weber Hale

BROAD

Shark stew full of snap

Corn soup with a bite

JAN NIXON'S RECIPE FOR A QUICK, easy, and delicious fish stew is based on shark, with tomato, celery, onion, and cilantro as adjuvants. She finds shark just as delicious as (and less expensive than) sea bass, the fish used in the original recipe. (Some people, the Nixon grandchildren among them, find the idea of eating shark exciting. It's a swimmer's revenge kind of thing.) If you suspect that your family or guests are squeamish about shark, just call it fish stew or, quoting Gilbert and Sullivan, simply a pretty kettle of fish.

Shark Stew

2 cups celery, cut into 1-inch pieces

2 medium-size (5 to 6 oz.) onions, chopped

3 tablespoons water

4 cans (14½ oz. each) stewed tomatoes with Mexican seasonings (or plain tomatoes with ½ teaspoon dried oregano leaves and ¼ teaspoon cumin seed)

½ cup chopped fresh cilantro (coriander)

2 pounds shark or other firm white fish, boned, skinned, and cut into pieces about 1½ by 3 inches

Hot cooked rice

Homemade or prepared salsa

Cilantro leaves

Unflavored nonfat yogurt or regular or nonfat sour cream

Lime wedges

Salt

In a 5- to 6-quart pan, combine celery, onions, and water. Stir often over medium-high heat until water evaporates and vegetables start to stick and brown slightly, about 10 minutes. Stir tomatoes and their liquid into pan along with chopped cilantro; bring to a boil on high heat. Push fish down into vegetables; cover and simmer on low heat until fish is opaque but still moist-looking in the center of the thickest piece (cut to test), about 20 minutes. Ladle stew into bowls and add rice, salsa, cilantro leaves, yogurt, lime juice, and salt to taste. Serves 4 to 6.

Per serving: 315 cal. (20 percent from fat); 35 g protein; 6.9 g fat (1.4 g sat.); 219 g carbo.; 1,116 mg sodium; 77 mg chol.

Jan Nixon

Phoenix

MEXICAN COOKS USE CORN, their national cereal, in many kinds of soup. As hominy, corn appears with tripe in *menudo*, the classic hangover remedy. In *pozole*, pork and hominy make soup. Corn flavors pozole in another way, and more delicately, as fried tortilla strips. These crisp strips also get dropped into any number of Mexico's chicken soups.

As just plain sweet corn, you may look for it in *sopa de elote*, the spiritual ancestor of Chuck Allen's soup.

Sweet Corn and Chili Soup

6 medium-size (about 8 in. long) ears of corn

2 medium-size (10 to 12 oz. total) onions, chopped

4 cloves garlic, minced or pressed

3 fresh jalapeño chilies, stemmed, seeded, and minced

2½ cups regular-strength chicken broth

About ½ teaspoon sugar

2 cups low-fat or regular milk

¾ cup finely chopped cooked ham

2 tablespoons lime juice

2 medium-size (10 to 12 oz. total) firm-ripe tomatoes, cored and diced

½ teaspoon balsamic vinegar

½ cup coarsely chopped fresh cilantro (coriander)

Unflavored nonfat yogurt or nonfat sour cream (optional)

Salt

Shuck corn and remove silk. With a sharp knife, cut corn kernels from the cobs. With the back of the knife, scrape juice from cobs into a bowl.

In a 5- to 6-quart pan over high heat, combine onions, garlic, chilies, and ¼ cup water. Stir often until liquid evaporates and vegetables start to stick and brown, about 10 minutes. Stir in broth, ½ teaspoon sugar, corn, liquid scraped from cobs, and, if desired, cobs. Bring to boiling; cover and simmer gently to blend flavors, 8 to 10 minutes. Lift out and discard cobs, draining juices into pan.

With a slotted spoon, scoop about 1 cup corn and onions from the soup and set aside. In a blender or food processor, purée remaining soup until smooth in batches, adding the milk. Return soup with reserved corn and onions to pan; if making ahead, cover and chill up to 1 day. Heat soup with ham until steaming, stirring often. Remove from heat; mix in lime juice. In a bowl, mix tomatoes with vinegar and cilantro.

Ladle soup into wide, individual bowls, and spoon an equal portion of the tomato mixture into each. Add yogurt and salt to taste. Serves 6.

Per serving: 198 cal. (23 percent from fat); 12 g protein; 5g fat (1.9 g sat.); 30 g carbo.; 346 mg sodium; 17 mg chol.

Dana Point, California

By Joan Griffiths, Richard Dunmire

DIP INTO *soft, fluffy spoonbread with fresh berries. Top serving with more berries, whipped cream, and hot maple syrup.*

A spoonful of flavor

Two spoonbread entrées for brunch, lunch, or supper

A PUDDINGLIKE BREAD WITH A crunchy crust, spoonbread gets its lightness from baking powder and fluffy, stiffly beaten egg whites.

This recipe offers both sweet and savory versions. When served with sweetened fresh berries, whipped cream, and maple syrup, it makes an outstanding brunch entrée—or summer evening dessert. Whip up the Southwestern variation, with smoked chicken, cheese, and green chili flavors, for a brunch, lunch, or supper entrée.

Spoonbread with Berries

8 to 10 cups berries, such as blackberries, strawberries, and raspberries

⅓ cup sugar

4 cups 1%, low-fat, or regular milk

¼ cup (⅛ lb.) butter or margarine

2 tablespoons sugar

½ teaspoon salt

1 ⅓ cups yellow cornmeal

6 large eggs, separated

4 teaspoons baking powder

1 teaspoon cream of tartar

Fresh mint sprig (optional)

Whipped cream, sweetened to taste

About 1 cup hot maple syrup

Rinse berries and drain on towels. In a bowl combine berries and ⅓ cup sugar; set aside.

In a 4- to 6-quart pan, combine milk, butter, the 2 tablespoons sugar, and salt. Heat mixture over medium-low heat, stirring occasionally, until steaming hot. Reduce heat to low and gradually add cornmeal, stirring constantly; cook until cornmeal mixture is thick, 6 to 8 minutes. Remove from heat and let cool slightly. Thoroughly stir in egg yolks and baking powder; set aside.

In a large bowl, beat egg whites with cream of tartar until stiff. Blend 1 cup of the beaten egg whites into cornmeal batter; gently fold cornmeal mixture into remaining whites in large bowl. Scrape mixture into a buttered 2½- to 3-quart shallow oval baking dish or a 9- by 13-inch baking dish. Bake in a 350° oven until a toothpick inserted in center comes out clean and top is golden brown and firm to touch, 45 to 55 minutes.

Ladle some of the sweetened berries and their juices over hot spoonbread; garnish with mint and serve immediately from baking dish. Offer sweetened whipped cream and remaining berries to spoon over servings and maple syrup to drizzle over top. Serves 6 to 8.—*Sandee B. Cameron, Lafayette, California*

Per serving: 468 cal. (23 percent from fat); 12 g protein; 12 g fat (5.7 g sat.); 81 g carbo.; 555 mg sodium; 180 mg chol.

Savory Southwestern Spoonbread. Follow directions for Spoonbread with Berries, omitting the berries and the sugar. When folding in the stiff egg whites, add 1½ cups (6 oz.) shredded **smoked chicken** and 1 can (4 oz.) **diced green chilies.** Before baking, sprinkle ½ cup (about 2 oz.) shredded **cheddar cheese** over batter. Substitute **fresh cilantro sprigs** for fresh mint garnish. Serve immediately from baking dish with about 2 cups **salsa.**

Per serving: 335 cal. (40 percent from fat); 19 g protein; 15 g fat (7.7 g sat.); 30 g carbo.; 1248 mg sodium; 207 mg chol. ■

By Betsy Reynolds Bateson

Creative ways with everyday foods—submitted by *Sunset* readers,
tested in *Sunset* kitchens, approved by *Sunset* taste panels

Couscous Provençal

Ellen Nishimura, Fair Oaks, California

- 1 small (6 oz.) onion, chopped
- 1 teaspoon olive oil
- 1½ cups regular-strength chicken broth
- 1¼ cups couscous
- 1 can (8 oz.) water-packed artichoke hearts
- 1 medium-size (about 6 oz.) firm-ripe tomato
- 2 tablespoons chopped fresh basil leaves
- 1 tablespoon drained prepared capers
- ¼ teaspoon pepper

In a 2½- to 3-quart pan over medium-high heat, frequently stir onion and oil until onion is lightly browned, about 5 minutes. Add broth and bring to a boil over high heat. Stir in couscous. Cover pan and remove from heat; let stand until couscous absorbs broth, about 5 minutes.

Meanwhile, drain artichokes and cut into ½-inch chunks. Core and dice tomato. With a fork, stir artichokes, tomato, basil, capers, and pepper into couscous. Transfer to serving dish. Serve hot or warm. Serves 4 to 6.

Per serving: 187 cal. (7.7 percent from fat); 6.8 g protein; 1.6 g fat (0.3 g sat.); 36 g carbo.; 71 mg sodium; 0 mg chol.

COUSCOUS *makes a quick sidekick for roast chicken.*

Roasted Vegetable and Cheese Soup

Laura Sabo, Portland

- Roasted vegetables (directions follow)
- 1 quart regular-strength chicken broth
- 1 cup (¼ lb.) white cheddar cheese, shredded
- ¼ cup half-and-half (light cream)
- 1 teaspoon paprika

In a 4- to 5-quart pan over high heat, bring vegetables and broth to a boil; cover and simmer 10 minutes. Stirring to pan bottom, mix in cheese, a handful at a time, until melted. Add cream and paprika. Serves 4 to 6.

Per serving: 174 cal. (46 percent from fat); 8.8 g protein; 8.9 g fat (5 g sat.); 16 g carbo.; 168 mg sodium; 24 mg chol.

Roasted vegetables. Husk and remove silk of 1 large (about 10 in.) ear of **corn.** Peel 1 large (about ½ lb.) **onion** and cut in half. Trim ends from 2 medium-size (about ¼ lb. each) **leeks;** cut in half lengthwise, and rinse well. Peel 2 cloves **garlic.**

Place corn, onion, leeks, and garlic in a 10- by 15-inch pan with 1 large (½ lb.) **red bell pepper** and 2 large (3 to 3½ oz. each) **fresh Anaheim** (California or New Mexico) **chilies.** Broil 4 to 6 inches from heat until vegetables are well charred, up to 25 minutes; turn as needed. As each vegetable chars, remove from pan. Cut corn kernels from cob. Pull off and discard skins, seeds, and stems from bell pepper and chilies. Coarsely chop vegetables.

CHAR VEGETABLES *under broiler, simmer in broth; stir in cheese.*

Soba Noodle Salad

Maureen Valentine, SeaTac, Washington

- ½ pound dried soba noodles or dried capellini
- 1½ cups julienne slivers red or green bell peppers
- ½ cup thinly sliced celery
- ½ cup thinly sliced green onions
- Dressing (recipe follows)
- ½ cup roasted, salted cashews

In a 5- to 6-quart pan, bring about 3 quarts water to a boil over high heat. Add noodles and cook, uncovered, just until barely tender to bite, about 5 minutes for soba, 2 to 3 minutes for cap-

ellini. Drain noodles and rinse with cold water until cool; drain. In a serving bowl, mix noodles, bell pepper, celery, onions, and dressing; sprinkle with cashews. Serves 4.

Per serving: 332 cal. (26 percent from fat); 13 g protein; 9.6 g fat (1.8 g sat.); 55 g carbo.; 1,448 mg sodium; 0 mg chol.

Dressing. Mix together 1 teaspoon **Oriental sesame oil** and 2 tablespoons *each* **oyster sauce, soy sauce,** and **lemon juice.**

Compiled by Linda Lau Anusasananan, Paula Smith Freschet

ALICE HARTH

BUCKWHEAT NOODLES *form base for cool Asian salad with cashews.*

FOOD GUIDE

Risotto with corn, treating tomatoes right, Provence lunch, picking the right Pinots

By Jerry Anne Di Vecchio

Every summer in Kansas, before my family trekked West, we had an amazing kitchen garden. The corn, tomatoes, melons, and other foods we harvested daily made a firm imprint on my tender taste buds. My commitment to fresh foods must have been passionate, because wedged among my first memories of hot summer days is braving the prickly okra vine that towered over my 3- or 4-year-old head. I would race among the scratchy leaves to find the tiniest, tenderest okra pods, then dash through the garden sprinkler or jump into a tub of cool water to soothe the itch.

When we had a bumper crop of one thing or another, we feasted. One night it might be all the corn you could eat, another, all the tomatoes, and on it went until the garden bowed to frost.

The delicate corn risotto that Lance Dean Velasquez served last summer at Moose's Restaurant, on San Francisco's Washington Square, reminded me of those indulgent, sunny evening meals. I ordered the risotto as a starter, and the portion was generous. With the first taste, I decided this dish would be my whole meal, and as I relished the sensation of

tender sweet corn kernels popping gently with each bite, I sipped a companionable glass of Zinfandel. Corn risotto is an ideal vegetarian dish if you use Lance's vegetable broth, or you can squeak by with canned vegetable broth. I often switch to chicken broth for flavor variation and convenience.

Vegetable broth. Peel and coarsely chop 1 medium-size (½ lb.) **russet potato,** 1 large (about ½ lb.) **onion,** 1 large (about ¼ lb.) **carrot,** and 1 stalk **celery.** Put vegetables in a 3- to 4-quart pan and add 5 cups **water.** Cover and bring to a boil over high heat; simmer gently 45 minutes. Line a strainer with 2 layers of damp cheesecloth; pour liquid through cloth into a bowl. If making ahead, cover and chill up to 3 days; freeze to store longer. Makes about 4 cups.

Per cup: 38 cal. (2.3 percent from fat); 1 g protein; 0.1 g fat (0 g sat.); 8.5 g carbo.; 12 mg sodium; 0 mg chol.

BACK TO BASICS

Tips on tomatoes

If you've ever held a ripe tomato, and many haven't, you know that it has the firm softness of a baby's cheek. A ripe tomato is juicy

A TASTE OF THE WEST

Moose's Sweet Corn Risotto

2   medium-size (about 8 in. long) ears of fresh corn

2   cups finely chopped mild, sweet onion

1   to 3 teaspoons unsalted or salted butter

1   cup arborio rice or short-grain white rice (such as pearl)

4 cups fresh (directions at left) or canned vegetable broth or regular-strength chicken broth

About ¼ cup lime juice

1 or 2 tablespoons thinly sliced green onion tops or chives

Finely shaved parmesan cheese

Salt and freshly ground pepper

Husk corn, pull off silk, and rinse ears. In a shallow pan, hold ears of corn upright and, with a sharp knife, cut kernels from cobs. Then with blunt edge of the knife, scrape juice from cobs; reserve juice. Discard cobs, husks, and silk.

In a 10- to 12-inch frying pan, combine 1 cup onion, butter, and 2 tablespoons water. Stir often over medium-high heat until liq-uid has evaporated and onion is limp, about 5 min-utes. Add rice and stir often until it turns opaque, about 3 minutes. Also heat veg-etable broth to simmering; keep warm.

Add 2 tablespoons lime juice and 3 cups broth to rice. Stir often until liquid is ab-sorbed, about 10 minutes. Add 1 more cup broth, corn kernels and juice, and re-maining onion. Stir often un-til rice is tender to bite and mixture is creamy, 6 or 7 minutes.

Spoon risotto into warm, wide soup bowls; sprinkle with green onion and top with parmesan slivers. Sea-son to taste with remaining lime juice, salt, and pepper. Makes 2 servings.

Per serving: 593 cal. (5.9 percent from fat); 14 g protein; 3.9 g fat (1.5 g sat.); 129 g carbo.; 60 mg sodium; 5.2 mg chol.

to bite, the flavor is as good as it gets, and the skin is ready to slip away. But if you don't treat tomatoes properly, the memorable taste and texture of ripeness will never be yours.

Keep in mind when you pick your own tomatoes, or buy them from a farm stand or at a farmers' market, that a tomato is programmed to ripen. But its potential is often thwarted permanently by misdirected good intentions. If a tomato is refrigerated (55° or colder) before fully ripe in order to keep it "fresh," an enzyme in the tomato sends an irreversible message to the fruit to quit developing flavor. Back at room temperature, the fruit does change, and looks and feels as if it is ripening—but its texture is apt to be cottony and the taste flat. The tomato industry has campaigned long and hard to keep tomatoes out of supermarket refrigerators—and your own. But once tomatoes are ripe, you can prolong their prime state by refrigerating for a few days.

In this month of tomato abundance, some of the finer points about preparing them deserve airing:

To peel or not to peel. It's up to you, but peeling is easy and I find the skins on sliced tomatoes surprisingly tough. Immerse tomatoes in boiling water for as little as 5 or up to 15 seconds; the riper they are the less time they take. Lift out, let cool briefly, then slip off the skins.

To seed or not to seed. Seeded tomatoes don't leak as much, and if you heat them only briefly, they get less soupy. Also, some people don't like the seeds (or can't eat them). Some situations where seeded tomatoes make sense are on toast for bruschetta, in salads when you don't want the dressing diluted, in salsas that you don't want to run all over the plate, and in sauces where the tomatoes are cooked just enough to get hot. To remove seeds, cut tomatoes in half crosswise, then

gently squeeze, pressing the juice and seeds from their pockets in the tomato. The pulpy mixture tastes as good as the tomato, and I often add it to commercial plain or seasoned tomato juice (such as Bloody Mary mix) to give it a fresher flavor.

One of my favorite ways to use seeded, chopped tomatoes is on a special open-faced BLT, without the bacon.

BLT bruschetta—sort of. Toast 1 slice **whole-wheat bread,** drizzle it with **extra-virgin olive oil,** and sprinkle it with **cumin seed.** Then lay a slice of **iceberg lettuce,** about as thick as the bread, on the toast. Mound chopped seeded **tomatoes** on the lettuce, sprinkle on a few more cumin seeds, **salt and pepper,** and a wee bit more of the extra-virgin olive oil. It's a knife-and-fork sandwich that's curiously refreshing for lunch, snack, or breakfast.

GREAT TOOL

More than a toy

The first 6-inch-long wire whisk I owned came tied up with a bow as decoration

THE TINIEST WHISK *is much more than a cute accessory. You will use it often.*

on a gift. I have no memory of the gift, but the whisk has proven many times over that it is more than a trinket. Where I once resorted to a fork for mixing little dabs of this or that, I now use the tiny whisk. It does a much better job.

I use it to mix mayonnaise and lemon juice with the last dab of mustard in a Dijon jar to make a sauce for cracked crab. It smooths stiff-looking yogurt or sour cream in the carton, and it does a superb job of blending a little cornstarch or flour with water. And best of all, it's much easier to wash than a big whisk. Look for little wire whisks in the bins and baskets of cookware stores, along with nutcrackers, mushroom brushes, and citrus zesters; expect to spend about $1.50.

GREAT INGREDIENT

Mexico's panela vs. Italy's mozzarella

Mexican-style cheeses have long been made in the West by a number of small manufacturers who sell to Latino food markets. But now these cheeses are moving into the mainstream. Nine kinds are made by the Estrella Cheese Company (a division of Stella Foods Company, well known for its wedges of parmesan and romano in the dairy case).

Of particular interest is panela. Its smooth, almost squeaky texture and fresh taste make it a delicious switch from mozzarella as the cheese to serve with sliced tomatoes and basil. Panela on pizza doesn't get stringy like melted mozzarella, but stays in a soft creamy puddle.

Another Mexican-style cheese that's great for summer meals is cotija. Firm, white, and salty, it crumbles readily and is a grand alternative to parmesan in salads or sprinkled over vegetables. When heated, cotija doesn't melt; it just gets a little softer.

Two meals from one in Provence

For me, September doesn't come soon enough or last as long as it should. This is because it is spent in Provence in a big, two-centuries-old farmhouse we've rented with another family for a number of years. The rest of the time we leap at any opportunity to rave about our stay, and extend invitations to all who appear properly attentive. Through the years, the invitations have been accepted by many and dinner is always an adventure.

I cook most nights, with lots of help and good company. But once a day is enough, and we have fallen into a comfortable system by which dinner regularly rolls over into the next day's lunch. (Breakfast is on your own, at your own pace.) I relish the menu planning as much as the preparation.

One meal often requested by repeat guests starts as roasted leg of lamb, roasted garlic, roasted onions, and little boiled potatoes and tiny green beans. These ingredients, as cold leftovers, are laid out on the kitchen table about noontime the next day. Each person creates an individualized extravaganza.

There's always a basket of ripening tomatoes from the garden, and some get sliced onto plates. A few oil-cured olives from the crock on the table might be added. There's a spray of fresh thyme snipped from the doorstep. Leaves of it are crumbled over salads, and then the ingredients are moistened with a little olive oil from Nyons, just north, and balsamic vinegar. As we take our lunch outside to enjoy it in the cool shade, our talk turns to dinner once again.

Roasted onions. Cut 6 to 8 unpeeled **onions** (2½ to 3 in. wide) in half from tip to stem end. Choose a pan they almost fill, cut side down (9 by 13 in.

or 10 by 15 in.). Before you put the onions in the pan, mix in ⅓ cup **balsamic vinegar,** ¼ cup **regular-strength chicken broth,** and 4 teaspoons **sugar.** Put onions, cut side down, in liquid. Bake in a 450° oven until liquid has evaporated and drippings around edges are beginning to brown, 20 to 30 minutes (keep an eye on them when liquid is almost gone to avoid scorching). Add about ¼ cup more regular-strength chicken broth or water to pan. Gently shake to loosen browned drippings, and stir to free those at edges. Bake until onions give when pressed, 20 to 30 minutes more, and until pan is dry again. Remove from oven and add 2 or 3 tablespoons water to pan, tilting to moisten it. Let onions stand at least 10 minutes to soak up juices before serving; serve hot or at room temperature. To keep until next day, cover and let stand at room temperature. Salt to taste. Makes 6 to 8 servings.

Per ½ onion: 59 cal. (3 percent from fat); 1.5 g protein; 0.2 g fat (0 g sat.); 13 g carbo.; 6 mg sodium; 0 mg chol.

A DINNER OF ROASTED LEG OF LAMB *can easily become the next day's lunch with a little planning and very little effort.*

BOB THOMPSON ON WINE

Personable Pinot Noirs

Pork tenderloin with apples in cream sauce and a ripe Pinot Noir could make a movie fan decide to skip a night at the theater. Roasted quail and a soft, smoky Pinot Noir could have the same effect. And coq au vin and the most velvety of Pinot Noirs could lead a romantic to sacrifice one last chance to see the restored print of *Gone With the Wind*.

To put it more plainly, where Cabernet Sauvignon stimulates the intellect, Pinot Noir caresses the senses.

On its own, ripe Pinot Noir tends to taste something like-

black cherries left on the tree until they begin to soften. Ripe Pinot Noir aged in lightly charred oak barrels can develop flavors so rich they call to mind tender, juicy beef sooner than they do fruit. Naturally low tannins add a velvety texture not so different from that of tender beef. Together, these riches make Pinot Noirs perfect foils for grainy-meated game birds, lean pork, and lean beef.

There is a catch. Pinot Noir has to be on its best behavior to deliver such goods. The French learned long ago in Burgundy that Pinot Noir gives gratifying wines only when the vines grow within a narrow range of soils and slopes and weathers. Only in the last decade or so have

American growers found sites where Pinot Noir begins to live up to its Burgundian heritage.

In northern California, a great majority of them are in sea-fogged coastal valleys, especially the Russian River Valley, Anderson Valley, and Carneros. In Oregon, the northern half of the Willamette Valley is the place.

Most of the wines that play rich flavors against richer textures come from small, hard-to-tend vineyards, fair warning that their price tags are not modest and supplies of any one wine are scarce. At $14 to $32 a bottle, these are exemplary Californians: Gary Farrell Russian River Valley "Allen Vineyard," Dehlinger Russian River Valley Estate

Bottled, Acacia Carneros "St. Clair Vineyard," Husch Anderson Valley Estate Bottled, Au Bon Climat Santa Barbara County "La Bauge Audessus," and Byron Santa Barbara County Estate Reserve.

Two Oregon counterparts in the same price range: Adelsheim Yamhill County Elizabeth's Reserve and Bethel Heights Willamette Valley.

Some modestly priced Pinot Noirs—$7 to $10 a bottle—show enough succulence to satisfy: Chateau De Baun Russian River Valley, Seghesio Russian River Valley, Saintsbury Carneros "Garnet," Carneros Creek "Fleur de Carneros," and Pepperwood Springs Anderson Valley "Pepperwood Cuvée." ■

More than just a pretty bottle

Flavored vinegars add zip to late-summer cooking

T ODAY'S GOURMET vinegars might seem better suited to a still life than to a green salad. With gleaming sprigs of herbs and flowers suspended behind watery windows of glass, they're almost too beautiful to open. And like other works of art, the price can be dear. But these condiments are too good—and useful—to be only decorative.

Painted on grilled meats, drizzled onto fresh fruit, even splashed into sparkling water, flavored vinegars add pizzazz and nearly no calories to quick, casual meals.

Most start with white wine vinegar as the base. The added seasonings that flavor, and sometimes tint, the vinegar run the gamut from berries and citrus to herbs, lemon grass, chilies, and garlic. Some fruit vinegars also have sugar or juice added; these are especially good with fish, poultry, and fruit.

Because the level of flavor varies greatly from brand to brand, you'll want to experiment to find ones that suit you. Boldly flavored vinegars stand on their own to season a dish. More subtle vinegars make a good background canvas; with these, you may want to offer additional vinegar at the table for seasoning.

In the recipes that follow, let the artist in you—or the contents of your cupboard— decide which vinegar to try.

Beef, Fennel, and Arugula with Garlic Vinegar

Olives labeled "cracked" are easier to pit. To pit cracked olives, place flat side of a large knife blade over 1 olive at a time and hit with fist. Pull loosened meat from pits. You can use regular olives, but you must cut meat from pits.

  1 large (about 1¼ lb.) bulb fennel

  1 pound New York (top loin) steak

  6 tablespoons garlic, onion, or herb vinegar

  1 tablespoon minced fresh garlic

  3 tablespoons extra-virgin olive oil

  1½ quarts (about ⅓ lb.) arugula leaves (any tough stems removed), rinsed and crisped

  1 cup pitted, cracked or uncracked green olives

  Salt and pepper

START WITH GREAT vinegars (shown from left): raspberry, oregano with flowers, blueberry, carrot, garlic-chili, lime, rosemary-chili, or mixed herbs. Use to enliven (from left) a raspberry cooler, grilled beef and arugula salad, and ripe multicolored tomatoes.

DEBORAH JONES

DEBORAH JONES

ACCENTUATE *the succulence of summer fruits with sweet-tart raspberry vinegar.*

Trim root end of fennel; cut off and discard leaves and stems. Halve bulb vertically. Very thinly slice crosswise into strips ⅛ inch by 3 inches.

Trim and discard fat from steak; cut across the grain in ¼-inch-thick strips. In a bowl, mix meat with 3 tablespoons vinegar, garlic, and 1 teaspoon oil. Separately, combine remaining vinegar and oil. Place arugula and fennel in a shallow serving dish.

Place meat on a greased grill over a solid bed of hot coals (you can hold your hand at grill level about 3 seconds). Cook, turning once, until done to your liking, 3 to 4 minutes for medium-rare.

Arrange meat and olives with greens. Drizzle with vinegar mixture and add salt and pepper to taste. Toss gently to serve. Serves 4.

Per serving: 335 cal. (62 percent from fat); 27 g protein; 23 g fat (5 g sat.); 5.8 g carbo.; 1,003 mg sodium; 65 mg chol.

Grilled Fish with Fruit and Citrus Vinegar

1½ pounds (1 in. thick) Pacific halibut, sturgeon, or swordfish

1 tablespoon salad oil

1 cup chopped ripe mango

1 cup rinsed, drained blackberries

2 tablespoons chopped fresh cilantro (coriander)

About 1 cup grapefruit, other citrus, or chili vinegar

Salt and pepper

Rub fish with oil. Place on a greased grill over a solid bed of medium-hot coals (you can hold your hand at grill level 4 to 5 seconds). Turn occasionally until fish is no longer translucent in center (cut to check), about 10 minutes.

Place fish on 4 plates. Top with mango, blackberries,

cilantro, and half of the vinegar. Season with salt, pepper, and remaining vinegar to taste. Serves 4.

Per serving: 271 cal. (25 percent from fat); 36 g protein; 7.5 g fat (1 g sat.); 14 g carbo.; 93 mg sodium; 54 mg chol.

Zingy Fruit Cooler

Stir 2 tablespoons **berry** or citrus **vinegar** and 2 teaspoons **sugar** until sugar dissolves. Pour 1½ cups cold **sparkling water** into a 16- to 20-ounce glass, then pour in vinegar syrup and add **ice cubes.** Serves 1.

Per serving: 36 cal. (0 percent from fat); 0 g protein; 0 g fat (0 g sat.); 9.3 g carbo.; 0.1 mg sodium; 0 mg chol.

Fruit with a Splash

Cut a 4-pound **honeydew melon** into 6 wedges; remove seeds. Rinse and halve 9 ripe **figs.** Rinse and drain 1 cup **raspberries.** Arrange fruit on 6 dessert plates. Pour ½ cup **berry** or citrus **vinegar** over top, equally distributing among 6 plates. If desired, add **powdered sugar** and up to ½ cup more vinegar to taste. Serves 6.

Per serving: 120 cal. (3.8 percent from fat); 1.4 g protein; 0.5 g fat (0 g sat.); 31 g carbo.; 15 mg sodium; 0 mg chol.

Grilled Vegetables Provençal

¾ pound 2-inch-diameter thin-skinned potatoes

2 large (about 1½ lb. total) red bell peppers

6 medium-size (about ¾ lb. total) yellow or green pattypan squash

2 medium-size (about 1 lb. total) onions

3 tablespoons extra-virgin olive oil

¼ cup finely shredded parmesan cheese

¼ cup fresh basil shreds, thinly sliced crosswise

Fresh basil sprigs

½ cup herb, onion, or garlic vinegar

Salt and pepper

Halve potatoes. Place in a 2-quart pan; cover with water. Simmer, covered, until just tender when pierced, about 8 minutes; drain.

Stem and seed peppers; cut each lengthwise into sixths. Halve squash horizontally. Cut onions crosswise into ½-inch rounds. Divide all vegetables between 2 large bowls. Drizzle oil equally over each; mix to coat.

Place vegetables (part at a time, if necessary) on a greased grill over a solid bed of medium-hot coals (you can hold your hand at grill level 4 to 5 seconds). Cook, turning often, until all are streaked brown, 10 to 12 minutes.

Arrange on platter. Scatter cheese and basil on top; garnish with basil sprigs. Pour vinegar on top; season with salt and pepper. Serves 6.

Per serving: 190 cal. (40 percent from fat); 4.9 g protein; 8.5 g fat (1.7 g sat.); 26 g carbo.; 71 mg sodium; 2.6 mg chol.

Chili Eggplant and Corn

6 medium-size (about 1 lb. total) Asian eggplant

2 large ears (about 1 lb. total) yellow corn

3 tablespoons extra-virgin olive oil

About ½ cup chili, onion, garlic, or lemon grass vinegar, or a combination

2 tablespoons minced fresh parsley or fresh cilantro (coriander)

Salt and pepper

Halve eggplant lengthwise from base to within ½ inch of stem; press pieces to flatten and spread apart. Remove husks and silk from corn; cut into 1- to 1½-inch rounds. Rub corn and the cut surfaces of eggplant with oil.

Place vegetables on a greased grill over a solid bed of medium-hot coals (you can hold your hand at grill level 4 to 5 seconds). Cook, turning often, until eggplant are tender when pressed (8 to 10 minutes) and corn ears are golden, 10 to 12 minutes.

Lift to a platter. Pour half of vinegar on top. Sprinkle with parsley; add salt, pepper, and remaining vinegar to taste. Serves 4.

Per serving: 159 cal. (62 percent from fat); 2.6 g protein; 11 g fat (1.7 g sat.); 16 g carbo.; 11 mg sodium; 0 mg chol. ∎

By Elaine Johnson

PAUL HAMMOND

SPINACH, *chicken, and tomato salad with pesto dressing cascades over mozzarella pizza.*

Salad
on a crust

Pizza-inspired—cold on top, warm beneath

T HE PLAYFUL contrast of temperature and texture— cool salad on a hot crust—adds yet another dimension to popular pizza. Heat-softened cheese on the crust unifies the combination.

The shortcut crusts, made with frozen bread dough, are toasted in a dry pan. Although they cook quickly, you can make them ahead and reheat.

Salad pizza is a fresh approach to a casual meal on a warm day. You have two salad choices: chicken with spinach and tomatoes, or shrimp with avocado, artichoke hearts, and prosciutto.

Chicken Salad Pizza

2 cups bite-size pieces skinned cooked chicken or turkey

1½ pounds firm-ripe Roma-type tomatoes, rinsed, cored, and chopped

2 cups firmly packed (about 3 oz.) rinsed and drained spinach leaves, cut into fine slivers

⅓ cup prepared pesto sauce

2 tablespoons seasoned rice vinegar (or 2 tablespoons rice vinegar with ½ teaspoon sugar)

Frying pan pizza crusts (recipe follows)

¼ to ½ pound mozzarella cheese, thinly sliced

Salt

In a bowl, mix chicken, tomatoes, spinach, pesto, and vinegar. If making ahead, cover and chill up to 2 hours.

Place crusts, warm or cool, in a single layer on a 12- by 15-inch baking sheet. Cover equally with the cheese and heat in a 350° oven until hot, 5 to 10 minutes. Place crusts on dinner plates; using a slotted spoon, top crusts equally with chicken mixture. Add salt to taste. Makes 4 servings.

Per serving: 660 cal. (37 percent from fat); 37 g protein; 27 g fat (4.7 g sat.); 66 g carbo; 926 mg sodium; 91 mg chol.

Frying pan pizza crusts. Thaw 1 loaf (1 lb.) **frozen white** or whole-wheat **bread dough** and divide into 4 equal pieces. On a floured board, roll each piece into a 7- to 8-inch round. As rolled, cover with plastic wrap to prevent drying.

Place an 8- to 10-inch nonstick frying pan over medium-high heat. When pan is hot, add 1 dough round (or use 2 frying pans, simultaneously). Cook dough until bottom side looks dry and is covered with large brown spots, about 4 minutes. Turn bread over and cook until bottom is browned, 2 or 3 more minutes. If bread puffs, pierce bulges to release steam and gently press flat with a spatula. Use crusts as cooked, or transfer to a 10- by 15-inch pan and keep warm in a 300° oven up to 10 minutes. To make ahead, let crusts cool on racks, store airtight at room temperature up to 1 day. Makes 4.

Shrimp and Avocado Salad Pizza

3 ounces very thinly sliced prosciutto, finely chopped

1 jar (6 oz.) marinated artichoke hearts

½ pound shelled cooked tiny shrimp

4 green onions, ends trimmed, chopped

3 tablespoons lemon juice

Frying pan pizza crusts (recipe precedes)

¼ pound crumbled feta cheese

1 medium-size (about ½ lb.) firm-ripe avocado

In an 8- to 10-inch nonstick frying pan over medium-high heat, stir prosciutto often until browned and crisp, 7 or 8 minutes. Drain meat on paper towels.

Drain artichokes and pour 1 tablespoon marinade into a bowl. Cut artichokes in ½ and put in bowl. Add shrimp, onions, and 2 tablespoons lemon juice; mix. If making ahead, cover and chill up to 2 hours.

Place crusts, warm or cool, in a single layer on a 12- by 15-inch baking sheet. Cover equally with the prosciutto and cheese and heat in a 350° oven until hot, 5 to 10 minutes.

Meanwhile, peel, pit, and cut avocado lengthwise into 12 slices. Sprinkle slices with remaining lemon juice. Place warm crusts on dinner plates and top equally with artichoke mixture and avocado slices. Makes 4 servings.

Per serving: 599 cal. (38 percent from fat); 33 g protein; 25 g fat (7.9 g sat.); 63 g carbo; 1,612 mg sodium; 159 mg chol. ∎

By Christine Weber Hale

DEBORAH JONES

JUICY PEACHES *and honeydew in tiny cubes, sparked by mint, tarragon, lemon, and rice vinegar, become a new-wave salsa for grilled fish.*

Salsa redefined

Exploring flavors or combinations beyond tomatoes and chilies

W ESTERNERS' LOVE affair with salsa has redefined this lively condiment. The classic tomato-based salsa has evolved to encompass a veritable free-for-all of fruit and vegetable combinations. Fruit salsas, in particular, have grown in popularity. The sweetness of fruit paired with piquant-hot seasonings makes these salsas especially refreshing with grilled chicken, fish, and meats. They even shine when used the old-fashioned way—scooped onto chips for snacking.

Tropical Fruit Salsa

- 1 cup ¼-inch-dice peeled pineapple
- ¾ cup ¼-inch-dice firm-ripe peeled papaya
- ½ cup ¼-inch-dice firm-ripe peeled mango
- ½ cup ¼-inch-dice red bell pepper
- 3 tablespoons minced crystallized ginger
- 2 tablespoons minced green onion
- 2 tablespoons lime juice
  Salt

In a bowl, gently mix together pineapple, papaya, mango, bell pepper, ginger, onion, and lime juice, and add salt to taste.

Serve salsa, or if making ahead, cover and chill up to 2 hours. Makes about 3 cups.

Per ½ cup: 60 cal. (3 percent from fat); 0.4 g protein; 0.2 g fat (0 g sat.); 15 g carbo.; 7.2 mg sodium; 0 mg chol.

Watermelon Salsa

- 2 cups ¼-inch-dice seeded red or yellow watermelon
- 1 cup ¼-inch-dice peeled jicama
- 1 fresh jalapeño chili, stemmed, seeded, and minced
- 2 tablespoons minced fresh cilantro (coriander)
- 3 tablespoons lime juice
  Salt

In a bowl, gently mix together watermelon, jicama, jalapeño, cilantro, and lime juice, and add salt to taste.

Serve salsa, or if making ahead, cover and chill up to 2 hours. Makes about 3 cups.

Per ½ cup: 28 cal. (9.6 percent from fat); 0.7 g protein; 0.3 g fat (0 g sat.); 6.3 g carbo.; 3.8 mg sodium; 0 mg chol.

Peach and Honeydew Salsa

- 1½ cups ¼-inch-dice honeydew melon
- 1½ cups ¼-inch-dice peeled firm-ripe peaches
- 2 tablespoons seasoned rice vinegar (or 2 tablespoons rice vinegar with ½ teaspoon sugar)
- 2 tablespoons minced fresh mint leaves
- 1 tablespoon lemon juice
- 1 tablespoon minced fresh or ½ teaspoon dried tarragon leaves
  Salt

In a bowl, gently mix together melon, peaches, vinegar, mint, lemon juice, and tarragon; add salt to taste.

Serve salsa, or if making ahead, cover and chill up to 2 hours. Makes about 3 cups.

Per ½ cup: 38 cal. (2.4 percent from fat); 0.5 g protein; 0.1 g fat (0 g sat.); 9.9 g carbo.; 104 mg sodium; 0 mg chol.

Bold Berry Salsa

- 2 cups raspberries, rinsed and drained
- 1 small (about ½ lb.) firm-ripe Bartlett pear, peeled and cut into ¼-inch dice
- ½ pound figs (about 4 large), peeled and cut into ¼-inch dice
- 3 tablespoons raspberry vinegar
- ¼ to ½ teaspoon pepper
  Salt

In a bowl, gently mix together raspberries, pear, figs, vinegar, and pepper, and add salt to taste.

Serve salsa, or if making ahead, cover and chill up to 2 hours. Makes about 3 cups.

Per ½ cup: 69 cal. (6.5 percent from fat); 0.8 g protein; 0.5 g fat (0 g sat.); 17 g carbo.; 0.4 mg sodium; 0 mg chol. ∎

By Christine Weber Hale

ESCAROLE, *tinged with a bite of bitterness, and earthy mushrooms tumble over linguine.*

Fabulously fast pasta

Few ingredients, fresh flavors add up to quick meals

LESS IS MORE IN THESE simple pasta main-dish combinations. They require just a few key ingredients and take little time to cook, both pluses on busy weeknights. However, the sophisticated Italian spareness of these dishes makes them fine enough to share with guests.

Linguine with Escarole

2   tablespoons olive oil

½   pound mushrooms (1 kind or a combination of common, porcini, shiitake, portabella, chanterelle), rinsed well and sliced

1   clove garlic, pressed or minced

¼   teaspoon crushed dried hot red chilies

¾   cup regular-strength chicken broth

½   pound dried linguine

¾   pound escarole, rinsed and cut in ¼-inch shreds

Grated parmesan cheese

Salt

In a 10- to 12-inch frying pan, combine oil, mushrooms, and garlic. Stir often over high heat until mushrooms lightly brown, about 8 minutes. Add chilies and broth and bring to a boil. Set aside, but keep warm.

Meanwhile, in a 5- to 6-quart pan, bring about 3 quarts water to a boil over high heat. Add linguine and cook until barely tender to bite, 7 to 9 minutes.

When pasta is done, stir escarole into boiling water. Drain pasta and escarole well and pour into a large bowl. Add mushroom mixture and mix. Spoon pasta onto warm plates; add cheese and salt to taste. Serves 2.

Per serving: 612 cal. (25 percent from fat); 20 g protein; 17 g fat (2.4 g sat.); 97 g carbo.; 70 mg sodium; 0 mg chol.

Ricotta Spaghetti

1   pound dried spaghetti

1   cup (8 oz.) ricotta cheese

⅓   cup (3 oz.) mascarpone cheese or cream cheese

2   cups regular-strength chicken or vegetable broth

Grated parmesan or pecorino cheese

½   cup thinly sliced chives

Salt and freshly ground pepper

In a 5- to 6-quart pan, bring about 3 quarts water to a boil over high heat. Add spaghetti and cook until barely tender to bite, about 7 minutes.

When pasta is done, pour into a colander to drain well. At once, add to pasta pan the ricotta and mascarpone; stir over medium heat until well mixed. With a whisk, stir broth into cheese. Stir until simmering. Ladle about 3 tablespoons of the hot mixture into each of 4 warm, wide, shallow bowls.

Return drained pasta to pan with sauce. Mix well with 2 forks, lifting to separate pasta strands. Serve pasta in bowls; sprinkle with parmesan and chives. Add salt and pepper to taste. Serves 4.

Per serving: 632 cal. (28 percent from fat); 23 g protein; 20 g fat (5.2 g sat.); 88 g carbo.; 95 mg sodium; 58 mg chol. ∎

By Linda Lau Anusasananan

Today's pig is raised with breeding

And Thai pai is made with apples

WE IMPUTE TO FARM ANIMALS human virtues and vices: the strong and patient ox, the cowardly chicken, the angry bull, the innocent lamb. But alas, the poor pig—we brand him as dirty, greedy, selfish, and deplorably deficient in muscle tone. In fact, pork is a synonym for government contracts awarded as political favors. (The old-fashioned pork barrel was just that—a barrel in which fresh pork was preserved for the winter by immersing it in lard.) Yesterday's pig was indeed likely to be fat; lard was more widely used then than now, and 1,000-pound pigs were not unknown.

Today's pig is raised in clean surroundings and is leaner than its slovenly ancestors, the result of breeding for meat quality rather than size. The pig is also coming to the market at a younger age, so its meat is leaner.

Katherine Logan pushes this quality to the ultimate, by sautéing tenderloin cutlets with only a brush stroke of oil and making the sauce with a fat-free nondairy creamer. If we hadn't told you about her spartan approach, you probably wouldn't guess from the taste. Diehards can substitute cream in the recipe.

Pork Tenderloin Cutlets with Mustard Cream

2   pork tenderloins (each ¾ to 1 lb.), fat trimmed

About ½ teaspoon salad oil

1   pound mushrooms, rinsed and sliced thinly

2   tablespoons minced shallots or green onion

3   cloves garlic, minced or pressed

2   tablespoons balsamic vinegar

½   cup liquid nonfat, nondairy creamer or whipping cream

3   tablespoons Dijon mustard

1   teaspoon Worcestershire

½   teaspoon dried rubbed sage leaves

1   tablespoon lemon juice

¼   teaspoon sugar

About ¼ cup minced chives or green onion tops

Salt and pepper

Cut tenderloins across the grain into 1-inch-thick slices. Place pieces of meat well apart between sheets of plastic wrap. Pound firmly and gently with a flat mallet until meat is evenly about ¼ inch thick; if making ahead, roll up meat in plastic wrap and seal in a plastic bag. Chill up to 1 day.

Rub bottom of a nonstick 10- to 12-inch frying pan with a light coating of oil. Place pan over medium-high heat; add mushrooms, shallots, garlic, and vinegar; stir often until mushroom liquid evaporates and slices begin to brown lightly, 10 to 12 minutes. Pour from pan into a container and keep warm.

Rub pan bottom lightly with more oil and place over high heat. When pan is hot, fill with some of the pork (do not crowd). Turn pieces just as edges turn white; cook until no longer pink in center (cut to test), about 1½ to 2 minutes total. As cooked, transfer pork to container with mushrooms. Repeat until all the pork is cooked.

To pan, add the creamer, mustard, Worcestershire, sage, lemon juice, and sugar. Stir over high heat until boiling vigorously; drain any liquid from pork and mushrooms into pan and return to a boil. Remove sauce from heat. Quickly arrange on warm dinner plates equal portions of the meat with mushrooms on top. Pour sauce over servings and sprinkle with chives. Season to taste with salt and pepper. Serves 6 to 8.

Per serving: 141 cal. (24 percent from fat); 19 g protein; 3.8 g fat (1 g sat.); 5.6 g carbo.; 226 mg sodium; 55 mg chol.

Katherine Logan

Corona del Mar, California

CHEFS DO NOT OFTEN SUBMIT dessert recipes, but Arthur R. Vinsel, a frequent and fearless contributor, dares to tamper with that American classic, apple pie. He calls his version Surfside Fats' Thai Apple Pai, and it is unlikely that Mom ever made it. What makes it Thai? Fresh ginger and lime juice.

Surfside Fats' Thai Apple Pai

5 large (about 2½ lb. total) Granny Smith apples, peeled, cored, and sliced ¼ inch thick

1 cup granulated sugar

3 tablespoons firmly packed brown sugar

¾ teaspoon minced fresh ginger

6 tablespoons lime juice

¾ cup all-purpose flour

¾ teaspoon ground cinnamon

¼ teaspoon pepper

3 tablespoons butter or margarine

Coconut or vanilla ice cream (optional)

In a 9-inch square pan, mix apples with ⅓ cup granulated sugar, the brown sugar, ginger, and lime juice. Shake pan to level fruit.

In a small bowl, rub together remaining granulated sugar, flour, cinnamon, pepper, and butter to form fine crumbs, then squeeze into lumps and scatter evenly over apple mixture.

Bake in a 375° oven until apples are tender when pierced and topping is golden brown, 50 to 55 minutes. Serve hot or cool, spooned into bowls and topped with ice cream. Makes 6 to 8 servings.

Per serving: 269 cal. (16 percent from fat); 1.5 g protein; 4.8 g fat (2.8 g sat.); 58 g carbo.; 48 mg sodium; 12 mg chol.

Arthur R. Vinsel

San Pedro, California

By Joan Griffiths, Richard Dunmire

Argentina's steek sauce

ASK AN ARGENTINE WHAT'S good with steak, and you'll hear about *chimichurri*. The zesty mixture of herbs, garlic, and olive oil makes an excellent basting and table sauce. Most Argentines use chimichurri with a mixed grill that reads like a butcher's inventory: beef short ribs, skirt steak, filet mignon, chorizo, Italian and blood sausage, sweetbreads, and tripe. Sylvina Bonvehi, an Argentine living in California, also suggests the sauce with chicken, fish, and baguettes.

To prevent flare-ups when barbecuing, baste meat or fish with the sauce only at the last minute.

Chimichurri Sauce

1 cup minced parsley

½ cup extra-virgin olive oil

¼ cup minced fresh or 1 tablespoon dried oregano leaves

3 tablespoons white wine vinegar

1 tablespoon minced garlic

¼ teaspoon crushed dried hot red chilies

Salt

In a container, mix parsley, oil, oregano, vinegar, garlic, and chilies. Use, or chill up to 3 days; use at room temperature. Add salt to taste. Makes 1 cup, enough to baste and serve with 1½ pounds meat.—*Sylvina Bonvehi, Van Nuys, California*

Per tablespoon: 63 cal. (100 percent from fat); 0.1 g protein; 7 g fat (1 g sat.); 0.7 g carbo.; 1.6 mg sodium; 0 mg chol. ■

By Elaine Johnson

NORMAN A. PLATE

PESTO LOOK-ALIKE *gets its color from parsley and oregano.*

NORMAN A. PLATE

BURGUNDY-COLORED *catsup? It is if you start with berries.*

A new flavor for catsup

CATSUP, IN THE HANDS OF Harolyn Thompson, rises well above tomatoes. Inspired by the abundance of wild blackberries that grow near her home in St. Helena, California, she created a new version of this popular condiment. It's tart-sweet and slightly hot, and clings well when splashed onto grilled pork, lamb, poultry, and even fish.

Blackberry Catsup

8 cups blackberries, rinsed and drained

1¾ cups red wine vinegar

1 cup firmly packed brown sugar

1 cup granulated sugar

2 teaspoons ground cinnamon

1½ teaspoons ground allspice

1 teaspoon ground ginger

½ teaspoon pepper

¼ teaspoon cayenne

In a 4- to 5-quart pan, stir berries often over medium-high heat until they get juicy and begin to fall apart, about 10 minutes. Rub berries and juice through a fine strainer into a bowl; discard seeds. Return berry juice to pan and add vinegar, brown sugar, granulated sugar, cinnamon, allspice, ginger, pepper, and cayenne. Bring mixture to a boil over high heat; simmer gently, uncovered and stirring often, until berry catsup is reduced to 2½ cups, about 1 hour.

Cool catsup and serve, or chill airtight up to 2 weeks; freeze to store longer. Makes about 2½ cups.

Per tablespoon: 57 cal. (1.6 percent from fat); 0.2 g protein; 0.1 g fat (0 g sat.); 15 g carbo.; 2.3 mg sodium; 0 mg chol. ■

By Christine Weber Hale

SWIRLS OF RASPBERRY *purée make a striking pattern in golden watermelon soup. With a garnish of prosciutto, the soup becomes a first course; without it, consider for dessert.*

much more subtle.

If you omit the prosciutto, you can serve the soup as dessert.

Yellow Watermelon Soup

    3 ounces very thinly sliced
       prosciutto
    1 medium-size (7 to 8 lb.)
       yellow-flesh
       watermelon, chilled
    1 cup raspberries, chilled
    ¼ cup minced fresh mint
       leaves

Cut prosciutto into very thin shreds. Place shreds in an 8- to 10-inch nonstick frying pan over medium-high heat. Stir often until prosciutto is browned and crisp, about 10 minutes. Drain on paper towels until cool.

Cut watermelon into pieces. Trim off rind and discard with seeds. In batches, purée watermelon flesh in a blender or food processor. Pour purée into a large bowl. If making ahead, cover and chill up to 1 day; stir to mix before using.

Rinse berries, drain, then purée in a blender or food processor. Rub purée through a fine strainer into a bowl. Discard raspberry seeds. If making ahead, cover and chill up to 1 day.

Pour melon purée equally into 6 to 8 wide soup bowls. With a small spoon, dollop raspberry purée into bowls, spacing drops well apart and adding equal amounts to each portion. With the tip of a skewer or small knife, pull through raspberry dots, drawing them out into swirls through yellow melon purée. Sprinkle prosciutto and mint equally onto soups. Makes 8 cups, 6 to 8 servings.

Per serving: 98 cal. (23 percent from fat); 4.4 g protein; 2.5 g fat (0.4 g sat.); 17 g carbo.; 201 mg sodium; 8.6 mg chol. ∎

By Christine Weber Hale

Striking gold in minutes

Make-ahead soup has only four ingredients

BRIGHTLY HUED, COOL, and refreshing, this yellow-flesh watermelon soup is an eye-catching way to start a summer meal.

With only four ingredients, preparation could hardly be easier. Purée watermelon in a blender or food processor, then chill. Do the same with raspberries. When you swirl dots of raspberry purée through bowlfuls of the melon, the presentation is much more impressive than the effort. Garnish with aromatic mint and sprinkle with bits of crisp, browned prosciutto; its saltiness is a sophisticated contrast to the melon and berries.

Red watermelon can be used if yellow is unavailable. The soup flavors will be the same but the color contrasts

Creative ways with everyday foods—submitted by *Sunset* readers,
tested in *Sunset* kitchens, approved by *Sunset* taste panels

Pear Crumble Pie

Cynthia Biondi, Jacksonville, Oregon

    4   medium-size (about 2 lb. total)
        firm-ripe Bartlett pears
    1   cup nonfat sour cream
    1   large egg, slightly beaten
    ½   cup sugar
    2   tablespoons all-purpose flour
    1   teaspoon vanilla
    ½   teaspoon *each* ground cinnamon
        and ground nutmeg
    1   unbaked 9-inch pie shell
        Crumble topping (recipe follows)

Peel and core pears; cut into ¼-inch slices. In a bowl, combine pears, sour cream, egg, sugar, flour, vanilla, cinnamon, and nutmeg. Spoon pear mixture into pie shell. Bake in a 375° oven until filling is thick and bubbling, about 40 minutes.

Evenly distribute crumble topping over filling. Continue baking until topping is golden brown (if crust edge is getting too brown, cover with foil), about 20 minutes more. Serve cool or chill until next day. Makes 6 to 8 servings.

Crumble topping. Combine ½ cup **all-purpose flour**, ⅓ cup **sugar**, 3 tablespoons **butter** or margarine, and ½ teaspoon **ground cinnamon**. Rub mixture with fingers until large crumbs form.

Per serving: 362 cal. (32 percent from fat); 5.6 g protein; 13 g fat (4.8 g sat.); 57 g carbo.; 189 mg sodium; 38 mg chol.

SWEET-SPICY CINNAMON CRUMBLE *tops a Bartlett pear–cream pie.*

New Mexican Chili Bean Salad

Jane E. Cook, Albuquerque

    1   can (15 to 17 oz.) *each* garbanzos,
        kidney beans, pinto beans, and
        whole-kernel corn
    ½   cup chopped green onion
    ⅓   cup chopped fresh cilantro
        (coriander) leaves
    1   large (about 8 oz.) red bell pepper,
        stemmed, seeded, and coarsely
        chopped
    1   can (4 oz.) diced green chilies
        New Mexican dressing (recipe
        follows)

In a colander, rinse garbanzos, kidney beans, pinto beans, and corn; drain well. Mix bean and corn mixture with green onion, cilantro, red bell pepper, green chilies, and New Mexican dressing. Cover and chill at least 1 hour or until the next day, stirring occasionally. Makes 8 cups, about ½ cup per serving.

Per serving: 95 cal. (25 percent from fat); 4.2 g protein; 2.6 g fat (0.3 g sat.); 15 g carbo.; 223 mg sodium; 0 mg chol.

New Mexican dressing. Combine ¼ cup **red wine vinegar**, 2 tablespoons **salad oil**, ¼ teaspoon **pepper**, and 1 teaspoon *each* **chili powder, dried oregano leaves,** and **ground cumin.**

CILANTRO AND RED BELL PEPPER *accent Southwestern bean salad.*

Pacific Pizza

Randall Francisco, Honolulu

    1   tablespoon olive oil
    2   teaspoons hot curry powder
    1   large (1 lb.) baked Italian bread
        shell
    2   cups (6 to 8 oz.) lightly packed
        shredded mozzarella cheese
    ⅓   cup *each* chopped fresh cilantro
        (coriander) and fresh basil
        leaves
    ¼   pound smoked salmon or trout, cut
        into about ¼-inch-wide strips
    1   cup (about 3 oz.) enoki mush-
        rooms, root ends trimmed

Combine olive oil and hot curry powder. Place bread shell on a 12- by 15-inch baking sheet; spread curry mixture over crust. Sprinkle mozzarella cheese, then cilantro and basil leaves, evenly over crust. Top with salmon pieces and enoki mushrooms.

Bake pizza in a 400° oven until hot throughout and cheese bubbles, about 12 minutes. Cut into wedges and serve. Makes 4 servings.

Per serving: 497 cal. (38 percent from fat); 28 g protein; 21 g fat (6.3 g sat.); 53 g carbo.; 1,005 mg sodium; 45 mg chol.

Compiled by Betsy Reynolds Bateson

ALICE HARTH

A QUICK PIZZA *features smoked salmon, enoki mushrooms, and curry seasoning.*

FOOD GUIDE

Savor pomegranates and persimmons, put bones to work, and the right wines with oysters

By Jerry Anne Di Vecchio

O
ne of my favorite paintings is a watercolor on my living room wall by Phoebe Ellsworth—of a bowlful of red pomegranates, showing their crown-shaped bud ends. If there were wall space, I also would have an oil of gleaming orange gold persimmons by Judith Gaulke that captured my fancy at one of her recent shows.

But real fruit moves in every fall, as I set out bowls or trays of it to admire. This is a routine I borrowed from Helen Evans Brown. Helen wrote many cookbooks, including her pioneering, and still timely, *California Cooks;* she also wrote *Sunset*'s Adventures in Food column until her death in the early 1960s. Annually, she mounded persimmons in a big blue and white Chinese bowl and, until the season ended, replenished the fruit as it softened. Although not a fan of raw persimmons, she did cook with them.

In those days, if you bit into a big, beautiful, firm persimmon, it was most likely a pointed-tip Hachiya (which once dominated the market and home gardens), and you were in for a shock. Unless this variety is jelly-soft ripe, it's as astringent as a bar of soap. Now the flat-bottom Fuyu persimmon is widely available, and it's wonderfully sweet while still firm and crisp, and good when soft, too.

Pomegranates can hang around forever. Their red to russet, leathery hide is so tough that the fruit doesn't rot—the interior just dries up. But as long as the skin is still taut and flexible enough to pull free, the shining seeds inside are like a heap of glowing rubies. The tart, transparent red flesh around each seed is very juicy. Getting at the seed is a messy, staining chore if you don't break pomegranates apart under water and work the seed free. Directions for doing this are at right. Use pomegranate seed in this refreshing refrigerator tart inspired by a recipe from Mary E. Pang of Ripon, California.

BACK TO BASICS

Bones make magic

I save bones—raw, cooked, carved from roasts, chops, shanks, and birds—and stow them in the freezer. I do it because I have discovered the treasure that bones yield—

A TASTE OF THE WEST

Pomegranate Tart

- ¾ cup sugar
- 2 envelopes (4 teaspoons total) unflavored gelatin
- 2 cups unflavored nonfat yogurt
- ½ cup regular or reduced-fat sour cream
- 1 teaspoon grated orange peel
- ½ teaspoon grated lemon peel
- 3 tablespoons lemon juice
- 1 teaspoon vanilla
  Cookie crust (recipe follows)
- 1 small package (3 oz.) raspberry-flavor gelatin dessert
- 2 cups raspberry-cranberry juice blend
  Pomegranate seed (directions follow)

In a 1- to 1½-quart pan, mix ½ cup sugar and 1 envelope gelatin. Stir in ½ cup water. Bring to a boil on high heat, stirring. Remove from heat. Add yogurt, sour cream, orange peel, lemon peel, 1 tablespoon lemon juice, and vanilla; whisk to blend smoothly (to speed thickening, set pan in ice water and stir until mixture just begins to thicken). Pour into cool cookie crust. Cover and chill until firm to the touch, 4 to 6 hours.

Rinse pan; in it mix remaining ¼ cup sugar, envelope of gelatin, raspberry-flavor gelatin dessert, juice blend, and remaining 2 tablespoons lemon juice. Bring to a boil on high heat, stirring. Chill until cold to touch but still liquid (to hasten, set pan in ice water and stir often). Stir in pomegranate seed, and gently pour mixture over firm yogurt filling. Cover and chill tart until firm enough to cut, at least 4 hours or up to 1 day.

Run a knife between pan and rim; remove rim. Use a sharp knife to cut tart into wedges (for clean cuts, dip blade in hot water and wipe dry). Serves 10 to 12.

Per serving: 222 cal.(23 percent from fat); 4.9 g protein; 5.6 g fat (3.3 g sat.); 39 g carbo.; 101 mg sodium; 14 mg chol.

PETER CHRISTIANSEN

Cookie crust. In a bowl, crush enough **zwieback toast** to make 1⅓ cups finely crushed crumbs. Mix crumbs with 3 tablespoons melted **butter** or margarine and 2 tablespoons **sugar.** Press crumb mixture firmly over bottom of a lightly oiled 9-inch cheesecake pan with removable rim. Bake in a 300° oven until crust smells toasted and is slightly firmer when pressed, about 30 minutes. Cool; if making ahead, chill airtight up to 6 hours.

Pomegranate seed. Cut crown ends off 2 medium-size (about 8 oz. each) **pomegranates.**

Score skin lengthwise all around fruit. Immerse fruit in a bowl of cool water and break apart with your fingers, separating seed, skin, and membrane. With a strainer, skim and discard floating skin and membrane. Scoop seed from water, and pick out any skin and membrane; drain on towels. Makes 1½ to 1⅔ cups.

something I call meat glaze. The French have a much more rarefied version, *glacé de viande,* and by their standards my method is both lazy and sloppy. But it works, and I'd never bother otherwise. The goal is to trap intense flavor, not to make sparkling clear broth or aspic. Even some of my noncook friends are now convinced that such a potent flavoring additive is worth the effort.

I cut the meat glaze into chunks and keep it in the freezer, ready to pull out and pop into everything from pan juices, soups, braised dishes, stews, and gravies to sauces for meat, poultry, game, and vegetables.

In making meat glaze, I have only one rule: *do not add salt.* There's enough lingering on cooked bones, or you can add it to a finished dish; too much salt will ruin your glaze.

As you make the glaze, you can stop and start again at almost any point. Here are the steps:

1. Accumulate bones. When you bone (or have boned) a chicken or any piece of meat, put the bones in the freezer. Save bones left from carved meats (I even take them off plates, if they haven't been gnawed), and bones from cooked cuts such as veal, beef, and lamb shanks. Occasionally, I even buy some of the bones I suspect most people purchase for their dogs to chew on.

2. When I have enough bones, I dump the frozen, lumpy mounds into a roaster pan. Then I add several cut-up onions and carrots (don't bother to peel either). Roast bones and vegetables, uncovered, in a 450° oven, stirring as bones thaw, and cook until they are well browned; time varies with volume. Occasionally, pour enough water in pan to keep drippings from scorching.

3. Now transfer the bones to a deep pan big enough to hold them all (if you don't want to handle the bones hot, let them cool first). Pour some

water in the roasting pan and scrape browned bits free. Add this liquid to the bones along with enough water to cover them. For part of the liquid, you can add odds and ends of leftover wine. You may also want to add more vegetables and herbs for additional flavor.

Bring to a boil, cover, and simmer at least 2 hours. Then uncover and boil until liquid is reduced by about half. Replenish water and continue to boil until liquid is again reduced by about half. Usually I let the broth bubble away for at least 4 hours, or all afternoon; it takes no watching. If you have to leave the house, just turn off the heat and let bones stand up to 4 hours, then return to a boil and continue. If you have to be gone longer, let liquid cool, then cover pan and stick in the refrigerator up to 2 days.

4. Let broth and bones cool to lukewarm (if chilled, heat to melt), then pour through a colander into a large bowl; let drain. Discard bones. Rinse the pan; pour broth through a fine strainer back into it. If you have time, cover and chill until fat layer is hard, then lift it off and discard. Or skim off and discard melted fat. The broth will look murky and not very appealing.

5. Boil broth, uncovered, over high heat. Stir occasionally to free browned drippings stuck to the pan sides. When reduced to my meat glaze stage, the liquid will be translucent, the boiling bubbles large and shiny; it will feel sticky, taste great, and usually have a rich brown color. You don't have to skim foam off the reducing broth because it eventually disappears, but I do sometimes because the foam usually contains some fat that's trapped as an emulsion in the churning broth.

Scraping to get all the liquid, pour meat glaze into a rimmed pan and chill until cold; natural gelatin makes the glaze firm. Cut into cubes, package for freezing, and

store in the freezer. Pull out cubes to use as you like.

GREAT INGREDIENT

The great pumpkin casserole

Jack-o'-lantern pumpkins, despite their gorgeous orange shells, have watery, pale, blah-tasting flesh. Not so with the miniature pumpkin varieties, which are quite good to steam and eat.

But for a really memorable pumpkin casserole, I turn to the kabocha squash. This green Japanese vegetable is round and squat; the flesh is exceptionally orange and very sweet. It makes a natural bowl, and I like to serve the squash, seasoned, from its own shell.

Pumpkin casserole. Cut the top third off 2 **kabocha squash** (each about 6 in. wide and 2 lb.). Scoop out and discard seeds. Lay squash (including tops) cut side down in a 10- by 15-inch pan. Put pan in a 375° oven and add ¼ inch **water.** Bake, uncovered, until squash is tender when pierced with the tip of a sharp knife, 35 to 45 minutes.

Meanwhile, heat 1 tablespoon **butter** or olive oil in a 10- to 12-inch frying pan. Place over high heat, and when fat is hot, add 2 to 4 tablespoons **dried currants** and stir until they puff, about 1 minute. Remove from heat, and with a slotted spoon, put currants in a small bowl.

Mince 1 large (½ lb.) **onion.** In frying pan, combine onion, ½ cup **regular-strength chicken broth,** 1 teaspoon **curry powder,** 1 teaspoon minced **fresh ginger,** ¼ teaspoon *each* **ground nutmeg, ground cumin,** and **dried thyme leaves.** Stir often over high heat until liquid has evaporated; reduce heat to medium and stir often until onion is lightly browned, about 15 minutes total.

Let squash cool. Choose the prettiest base and set aside. Scoop flesh from skin of remaining squash pieces. Whirl squash with onion mixture in a food processor until smooth (or mash). Mound all the seasoned squash into the reserved squash bowl. (If making ahead, cover and chill up to 1 day.) Bake, uncovered, in a 375° oven until hot in center, 15 to 25 minutes.

GOLDEN, CURRY-SPICED *pumpkin casserole starts with green kabocha squash; sautéed currants make sweet, chewy topping.*
PETER CHRISTIANSEN

Just before serving, scatter currants on squash; season to taste with **salt** and **pepper**. Makes 4 to 6 servings.

Per serving: 91 cal. (24 percent from fat); 2.8 g protein; 2.4 g fat (1.4 g sat.); 18 g carbo.; 28 mg sodium; 5.2 mg chol.

TABLETOP

Deep thoughts on soup bowls

When I first saw the soup bowl I now consider essential, I wondered why it was so wide and shallow. It was on my future mother-in-law's table, and she called it a *piatto fondo,* or deep plate. It was an everyday dish; she maintained her supply through the general store in Half Moon Bay, California. This wide-rimmed bowl was her one-dish solution for workaday meals on the family farm. The family always started with soup, and pasta or salad followed. The depth of the plate accommodated the soup, and the width made it easy to gather up the pasta or to mix the salad with oil and vinegar to taste.

When I went seeking plates like these a few years ago, they were hard to come by—most were too small, too shallow, or not wide enough. But the deep plate has caught the fancy of some of our most imaginative restaurateurs, and manufacturers have responded by bringing more examples to market. From the expanding selection, a few are shown above that function well for soup, pasta, or salad, as well as stews and other hearty dishes such as chili.

I've developed my own one-bowl salad for a really fast dinner: Fill the bowl with tender mixed salad leaves or arugula. Set a hot broiled rare beef patty on top, and moisten with bottled Asian-style peanut sauce. The piquant sauce and the meat juices make a wonderful dressing for the leaves.

HANDSOME SOUP BOWLS, *wide and shallow, with and without rims, have amusing patterns, whimsical shapes, many uses.*

SEASONAL NOTE

Dried persimmon slices

Timber Crest Farms' dried tomatoes were one of my favorite snacks until I tried their dried Fuyu persimmon slices. To me, the dark golden slices taste just like cookies—chewy, sweet, and faintly spicy—but they are much more wholesome, and contain no fat.

Now that persimmons are ripe, the new crop of dried slices is just appearing, though the fruit can be hard to find as it is distributed mostly to health and natural-food stores. The solution is to order by mail. A 3-ounce package (equal to about 2 lbs. fresh fruit) costs $4.40, including shipping and handling. To order, write or call Timber Crest Farms, 4791 Dry Creek Rd., Healdsburg, Calif. 95448; (707) 433-8251, fax (707) 433-8255. ■

BOB THOMPSON ON WINE

October and oysters

It's that time of year when the names of months with the letter *r* again roll softly off the tongue, a sure sign that oysters are with us once more.

With them comes one of the enduring fascinations for people who like to match food and drink to a nicety. The interplay between oysters and wine has spawned an abundance of theories as to why one wine glorifies the oyster while another does not. Some say it is the acidity of tart wines that does the trick, but this notion overlooks *fino* sherries and manzanillas. Others hold out for flavors that echo one another, but their idea skips past applelike Chardonnay.

Maybe it comes down to texture, or structure. All of the classic pairings with oysters share a certain firmness. Hold a sip of a structured wine on your tongue, and it feels like something with edges and angles, not like something smooth and round such as, well . . . such as an oyster. In short, when everything is going exactly right, you turn things upside down. You eat the wine and drink the oyster.

Several such pairings are French-born classics, but they are not the only triumphs.

Sparkling wines can have the steely edge and understated flavors that go perfectly with oysters. Among champagnes: Taittinger Blanc de Blancs. Among Californians: Domaine Chandon Brut, Mumm Napa Valley Brut Prestige, Maison Deutz Brut.

Chablisiens believe no finer companion exists than dry, firmly built Chablis, grown as it is in old seabed full of fossilized oysters. Moreover, its inimitable aromatic union of perfumey apple with burnt match sings close harmony with the salty flavor of an oyster. (The French say "gunflint" rather than burnt match, but that smell has become too rare for most of us to recognize.) To try: A. Moreau Chablis, Domaine Laroche Chablis Premier Cru "Les Vaudevey" or "Les Fourchaumes."

If there is a closer harmony of flavor than that between oysters and Chablis, then it must be that between oysters and Washington State Semillon. Its faint echo of herbs is as right with the salt-sea taste of oysters as can be. Make the oyster an Olympia, and it is perfect. Try: The Hogue Cellars Columbia Valley, Columbia Winery Columbia Valley Semillon (not Chevrier), Chateau Ste. Michelle Columbia Valley.

CRUSTY RICE CAKES *are shaped from a creamy risotto and pan-browned. For lunch, serve them with tomato-basil sauce and sautéed shrimp.*

California rice, sweet or wild?

This diverse grain doesn't have to be a boring side dish

CALIFORNIA'S FERTILE Sacramento Valley is one of the world's most productive rice-growing areas. Its rich soil and temperate climate host an astonishing array of rices.

Many varieties of short-, medium-, and long-grain rices, including aromatic rices and sweet (glutinous) rices, get finished one of two ways: hulled but with bran (brown or colored rice) or hulled and bran removed (white rice). Wild rice, even though it is not a true rice but a grass seed, grows abundantly in this area, too.

While there are enough different rices produced to provide the cook with many choices, there is so much medium-grain Calrose it actually accounts for 80 percent of the harvest, and the bulk of it is consumed domestically.

Why so many kinds? Rice is rice, isn't it? The answer is definitely no. The West's diverse ethnic populations have strong loyalties to particular kinds of rice. And the many different flavors and textures of rice bring rich variety to different menus.

Each of the following recipes emphasizes the unique character of the rice that is used. Medium-grain rice is inclined to stick and has a firm-soft bite; this makes it suitable for shaping as cakes to pan-brown. Sweet rice works well for dessert, particularly with coconut milk and mangoes.

Aromatic rice lends complexity to spices that season pilaf. Boldly flavored wild rice holds up well to lively Chinese seasonings, and the chewy, nutty quality of a colored rice supplements the meat and fennel filling in baked squash.

Supermarkets usually have white and brown rices in short, medium, and long grain; most also have aromatic rice and wild rice. Colored rices are more likely to be found in natural-food or health stores and gourmet shops. Glutinous rice is available in Asian markets.

California Risotto Cakes

2 tablespoons butter or olive oil

1¼ cups medium-grain white rice

1¾ cups regular-strength chicken broth

1½ cups water

⅓ pound mozzarella cheese, shredded

¼ cup freshly grated parmesan cheese

4 green onions, ends trimmed, minced

Tomato-basil sauce (recipe follows)

Basil sprigs (optional)

In a 3- to 4-quart pan over medium-high heat, combine 1 tablespoon butter and rice. Stir until rice is opaque, 3 minutes. Add broth and water; stir occasionally until boiling. Reduce heat and simmer, uncovered, until rice is tender to bite and liquid has been absorbed, 25 to 30 minutes; stir frequently, and more often as mixture thickens. Remove from heat and stir in mozzarella, parmesan, and green onions. Let cool, uncovered. If making ahead, cover and chill up to 1 day.

Divide rice mixture into 12 equal portions. With your hands, shape each into ¾-inch-thick cakes. Melt 1 teaspoon butter in a 10- to 12-inch nonstick frying pan over medium-high heat. Fill pan with risotto cakes, but do not crowd. Brown cakes until golden color on each side, about 20 minutes total; turn once with a wide spatula. As cooked, transfer cakes, in a single layer to a shallow pan (9 by 13 in. or 10 by 15 in.), drape with foil, and keep warm in a 300° oven. Add remaining butter to pan and brown remaining risotto cakes (or you can brown cakes in 2 frying pans, simultaneously).

Spoon cakes onto plates, ladle an equal portion of tomato-basil sauce alongside, and garnish with basil sprigs. Serves 4 to 6.

Per serving: 302 cal. (33 percent from fat); 11 g protein; 11 g fat (6.6 g sat.); 38 g carbo.; 345 mg sodium; 33 mg chol.

Tomato-basil sauce. In a blender or food processor, whirl 1 can (14½ oz.) **diced tomatoes** and their juice with ¼ cup **nonfat unflavored yogurt** and ¼ cup coarsely chopped fresh **basil**. If making ahead, let stand at room temperature up to 1 hour, or cover and chill, but serve at room temperature.

Sweet Rice and Coconut Milk with Mangoes

2 cups sweet (glutinous) white or brown rice

2½ cups low-fat milk

2 tablespoons sugar

1 teaspoon coconut extract

1 can (14 oz.) light or regular coconut milk

2 large (about 2 lb. total) firm-ripe mangoes, peeled, pitted, and sliced

Chopped roasted, salted peanuts

Brown sugar

In a 2-to 3-quart pan, cover rice with cool water and let stand at least 30 minutes or up to 1 day. Drain, and rinse rice with more cool water and drain several times, until the water is clear. Drain rice and add to pan the milk, sugar, and coconut extract.

Bring to a boil over medium-high heat. Simmer, uncovered, until rice is creamy-looking and most of the liquid is absorbed, about 15 minutes for white rice, about 25 for brown rice; stir often.

Transfer rice to a steamer basket (or a metal colander) lined with cheesecloth. Nest basket in a 5- to 6-quart pan above ½ to 1 inch boiling water. Cover basket and steam until rice is tender to bite, about 20 minutes. Serve rice hot or let stand until warm or room temperature. Pour coconut milk into a small pitcher. Spoon rice into wide bowls and top with mango slices. To taste, add coconut milk, chopped peanuts, and brown sugar. Serves 6 to 8.

Per serving: 370 cal. (29 percent from fat); 7.1 g protein; 12 g fat (10 g sat.); 59 g carbo.; 49 mg sodium; 6.1 mg chol.

Spiced Aromatic Pilaf

1 tablespoon butter or margarine

3 cups white or brown aromatic rice

3 cloves garlic, minced or pressed (optional)

2 tablespoons mustard seed

4 teaspoons minced fresh ginger

½ teaspoon hulled cardamom seed

6 cups regular-strength chicken broth

½ cup dried cranberries

½ cup golden raisins

2 cinnamon sticks (each about 3 in.)

2 tablespoons grated orange peel

1 dried bay leaf

1 small (about 3 oz.) carrot, peeled and cut into very fine matchstick-size pieces

Salt

In a 5- to 6-quart pan over medium-high heat, melt butter. Add rice, garlic, mustard seed, ginger, and cardamom; stir often until rice is lightly browned, about 10 minutes.

Add broth, cranberries, raisins, cinnamon, orange peel, bay leaf, and carrot; bring to boiling on high heat. Cover and simmer gently, stirring occasionally, until liquid is absorbed and rice is tender to bite, about 20 minutes for white rice, 45 minutes for brown. If desired, discard bay leaf. Spoon rice into a bowl and lay cinnamon sticks on top to garnish. Add salt to taste. Serves 10 to 12.

Per serving: 239 cal. (9.7 percent from fat); 5.2 g protein; 2.6 g fat (0.9 g sat.); 48 g carbo.; 42 mg sodium; 2.6 mg chol.

Wild Rice, Mandarin-style

1½ cups wild rice, rinsed and drained

3 cups regular-strength chicken broth

½ cup dried shiitake mushrooms

1 can (8 oz.) whole or sliced water chestnuts, drained and chopped

1 tablespoon soy sauce

1 tablespoon rice vinegar

2 teaspoons Oriental sesame oil

½ teaspoon sugar

¼ teaspoon pepper

Fresh cilantro (coriander) sprigs (optional)

In a 3- to 4-quart pan, combine rice and broth; bring to boiling over high heat. Cover and simmer gently until rice grains are tender to bite, 45 to 50 minutes.

Meanwhile, in a bowl, combine mushrooms and 1½ cups boiling water. Let stand until mushrooms are soft, at least 20 minutes. Reserving liquid, drain mushrooms. Trim off and discard mushroom stems; chop mushrooms.

In a 1- to 1½-quart pan, combine chopped mushrooms, ¼ cup mushroom soaking liquid, water chestnuts, soy sauce, vinegar, sesame oil, sugar, and pepper. Drain any liquid from cooked rice into pan. Bring mushroom mixture to boiling over high heat; boil 2 minutes to blend flavors, then mix with rice. Pour into a bowl and garnish with cilantro. Serves 6 to 8.
—*Julian Mao, owner, The Mandarin Restaurant, San Francisco.*

Per serving: 151 cal. (13 percent from fat); 5.8 g protein; 2.1 g fat (0.4 g sat.); 29 g carbo.; 154 mg sodium; 0 mg chol.

Mahogany Rice, Sausage, and Fennel in Squash Bowls

2 medium (about 1½ lb. each) acorn squash

1 large (about 3 in. wide) head fennel, with feathery green leaves

½ pound mild Italian sausages, casings removed

4½ cups regular-strength chicken or beef broth

2 tablespoons balsamic vinegar

1 cup red or black (Wehani or Black Japonica) rice, rinsed and drained

Salt

Cut squash in half lengthwise; scoop out and discard seeds and strings. Place squash, cut side down, in a 9- by 13-inch pan. Add about ½ inch water. Bake in a 400° oven until squash is tender when pierced, about 50 minutes. (If squash is done before rice, drain off water and keep squash warm.)

Meanwhile, trim and reserve feathery green fennel leaves; discard coarse stem. Trim stem end and any bruises from fennel; thinly slice fennel. In a 5- to 6-quart pan, combine fennel and sausages. Stir often over medium-high heat until mixture is well browned, about 15 minutes. Spoon out and discard any fat. Add to pan ½ cup broth and the vinegar; stir to release browned bits. Boil, and stir often until liquid evaporates and browned bits begin to stick. Stir free with ½ cup broth and boil until it begins sticking again, about 10 minutes total. Add remaining broth and rice to pan, stirring browned bits free. Bring to boiling over high heat; cover and simmer gently until rice is tender to bite, about 50 to 60 minutes.

Meanwhile, mince about half the reserved fennel leaves. When rice is done, remove from heat and stir in minced fennel.

Place squash, cupped side up, on platter or plates. With slotted spoon, fill squash with rice mixture, mounding. Sprinkle with remaining fennel leaves, accompany with any remaining juice, and add salt to taste. Serves 4.

Per serving: 529 cal. (36 percent from fat); 18 g protein; 21 g fat (7.2 g sat.); 69 g carbo.; 623 mg sodium; 43 mg chol. ∎

By Christine Weber Hale

STURDY LOAVES (bottom up) of sauerkraut-caraway rye, whole-wheat molasses nut, and extra whole-wheat are great for sandwiches, for spreads, or with soups.

Hearty loaves with simple surprises

Nuts and raisins, cereal, and sauerkraut make them taste even better

COMBINING FLOURS and flavorful additions gives character to these wholesome breads. To store, wrap airtight up to four days, or freeze.

Sauerkraut-Caraway Rye Bread

1 can (1 lb.) sauerkraut

2 packages active dry yeast

¼ cup sugar

2 cups rye flour

3 tablespoons caraway seed

About 5 cups all-purpose flour

Drain sauerkraut; reserve ½ cup juice. Rinse kraut with cool water in a fine strainer; press dry.

In a 1- to 1½-quart pan over medium heat, warm 1½ cups water and reserved ½ cup juice to 110°. In a large bowl, combine juice mixture, yeast, and sugar; let stand until bubbling, about 10 minutes. Add rye flour, caraway, and 1 cup all-purpose flour. With an electric mixer, beat on low speed until flour is moistened; beat on medium speed until stretchy, about 5 minutes. Stir in sauerkraut and 4 cups all-purpose flour.

If using a dough hook, beat on high speed until dough pulls cleanly from bowl, 5 to 8 minutes; if dough still sticks, add all-purpose flour, 1 tablespoon at a time, until dough pulls free.

If kneading by hand, scrape dough onto a lightly floured board; knead until smooth and elastic, about 10 minutes, adding all-purpose flour as required to prevent sticking. Place in oiled bowl.

Cover dough with plastic wrap. Let rise in a warm place until doubled, about 1 hour. Knead on a lightly floured board to expel air. Halve dough; shape into 2 loaves. Place each in an oiled 5- by 9-inch loaf pan. Cover loosely and let rise in a warm place until almost doubled, about 45 minutes.

Bake in a 350° oven until brown, 40 to 45 minutes. Invert loaves onto racks. Makes 2 loaves, about 1¾ pounds each.—*A. J. Stefani, Cobb Mountain, California*

Per ounce: 61 cal. (3 percent from fat); 1.7 g protein; 0.2 g fat (0 g sat.); 13 g carbo.; 36 mg sodium; 0 mg chol.

Extra Whole-wheat Bread

2 packages active dry yeast

1½ cups warm water (110°)

2 tablespoons sugar

¾ cup milk

⅓ cup *each* molasses and salad oil

4 cups whole-wheat flour

About 1½ cups all-purpose flour

1 cup finely crushed shredded whole-wheat cereal biscuits

½ cup dried potato flakes

1½ teaspoons salt

In a large bowl, combine yeast, water, and sugar; let stand until bubbling, about 10 minutes. Stir in milk, molasses, and oil.

Stir together whole-wheat flour, 1½ cups all-purpose flour, shredded wheat, potato flakes, and salt. Add 4 cups flour mixture to yeast. With an electric mixer, beat on low speed until moistened; then beat on medium until stretchy, about 4 minutes. Stir in remaining flour.

If using a dough hook, beat on high speed until dough pulls cleanly from bowl, 5 to 8 minutes; if dough still sticks, add all-purpose flour, 1 tablespoon at a time, until dough pulls free.

If kneading by hand, knead dough on a lightly floured board until smooth and elastic, about 10 minutes. Add all-purpose flour, as required, to prevent sticking. Place in an oiled bowl.

Cover dough with plastic wrap; let rise in a warm place until doubled, about 1½ hours. Knead on a lightly floured board. Halve dough; shape into 2 loaves. Place each in an oiled 5- by 9-inch loaf pan. Cover lightly; let rise in a warm place until almost doubled, about 45 minutes.

Bake in a 350° oven until loaves are a rich brown, 40 to 45 minutes. Invert onto racks. Makes 2 loaves, 1¾ pounds each.—*Mary Ann Fransen, Chandler, Arizona*

Per ounce: 66 cal. (22 percent from fat); 1.8 g protein; 1.6 g fat (0.3 g sat.); 12 g carbo.; 61 mg sodium; 0.4 mg chol.

Whole-wheat Molasses Nut Loaf

1 cup chopped pecans

1 cup dark molasses

¾ cup milk

½ cup water

2 tablespoons firmly packed dark brown sugar

2 cups whole-wheat flour

1 cup all-purpose flour

2 teaspoons baking powder

1 teaspoon baking soda

½ teaspoon salt

½ cup raisins

In an 8- to 9-inch-wide pan, bake nuts in a 325° oven until golden under skin, about 10 minutes; set aside.

In a bowl, beat molasses, milk, water, and sugar until blended. Stir together the 2 flours, baking powder, soda, and salt; add to molasses mixture and beat until blended. Stir in nuts and raisins. Scrape into an oiled 5- by 9-inch loaf pan.

Bake loaf in 325° oven until toothpick inserted in center comes out clean, 1 to 1¼ hours. Cool in pan on rack 10 minutes; invert loaf onto rack. Makes 1 loaf, about 3½ pounds.—*Pat Tompkins, San Mateo, California*

Per ounce: 58 cal. (25 percent from fat); 1.2 g protein; 1.6 g fat (0.2 g sat.); 10 g carbo.; 59 mg sodium; 0.5 mg chol. ∎

By Betsy Reynolds Bateson

NORMAN A. PLATE

PEARS *(from left) are Yellow Bartlett, Bosc, Green Anjou, Red Anjou, and Comice.*

Prime time
for pears

Savor them fresh, poached, in pies and cobblers—the same ways you enjoy apples

SPECIALTY PEARS *include (clockwise from upper left) Nelis, Forelle, and Seckel. These pears are particularly sweet, great for eating fresh, and good for canning.*

RED BARTLETT PEARS *are poached and served in a glistening port-citrus syrup with crystallized ginger.*

PETER CHRISTIANSEN

WESTERNERS WILL FIND a terrific assortment of pears in markets this month. In fact, all common varieties grown in pear country (Oregon, Washington, and California produce 95 percent of the nation's pears) are available in October. You can get some pears year-round, but the greatest selection is from September through February. Pear season begins in early August with the juicy, aromatic summer Bartletts. Then the nutty, firm-textured, russet brown Bosc and sweet, juicy Comice make the scene in early September. With the arrival of Anjou, Nelis, Forelle, and Seckel pears in mid-October, the full cast of the most common varieties is in place. Specialty markets and farmer's markets may have a couple of additional pear varieties, such as the Packham and the Eldorado, the latter a winter pear that resembles the Bartlett.

JUST BAG 'EM FOR
QUICK RIPENING

Because pears bruise easily, they are picked and shipped in an unripened state. If you find pears a bit on the hard side when you shop, don't despair. They'll actually ripen better on your counter than in the store or on the tree, where they tend to become mushy. Just remember to select pears a couple of days before you want to eat or cook them.

Choose uniformly firm fruit without soft spots (a skin blemish, however, is only "skin deep"), then take them home for some TLC. To speed ripening, place the pears in a paper bag (fold the top over) or in a ripener for two to seven days. Gently press near the base of the stem to test for ripeness: if the pear yields to gentle pressure, it's ripe. Once ripe, refrigerate until ready to use, up to a week.

Color is another ripeness indicator, but not as dependable. As the summer Bartlett ripens, it turns from green to a golden yellow, the red Bartlett from a dark to a brilliant red. When the greenish Forelle ripens, its crimson freckles deepen in color. But the Bosc, Comice, and green and red Anjou don't change color when ripe.

You can use most pear varieties interchangeably. Try them in pies and cobblers, or fresh with cheese, or eat them out-of-hand—the easiest and most gratifying way to enjoy a pear when it's perfectly ripe. The Comice is exceptional when eaten fresh, but because it doesn't keep well in cold storage, its availability is limited, and it's not the best choice for pies or jams.

Cooking possibilities are as varied for pears as for apples. For poaching, baking, and canning, Bartlett, Anjou, and Bosc pears are excellent. The smaller pears—Seckel, Nelis, and Forelle—can be used in the same ways, but their smaller size makes them especially good for canning. And remember, whether you're eating them fresh or using them in cooking, pears should be ripe.

Poached Pears in
Port-Citrus Syrup

- 2 cups port
- ½ cup sugar
- 1 tablespoon grated orange peel
- ¼ teaspoon ground nutmeg
- 4 Anjou (green or red), Bartlett (yellow or red), Bosc, or Comice pears, or 6 to 8 Forelle, Nelis, or Seckel pears (about 2 lb. total)
- 1 tablespoon lemon juice

In a 3- to 4-quart pan over medium heat, combine port, sugar, orange peel, and nutmeg. Stirring, heat mixture until sugar dissolves, then bring to a boil.

Add pears, cover, and simmer until very tender when pierced, 15 to 30 minutes; turn pears over halfway through cooking. With a slotted spoon, transfer to a wide bowl or platter; set aside.

Bring port mixture to a boil over high heat; continue to boil, uncovered, until liquid thickens and reduces to about ½ cup, 10 to 12 minutes.

Stir lemon juice into reduced syrup in pan and pour over pears. Serve warm or at room temperature. Makes 4 servings.

Per serving: 281 cal. (2.9 percent from fat); 1.1 g protein; 0.9 g fat (0.1 g sat.); 71 g carbo.; 12 mg sodium; 0 mg chol.

Ginger and orange poached pears. Follow recipe instructions as suggested, but reduce **orange peel** to 2 teaspoons and add 1 tablespoon minced **crystallized ginger** instead of the nutmeg. ∎

By Betsy Reynolds Bateson

SAUTÉED DRIED CRANBERRIES *give a lively, chewy dimension to a simple sauce for braised chicken.*

The great raisin substitute

Dried cranberries pack a punch at breakfast, lunch, and dinner

D RIED CRANBERRIES are proof that you can improve upon nature. Fresh cranberries are too sour and pulpy to eat raw, but dried they become pleasantly chewy, refreshingly sweet-tart, and almost addictive. Better yet, they are available all year.

When you're not snacking on dried cranberries, try them in cooking as an alternative to raisins. Or take them a step further and use their complementary tang with meat and poultry dishes.

QUICK TRICKS WITH DRIED CRANBERRIES

Cornbread. Stir dried cranberries into cornbread batter; allow ½ to 1 cup dried cranberries for an 8- to 9-inch square pan of cornbread.

Muffins. Instead of fresh blueberries, add an equal measure of dried cranberries to muffin batter.

Toppings. Sprinkle dried cranberries over prepared cereal, granola, or hot oatmeal.

Yogurt. Stir dried cranberries into vanilla or fruit-flavor yogurt.

Cookies. Instead of raisins, add an equal measure of dried cranberries to dough.

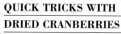

PETER CHRISTIANSEN

Braised Chicken with Dried Cranberries

6 whole chicken legs (drumsticks with thighs, 3 to 3¼ lb. total)

1½ cups regular-strength chicken broth

1 cup dry white wine

4 cloves garlic, minced or pressed

2 tablespoons minced fresh ginger

1 tablespoon grated lemon peel

1 cup dried cranberries

2 teaspoons butter or margarine

1½ tablespoons cornstarch mixed with 3 tablespoons water

Couscous (directions follow)

Salt

In a 12-inch frying pan or 5- to 6-quart pan over high heat, brown chicken legs, turning often, 15 to 20 minutes total. Do not crowd pan; remove pieces as browned. Discard fat in pan, wipe clean, and return chicken to pan. Add broth, wine, garlic, ginger, and lemon peel. Cover pan and bring to simmer over high heat; reduce heat and simmer until chicken is no longer pink at thigh bone (cut to test), about 25 minutes.

Meanwhile, combine cranberries, butter, and 2 tablespoons water in an 8- to 10-inch frying pan. Boil over high heat, stirring often, until water evaporates and cranberries are glazed, about 3 minutes. Set aside.

With a slotted spoon, transfer cooked chicken to a platter and keep warm. Spoon off and discard fat from pan juices. Boil juices on high heat, uncovered, until reduced to 1½ cups. Stir cornstarch mixture into boiling sauce and stir until boil resumes; add ½ the cranberries. Pour sauce into a small pitcher. Spoon couscous onto platter with chicken; sprinkle with remaining cranberries. Accompany chicken and couscous with sauce; add salt to taste. Serves 6.

Per serving: 546 cal. (30 percent from fat); 38 g protein; 18 g fat (5.5 g sat.); 56 g carbo.; 157 mg sodium; 111 mg chol.

Couscous. In a 1½- to 2-quart pan, bring 2¼ cups **regular-strength chicken broth** to a boil on high heat. Stir in 1½ cups **couscous.** Cover pan, remove from heat, and let stand 5 to 10 minutes. Stir with a fork and serve hot.

Dried Cranberry Dessert Sauce

Spoon over ice cream or orange slices.

1 cup dried cranberries

1½ cups port

1 cup water

¾ cup sugar

2 cinnamon sticks, each about 3 inches

1 tablespoon grated orange peel

2 tablespoons orange-flavor liqueur (optional)

In a 1½- to 2-quart pan, combine cranberries, port, water, sugar, cinnamon sticks, and orange peel. Boil over high heat, stirring often, until reduced to 2 cups, about 20 minutes. Remove from heat and stir in liqueur. Use hot, warm, or cold. If making ahead, cool, cover, and chill up to 1 week; reheat if desired. Makes 2 cups.

Per ¼ cup: 138 cal. (0 percent from fat); 0.2 g protein; 0 g fat; 36 g carbo.; 4.9 mg sodium; 0 mg chol. ∎

By Christine Weber Hale

BROAD

Tender treatment pulls the best out of oxtails

While fresh ginger and capers dress chicken breasts

N O CUT OF BEEF IS MORE consistently close to the bone than oxtail, and the meat truly has excellent flavor. However, it is tough, the result of constant exercise in such endeavors as driving off flies and annoying the milker. This toughness can be overcome by long, slow braising, which Henry Woo uses in his Oxtail Stew. He combines the ingredients of a classic French *daube* with the Oriental flavors of soy and oyster sauces.

Oxtail Stew

3½ to 4 pounds oxtails, cut about 1½ inches thick

4 teaspoons reduced-sodium soy sauce

2 tablespoons vodka, gin, or regular-strength beef broth

2 tablespoons oyster sauce

1 clove garlic, minced or pressed

1 small (3 or 4 oz.) onion, coarsely chopped

2 dried bay leaves

1 teaspoon dried oregano leaves

1¾ cup (1 can, 14½ oz.) regular-strength beef broth

1½ cups sliced celery

4 large (about 1 lb. total) carrots, cut into ½-inch-thick slices

1 tablespoon cornstarch blended smoothly with 2 tablespoons water

Trim and discard surface fat from oxtails. Put oxtails in a 5- to 6-quart pan; mix in the soy sauce, vodka, and oyster sauce. Cover and let stand 45 minutes to 1 hour.

Place oxtails over medium-high heat and cover; cook 30 minutes to draw out juices. Uncover and boil until liquid evaporates and oxtails are browned well; turn often. Add garlic, onion, bay leaves, oregano, and beef broth; stir well to release browned bits. Cover and simmer gently until meat is tender when pierced, 2½ to 3 hours.

Add celery, carrots, and 1 cup water to oxtails, mix, and continue to simmer, covered, until the vegetables are tender when pierced, about 15 minutes.

With a slotted spoon, transfer meat and vegetables to a serving bowl; keep warm. Skim and discard fat from pan juices. Measure juices and add water to make 1⅓ cups total. Return juices to pan and bring to boiling over high heat; stir in cornstarch mixture and stir until boil resumes. Pour sauce over meat and vegetables. Makes 4 servings.

Per serving: 297 cal. (36 percent from fat); 27 g protein; 12 g fat (0.1 g sat.); 20 g carbo.; 771 mg sodium; chol. not available.

Los Angeles

Q UICK TO COOK, LOW IN fat, useful cold or hot, and friendly to all sorts of sauces, the skinned, boned chicken breast is the ultimate in versatility. There are 1,000 ways to prepare it. A. J. Marineau gives us number 1,001: chicken breast cutlets with ginger-orange sauce and, surprisingly, capers.

Ginger Chicken

1 whole (about 1 lb.) chicken breast, split, skinned, and boned

2 tablespoons nonfat sour cream

½ teaspoon all-purpose flour

1 tablespoon minced fresh ginger

1 tablespoon drained prepared capers

2 teaspoons butter or margarine

¼ cup orange-flavor liqueur such as triple sec or Cointreau

Chopped parsley

Lime wedges

Salt

Place each chicken half between 2 sheets of plastic wrap. Pound chicken with a flat mallet until about ¼ inch thick.

In a small bowl, stir together sour cream and flour until smooth; add ginger and capers.

Melt butter in a 10- to 12-inch frying pan over medium-high heat. Add chicken, and brown lightly on each side, 1 to 2 minutes total. Lift chicken from pan and set aside. To pan, add liqueur; stir to loosen browned bits. Stir in the sour cream mixture, and add chicken and any juices. Simmer until chicken is no longer pink in center (cut to test), 3 to 4 minutes; spoon sauce over meat several times as it cooks. Transfer chicken to plates, and pour sauce over portions. Sprinkle chicken with parsley and garnish with lime wedges. Season to taste with lime and salt. Makes 2 servings.

Per serving: 293 cal. (18 percent from fat); 35 g protein; 5.7 g fat (2.9 g sat.); 11 g carbo.; 255 mg sodium; 96 mg chol.

Moscow, Idaho

By Joan Griffiths, Richard Dunmire

Sunset's Kitchen Cabinet

Creative ways with everyday foods—submitted by *Sunset* readers,
tested in *Sunset* kitchens, approved by *Sunset* taste panels

BUTTER CAKE *squares with parmesan are "quesadillas" in El Salvador.*

Salvadoran Quesadillas

Linda Dueñas, Fontana, California

6 tablespoons butter or margarine, softened

1 cup sugar

2 large eggs

½ cup milk

1 cup all-purpose flour

½ cup grated parmesan cheese

1 teaspoon baking powder

2 tablespoons sesame seed

In the bowl of an electric mixer, beat butter and sugar until fluffy. Beat in eggs well, then beat in milk. Mix flour, cheese, and baking powder; beat into butter mixture until smooth.

Scrape batter into a buttered and floured 8-inch square pan. Sprinkle with sesame seed and bake in a 350° oven until cake begins to pull from pan sides, about 30 minutes. Let cake cool on a rack, then cut into squares. Serve, or store airtight up to 1 day. Makes 9 servings.

Per serving: 261 cal. (41 percent from fat); 5.5 g protein; 12 g fat (6.4 g sat.); 34 g carbo.; 236 mg sodium; 73 mg chol.

Dilled Crab and Shrimp Cakes

Joyce Albert, Seattle

SERVE GOLDEN SEAFOOD *and bell pepper cakes as an appetizer or entrée.*

1 large egg plus 1 large egg white

1 tablespoon chopped fresh dill or 1 teaspoon dried dill weed

2 teaspoons Worcestershire

½ teaspoon dry mustard

6 ounces (1 cup) shelled cooked crab, flaked

6 ounces (1 cup) chopped, shelled, cooked tiny shrimp

1 cup fine dried bread crumbs

1 cup diced red bell pepper

¼ cup light mayonnaise

2 tablespoons sliced green onion

1½ tablespoons butter or margarine

Fresh dill sprigs (optional)

Lemon or lime wedges

In a bowl, beat egg and egg white; add dill, Worcestershire, mustard, crab, shrimp, bread crumbs, bell pepper, mayonnaise, and green onion. Shape into 12 equal flat rounds about ½ inch thick.

In a 10- to 12-inch nonstick frying pan over medium heat, melt ½ tablespoon butter. Place 4 crab cakes in pan; cook until golden, turning halfway through cooking, 3 to 5 minutes per side. Keep warm in a 200° oven while cooking remaining cakes in remaining butter. Garnish with dill sprigs and offer with lemon wedges. Makes 12 cakes, 6 appetizer or 3 entrée servings.

Per cake: 102 cal. (36 percent from fat); 7.9 g protein; 4.1 g fat (1.5 g sat.); 7.7 g carbo.; 210 mg sodium; 65 mg chol.

Quick Chicken-Vegetable Chowder

Bonnie E. Peterson, Tucson

BOW-TIE PASTA, *chunks of chicken, and sliced vegetables go into a creamy soup.*

1 cup chopped onion

1 cup thinly sliced carrots

1 cup diced celery

1¼ cups sliced small mushrooms

1 quart regular-strength chicken broth

2 cups (4 oz.) dried bow-tie pasta

1½ teaspoons dried tarragon leaves

1½ pounds boned chicken breasts, skinned and cut into 1-inch chunks

2½ cups milk mixed with 1 tablespoon cornstarch

3 tablespoons chopped parsley

Salt and pepper

In a 5- to 6-quart pan over high heat, boil onion, carrots, celery, mushrooms, and ¼ cup broth, stirring occasionally, until liquid evaporates and vegetables start to stick and brown, about 10 minutes. Add ¼ cup more broth and repeat until vegetables are well browned, 3 to 5 minutes.

Add remaining broth and bring to a boil. Stir in pasta and tarragon; boil over medium-high heat, covered, until pasta is barely tender to bite, about 6 minutes. Stir in chicken and milk mixture. Bring to simmering, stirring occasionally, about 6 minutes. Add parsley; season to taste with salt and pepper. Makes about 9 cups, 4 to 6 servings.

Per serving: 286 cal. (19 percent from fat); 30 g protein; 6 g fat (2.7 g sat.); 27 g carbo.; 173 mg sodium; 68 mg chol.

Lentil-Nut Shepherd's Pie

Patricia Stearns, Fresno, California

1½ cups lentils, sorted of debris and rinsed

2 cloves garlic, minced or pressed

1½ teaspoons *each* dried thyme leaves and dried savory leaves

½ teaspoon dried rubbed sage leaves

5½ cups vegetable broth

1 cup chopped walnuts

2 cups soft whole-wheat bread crumbs

2 pounds thin-skinned potatoes, peeled and cut into 2-inch chunks

1 cup (¼ lb.) shredded sharp cheddar cheese

In a 3- to 4-quart pan, bring lentils, garlic, thyme, savory, sage, and 3½ cups broth to a boil over high heat. Cover and simmer until lentils are tender to bite, 35 to 40 minutes. Remove from heat and stir in nuts and bread crumbs.

In a 2- to 3-quart pan, bring potatoes and remaining 2 cups broth to a boil; simmer, covered, until potatoes mash easily when pressed, about 15 minutes. Drain, reserving liquid. In pan, beat or mash potatoes until no lumps remain; mix in ⅓ cup reserved liquid. Stir in cheese.

Stir remaining potato liquid into lentil mixture; spoon into an oiled shallow 2- to 2½-quart baking dish. Drop potatoes in spoonfuls onto lentil mixture. Bake in a 375° oven until tops of potatoes are deep golden, 35 to 40 minutes. Serves 6.

Per serving: 550 cal. (34 percent from fat); 27 g protein; 21 g fat (5.7 g sat.); 66 g carbo.; 258 mg sodium; 20 mg chol.

PUFFS OF POTATOES *with cheddar cheese crown a baked lentil casserole.*

Fruit Spinach Salad

Diana R. Glassman, Tacoma

2 large (about 1¼ lb. total) seedless oranges

3 quarts lightly packed rinsed, crisped spinach leaves

1 cup *each* chopped red and green bell peppers

½ cup thinly sliced red onion rings

1 large (about ⅔ lb.) banana, sliced

½ cup roasted salted cashews (optional)

Cumin dressing (recipe follows)

Salt and pepper

Cut off and discard orange peels and outer white membranes. Working over a bowl, cut between inner membranes to free segments. Squeeze juice from membranes into bowl; discard membranes. Drain juice; reserve.

Place spinach in a large bowl; top with orange segments, red and green bell peppers, onion, banana, and cashews. Mix gently with dressing. Add salt and pepper to taste. Serves 6.

Per serving: 155 cal. (31 percent from fat); 5.2 g protein; 5.4 g fat (0.7 g sat.); 26 g carbo.; 107 mg sodium; 0 mg chol.

Cumin dressing. To reserved **orange juice** add 2 tablespoons **red wine vinegar,** 2 tablespoons **salad oil,** 1 teaspoon minced **garlic,** and 1 teaspoon **ground cumin.**

ORANGES, BANANAS, *cashews, and a citrus dressing accent a leafy salad.*

Cheesecake Apple Torte

Angie Berberian, Fresno, California

½ cup (¼ lb.) butter or margarine

About 1 cup sugar

1 teaspoon vanilla

1 cup all-purpose flour

1 large package (8 oz.) cream cheese

1 large egg

½ cup raisins

1 teaspoon ground cinnamon

½ teaspoon grated lemon peel

2 cups ¼-inch-thick slices peeled Granny Smith apples

In a bowl, beat butter, ⅓ cup sugar, and vanilla until fluffy. Add flour; stir until dough holds together. Spread over bottom and 1½ inches up sides of a 9-inch cake pan with a removable rim. Bake in a 350° oven until golden, about 20 minutes.

In bowl, beat cream cheese, ¼ cup sugar, and egg until smooth. Spread over bottom of crust; top with raisins. Mix ¼ cup sugar, cinnamon, lemon peel, and apples; arrange apples, slightly overlapping, on raisins. Bake until filling is set in center when pan is gently shaken, and apples are tender, about 40 minutes. Cool at least 30 minutes; push from pan rim. Serves 8.

Per serving: 412 cal. (48 percent from fat); 5 g protein; 22 g fat (14 g sat.); 49 g carbo.; 211 mg sodium; 89 mg chol.

Compiled by Elaine Johnson

HANDSOME DESSERT *tastes like a cross between cheesecake and apple pie.*

FOOD GUIDE

Roasting chestnuts, Meyer lemons, fila tips, and nouveau wine

By Jerry Anne Di Vecchio

In many ways, chestnuts are like potatoes—or maybe even oatmeal. Rarely do trumpets go off with the first taste; *bland* is usually the adjective that comes immediately to mind. But a second bite leads to another, then another, and the next thing you know, the quiet subtleties, the comforting mellow flavor, and the smooth texture work their way into your subconscious appetite.

At least, that's how I grew to love chestnuts. They've earned their place alongside mashed potatoes as a food that soothes and satisfies. But more important, their appearance primes my spirit for the onset of winter and the joys of the holidays.

Fresh chestnut season is brief. Most chestnuts are imported from Italy, but some are grown commercially in Northern California, mostly near Mendocino, and also in various locations in Washington. In Oregon, a few chestnuts are locally grown and distributed. I like to seek out the West Coast chestnuts because they are fresher.

Chestnuts are graded by size. Yoshiko Hug of San Diego, whose fondness for chestnuts prompted her to write encouraging us to use them more often, says that if you want large chestnuts, look for them in Asian markets.

When buying chestnuts, pick out ones that feel heavy and solid. The nuts are moist and starchy, so they're quite perishable. When they get moldy, shrivel, or dry up inside, they feel light.

You can't crack and shell chestnuts like other nuts; the shells are too soft, and the raw nut is covered by a coarse brown skin that sticks tightly. Roasting is the easiest, though not the only, method that will loosen the skin.

The old-fashioned way of roasting is to shake the nuts in a long-handled chestnut pan over an open fire until the shells are scorched and smell toasted. The simple way is to bake them in the oven.

With a glass of port, warm chestnuts make a lovely way to end dinner. But the roasted nuts, with seasoning, also make this fabulous soup to begin a meal; it's much like one I enjoyed last winter at Wolfgang Puck's restaurant Spago in Los Angeles.

BACK TO BASICS

Roasting chestnuts

Pierce the shells before roasting chestnuts, or they will likely explode as they cook. The fragmented hot nut can cause serious burns because it sticks to anything it hits. Cooked, the nuts are easiest to shell and skin while still warm. Finally, a little discovery for stretching the nuts beyond the holidays: Last year, I froze some fresh chestnuts in their shells. Later on, I thawed the nuts in the refrigerator and roasted them; the results were fine. You can also freeze roasted, shelled chestnuts.

To roast chestnuts. Pierce shells (it's easiest to do on the flat side). I make an X-shaped cut so the shell corners can curl back as the nuts roast and give me something to pull on when I'm shelling them.

Place chestnuts in a rimmed pan that's large enough to hold them in a single layer. Bake in a 400° oven until nuts are no longer starchy-tasting (taste to test), about 30 minutes. Dump nuts onto a towel, fold to enclose, and seal in a plastic bag. Let stand until nuts

A TASTE OF THE WEST

Chestnut Soup

- ½ to ¾ cup minced shallots or onions
- ½ teaspoon dried thyme leaves
- About 6 cups regular-strength chicken broth

PETER CHRISTIANSEN

3 cups peeled roasted chestnuts (about 1½ lb. unshelled, see Back to Basics opposite page)

Sour cream

Salt

In a 4- to 5-quart pan over high heat, stir shallots, thyme, and ¼ cup broth until vegetables are dry and start to brown. Stir in another ¼ cup broth; boil away and stir often until vegetables are darker brown. Stir in 5½ cups broth; add chestnuts. Cover, bring to a boil, then simmer until chestnuts mash easily, about 30 minutes. Whirl mixture, a portion at a time, in a blender until smoothly puréed; or skim chestnuts and vegetables from broth, and purée in a food processor. Return to pan.

Measure soup; you need 5 cups. If you have less, add broth to make this amount. If you have more, boil, stirring, until reduced. Serve, or if making ahead, cover and chill up to 3 days; freeze to store longer. Ladle hot soup into bowls; add to each a spoonful of sour cream and salt to taste. Serves 4.

Per serving: 342 cal. (13 percent from fat); 7.7 g protein; 4.8 g fat (1.1 g sat.); 67 g carbo.; 85 mg sodium; 0 mg chol.

PETER CHRISTIANSEN

CUT THROUGH *the thin chestnut shell before baking. While nut is warm, pull off shell and brown skin.*

are cool enough to touch, about 10 minutes.

Take out 1 nut at a time; with a short-bladed knife (better still, a short, curved-tip chestnut knife), pull off shell and as much of the slightly bitter brown skin as you can. The nuts waiting in the bag stay steamy, and the shells remain pliable.

Buying guide: 3 pounds chestnuts (about 1½ in. wide) equal about 2 quarts; roasted and peeled, they yield 6 cups chestnuts.

Per cup: 371 cal. (8 percent from fat); 4.8 g protein; 3.3 g fat (0.6 g sat.); 80 g carbo.; 3 mg sodium; 0 mg chol.

GREAT TOOL

Cooking thermometer: A wise investment

About once a year, usually during the holidays when the kitchen is full of people and I'm trying to visit as I put the finishing touches on dinner, I forget and leave an in-

stant-read thermometer in a roasting turkey or hunk of meat. Naturally, the plastic cover melts and the thermometer is ruined, but not before I can determine when the meat is ready to serve. You might think I could solve the problem by using a meat thermometer that can go in the oven. In fact, usually I do; the instant-read is for double-checking.

This sounds rather obsessive, perhaps, but because thermometers are fragile and break easily, and temperature is often critical to the quality of food, it's wise to check the accuracy of thermometers frequently. To do this, you need a cooking thermometer with a range above 212° (boiling at sea level). Put the thermometer in boiling water and give it time to register. If it reads 212° (or the correct temperature for boiling at your altitude), no problem. If the thermometer reads above or below boiling, it's still useful, but you must factor in the difference when you use this thermometer to check others.

Most meat thermometers don't register above 200°; if they get hotter, they will either break or give weird readings. So let the hot water containing the control thermometer cool below 200°, put the meat thermometers in the water, and give them a few minutes to register. Give instant thermometers about 1 minute to register; they're fast but not really instant. Compare readings with the control thermometer and discard thermometers more than 5° off.

One controversy that frequently comes up when roasting meat is what happens when the meat comes out of the oven. Does the internal temperature rise or not? Through many years of testing in *Sunset's* kitchens, we have observed that the temperature rarely changes more than 1° or so, and usually it drops in roasts of the size you cook in a home oven. We recommend that you cook meat to the desired temperature,

then let it rest 10 to 20 minutes before serving. As the meat stands, internal juices redistribute themselves and the meat firms.

Another point to keep in mind: Some thermometers have written on them specific temperatures for certain meats. Some of these temperatures are higher than needed for safety and today's taste; for example, pork is best at 150° to 155°, even though the thermometer might indicate it should be cooked to 170° or higher. When instructions conflict, go with the temperature the recipe recommends.

SEASONAL NOTE

Meyer lemons to sip

Meyer lemons have a more floral aroma and taste than their commercial counterpart, the tart Eureka. Meyers are appearing more frequently in markets, and pastry chefs in the West's leading restaurants favor them in desserts.

Lindsey Shere at Chez Panisse in Berkeley takes another approach: she offers a refreshing, nonalcoholic beverage, using the zest of the peel to reinforce the unique flavor. I've presented this version at parties, letting guests mix their own by the glass to suit their tastes.

Meyer lemon spritzer. Finely grate yellow part of the peel from 2 **Meyer lemons.** In a 1½- to 2-quart pan, combine peel and 1 cup **sugar;** mash them together with a spoon until sugar is colored lightly by the peel. Let stand for 1 to 2 hours. Add 1 cup **water;** bring to a boil over high heat, stirring until sugar dissolves, 2 to 3 minutes. Pour syrup through a fine strainer into a bowl or pitcher. Cover and chill until cold, at least 1 hour or up to 4 days. Pour 2 to 3 tablespoons syrup into a tall glass (about 8 oz.) filled with ice. Add 2 to 3 tablespoons freshly squeezed **Meyer**

lemon juice, to taste, and **sparkling mineral water** or part Chenin Blanc or Riesling to fill glass.

Per serving: 78 cal. (0 percent from fat); 0 g protein; 0 g fat; 20 g carbo.; 0.2 mg sodium; 0 mg chol.

GREAT INGREDIENT

Turning over a new leaf with fila

Fila, phyllo, or fillo: how you spell the name of these large, useful pastry sheets matters much less than how you handle them.

The thin sheets or leaves, lightly buttered and stacked, can be folded around fillings, used to top casseroles, or cut into small pieces and baked to make flaky pastries, which are not nearly as rich as regular pastry or puff pastry. And fila pastries are certainly quicker and easier—real boons during this season of entertaining.

Fila is sold in 1-pound packages of 18 to 20 sheets. You'll find them in the refrigerator or freezer section of most supermarkets. If you have access to a good Middle Eastern delicatessen, you may be able to get freshly made fila. Whether fresh or frozen, you'll still have to buy a pound; that's the way it always comes.

Such quantities present problems. A pound is enough to make a big roasting pan of baklava—dessert for a month for most families.

Until fila producers rethink their packaging, you might want to try a method I use to keep fila flexible and useful longer. Instead of removing the wrapper to get at large sheets, I cut off a desired width right through the plastic-wrapped and folded fila. Then I immediately seal the remaining portion airtight in a plastic bag (foil doesn't work as effectively) and return it to the refrigerator for up to 1 week, or freeze it to store longer for later use.

As you work with fila, you'll get flaky, buttery results by lightly streaking sheets with melted butter as you stack them. Sheets that touch moisture should be buttered more generously to keep them from getting soggy.

It's a safe bet to bake fila dishes in a 350° oven; if hotter, thin fila edges may scorch and center layers won't get as crisp.

Faux Napoleons. Cut **fila dough** into 10 to 12 strips, about 18 inches long and about 2½ inches wide. Using about 2 tablespoons melted **butter** or margarine, lightly and quickly brush over each strip and stack them. Cover fila strips not in use with plastic wrap to prevent drying. Cut stack into 3-inch lengths, and place them slightly apart on a lightly buttered 10- by 15-inch pan. Bake in a 350° oven until pastry is golden

FAST FLAKY PASTRIES *start with fila dough. To preserve freshness, cut fila in desired widths without unwrapping the package; seal and store unused portions. Lightly butter strips of dough, stack, cut, and bake. Separate each stack into several portions, then restack with filling.*

brown, about 20 minutes. Let fila cool slightly. Separate each rectangle, lifting apart to make 3 layers. Spoon about 2 tablespoons **sweetened whipped cream** or ice cream on the first layer, adding fresh sliced or cooked **fruit** as filling. Top with middle layer of pastry, add more of the same filling, then cover with the pastry top and dust generously with **powdered sugar.** Makes 6 servings.

Per serving, no fruit: 194 cal. (79 percent from fat); 1.3 g protein; 17 g fat (10 g sat.); 10 g carbo.; 109 mg sodium; 55 mg chol.

BOB THOMPSON ON WINE

What's new in nouveau?

The Thanksgiving feast is a small farmer's idea of big spending—a lavish use of food that might have been scarce until one more victory over capricious weather brought one more crop safely to the barn.

For the celebratory toast? Forget champagne. For the festive board? Forget old bottles long in the cellar. Seize the day with something so close to the season you think you can smell and taste the last dusty, ripening warmth of September and October, and you certainly can smell and taste the edgy bite of fruit just off the vine. In short, salute the new crops with a 1994 *nouveau,* made from grapes brought in while other farmers were busy with the last of their tomatoes or still waiting for the squash.

The French invented the idea of nouveau. For them, of course, it must be made in Beaujolais using Gamay

grapes, and it ought to be drunk straight from the barrel beginning in mid-November, when it is still a tiny bit fizzy from the last step of fermentation.

When Californians first took up the idea in the 1970s, they created so much expectation and served so much disappointment that the craze collapsed faster than it sprang up. French approaches to fermentation did not quite suit California grapes.

Bottling—and the U.S. government, unlike the French, insists on bottles—proved difficult to do without muting nouveau's freshness. However, a handful of stubborn souls kept trying until they got it right. A slow second flowering has produced enough delicious nouveau to supply a good many of this year's Thanksgiving tables. All cost a modest $5 to $8 a bottle.

The major producers: Beringer Vineyards North Coast Nouveau and Robert Pecota Gamay Beaujolais Napa Valley.

Limited production: Preston Vineyards & Winery Dry Creek Valley Gamay Beaujolais.

Local production most easily found at the tasting rooms or in local restaurants: Sebastiani Gamay Nouveau, Castoro Cellars Paso Robles Gamay Beaujolais Nouveau, Perry Creek Sierra Foothills Zinfandel Nouveau, Maurice Car'rie Temecula Nouveau Gamay Beaujolais.

Wherever it comes from, however it is made, nouveau must be intensely fruity and low in tannins, the two qualities that give it its particular appeal with turkey and all the fixings.

Gamay is the obvious first choice of grape variety, no surprise given its history in Beaujolais, but it is rare in this country. Napa Gamay, Zinfandel, and the strain of Pinot Noir we call Gamay Beaujolais have all done well as sources of nouveau from Western vineyards.

Careful fermentation takes care of the rest. Most nouveaus ferment as whole clusters rather than crushed

grapes, in effect turning each berry into its own miniature fermenting vessel. However, with careful crushing and cooling, a conventional fermentation can temper tannins just as well. Preston's Gamay Beaujolais is a case in point.

Because they are so young and frisky, serving nouveaus lightly cooled adds to the pleasure. ■

NOUVEAU WINES *are priced right at $5 to $8 a bottle.*

IN CALIFORNIA GOLD COUNTRY, *the sun shines through brilliant foliage as the Parsons family of Sutter Creek enjoys a backyard stream.*

HAZELNUTS *from the Evonuk farm near Eugene, Oregon, could end up in the family's special chocolate-nut tart.*

ON THE HARDER RANCH *in eastern Washington, Jake Harder and his grandson, Jacob, prepare to feed the calves.*

GOLDEN TURKEY, *garlicky Swiss chard, Yukon gold potatoes, and garden salad star at the Sansones' Thanksgiving table in Oregon.*

A Western Country Thanksgiving

Favorite family recipes from eastern Washington, western Oregon, California Gold Country, and Santa Barbara County

SANTA BARBARA COUNTY *winery owner Jim Clendenen tucks rosemary branches around a turkey he's grilling in the backyard.*

Back to the country—that's where our thoughts turn at Thanksgiving: to the rural roots of many groups that make up the West, to our region's pastoral beauty, and to its rich agricultural bounty. We asked families in four regions of the West to share the recipes and traditions that help to make a

By Linda Lau Anusasananan, Betsy Reynolds Bateson, Christine Weber Hale, Elaine Johnson

Photography by Peter Christiansen

Western country Thanksgiving special.

In the California Gold Country, Santa Barbara County, eastern Washington, and western Oregon, we visited with people who gather good foods from the source. These are families who grow their own vegetables, bake their bread, raise meat, catch fish, produce wine, and run country restaurants.

Each group celebrates in different ways, with meals that encompass family favorites and new holiday choices. Their recipes are as diverse as the West, but all have the honest good flavor that we expect from down-to-earth cooking.

THE HARDER FAMILY *gathers in eastern Washington.*

Thanksgiving Dinner Checklist

Starters (Pick one or both)
Grilled Vegetable Appetizer** (page 210)
Spicy Squash Soup** (page 213)

Salads (Choose one or both)
Cranberry-Waldorf Molded Salad* (page 200)
Thanksgiving Salad (page 208)

The Starring Attraction (Pick one)
Beef Tenderloin with Cabernet-Cherry Sauce (page 204)
Lemberger-marinated Steelhead (page 207)
Rosemary Smoked Turkey (page 213)

The Gravy (To go with turkey and trimmings)
Rich Brown Giblet Gravy** (page 203)

Dressings (One is enough)
Artichoke-Parmesan Sourdough Stuffing (page 199)
Pilaf Dressing with Fruits and Nuts** (page 205)
Spiced Basmati Rice with Chayote Squash** (page 214)

Vegetables (Make at least two, maybe more)
Citrus-sauced Green Beans*** (page 201)
Yam Puff*** (page 201)
Yukon Gold Herbed Mashed Potatoes* (page 209)
Italian-style Swiss Chard (page 209)
Sautéed Mushrooms with Apple Eau-de-Vie (page 209)

Desserts (It's up to you)
Zinfandel Port Cookies (page 202)
Pecan-Cranberry Tart (page 203)
Russian Cream with Cranberries*** (page 206)
Hazelnut-Chocolate Tart (page 211)

Wines (For selections, see page 195)

***10 percent, **20 percent, or *30 percent or fewer calories from fat

Natives and newcomers revive Gold Country holiday traditions

Yams, cranberries, and stuffing grace the table in new ways

A long every rolling road in the California foothills, trees are ablaze with brightly colored leaves of burnt red and squash yellow. Leslie Jo and Brent Parsons fell in love with this beauty, and moved to Sutter Creek in California's Gold Country in 1989. Brent bought an art gallery, and Leslie Jo found an old house with porches and a backyard creek—even ducks.

In the front yard, a fall garden with broccoli, cauliflower, cucumbers, brussels sprouts, and herbs is bordered by a picket fence. Leslie Jo loves to cook, and she bakes sourdough bread twice a week in a clay cloche that she swears makes the best crust ever. Her sourdough bread, an Amador County Fair prizewinner, is the base for her artichoke-parmesan sourdough stuffing. But the stuffing tastes terrific with purchased sourdough bread as well.

Another family favorite is the cranberry-Waldorf molded salad, a Thanksgiving tradition from Leslie Jo's great-grandmother that's been updated with a low-fat yogurt topping and a reduction in sugar. Says Leslie Jo about the salad, "Brent would die if I forgot it." For their Thanksgiving feast, she serves beans or another vegetable with a light citrus sauce. Here she shares two options: orange-sherry and lemon-dill.

LESLIE JO PARSONS, *of Sutter Creek, typically prepares the Thanksgiving meal for about 15 family members.*

Artichoke-Parmesan Sourdough Stuffing

2 pounds sourdough bread (about 2 loaves), cut into ¾- to 1-inch cubes (8 quarts *total*)

3 tablespoons butter or margarine

2 large (about 1¼ lb. *total*) onions, chopped

1 pound mushrooms, rinsed and sliced

2 cups chopped celery

¼ cup (about 12 cloves) minced garlic

3½ cups regular-strength chicken broth

4 jars (6 oz. *each*) marinated artichoke hearts, drained

1 cup grated parmesan cheese

1 tablespoon poultry seasoning

1 tablespoon minced fresh or 1½ teaspoons dried rosemary

¾ teaspoon *each* salt and pepper

2 large eggs, beaten

Spread bread cubes in a single layer on 12- by 15-inch baking sheets (you'll need 4 sheets, or do in sequence). Toast in a 350° oven until very crisp and golden brown, about 25 minutes; shake cubes after 15 minutes and switch pan positions. (If making ahead, cool cubes and store airtight for up to 2 days.)

In a 12-inch frying pan or 6- to 8-quart pan, melt butter over medium heat; add onions, mushrooms, celery, and garlic. Cook, stirring often, until vegetables are soft and tinged golden brown, about 25 minutes. To release brown bits from bottom of pan, add ½ cup broth; using a wooden spoon, scrape all brown bits from pan bottom. In a large bowl, mix cooked vegetables with toasted bread cubes, artichoke hearts, cheese, poultry seasoning, rosemary, and salt and pepper. Whisk together remaining broth and eggs, and pour over vegetable-bread mixture; stir until

ARTICHOKE-PARMESAN SOURDOUGH STUFFING *is based on prizewinning homemade bread. Half the stuffing is baked in the bird, half in a casserole; then the two are mixed to serve with the holiday dinner.*

ingredients are well coated.

Use to stuff an 18- to 22-pound turkey, roasting turkey according to chart instructions on page 203, adding 30 to 50 minutes roasting time because bird is stuffed. Bake any remaining stuffing mixture in a 2-quart baking dish alongside turkey during the last 45 minutes of roasting time. Or bake stuffing in a 4½- to 5-quart baking dish in a 350° oven for 30 minutes, covered, and 20 minutes more uncovered. Makes 12 to 16 servings.

Per serving: 281 cal. (31 percent from fat); 11 g protein; 9.8 g fat (3.4 g sat.); 39 g carbo.; 818 mg sodium; 36 mg chol.

Cranberry-Waldorf Molded Salad

1 small package (3 oz.) lemon-flavor gelatin

2 cups boiling water

2 cups fresh cranberries

1 large (about ¾ lb.) orange, peeled and seeded

1 large (about ½ lb.) red apple, cored

1 cup chopped celery

½ cup chopped walnuts or almonds

Lettuce leaves, rinsed and crisped (optional)

Creamy yogurt dressing (recipe follows)

Mix gelatin with boiling water, stirring until dissolved; chill until thick, about 20 minutes.

Meanwhile, coarsely chop cranberries; chop orange and apple into about ¼-inch cubes. Mix fruit with thickened gelatin; add celery and

nuts. Spoon into a 5- to 6-cup mold or fancy glass bowl. Chill for at least 4 hours or until the next day.

To remove salad from mold, dip mold in warm water and wait until salad breaks away from side of mold when gently shaken, about 2 minutes. Invert serving platter on top of mold. Holding tightly together, flip mold over onto platter; remove mold. Tuck lettuce leaves under edge of salad. Or serve salad directly from fancy bowl. Offer yogurt

dressing to add as desired.
Serves 8.

Per serving: 167 cal. (27 percent from fat); 4 g protein; 5 g fat (0.5 g sat.); 29 g carbo; 63 mg sodium; 0.6 mg chol.

Creamy yogurt dressing. Combine 1 cup **nonfat unflavored yogurt,** 2 tablespoons **honey,** and 1 tablespoon grated **orange peel.** Chill until ready to use, up to 2 days.

Citrus-sauced Green Beans

Orange-sherry sauce or lemon-dill sauce (recipes follow)

About 1½ pounds green beans, rinsed, ends snapped

½ cup sliced almonds, toasted, or fresh dill sprigs or fennel tops

Make orange-sherry or lemon-dill sauce. In a 4- to 5-quart pan, bring about 2 quarts water to a boil over high heat. Add beans, reduce heat, and simmer until beans are bright green and just tender to bite, about 6 minutes. Drain; place on a serving dish.

Pour warm orange-sherry sauce over beans and top with toasted almonds; or pour warm lemon-dill sauce over beans and garnish with fresh dill sprigs or fennel tops. Serves 6 to 8.

Per serving: 56 cal. (3 percent from fat); 1.6 g protein; 0.2 g fat (0 g sat.); 12 g carbo.; 41 mg sodium; 0 mg chol.

Orange-sherry sauce. In a 1- to 2-quart pan over medium heat, combine ¾ cup **orange juice,** 3 tablespoons **cream sherry,** 1 tablespoon **lemon juice,** and 1½ teaspoons **cornstarch.** Cook, stirring often, until sauce is just bubbling, about 4 minutes. Remove from heat; cover and keep warm.

Lemon-dill sauce. In a 1- to 2-quart pan over medium heat, combine ½ cup **lemon juice,** ¼ cup regular-strength **vegetable broth,** 1 tablespoon **sugar,** and 1½ teaspoons **cornstarch.** Cook, stirring often, until sauce is just bubbling, about 4 minutes. Remove from heat and stir in 2 tablespoons minced **fresh dill** or fresh fennel tops; cover and keep warm.

AN UPDATED FAMILY FAVORITE, *the Parsonses' cranberry-Waldorf molded salad is served with a creamy yogurt dressing.*

A zesty lemon-orange yam puff

Barbara Toma, a fifth-generation Italian-American, grew up in Sutter Creek, where her grandparents had a dairy that at one time delivered to half the town. On Thanksgiving, she always serves a family favorite, whipped yams with orange and lemon peel and juice.

Yam Puff

4 pounds (about 8 medium-size) yams

½ cup firmly packed brown sugar

About 3 tablespoons butter or margarine, melted

2 teaspoons *each* grated orange and lemon peel

¼ cup orange juice

2 tablespoons lemon juice

½ teaspoon salt

In a 6- to 8-quart pan, bring about 3 quarts water to a boil over high heat. Add yams, reduce heat, cover, and simmer until yams are tender when pierced with a fork, about 20 minutes. Drain and cool.

When yams are cool

BARBARA TOMA'S *whipped yam casserole is a great-tasting, healthful side dish.*

THE PARSONS FAMILY *has lived in its Sutter Creek home for five years.*

A glass of wine, and cookies, at Greenstone Winery

Eight miles west of Sutter Creek, near Ione, Greenstone Winery is tucked gently between grapevine-covered bluffs. Its name derives from the green stone found in the Sierra foothills. Thirteen years ago, Stan Van Spanje and Durward Fowler moved their families from Southern California to start a new life in the country, making wine. One of their favorites is a port made from grapes from a 100-year-old vineyard. Alongside, they enjoy Zinfandel port balls, a delicious, easy cookie that a close friend, June Copper, developed with their Zinfandel port in mind.

Zinfandel Port Cookies

1 package (12 oz.) vanilla wafer cookies

½ cup Dutch cocoa

1 cup pecans

¼ cup dark corn syrup

½ cup Greenstone Zinfandel port or other port

About ½ cup powdered sugar

In a food processor, combine cookies, cocoa, and pecans. Whirl until reduced to fine crumbs; pulse for several seconds.

Or by hand, put cookies in a heavy-duty plastic bag, seal shut, and crush cookies with a rolling pin. Finely chop pecans and mix with cookie crumbs and cocoa.

Add corn syrup and port. Continue to blend or mix until well blended, about 15 seconds if using a food processor.

Using your hands, form dough into 1-inch balls; roll in powdered sugar. Serve, or store airtight up to 1 month; for longer storage, freeze up to 2 months. Just before serving, roll balls in more powdered sugar if a white snowball effect is desired. Makes about 4 dozen cookies.

Per cookie: 62 cal. (40 percent from fat); 0.7 g protein; 2.8 g fat (0.5 g sat.); 8.9 g carbo.; 31 mg sodium; 0 mg chol.

GUESTS RELAX *with Zinfandel port and port balls at Greenstone Winery near Ione, California.*

enough to touch, peel them and cut into quarters. In a large bowl, mash yams until smooth. Add brown sugar, 2 tablespoons of the butter, the orange and lemon peel, orange and lemon juices, and salt. With an electric mixer, beat yam mixture until light and fluffy. Scrape the mixture into a buttered 2- to 2½-quart or 8- by 10-inch baking dish. (If making ahead, cover and chill up to 2 days.)

Bake yam puff in a 350° oven until warm throughout and peaks are tinged brown, about 25 minutes (if chilled, allow about 15 more minutes). If desired, drizzle baked puff with remaining melted butter. Makes 8 to 10 servings.

Per serving: 250 cal. (9 percent from fat); 2.5 g protein; 2.6 g fat (1.5 g sat.); 55 g carbo.; 152 mg sodium; 6.2 mg chol.

A LUSCIOUS *pecan-cranberry tart is the work of Amador City pastry chef Ingrid Fraser.*

A pastry chef sweetens Thanksgiving

Down U.S. Highway 49, a few miles from Sutter Creek, the Imperial Hotel in Amador City is well known for the handiwork of pastry chef Ingrid Fraser. On Thanksgiving, she serves her pecan-cranberry tart with homemade crème fraîche at home as well as at the hotel dining room.

Pecan-Cranberry Tart

2   cups pecan halves

4   large eggs

1   cup firmly packed brown sugar

⅔   cup light corn syrup

¼   cup (⅛ lb.) butter or margarine, melted and cooled

2   teaspoons grated orange peel

1   teaspoon vanilla

½   teaspoon salt

1   cup fresh cranberries

    Baked tart crust (recipe follows)

    About 1 cup crème fraîche or whipped cream (optional)

Spread pecans in a single layer in a 10- by 15-inch baking pan. Toast in a 300° oven until crisp and golden (break nuts open to check color), about 20 minutes; shake pecans after 10 minutes. Let cool.

In a bowl, whisk together eggs, brown sugar, corn syrup, butter, peel, vanilla, and salt until well blended. Fold in toasted pecans and cranberries. Place baked tart crust on a baking sheet; pour pecan-cranberry mixture into crust.

Place filled tart on sheet on middle rack in a 350° oven; bake until filling is just firm, 40 to 45 minutes. Remove from oven; cool to room temperature, about 4 hours. Push tart from rim to serve. Add crème fraîche if desired. Makes 12 to 14 servings.

Per serving: 403 cal. (49 percent from fat); 5 g protein; 22 g fat (7.6 g sat.); 49 g carbo.; 228 mg sodium; 103 mg chol.

Baked tart crust. In a food processor or with an electric mixer, mix together ½ cup **sugar** and ½ cup (¼ lb.) **butter** or margarine until light and fluffy. Thoroughly mix in 1 **large egg**, then 1½ cups **all-purpose flour.** (If making ahead, cover dough and chill up to 3 days. Freeze to store longer; use at room temperature.)

In an 11-inch tart pan with removable bottom and fluted ring, evenly press dough over bottom and up side. Bake in a 325° oven until edges are lightly browned, about 25 minutes. Cool.—*B. R. B.*

Turkey and Gravy Basics

Turkey and trimmings don't go far without a rich turkey gravy. This gravy tastes rich but is low-fat. Consult the chart for cooking times for barbecued or oven-roasted turkey.

Barbecued* or Oven-roasted Turkey

Turkey weight with giblets	Oven temp.*	Internal temp.**	Cooking time***
10 to 13 lb.	350°	160°	1½ to 2¼ hr.
14 to 23 lb.	325°	160°	2 to 3 hr.
24 to 26 lb.	325°	160°	3 to 3¾ hr.
28 to 30 lb.	325°	160°	3½ to 4½ hr.

* See Rosemary Smoked Turkey, page 213, for heat control for a charcoal barbecue.
** Insert meat thermometer through thickest part of breast to bone.
*** Add 30 to 50 minutes to cooking time for a stuffed, oven-roasted turkey.

Rich Brown Giblet Gravy

For more gravy to go with birds 18 pounds or larger, increase broth to 7 cups, wine to 1 cup, and cornstarch to 7 tablespoons. Adjust final measure of broth to make 6 cups, adding water if needed. These changes yield 6 to 6½ cups gravy.

    Giblets from a 12- to 24-pound turkey

2   medium-size (about ¾ lb. total) onions, quartered

2   large (about ½ lb. total) carrots, cut into chunks

¾   cup sliced celery

5   cups regular-strength chicken broth

½   cup dry white wine

½   teaspoon pepper

⅓   cup cornstarch

    Salt

Rinse giblets and cut neck into 3 or 4 sections; chill liver airtight. Combine remaining giblets, neck pieces, onions, carrots, celery, and ½ cup broth in a 5- to 6-quart pan over high heat. Boil, uncovered, stirring often as liquid evaporates; cook until giblets and vegetables are browned and browned bits stick to pan, 15 to 20 minutes. Add another ½ cup broth and stir to loosen browned bits; boil and brown, uncovered, as directed in preceding step. Add remaining broth, wine, and pepper to pan; stir to scrape browned bits free. Cover pan and simmer gently until gizzard is tender when pierced, about 1½ hours. Add liver and cook 10 minutes.

Pour broth through a fine strainer into a bowl; discard vegetables. Save giblets for gravy or other uses. If using giblets, pull meat off neck and finely chop neck meat and giblets. Measure broth; if needed, add water to make 4 cups. (If making ahead, cover and chill liquid and giblets up to 1 day.)

In the pan, mix cornstarch with ¼ cup water until smooth; add broth and chopped giblets. Stir over high heat until boiling, about 5 minutes. Season to taste with salt. Makes 4 to 5 cups.

Per ½ cup: 51 cal. (18 percent from fat); 2.6 g protein; 1 g fat (0.3 g sat.); 7.7 g carbo.; 41 mg sodium; 16 mg chol.

ON A BRISK MORNING HIKE, *members of the Harder clan scamper over rough basalt and dry grass hills, surveying the broad, bare beauty of their cattle ranch in eastern Washington's high desert.*

Back to the land in eastern Washington

At the Harder ranch, it's elegant beef; at the Kiona family winery, a barbecued steelhead trout

In the high desert of eastern Washington known as the Channel Scablands, rough boulders punctuate the rugged basalt landscape. Cattle ranchers Joan and Jake Harder live on land that Jake's grandfather settled in 1873.

On Thanksgiving, ranch activities—feeding the calves, hunting birds, and going for hayrides—give city guests a bit of country flavor. If it's cold enough—and it often is—kids skate on frozen ponds nearby.

For the big holiday meal, guests sit down to an elegant table covered with pressed autumn leaves, fine china, crystal, and silver. "Although we dress casual for the ranch, we like to set a formal dinner," says Joan.

Foods from the ranch and the area highlight the menu.

It's not surprising that, as cattle ranchers, they prefer beef over turkey for their feast. They coat a tenderloin with spices, roast it, and serve it with a sauce made from Washington's dried sour cherries. Wild and long-grain rice studded with local apples and nuts complements the cherry sauce. Traditional choices reign for dessert: pumpkin and apple pies and a family favorite, a molded cream with refreshing cranberry sauce.

Beef Tenderloin with Cabernet-Cherry Sauce

Spice mixture (recipe follows)

1 trimmed and tied center-cut beef tenderloin (about 5 lb.)

3 cups regular-strength beef broth

1½ cups Cabernet Sauvignon

1½ cups dried tart cherries, such as Montmorency

2½ tablespoons red currant jelly

2 tablespoons cornstarch mixed with ¼ cup water

Thin orange slices (optional)

Salt and pepper

Rub spice mixture over beef. Set beef in a 10- by 15-inch roasting pan. Roast in a 450° oven until a thermometer inserted in the center of the thickest part of the meat registers 135° for rare to medium-rare, 35 to 40 minutes, or 140° for medium, about 50 minutes

Meanwhile, in a 3- to 4-quart pan, combine 2 cups broth, wine, cherries, and jelly; bring to a boil over high heat. Cover and simmer over low heat until cherries soften, 15 to 20 minutes.

When done, transfer roast to a warm platter. Snip strings free; remove. Let roast stand in a warm place for about 15 minutes.

Meanwhile, add remaining 1 cup broth to roasting pan; stir over medium heat to scrape browned bits free. Pour broth mixture into cherry mixture; bring to a boil. Add cornstarch mixture, and stir until sauce boils. Pour into a bowl.

Garnish beef with orange slices. Cut roast into thick or thin slices as desired; serve with sauce. Add salt and pepper to taste. Makes 10 to 12 servings.

Per serving: 388 cal. (35 percent from fat); 40 g protein; 15 g fat (5.6 g sat.); 18 g carbo.; 108 mg sodium; 117 mg chol.

AT JOAN AND JAKE HARDER'S *table, the main event is a spice-coated beef tenderloin with Cabernet-cherry sauce, and rice with local fruits and nuts.*

Spice mixture. Mix 1½ teaspoons *each* **whole black pepper, dried thyme leaves,** and **grated orange peel,** ½ teaspoon *each* **dried oregano leaves** and **whole coriander,** ¼ teaspoon **ground cinnamon,** ⅛ teaspoon **ground allspice,** and **4 cloves garlic,** pressed or minced.

Pilaf Dressing with Fruits and Nuts

½ cup chopped walnuts or almonds

1 tablespoon butter or margarine

1 large (about ½ lb.) onion, chopped

1 teaspoon ground coriander

1 quart regular-strength chicken broth

2 cups apple juice

2 cups wild rice, rinsed

1½ cups long-grain white rice

⅓ cup raisins

1 large (about ½ lb.) Red Delicious apple, cored and diced

Chopped parsley or apple slices dipped in lemon juice

In a 5- to 6-quart pan, stir nuts over medium-low heat until toasted, about 7 minutes. Remove from pan.

Add butter and chopped onion; stir over medium-

rice. Garnish with parsley or apple slices. Makes about 4 quarts, 10 to 12 servings.

Per serving: 279 cal. (17 percent from fat); 7.4 g protein; 5.1 g fat (1.1 g sat.); 52 g carbo.; 33 mg sodium; 2.6 mg chol.

Russian Cream with Cranberries

1⅓ cups sugar

2 envelopes unflavored gelatin

1½ cups water

2 cups milk or half-and-half

2 cups nonfat unflavored yogurt or nonfat or regular sour cream

2 teaspoons vanilla

Fresh cranberries (optional)

Poached cranberries (recipe follows)

In a 3- to 4-quart pan, mix sugar and gelatin. Stir in water; let stand for about 5 minutes to soften gelatin. Bring to a boil over high heat, stirring constantly, until sugar and gelatin dissolve. Remove from heat; stir in milk. Gradually whisk yogurt and vanilla into the hot gelatin mixture. Pour mixture into an 8- to 10-cup metal mold. Cover and chill until set, at least 5 hours or until next day.

To unmold, dip container up to rim in hot-to-touch tap water until edges of cream just begin to liquefy; it takes only a few seconds. Quickly dry mold and invert it onto a serving dish. The cream will slowly slip free; if it's stubborn, return it briefly to hot water bath. If you unmold dessert before serving time, return to refrigerator until surface firms, then cover lightly.

Garnish with fresh cranberries, if desired. Slice in wedges and serve with poached cranberries. Makes 8 servings.

Per serving: 278 cal. (7 percent from fat); 6.8 g protein; 2.2 g fat (1.3 g sat.); 59 g carbo.; 77 mg sodium; 9.7 mg chol.

Poached cranberries. In a 1- to 2-quart pan, combine 2 cups **fresh** or frozen **cranberries,** ½ cup **sugar,** and ½ cup **cranberry juice cocktail.** Cook over medium-high heat, stirring occasionally,

BESIDES TRADITIONAL PIES, *the family often requests a molded cream with tangy cranberry sauce. Adjust the dessert's richness by choosing cream or milk, sour cream or yogurt.*

high heat until onion is tinged with brown, about 5 minutes. Stir in coriander. Add broth and juice; bring to a boil. Add wild rice; cover and simmer over low heat for 25 minutes. Stir in white rice; cover and cook over low heat

until rice is tender to bite, about 20 minutes.

(If making ahead, cool, cover, and chill until next day. Reheat, covered, over low heat, adding about ¾ cup water, until hot. Or heat, covered, in a microwave-safe

bowl in a microwave oven on full power [100 percent] for 3 minutes. Stir and continue heating, stirring every minute, adding a little water if too dry, until hot.)

Shortly before serving, stir raisins, apple, and nuts into

until berries begin to pop, about 7 minutes. Cool, cover, and chill until cold, at least 2 hours or up to 3 days. Makes about 2 cups.

With luck, a holiday potluck features the catch of the day

In the arid Red Mountains, Ann and John Williams, Jr., celebrate the holiday with a big, multigeneration potluck party at Kiona, their small family winery near Benton City, Washington. Four great-grandparents and seven grandkids are among the 40-plus guests at the Williamses' family gathering.

Ann handles the major entrées. As relatives arrive, they place their contributions on the generous counter that serves as a buffet in the open kitchen. If the family fishermen were lucky, daughter-in-law Vicky Williams will bring a steelhead trout that has been marinated in the family's Lemberger wine and barbecued. Carrie, Ann and John's daughter, offers a fruit salad made with pineapple to remind her of when she lived in Hawaii. Great-grandmother Ethel Williams, 80, always brings her specialty, homemade yeast rolls.

Lemberger-marinated Steelhead

1 bottle (750 ml.) Kiona Lemberger or other dry red wine

¼ cup soy sauce

3 tablespoons olive oil

¼ cup honey

2 tablespoons minced fresh ginger

1 tablespoon Worcestershire sauce

1 tablespoon mustard seed

1 teaspoon black peppercorns

3 cloves garlic, pressed or minced

1 whole (6 to 8 lb.) steelhead or salmon, cleaned, head and tail removed, and cut

BARBECUED STEELHEAD FILLETS *glow with a rich bronze sheen after a long bath in Kiona's Lemberger, a medium-body, spicy red wine that originated in Eastern Europe.*

lengthwise in half into 2 boneless fillets

In an 11- by 17-inch non-corrodible roasting pan (if pan is corrodible, line with plastic wrap), mix together wine, soy sauce, oil, honey, ginger, Worcestershire sauce, mustard seed, peppercorns, and garlic.

Rinse fish and pat dry. Immerse fillets, skin side up, in marinade. Cover and chill at least 8 hours or up to 1 day.

Lift fillets from marinade and drain briefly. Discard marinade.

Place each fillet, skin side down, on a double piece of heavy-duty foil. Cut the foil to follow the outlines of the fish, leaving a 1-inch border. Crimp foil edges.

Ignite 50 charcoal briquets on firegrate of a barbecue with a lid. Let briquets burn until coals are barely covered with gray ash, about 30 minutes. Bank about half the briquets on each side of the firegrate. Place a drip pan between banks of coals.

Set the cooking grill in place 4 to 6 inches above the pan. Set fish on grill in center so coals do not lie under fillets. Cover barbecue; adjust dampers to maintain even heat. Cook until fish is barely translucent in thickest part, 20 to 25 minutes.

Supporting fish with foil, transfer to a warm platter. To serve, cut through flesh of each fillet to the skin; slide a wide metal spatula between skin and flesh and lift off each portion. Makes 8 to 10 servings.

Per serving: 292 cal. (40 percent from fat); 35 g protein; 13 g fat (1.9 g sat.); 3 g carbo.; 87 mg sodium; 97 mg chol.—L. L. A.

ALONG THE BANKS *of the Columbia River, three generations of the Williams family—John, Sr., 82, his grandson, Scott, and Scott's 7-year-old son, J. J.—stand in the morning cold, hoping to hook a steelhead trout for Thanksgiving dinner.*

The freshest of western Oregon

Fine greens, great vegetables, and homegrown hazelnuts define the day

EDIBLE FLOWERS, *such as calendula, chrysanthemum, borage, and nasturtium, and greens from her specialty gardens go into Margaret Sansone's Thanksgiving salad.*

Margaret Sansone need only step outside to gather ingredients for Thanksgiving dinner. At her home surrounded by Douglas firs and autumn gold wisteria in Beaver Creek, 30 miles southeast of Portland, she has 5 acres of gardens and three greenhouses. The vegetable beds supply her family and Margaret's specialty produce business, Phoenix Gardens.

Growing up in an Italian-American family, Margaret learned to love fresh produce long before nutritionists touted its benefits. Her contributions to Thanksgiving dinner, shared with neighbors, always include a big salad with edible flowers and fresh herbs; rich-flavored Yukon gold potatoes, mashed and seasoned with chives and parsley; and Swiss chard cooked as her Italian mother taught her, with balsamic vinegar and a generous shot of garlic.

Thanksgiving Salad

3 quarts (about 10 oz.) lightly packed mixed salad greens (with edible flowers, if available)

½ cup chopped Italian parsley sprigs

3 tablespoons balsamic vinegar

1 tablespoon red wine vinegar (or use more balsamic)

3 tablespoons extra-virgin olive oil

1 small clove garlic, minced or pressed

2 teaspoons Dijon mustard

3 tablespoons chopped fresh or 1 teaspoon dried tarragon leaves

1 teaspoon chopped fresh or ½ teaspoon dried rosemary

Salt and pepper

Rinse salad greens; drain. Wrap greens in towels, and seal in plastic bags to crisp, at least 15 minutes or up until next day.

In a large salad bowl (at least 2½ quarts), combine parsley, balsamic and red wine vinegars, oil, garlic, mustard, tarragon, and rosemary. Season to taste with salt and pepper. Add greens; mix gently to coat. Serves 8.

Per serving: 56 cal. (88 percent from fat); 0.6 g protein; 5.5 g fat (0.8 g sat.); 2.1 g carbo.; 43 mg sodium; 0 mg chol.

Yukon Gold Herbed Mashed Potatoes

4 pounds Yukon gold or other thin-skinned potatoes, peeled

1½ cups low-fat milk

3 tablespoons butter or margarine

⅓ cup sliced chives

¼ cup chopped Italian parsley

Salt and pepper

Italian parsley sprigs

Place potatoes in a 6- to 8-quart pan with water to cover. Bring to a boil over high heat, cover, and simmer until tender when pierced, about 20 minutes; drain.

Meanwhile, in a 1- to 2-quart pan over medium heat, stir milk and butter until steaming, about 3 minutes. (Or in a quart-size microwave-safe measuring cup, cook uncovered in a microwave oven on full power [100 percent] until steaming, 2 to 3 minutes.)

In the large bowl of an electric mixer, or in cooking pan, beat or mash potatoes until very smooth. Add milk mixture and beat or stir until fluffy. Stir in chives, parsley, and salt and pepper to taste. Garnish with Italian parsley sprigs. Serves 8.

ITALIAN-STYLE SWISS CHARD *and herbed mashed potatoes have roots in Sansone's gardens.*

Per serving: 227 cal. (22 percent from fat); 5.6 g protein; 5.6 g fat (3.2 g sat.); 39 g carbo.; 83 mg sodium; 15 mg chol.

Italian-style Swiss Chard

3 pounds Swiss chard (both red and green, or all of one color), rinsed and drained

2 tablespoons extra-virgin olive oil

1½ tablespoons minced or pressed garlic

6 chopped anchovies

3 tablespoons balsamic vinegar

Salt and pepper

Trim stem ends of chard. Thinly slice stems crosswise up to base of leaves; set slices aside. Reserve a few whole leaves to line serving dish; coarsely chop remaining leaves.

In a 6- to 8-quart pan over medium-high heat, stir oil, garlic, and anchovies until garlic is slightly softened, about 2 minutes. Add chard stems; stir until softened, about 2 minutes. Stir in chopped leaves (part at a time if pan is full), cover, and cook until wilted, about 4 minutes. Mix in vinegar; season to taste with salt and

pepper. Garnish a serving dish with reserved chard leaves; spoon greens alongside. Serves 8.

Per serving: 70 cal. (53 percent from fat); 3.8 g protein; 4.1 g fat (0.6 g sat.); 6.6 g carbo; 444 mg sodium; 1.7 mg chol.

Mushrooms and eau-de-vie in Dundee

In the wine-producing Willamette Valley, Tina Landfried and David Bergen, owners of Tina's Restaurant in Dundee, have built their reputation cooking local products in a country French style. Foods like wild chanterelles from Oregon's damp woods figure prominently on their home table, too. In this simple sauté, high-quality ingredients make a difference; Tina flavors the mushrooms with apple eau-de-vie from Portland's Clear Creek Distillery.

Sautéed Mushrooms with Apple Eau-de-Vie

1 pound chanterelle mushrooms

1 pound large common mushrooms

1½ tablespoons minced or pressed garlic

1½ tablespoons chopped fresh thyme or 1½ teaspoons dried thyme leaves

¼ cup (⅛ lb.) butter or margarine

¼ cup good-quality cream sherry

¼ cup apple eau-de-vie or apple brandy

Fresh thyme sprigs (optional)

Salt and pepper

Rinse mushrooms and gently scrub if needed; pat dry. Slice ¼ to ½ inch thick. In a 12-inch frying pan or wok over medium-high heat, stir garlic, chopped thyme, and butter until sizzling, 1 to 3 minutes. Add mushrooms and stir often over high heat until pan is dry and mushrooms are browned, 20 to 25 minutes. Add sherry and eau-de-vie; stir until liquid evaporates. Spoon into a bowl and garnish with thyme sprigs. Add salt and pepper to taste. Serves 8.

Per serving: 117 cal. (50 percent from fat); 2.6 g protein; 6.5 g fat (3.8 g sat.); 9.2 g carbo.; 67 mg sodium; 16 mg chol.

GRILLED VEGETABLES *served with Pinot Gris is Paul Hart's favorite Thanksgiving appetizer.*

A Newberg winery owner's Thanksgiving appetizer

Not far north of Dundee, Paul Hart, co-owner of Rex Hill Vineyards and Winery outside Newberg, Oregon, loves to pull out all the stops when he entertains. Lavish parties take place in the lush flower gardens designed by his artist wife, Jan Jacobsen, or, in cooler weather, in the intimate private wine cellar. But Thanksgiving Day, the prelude to the Willamette wineries' busiest retail weekend of the year, necessitates a more practical, family-only meal.

Hart's grilled vegetable appetizer allows a great deal of flexibility, important with his hectic schedule. He slowly grills elephant garlic and multicolored vegetables to sweetness, hours in advance, then serves them at room temperature with toast and the winery's Pinot Noir or Pinot Gris.

Grilled Vegetable Appetizer

4 medium-size (about ¾ lb. total) slender eggplant, such as Asian or Italian, or 1 small (about ¾ lb.) globe eggplant, halved

2 medium-size (about 1¼ lb. total) sweet potatoes, scrubbed

A GENTLE RINSE *removes dirt from chanterelles and common mushrooms for Tina Landfried's sauté.*

1 large (about ¾ lb.) onion, unpeeled and quartered lengthwise

3 tablespoons extra-virgin olive oil

2 large red bell peppers (about 1¼ lb. total), stemmed and seeded

2 large heads (about 1 lb. total) elephant garlic, unpeeled and broken into cloves; or 3 large heads (about ¾ lb. total) regular garlic, whole and unpeeled

   Whole herb leaves (optional)

1½ teaspoons minced fresh rosemary or ½ teaspoon dried rosemary

1½ teaspoons minced fresh sage leaves or ½ teaspoon dried rubbed sage

2 slender baguettes (8 oz. each), diagonally sliced ½ inch thick, toasted

   Salt and pepper

Trim ends from eggplants and sweet potatoes. Lightly brush cut surfaces of onion and globe eggplant, if used, with a little oil.

Ignite 70 charcoal briquets in a large barbecue with dampers open, then spread into a solid layer and let burn until you can hold your hand at grill level for 10 seconds; if fire is hotter, vegetables will scorch.

Place eggplant, sweet potatoes, onion, peppers, and garlic on a greased grill over coals. Cover barbecue and turn vegetables every 5 minutes; after 30 minutes, add 10 more briquets to fire, and turn vegetables every 10 minutes. Cook vegetables until very tender when pressed: about 40 minutes for eggplant and peppers, 50 to 60 minutes for onion and garlic, and 1 hour for sweet potatoes. Remove vegetables as they are cooked.

Remove any tough peel from sweet potatoes, and all of peel from onion, peppers, and elephant garlic; for regular garlic, just halve heads horizontally. Coarsely chop eggplants, peppers, and sweet potatoes. Mince half of garlic; for regular garlic, squeeze out half of cloves and mince.

On a platter, place eggplant, peppers, and sweet potatoes in mounds. Arrange onion and whole garlic like petals of a flower; place minced garlic in the center. Garnish with whole herb leaves.

Drizzle vegetables with remaining oil, and sprinkle with minced rosemary and sage. Place baguette toasts in a basket. Serve, or if making ahead, let stand, lightly covered, up to 6 hours.

Spread toast with minced or whole cloves garlic, then spoon other vegetables on top. Season to taste with salt and pepper. Serves 8.

Per serving: 370 cal. (18 percent from fat); 10 g protein; 7.6 g fat (1.2 g sat.); 68 g carbo.; 364 mg sodium; 0 mg chol.

A chocolate-nut tart from hazelnut country

Rows of brilliant orange pumpkins line the walkway and the white spindles along the spacious front porch at the Evonuk family's farmhouse in Junction City, just north of Eugene. This is where the Evonuks, third-generation hazelnut and pumpkin farmers, gather on Thanksgiving Day, taking a break from the bustling holiday season.

210

The original owners of the Evonuks' 1910 farmhouse purchased it from the Sears Roebuck catalog, and the house still has the original cookstove. The Evonuks use it to cook much of the Thanksgiving dinner, including Shannon's special tart. This is a tart for serious dessert lovers: reminiscent of a pecan pie, but with a generous measure of hazelnuts and chocolate.

Hazelnut-Chocolate Tart

To keep tart from overbrowning, you'll need to tent it with foil, supporting foil on either side of pan with an empty can (1-lb. size works well) so foil doesn't fall and stick to filling. If you don't have a deep 10-inch quiche pan, you can use a 10-inch cheesecake pan with a removable rim. Roll crust to 14 inches, ease into pan to make a 1¾-inch side, and bake blind as directed for quiche pan. Cheesecake pan rim will keep foil from falling.

1¾ cups hazelnuts, toasted (directions follow)

5 ounces bittersweet chocolate bars, cut into ½-inch chunks

3 tablespoons all-purpose flour

¾ cup firmly packed brown sugar

½ cup butter or margarine, softened

3 large eggs

⅔ cup dark corn syrup

3 tablespoons dark molasses

2 tablespoons hazelnut liqueur

2 teaspoons vanilla

Baked pastry crust for a deep (1¾ in.) fluted 10-inch quiche pan (see recipe, page 216).

Combine nuts with chocolate and flour. In a bowl of an electric mixer, beat brown sugar and butter until very smooth. Add eggs 1 at a time, beating until combined. Beat in corn syrup, molasses, liqueur, and vanilla until smooth. Stir in nut mixture. Pour into crust and bake in a 325° oven until deep golden, about 20 minutes. Tent tart with foil (see preceding) and continue to bake until edges are set but center still jiggles slightly when gently shaken, 40 to 45 minutes more.

Let cool on a rack, then cover airtight and chill at least 4 hours to firm, or up to 1 day. Push tart from rim to serve. Serves 12.

Per serving: 492 cal. (57 percent from fat); 5.9 g protein; 31 g fat (11 g sat.); 53 g carbo.; 258 mg sodium; 83 mg chol.

To toast hazelnuts, place in a 9- or 10-inch pan and bake in a 350° oven until golden beneath skins, about 15 minutes. Rub in a towel to remove loose skins.—*E. J.* ■

HAZELNUT-STUDDED *tart with soft chocolate chunks is baked in the Evonuks' cast-iron stove. On the front porch, Hilary and Rose crack nuts the old-fashioned way.*

THANKSGIVING *on Sarah Chamberlin and Jim Clendenen's porch begins with a robust squash soup spiked with four kinds of chilies. A dollop of sour cream adds a cooling touch.*

An outdoor feast from Santa Barbara County

A potter and a vintner celebrate with rosemary smoked turkey and a spicy squash soup

ROSEMARY-SCENTED SMOKE *surrounds the turkey as it grills.*

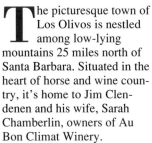he picturesque town of Los Olivos is nestled among low-lying mountains 25 miles north of Santa Barbara. Situated in the heart of horse and wine country, it's home to Jim Clendenen and his wife, Sarah Chamberlin, owners of Au Bon Climat Winery.

Jim's culinary expertise and creativity are well known among the winemaking community, and he cooks in the kitchen of his eclectic ranch-style home with contagious passion. The Thanksgiving meal at the couple's home is hearty and full-flavored, with vegetables and herbs harvested from their extensive garden. Jim's specialty is chili peppers: he grows several varieties, and even smokes his own jalapeños to make the chipotle chilies used in the spicy squash soup. Rosemary branches for smoking the turkey come from an enormous rosemary plant that shades an edge of the garden.

While Jim mans the kitchen, Sarah, a ceramic artist, provides the feast's setting with her stunning handmade majolica platters, plates, and mugs. Sarah's ceramics are sold under the Art in Your Home label, and are all made in the studio adjoining their house.

Sarah and Jim's entertaining style matches their lifestyle—casual and comfortable—and Thanksgiving dinner is no exception. Weather permitting, the appetizers and first course are served in the yard or on the sheltered porch. Guests move indoors to the big wooden dining table for the smoked turkey and trimmings. When asked what wines he serves with dinner, Jim quips, "They are copious, local, and mine."

Spicy Squash Soup

2 large (about 4 lb. total) butternut squash, halved lengthwise and seeded

3 pounds banana squash, seeded and cut into large pieces

1 dried chipotle chili

5 cups regular-strength chicken broth

2 tablespoons ancho chili powder or 1 large (about ½ oz.) dried ancho chili, stemmed and whirled in a blender or food processor until finely ground

1 fresh habanero chili, stemmed and seeded (optional)

¼ cup lime juice

2 medium-size (about ½ lb. total) zucchini, ends trimmed, diced

Two-color chili garnish (recipe follows)

Sour cream or unflavored yogurt (optional)

Place butternut and banana squash, cut side up, in an 11- by 17-inch roasting pan (or divide squash evenly between two 9- by 13-inch baking pans). Add about ½ inch of boiling water to pan; cover tightly with foil. Bake in a 400° oven until squash is very soft when pierced, about 1 hour. Remove squash from pan, drain briefly, and set aside until cool enough to handle.

Place chipotle chili in a small bowl; add boiling water to cover. Let stand 5 minutes; drain.

Combine chipotle, broth, ancho chili powder, and habanero in a 5- to 6-quart pan over high heat. Bring to a boil, cover, and simmer 20 minutes. With a slotted spoon, remove chipotle and habanero chilies; discard.

Scrape cooked squash from rind. Whirl squash in batches in a blender or food processor until very smooth. Add squash purée and lime juice to broth mixture. If making ahead, cover and chill up to 1 day.

Add zucchini to soup and stir often over medium-high heat until soup simmers and zucchini are tender when pierced, about 10 minutes (20 minutes if reheating).

Ladle soup into 1 large bowl or individual serving bowls. Top decoratively with chili garnish and sour cream, or offer both to add to taste. Makes about 8 cups.

Per serving: 183 cal. (15 percent from fat); 6.2 g protein; 3.1 g fat (0.5 g sat.); 39 g carbo.; 69 mg sodium; 0 mg chol.

Two-color chili garnish. Stem and halve 2 large **fresh green jalapeño chilies** and 2 large **fresh red jalapeño chilies** or 1 small (about 6 oz.) red bell pepper; discard seeds. Set chilies cut side down in a 10- by 15-inch baking pan. Broil 4 inches away from heat until chili skins are mostly charred, 10 to 15 minutes. Set chilies aside until cool enough to handle; coarsely chop.

In a 10- to 12-inch pan, combine 1 small (about ¼ lb.) **chopped red onion** and 2 teaspoons **salad oil** over high heat. Stir often until onion softens slightly, about 5 minutes. Remove pan from heat and stir in chopped jalapeños. Use warm.

Rosemary Smoked Turkey

3 tablespoons olive or salad oil

2 tablespoons minced fresh rosemary

1 tablespoon minced Italian parsley

½ teaspoon black pepper

1 turkey, 16 to 18 pounds

¾ pound fresh rosemary bunches, rinsed and drained

AROMATIC BASMATI RICE, *baked with chayote squash, carrot and orange juices, white wine, and spices, complements the turkey's smoky flavor.*

bird is done, drape those areas with foil.

Per ¼ pound boneless cooked turkey, based on percentages of white and dark meat found in average turkey (including skin): 243 cal. (44 percent from fat); 32 g protein; 12 g fat (3.2 g sat.); 0.1 g carbo.; 83 mg sodium; 94 mg chol.

Spiced Basmati Rice with Chayote Squash

4 cups carrot juice

3 medium-size (about 10 oz. each) chayote squash, peeled, seeded, and cut into ½-inch cubes

3 3-inch cinnamon sticks

1 cup dry white wine

1 cup orange juice

1 tablespoon *each* orange peel and lemon peel

3 cups basmati or long-grain white rice

3 cloves garlic, minced or pressed

2 tablespoons olive or salad oil

1 large (about ½ lb.) onion, chopped

   Minced fresh cilantro (coriander)

   Salt and pepper

Combine carrot juice, chayote, cinnamon sticks, wine, orange juice, and orange and lemon peel in a 5- to 6-quart pan over high heat. Bring to a boil, cover tightly, and simmer for 20 minutes.

Meanwhile, combine rice, garlic, oil, and onion in a 12-inch frying pan over medium-high heat. Stir often until rice and onion brown lightly, 10 to 15 minutes.

Transfer rice and onion to a 4- to 4½-quart baking dish. Pour in hot carrot juice–chayote mixture; stir well. Cover dish very tightly with foil. Bake in a 350° oven until liquid is absorbed and rice is tender to bite, about 45 minutes; after 20 minutes, stir mixture, re-cover, and continue baking. If desired, remove cinnamon sticks. Sprinkle with minced cilantro. Add salt and pepper to taste. Serves 8 to 10.

Per serving: 293 cal. (13 percent from fat); 8.1 g protein; 4.1 g fat (0.4 g sat.); 62 g carbo.; 59 mg sodium; 0 mg chol.—C. W. H.

Mix together oil, minced rosemary, parsley, and pepper; set aside.

To prepare turkey, remove and discard leg truss. Pull off and discard lumps of fat, and remove giblets. Rinse bird inside and out; pat dry. Rinse giblets, drain, and reserve for gravy (see recipe, page 203). Insert a meat thermometer straight down through the thickest part of the breast to the bone.

In a large barbecue with a lid, mound and ignite 40 charcoal briquets on fire-

grate. When briquets are dotted with gray ash, about 15 minutes, divide in half and push to opposite sides of firegrate. Place a metal drip pan between coals. Add 5 briquets (10 total) to each mound of coals now and every 30 minutes while cooking. Set grill 4 to 6 inches above coals.

Place 3 or 4 rosemary sprigs inside the turkey cavity. Set turkey, breast side up, on grill over drip pan. Brush turkey evenly with oil-herb mixture. Push about ¼ of the

rosemary sprigs through grill so that they sit on and over coals; divide sprigs equally between two coal mounds. Add another ¼ of the sprigs each time you add new coals (every 30 minutes) until they are used up.

Cover barbecue and cook turkey until thermometer registers 160°, 2½ to 3 hours. Because temperature, heat control, and size and shape of the bird all can vary, start checking doneness after 2 hours. If parts of the turkey begin to get dark before the

RELAX BY THE FIRE *with a bowl of rich turkey soup made with a little help from Thanksgiving leftovers.*

Stone soup with turkey

Pebbles are off-limits, but you can throw in most anything else

I T SEEMED LIKE magic!… Never had there been such a soup. And fancy, made from stones!"

The soup in the folk tale "Stone Soup" may have started with stones—but a bounty of other foods was then added. And so goes this turkey soup, which takes advantage of a wealth of Thanksgiving leftovers.

First, make a rich-tasting broth with a turkey carcass and lots of herbs and vegetables: the secret is letting it simmer several hours. Then add Thanksgiving leftovers.

The choices you make among your leftovers determine the soup's flavors. Follow this recipe's suggested amounts, but otherwise let your creativity flow.

Of course, add only foods you like. If you think additions such as cranberry sauce or stuffing might prove controversial, offer them at the table to add as desired. Or turn soft bread stuffing into croutons to add when served. To make croutons, separate stuffing (about 4 cups) into bite-size pieces. Toast in a single layer on a baking sheet at 350° until crisp, about 25 minutes.

Turkey Stone Soup

1 large (about ½ lb.) onion, chopped

1 medium-size (about 7 oz.) red bell pepper, cored, seeded, and chopped

1 tablespoon olive oil

Turkey broth and meat (recipe follows)

6 cups leftover cooked vegetables, such as green beans, carrots, broccoli, mushrooms, and onions

1 cup leftover tomato-based dish or 1 can (14½ oz.) diced tomatoes, drained

2 cups leftover bread stuffing or rice stuffing (optional)

About ½ cup leftover gravy (optional)

Pepper

About 1 cup cranberry sauce (optional)

In an 8- to 10-quart pan, cook onion and bell pepper in oil over medium-high heat, stirring often, until onion is golden, about 5 minutes. Add broth; bring to a simmer, uncovered, about 10 minutes. Stir in reserved turkey meat, leftover vegetables, and tomato-based dish. Cover and simmer until in-

gredients are hot, about 5 minutes. Stir in stuffing and gravy. Add pepper to taste. Transfer to a tureen, if desired. Serve with cranberry sauce to stir into individual portions. Serves 8 to 10.

Turkey broth and meat. Pull meat off a roast **turkey carcass** (a 16-lb. or larger bird). Reserve meat (you need 4 to 5 cups bite-size pieces to use in soup). If doing ahead, wrap and chill meat up to 2 days.

Break carcass into quarters. Gather in cheesecloth (about 52 by 36 inches, doubled to make a 26- by 36-in. rectangle), and tie bundle shut with corners of cheesecloth. Place bundle in an 8- to 10-quart pan. Add 3½ quarts **regular-strength chicken broth;** 2 large (about 1 lb. total) **onions,** chopped; 4 large (about 1 lb. total) **carrots,** chopped; 4 large stalks (about ¾ lb. total) **celery,** chopped; 3 tablespoons minced **fresh sage** or 1 tablespoon dried rubbed sage; 1 tablespoon *each* minced **fresh rosemary leaves** and **fresh thyme leaves,** or 1 teaspoon *each* dried rosemary and thyme; 1 tablespoon **dried marjoram leaves;** 8 cloves **garlic,** minced or pressed; 3 **dried bay leaves;** and 1 teaspoon *each* **dried oregano leaves, fennel seed, mustard seed,** and **pepper.**

Bring to a boil. Cover, reduce heat, and simmer about 4 hours. Lift carcass from broth. Drain (add drained liquid back to broth); cool. Remove cheesecloth; separate meat from bones. If desired, add meat to reserved turkey to use in soup. (If making ahead, cover and chill up to 2 days.) Discard bones.

Pour remaining broth and vegetables through a cheesecloth-lined colander set over a large bowl. Then twist cloth tightly closed and squeeze remaining juices into broth; discard vegetables. Skim fat. If necessary, add water or boil, uncovered, to make 3½ quarts broth. (If making ahead, cool broth, cover, and chill up to 2 days. Spoon off any fat.)

Per serving: 230 cal. (26 percent from fat); 22 g protein; 6.6 g fat (1.7 g sat.); 20 g carbo.; 240 mg sodium; 43 mg chol. ■

By Betsy Reynolds Bateson

GOOD TO THE LAST CRUMB, *pie crust strikes the right balance between crisp, flaky, and tender.*

PETER CHRISTIANSEN

The perfect pie crust

A step-by-step guide for terrific roll-out pastry dough

MY QUEST FOR THE perfect pie crust began with an embarrassingly tough and soggy example. I hadn't expected the pecan-type pie to give me crust problems—but it certainly did. Whoever coined the phrase *easy as pie* must have been talking about the filling.

About 35 crusts later, I figured out what went wrong

with that pie, and mastered the basics for producing pastry for a single-crust pie that's flavorful, tender, and flaky, and doesn't stick during rolling. Here are some of the points I learned:

Proportions and accurate measuring are important. Too much flour or water will make a tough crust, too much fat can make a greasy and crumbly one.

Fat contributes tenderness and flakiness by coating the flour, separating the dough into layers. Butter or margarine alone makes a flavorful but tough crust (my first crust was all-butter). Lard makes the flakiest crust of all, with a distinctive flavor (and, surprisingly, less saturated fat than butter). Crusts from solid shortening are tender and flaky, with a neutral flavor. Our favorite crust? Half butter and half shortening (combining the best of each).

Cutting in the fat. For fat to do its job, it must be cold. You need to cut it into the flour to form distinct, pea-size particles.

I compared the effectiveness of using two knives with that of using fingers or a pastry blender for cutting in the fat. The knives worked, but progress was so slow I abandoned them in favor of my fingers, which warmed the fat so it no longer formed particles. The pastry blender made speedy work of cutting in the fat and produced just the right texture.

A food processor is a good alternative to a pastry blender,

Perfect Pie Crust

For a 9-inch regular pie pan or tart pan

About 1 cup all-purpose flour

¼ teaspoon salt

3 tablespoons cold butter or margarine, in ½-tablespoon chunks

3 tablespoons cold solid shortening, in ½-tablespoon chunks

3 to 4 tablespoons ice water

For a 9-inch deep-dish pie pan, 10-inch regular pie or tart pan, or 10-inch, deep quiche pan

About 1¼ cups all-purpose flour

½ teaspoon salt

3½ tablespoons cold butter or margarine, in ½-tablespoon chunks

¼ cup cold solid shortening, in ½-tablespoon chunks

4 to 5 tablespoons ice water

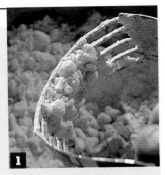

WITH PASTRY BLENDER, *cut in butter, then shortening, until particles are the size of peas.*

In a bowl, stir 1 cup of the flour (1¼ cups for larger crusts) and salt with a pastry blender. Cut in butter, then shortening, until fat particles are pea-size (photo 1); occasionally scrape fat from pastry blender, and use it to scrape bowl and gently stir flour.

Add the minimum

amount of water 1 tablespoon at a time; stir with a fork just until flour is evenly moistened. Gently squeeze a handful of dough (2); it should hold together and feel like clay. If not, add water ½ tablespoon at a time.

Gather dough into a ball. Flatten into a 4-inch disk (3), wrap in plastic, and chill at

least 1 hour or up to 2 days.

Lightly dust a countertop, the dough, and a rolling pin with flour. Using short, gentle strokes, and working from the center of dough outward (4), roll dough to the size circle required: 2 inches greater than the diameter of a regular pie or tart pan, 4 inches greater than the diameter of a deep-dish pie or quiche pan. Occasionally lift dough, rotate a quarter turn, and dust underneath with flour.

Fold dough in quarters and position in center of pan. Unfold, easing dough to line pan evenly without stretching (5).

For pie pans, cut off dough to an even ¾ inch beyond edge of pan. With fingers, turn overhanging dough under itself, making flush with pan edge. Pinch dough along rim to make a ridge. Then crimp (6).

For tart or quiche pans, run a rolling pin over the edge of the pan to cut off excess dough.

If you wish to bake filling in a raw crust, follow pie recipe instructions. To bake pastry blind, gently line dough with a piece of foil large enough to extend over edges. Fill pan nearly to top of crust with dried beans, dried rice, or pie weights (they're reusable); fold foil slightly over them (7).

Bake pastry in a 450° oven 15 minutes (20 minutes for a deep-dish pie pan or deep quiche pan). Lift out foil and weights, reduce heat to 350°, and bake crust until golden in center, 5 to 10 minutes more, depending on pan size.

Let crust cool on a rack. If cooking further with a filling, cover crust rim with foil partway through baking to prevent overbrowning.

Per serving (⅛ of 9-in. crust): 183 cal. (59 percent from fat); 2.2 g protein; 12 g fat (5.2 g sat.); 16 g carbo.; 149 mg sodium; 16 mg chol.

2

SQUEEZE *the dough; it should hold together without being sticky.*

3

A DOUGH DISK *rolls out more evenly than a ball. Chill first to minimize stickiness.*

4

PETER CHRISTIANSEN

TO PREVENT STICKING, *gradually roll the dough from the middle into a circle with short, light strokes.*

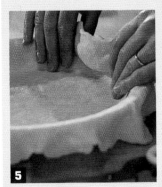

5

UNFOLD THE DOUGH *into a pan. Working from the center, fit gently into the inside edge without stretching.*

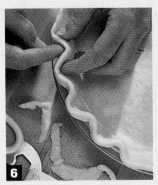

6

MAKE A WIDE CRIMP *on the edge by pinching the dough between 2 fingers while indenting with another.*

7

BAKING BLIND: *Line the crust with foil, weight to prevent bubbling, and cook until golden.*

if you take care to avoid overworking the dough. Follow the recipe here, using fat that's been frozen in ½-tablespoon portions. Pulse flour and fat just until particles are pea-size. Add the minimum amount of water with the motor running, then pulse just until the dough holds together.

Rolling the dough. In my tests, crusts rolled with a pastry cloth on the board and a stockinette over the pin actually stuck more than those rolled with a floured pin and board alone. Yet the real key to preventing sticking is technique (see techniques section below and photos at left).

My favorite rolling pin is the wooden kind with ball bearings, but you can use a solid wood cylinder, marble, or other kind if you prefer.

Pans. Both glass and matte-finish metal pans produce great crusts. With very shiny metal pans, which deflect heat, crusts took longer to bake and got tough.

Techniques. When adding water to flour, stir only enough to distribute water evenly; overstir, and the dough will be tough. Chill dough before rolling so it continues absorbing water evenly and is less sticky.

Finally, many recipes don't call for baking the crust blind (prebaking the crust filled with weights to prevent bubbling). But you can use this technique with a single-crust pie even if the recipe doesn't suggest it.

Baking blind before adding fillings traditionally baked in a raw shell improves crust flavor and prevents a soggy crust—especially with wet fillings such as pumpkin. But check the crust rim during the time you're baking the filling. Cover the rim with foil, if necessary, to prevent overbrowning.

For fillings that always go into a prebaked crust, such as lemon meringue, baking blind produces an evenly cooked shell. ∎

By Elaine Johnson

BIRUAD

Oat bran bread competes with the baguette

Plus salad with multicultural claims

T HINK OF THIS LOAF AS A wholesome species of peasant bread. In addition to hearty flavor, its pleasant, perfumed aroma combines a refreshing whiff of lemon peel and a hint of nutmeg; it's seductive enough to distract even the French from their baguettes. Just the right amount of oat bran adds complexity to the texture; a sprinkling of bran on the surface bespeaks the presence of more within.

Oat Bran Bread

1 tablespoon active dry yeast (about 1½ packages)

2 cups warm (110°) water

1½ teaspoons sugar

½ teaspoon salt

½ teaspoon grated lemon peel

2 tablespoons lemon juice

¼ teaspoon ground nutmeg

4½ to 5 cups unbleached all-purpose flour

About ⅓ cup oat bran

About 1 tablespoon melted butter or margarine

In a large bowl, sprinkle yeast over warm water; let stand until yeast softens, about 5 minutes. Stir in sugar, salt, lemon peel, lemon juice, nutmeg, 2 cups flour, and ¼ cup oat bran.

Using a heavy spoon or an electric mixer, beat dough until it is stretchy, about 5 minutes. Stir in 2 cups more flour, then knead dough.

To knead by hand, stir dough until it holds together, then scrape out onto a lightly floured board. Knead until dough is smooth and elastic, about 10 minutes; add flour, as required, to prevent sticking. Place dough in a large, oiled bowl; turn dough over to oil the top.

To knead with a dough hook, beat dough until it no longer feels sticky when lightly touched and it pulls cleanly from side of bowl, about 5 minutes. If required, add flour, 1 tablespoon at a time, until dough reaches this consistency.

Cover kneaded dough with plastic wrap. Let stand in a warm place until puffy, about 20 minutes.

Punch down dough to expel air bubbles. Divide dough in half, and shape each section into a round loaf. Place loaves smooth side up and well apart on an oiled 12- by 15-inch baking sheet. Pat to flatten each loaf until it's about 1 inch thick. Cover loosely with plastic wrap and let stand in a warm place until slightly puffed, about 20 minutes.

Uncover and bake in a 350° oven for 35 minutes. Brush tops with melted butter, and sprinkle lightly with remaining oat bran. Continue baking until bread is a rich brown, 15 to 20 minutes longer. Cool slightly or completely, then slice to serve. If making ahead, wrap cooled, unsliced loaves airtight and hold up to 1 day; freeze to store longer. Makes 2 loaves, each about 1 pound.

Per ounce: 144 cal. (7.5 percent from fat); 4.3 g protein; 1.2 g fat (0.5 g sat.); 29 g carbo.; 77 mg sodium; 1.9 mg chol.

John Bonnier

Pullman, Washington

K URT LARSEN HAD TO bring a dish to a potluck. In casting about the kitchen, he noticed a bunch of carrots that were hovering on the brink of limpness and crying out for immediate use.

With this as a beginning and a free-ranging imagination to guide him, he ransacked the cupboard for additional ingredients and came up with what might be described as an eastern Mediterranean chilled vegetable stew, a Mexican *ensalada,* or a substantial salad. Larsen calls it Carrot, Garbanzo, and Olive Salad with Feta Cheese.

Like most good potluck dishes, it is filling enough to be a one-dish meal.

Marinated Carrot, Garbanzo, and Olive Salad

3 large (about ¾ lb. total) carrots, thinly sliced

1 can (15 oz.) stewed tomatoes

1 can (15½ oz.) garbanzos, drained

1 can (6 oz.) pitted ripe olives, drained

1 can (4 oz.) diced green chilies

1 medium-size (5 oz.) mild onion, thinly sliced

2 tablespoons olive oil or salad oil

2 tablespoons white wine vinegar

2 cloves garlic, minced or pressed

½ teaspoon crushed hot dried red chilies

½ teaspoon ground cumin

1 tablespoon minced parsley

½ cup crumbled feta cheese

Salt and pepper

In a 1½- to 2-quart pan over high heat, cook carrots in about ½ inch boiling water until they are just tender when pierced, 3 to 4 minutes. Drain carrots and pour into a salad bowl; let cool.

Cut tomatoes into bite-size pieces with scissors or a knife; add with their juice to bowl along with garbanzos, olives, green chilies, onion, oil, vinegar, garlic, red chilies, and cumin; mix well (if making ahead, cover and chill up to 1 day). Mix in parsley and cheese. Serve salad with a slotted spoon, seasoning portions to taste with salt and pepper. Makes 6 to 8 servings.

Per serving: 159 cal. (48 percent from fat); 4.6 g protein; 8.5 g fat (2.1 g sat.); 18 g carbo.; 578 mg sodium; 7.5 mg chol.

Magalia, California

SCRAMBLED EGGS AT Reuben's was the traditional way to end a big night on the town in Manhattan, but the celebrated delicatessen is better known across the land for its eponymous sandwich, the Reuben. This, in its classic form, enfolds Swiss cheese, corned beef, and sauerkraut in rye bread, but variations exist, some substituting ham for corned beef, others adding tomato or other abominations. As a sandwich it is, in its original version, a lily that needs no gilding.

The original combination of ingredients remains a good one, as Susan Conwell demonstrates in her Reuben Squares appetizer. Here the meat, cheese, and kraut are embedded in a sort of flan, *torta,* or *clafoutis* of rye flour, cottage cheese, and eggs enlivened by caraway seed and dry mustard.

Reuben Squares

1 small can (8 oz.) sauerkraut

½ cup rye flour

2 teaspoons baking powder

1 teaspoon dry mustard

1½ cups nonfat cottage cheese

8 large eggs

2 cups (½ lb.) shredded Swiss cheese

About ¾ pound cooked corned beef, finely chopped

1 tablespoon caraway seed

Small or bite-size pieces lettuce leaves, rinsed, drained, and crisped

Drain sauerkraut and rinse well under cool running water; drain thoroughly and finely chop.

In a large bowl, mix flour with baking powder and mustard; set aside.

Whirl cottage cheese in a blender or food processor until smooth; add eggs, and whirl to blend. Pour into flour mixture, adding Swiss cheese, sauerkraut, and corned beef. Stir until evenly moistened.

Scrape mixture into an oiled 9- by 13-inch pan; sprinkle evenly with caraway seed.

Bake in a 350° oven until top is firm when gently pressed, 30 to 35 minutes. Let cool at least 10 minutes, then cut into 48 squares. Serve warm or at room temperature; pick up and eat, or use lettuce as holders. Makes 48.

Per piece: 59 cal. (53 percent from fat); 4.7 g protein; 3.5 g fat (1.5 g sat.); 1.7 g carbo.; 159 mg sodium; 47 mg chol.

Littleton, Colorado ∎

By Joan Griffiths, Richard Dunmire

DECORATIVE DECANTERS *of flavored oils make great gifts.*

Flavored oils from Napa Valley

They capture flavor and rich color of herbs

BOB ELLSWORTH, owner of the Compleat Winemaker in St. Helena, California, sells winemaking supplies. Recently, he was bursting with news about how some folks, including Michael Chiarello—chef-owner of the highly regarded Tra Vigne restaurant in town—were using some of his equipment to do wild things with oils.

Chiarello and the Napa Valley Kitchens group have taken flavor-infused oils to new heights. First, the oils are saturated with the flavoring element; then solids and moisture are removed, leaving a clear oil that's intensely colored and seasoned. Chiarello's Consorzio line offers basil olive oil, roasted garlic oil, rosemary olive oil, porcini mushroom oil, five-pepper oil, and oregano olive oil. Napa Valley Kitchens flavors oils with cilantro (the complexity of this herb transfers into the oil with exceptional freshness), garlic, jalapeño, and mustard.

Consorzio oils, based on olive oil, are $9.50 or $10 each (375 ml., 12.5 oz.). Napa Valley Kitchens oils, made with a blend of olive and canola oils, are about $6 for the same-size bottle. You'll find Consorzio oils in fancy food and cookware shops across the country. But you can order all the oils from Napa Valley Kitchens, 1236 Spring St., St. Helena 94574. Call (800) 288-1089 for details and costs. The oils also come in smaller bottles, in combination packages, or as a sampler kit.

What can you do with flavored oils? The simplest way to enjoy their character is to dunk crusty bread into them. Or try them in salads and on cooked vegetables, pasta, meats, poultry, and fish. In brief, use them anywhere their seasonings are at home. Good pairings include the porcini mushroom oil with hot cooked peas, the basil oil on tomatoes, the cilantro oil with hot corn and lime, and the roasted garlic and five-pepper oils with mashed potatoes.

Some of the oils are best used cool; the flavors of cilantro, basil, and oregano oils fade when heated. Once they're open, use oils within several months to enjoy their best qualities. In the meantime, keep them tightly closed and store in a cool, dark place to maintain flavor.

By Jerry DiVecchhio

SUNSET'S KITCHEN CABINET

Creative ways with everyday foods—submitted by *Sunset* readers,
tested in *Sunset* kitchens, approved by *Sunset* taste panels

Cranberry-Orange Cheese Bread

Rose Basim, Enumclaw, Washington

- 2 cups all-purpose flour
- 1 cup sugar
- 2 tablespoons grated orange peel
- 1½ teaspoons baking powder
- ½ teaspoon baking soda
- 3 tablespoons butter or margarine, cut into small pieces
- 1½ cups (6 oz.) shredded sharp cheddar cheese
- 1 cup fresh or frozen cranberries
- 1 large egg
- ¾ cup buttermilk

In a bowl, mix flour, sugar, peel, baking powder, and soda. Cut or rub in butter until coarse crumbs form. Add 1 cup cheese and cranberries, and mix. Beat egg to blend with buttermilk; stir into dry ingredients just until moistened. Spoon batter into a 5- by 9-inch loaf pan. Sprinkle top with remaining cheese.

Bake in a 350° oven until the bread is golden brown and loaf begins to pull away from pan sides, about 1 hour. Cool in pan 15 minutes, then invert onto a rack and let cool. If making ahead, wrap cool loaf airtight and chill up to 1 day. Bring bread to room temperature to serve. Makes 1 loaf, 2 pounds, 2 ounces.

Per ounce: 85 cal. (31 percent from fat); 2.4 g protein; 2.9 g fat (1.8 g sat.); 12 g carbo.; 89 mg sodium; 14 mg chol.

CHEDDAR-CRUSTED *bread goes well with orange muscat wine or a liqueur.*

Chorizo Soup

Sandy Szwarc, Albuquerque

- 1 pound firm-textured chorizo sausages
- 1 large (about ½ lb.) onion, chopped
- ½ cup dehydrated masa flour (corn tortilla flour) or yellow cornmeal
- 1 large can (7 oz.) chopped green chilies
- 7 cups regular-strength chicken broth
- ¾ cup shredded jack cheese

About ½ cup minced fresh cilantro (coriander)

Remove chorizo casings and crumble sausage into a 5- to 6-quart pan; add onion. Stir often over medium-high heat until meat and onion are browned, about 15 minutes. Mix masa with sausage mixture, then stir in chilies and broth. Stirring often, bring to a boil over high heat. Simmer gently 20 minutes to blend flavors; stir frequently. Skim fat from surface as it accumulates and discard.

Ladle soup into bowls; add cheese and cilantro to taste. Serves 4 to 6.

Per serving: 371 cal. (65 percent from fat); 16 g protein; 27 g fat (10 g sat.); 15 g carbo.; 829 mg sodium; 56 mg chol.

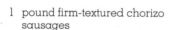

SPRINKLE CILANTRO *and cheese into soup; serve with warm corn tortillas.*

Acorn Squash with Spiced Apples

Linda Z. Riley, Glendale, Arizona

- 1 medium-size (about 1¾ lb.) acorn squash
- 2 large (about 1 lb. total) Granny Smith or Newtown Pippin apples, peeled, cored, and thinly sliced
- ¼ cup firmly packed brown sugar
- 1 tablespoon lemon juice
- 2 teaspoons minced fresh ginger
- ¾ teaspoon ground cinnamon
- ⅛ teaspoon ground nutmeg
- ⅛ teaspoon ground cloves
- ½ cup nonfat sour cream
- 1 teaspoon grated lemon peel

Pierce squash in several places with a sharp knife. Cook squash in microwave oven at full power (100 percent) for 6 minutes. Turn squash over; continue cooking at full power until squash is tender when pierced, 8 to 10 minutes more; test at 3-minute intervals. Remove from oven and set aside.

Mix apples, sugar, lemon juice, ginger, cinnamon, nutmeg, and cloves in a 1- to 1½-quart microwave-safe bowl; cover with a lid or plastic wrap. Cook at full power until apples are tender when pierced, 8 to 10 minutes; stir and test at 2- to 3-minute intervals.

Cut squash in half lengthwise; remove seeds and strings. Spoon apple mixture (with juices) equally into squash cavities. Mix sour cream and lemon peel; add to taste to squash and apples. Serves 2 to 4.

Per serving: 191 cal. (2.3 percent from fat); 3.4 g protein; 0.5 g fat (0.1 g sat.); 46 g carbo.; 31 mg sodium; 0 mg chol.

SQUASH *and apples cook separately, then join in a dish that goes with meats.*

Lemon Rosemary Chicken

Diane Peacock, Crockett, California

1¼ cups soft whole-wheat bread crumbs (2 to 3 bread slices whirled in a blender or food processor)

2 tablespoons minced fresh or 2 teaspoons crumbled dried rosemary

1 tablespoon minced parsley

1 teaspoon grated lemon peel

½ teaspoon pepper

6 boned and skinned chicken breast halves (about 2 lb. total)

1 tablespoon lemon juice

Lemon wedges (optional)

Salt

In a bowl, mix crumbs with rosemary, parsley, peel, and pepper. Arrange breasts slightly apart in an oiled 10- by 15-inch pan. Moisten top of chicken with lemon juice, and press an equal amount of crumbs over the surface of each piece, covering evenly.

Bake chicken, uncovered, in a 400° oven until crumb topping is browned and meat is white in the thickest part (cut to test), about 25 minutes. Accompany chicken with lemon wedges and salt to taste. Serves 6.

Per serving: 195 cal. (11 percent from fat); 36 g protein; 2.4 g fat (0.6 g sat.); 5.4 g carbo.; 154 mg sodium; 88 mg chol.

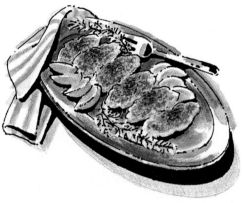

BREAD CRUMBS *bake crisp on moist, lemon-seasoned chicken breast halves.*

Red Cabbage and Orange Salad

Sharon Armstrong, Fallbrook, California

¼ cup sliced almonds

4 large (about 3 lb. total) oranges

5 cups (about ¾ lb.) very finely shredded red cabbage

½ cup minced onion

Honey dressing (recipe follows)

Large outer red cabbage leaves

Salt

Pour almonds into an 8- to 10-inch frying pan. Over medium-high heat, stir nuts often until lightly browned, 5 to 7 minutes. Pour from pan. If making ahead, store airtight up to 1 day.

Cut peel and white membrane off oranges. Over a bowl, cut between inner membranes of fruit to release segments into bowl; discard seeds. To bowl, add shredded cabbage, onion, and dressing; mix gently. Arrange cabbage leaves on a rimmed platter and spoon salad onto leaves. Sprinkle with almonds. Add salt to taste. Makes 4 to 6 servings.

Per serving: 171 cal. (28 percent from fat); 3 g protein; 5.3 g fat (0.9 g sat.); 32 g carbo.; 86 mg sodium; 3.3 mg chol.

Honey dressing. Mix together ¼ cup **reduced-calorie mayonnaise,** 2 tablespoons **honey,** 2 tablespoons **cider vinegar,** and 1 teaspoon **Dijon mustard.** If making ahead, cover and chill up to 1 day.

RED CABBAGE *and orange salad is refreshing with honey dressing.*

Rum-Bananas Streusel Sundaes

Linda Tebben, Menlo Park, California

¼ cup all-purpose flour

¼ cup chopped pecans or walnuts

½ teaspoon ground cinnamon

⅛ teaspoon ground nutmeg

1 cup firmly packed brown sugar

½ cup (¼ lb.) butter or margarine

3 medium-size (about 1½ lb. total) firm-ripe bananas

½ cup rum or orange juice

1 quart vanilla frozen yogurt or ice cream

In a food processor or bowl, whirl or rub with your fingers the flour, nuts, cinnamon, nutmeg, ¼ cup brown sugar, and 2 tablespoons butter until mixture forms coarse crumbs. Pour into an 8- or 9-inch square pan. Bake in a 350° oven, stirring occasionally, until streusel mixture is golden brown, about 15 minutes. Let cool in pan; if making ahead, wrap airtight when cool and chill up to 2 days.

Peel bananas and cut in ½-inch-thick slices. Melt remaining butter in a 10- to 12-inch frying pan over medium-high heat. Add remaining sugar and rum; stir until sugar dissolves. Add bananas and turn often with a wide spatula until sauce bubbles, about 3 minutes.

Divide frozen yogurt among 6 bowls; top equally with streusel and banana sauce. Serves 6.

Per serving: 568 cal. (32 percent from fat); 7.1 g protein; 20 g fat (9.9 g sat.); 82 g carbo.; 245 mg sodium; 48 mg chol.

Compiled by Christine Weber Hale

BROWN SUGAR *streusel and bananas in warm caramel sauce top frozen yogurt.*

Pheasant for Christmas, the ultimate supper for two, gracious ports

By Jerry Anne Di Vecchio

Choosing the main course for Christmas dinner is always a thoughtful exercise in our house, and stomachs rumble as the merits of various candidates for roasting are aired. Often we're inclined to indulge in the more exotic options from game farms. Will it be pheasant? Venison? Squab or quail? For the most part, these meats are best cooked very rare to rare at high temperatures, and they suffer significantly if overdone. The cook can't afford distractions at critical moments, as I have learned the hard way. If my oven is on full blast, I must also turn on the exhaust fan, or else searing, smoking fat invariably sets off the smoke alarm—usually just as the doorbell rings. During my first such episode (but, annoyingly, not my last), squab were sizzling madly, guests were gaping in the entry, and I, with broom handle waving, was battering the battery out of the ceiling alarm.

When we settle on pheasant for our holiday dinner, we order farm-reared ones from the market. They are plumper than their field-range brethren, easier to come by, consistently more tender, and we don't have to chew around bits of buckshot.

The firm white meat is a delicate background for a complex range of sauces. Pheasant, like other roasts that cook quickly, has few drippings, so the sauce is an independent production and can be made ahead. I particularly like a tangy orange sauce with these birds, and to set them off handsomely on the dinner platter, I surround them with a wreath of crisp, juicy green grapes, heated just enough to give them a gemlike sheen.

SEASONAL NOTE

Giblet pâté

Giblets are a bonus when you buy whole birds for festive meals. I like to use the giblets to make this smooth,

---

Roast Pheasant with Orange Sauce and Green Grapes

2   pheasants (2 to 2½ lb. each)
1   small (about ¼ lb.) orange, rinsed
    Orange sauce (recipe follows)
2   teaspoons butter or margarine
3   or 4 cups stemmed seedless green grapes
    Salt

Remove any giblets and pheasant necks for other uses (see mushroom-giblet pâté, page 224). Pull off and discard any fat lumps from pheasants. Rinse birds inside and out; pat dry. Cut orange in ½; put 1 piece in the body cavity of each bird. With small skewers, secure skin over body cavity to cover and pin neck skin to back.

Lay pheasants, breasts down, on a rack in a roasting pan (about 12 by 17 in.). Put 1 cup water in pan. Roast birds in a 450° oven for 15 minutes. Turn birds over, brush with orange sauce, and roast until a thermometer inserted in the thickest part of the breast to the bone is 135°, and meat at breastbone looks moist but not soft and wet (cut from shoulder joint to breastbone to test), about 15 minutes longer. Tilt birds to drain juices into pan, then set them on a platter and let stand at least 10 minutes before serving.

Meanwhile, skim and discard fat from drippings; add drippings to orange sauce and boil, uncovered, over high heat until reduced to 1 cup. Also melt butter in a 10- to 12-inch frying pan over high heat. Add grapes and swirl in pan until slightly brighter green and hot, about 3 minutes. Pour grapes onto platter around pheasants; scatter orange peel reserved from sauce on top of pheasants. Accompany with grapes and orange sauce; add salt to taste. The 2-pound pheasants make 4 to 6 servings; the larger ones serve 6 to 8.

Per serving: 614 cal. (38 percent from fat); 60 g protein; 26 g fat (8 g sat.); 30 g carbo.; 270 mg sodium; chol. data unavailable.

Orange sauce. With a vegetable peeler, cut orange part of skin from 2 large **oranges** (½ lb. each). Cut peel in thin slivers and put in a 3-

PETER CHRISTIANSEN

to 4-quart pan. Cover peel generously with **water** and bring to a boil over high heat. Drain peel and add to pan 1 cup **orange juice,** ½ cup **orange-flavor liqueur,** and 3 tablespoons **sugar.** Boil on high heat, uncovered, until liquid is almost gone,

10 to 15 minutes; watch carefully as liquid reduces to avoid scorching. Spoon out and set aside 2 tablespoons peel.

To pan, add another ½ cup **orange juice,** 2 tablespoons **Dijon mustard,** 1 tablespoon **currant** or raspberry **jelly,**

and 1 tablespoon **brandy.** Stir over medium heat until jelly melts. Use hot, or let cool, cover, and chill up to 1 day; also cover and chill reserved peel.

As an alternative, use 2 **chickens** (each 2½ to 3 lb.) instead of pheasant. Follow

preceding directions, but roast chickens breast down for 20 minutes, then breast up for 30 to 35 minutes, or until a thermometer at thigh joint reaches 185°. During the last 10 to 15 minutes of cooking, brush once with orange sauce. Makes 6 to 8 servings.

MUSHROOM-GIBLET PÂTÉ *can be made ahead and served as an appetizer or as cocktail party fare.*

mellow pâté as the dinner appetizer. Chickens nearly always come with liver, gizzard, heart, and neck neatly enclosed in a bag that's tucked into their body cavities. Giblets in other birds are less consistently included, but I use what comes, and supplement with chicken livers.

Mushroom-giblet pâté. You need 4 **chicken livers,** or pheasant or other poultry livers (or a combination, about ¼ lb. total). If available, also use **hearts, gizzards,** and **necks** (pull off and discard skin) from 2 chickens, pheasants, or other poultry.

Rinse giblets and pat dry. In a 10- to 12-inch frying pan on medium-high heat, melt 1 tablespoon **butter** or margarine. Cook livers first, until browned but still pink in center (cut to test), about 5 minutes; cover pan if the fat spatters. Lift livers from pan and set aside. Brown any remaining giblets in pan. Add about ⅓ pound coarsely chopped **mushrooms** and stir often until the juices evaporate and mushrooms are lightly browned. If mixture includes any giblets, add 1 cup **regular-strength chicken broth** and ½ cup **water;** cover pan and simmer until giblets are tender when pierced, about 40 minutes. Uncover and boil until liquid evaporates, stirring often. Lift out giblets and coarsely chop; pull meat off necks and discard bones. If

using only livers, add ½ cup regular-strength chicken broth to browned mushrooms and boil uncovered, stirring often, until broth evaporates.

In a blender or food processor, combine livers and their juices, remaining giblets, the mushroom mixture, and ¼ cup regular-strength chicken broth. Whirl until smoothly puréed, scraping container sides frequently. Then whirl in ¼ cup (⅛ lb.) butter or margarine. Add **salt** to taste. Scrape into a small container; cover and chill until cold, at least 1 hour or up to 3 days. With livers only, makes about 1¼ cups.

Per tablespoon, livers only: 37 cal. (80 percent from fat); 1.3 g protein; 3.3 g fat (1.9 g sat.); 0.6 g carbo.; 39 mg sodium; 33 mg chol.

GREAT GIFTS
For friends who like to cook and drink

New food and wine items I stumble across invariably evoke enthusiasm from those who receive them as gifts. Even better, these gifts get used, eaten, or drunk.

Wine has always proved complicated to deliver unless hand-carried. Although delivery services transport wine and some bottle shops will handle transactions for you, they tend to do so reluctantly.

However, one company is making a special effort: the Napa Valley Winery Exchange offers three-day air delivery of its wines to anyplace in the United States (except Utah). The exchange cellars an interesting collection of California wines in its retail shop at 415 Taylor St., San Francisco 94102. You can make a selection in person, or call (800) 653-9463 to request their quarterly newsletter with a dozen special selections, to learn about the many other wines they stock, and to place an order for one to as many bottles as you like. Shipping costs vary, but $10 should cover the transport of two bottles within this country.

Chef togs. First baseball caps knocked off chefs' tall white toques. Now wild prints and colors are getting the better of starched white chefs' jackets and traditional black-and-white checked pants. If you have a home chef who likes to stay chic, make wardrobe selections for them by mail. For catalogs and information:

Chefwear, 833 N. Orleans St., Fourth Floor, Chicago 60610; (800) 568-2433.

Fun Uniforms, 19229 Sonoma Hwy., Suite 215, Sonoma, Calif. 95476; in California (800) 773-8726, elsewhere (800) 723-8726.

Gourmet Gear, 2320 Abbot Kinney Blvd., Suites A & B, Venice, Calif. 90291; (800) 682-4635.

Or you can go one step further and have an artist hand-paint your own plain white gear. It's more costly than ready-to-wear, but it's truly tailored to your taste. Contact Pat Palmieri, owner of Bon Apepaint Studio, 287 Bay 14th St., Brooklyn, N.Y. 11214; (718) 331-0668.

Cheese-making kit. The venerable Tillamook County Creamery Association has been an Oregon institution for 85 years. In this lush green land of many rivers (as *Tillamook* translates from the local Native American lan-

guage), cows and people are about equal in number, and together they produce Tillamook cheese. This year, the Tillamook association is offering the perfect gift for the curious chef who likes to know how things work—but who doesn't want to make a career of cooking. Its cheddar cheese–making kit comes with culture and rennet (hard to come by in small amounts) to make a 2.6-pound batch of cheese; the kit sells for $8.95, plus handling. Write or call Tillamook Cheese, Box 313, Tillamook, Ore. 97141; (800) 542-7290.

GREAT INGREDIENT
Uniquely Western, teleme cheese

According to popular lore, teleme cheese was accidentally invented in Pleasanton, California, in the early part of this century. What was intended to become a crumbly, sharp feta cheese took a very different route. The new cheese was delicate and fresh, with a smooth, slightly tangy flavor and the texture of velvet.

The more mainstream teleme is sealed in plastic and ripens quickly, without a crust. When young, the teleme is sort of firm to bite; the more mature teleme is creamier and may be identified as semisoft.

But it's the premier version of this cheese, rice-flour teleme, that's enjoying a surge of popularity. Considerably more is being made now than in years past, and it's usually found among the specialty cheeses in upscale supermarkets and health and natural food stores. Rice-flour teleme takes its name from how it's handled: 5- to 6-pound and 10- to 12-pound blocks of the newly formed cheese are dusted with rice flour and aged unwrapped on shelves in a cool, controlled environment. A light crust

RICE-FLOUR TELEME *is good for dipping or spreading.*

forms as the interior ripens and eventually becomes so creamy it could flow right off the shelf. You can trim the crust away, but I don't usually bother. Once the block is cut, the cheese is quite perishable; after a week to 10 days, it tends to mold and lose its fresh taste.

Rice-flour teleme is wonderful slathered on crusty bread. Nothing is smoother baked on top of lasagne or cannelloni. And slices of teleme melted on gratin potatoes become a perfect sauce. It's also delightful stirred into cooked risotto.

But creamy rice-flour teleme also makes a natural fondue when heated, clinging like a second skin to chunks of bread, breadsticks, pieces of fennel, and tortellini.

To melt rice-flour teleme for fondue, you can bake it or warm it over hot water. To bake, lay slices of the cheese in a shallow baking dish and heat in a 400° oven until it melts, 5 to 10 minutes. Or put chunks of the cheese in a wide bowl and set over hot water until cheese warms; if you stir more than once or twice as cheese melts, it's inclined to get stringy like freshly made mozzarella.

If you have trouble locating rice-flour teleme, Peluso Cheese ships it during the cool months. Minimum order is 2 pounds at $5.35 a pound, plus handling. Write or call Peluso Cheese, 429 H St., Los Banos, Calif. 93635; (209) 826-3744.

MEMORABLE MOMENT
Caviar and fresh cherries for two

When the gentle man of my household needs a special show of affection during the stress of the holidays, and I'm feeling equally pressured, this ultimate buy-and-serve menu has become our private indulgence: fresh caviar—on thin white-bread toast with a squeeze of lemon—and champagne, followed by plump, juicy cherries.

To eat fresh cherries at Christmas was once impossible. But my yearning to do so was implanted way back when Frank Sinatra was crooning to bobby-soxers. At the same time, a lipstick called "Cherries in the Snow" was being heavily promoted. Glossy Bing cherries on a bed of snow in the background of the ad became my image of unattainable luxury.

Many years later, when I was invited to tour Chile, my only request was to visit when the cherries ripened—during our winter. The unattainable was thus achieved. And now those big Bing cherries are here every December.

Settling on fresh caviar as the main course was easy. This may sound very extravagant, but there are many levels from which to choose: salmon caviar, golden whitefish caviar, tobiko (flying fish caviar), and sturgeon caviars. From my first bite of fresh caviar, starting with salmon roe I salted myself, I was hooked. But only after a sampling of sturgeon caviars (beluga, sevruga, and osetra—staged by Daphne and Mats Engstrom at California Sunshine Fine Foods) was I able to discover, uninfluenced by the price tag, which one I enjoyed most. To be sure, all of them are delightful—incredi-ble, embryonic bursts of the sea on your tongue. But the tiny, dark sevruga eggs—which have distinctly nut-rich overtones and which cost half as much as big-egg beluga—won out. For two, a 7- or 8-ounce tin of sevruga caviar is adequate, and you should be able to find one for $120 to $140. For more moderate occasions, we settle on fresh salmon caviar, golden caviar, or tobiko—they all cost about $20 to $30 for a half-pound. Or we have less sturgeon caviar and stretch it out with toppings of minced hard-cooked egg, sour cream, chopped onions, and lemon wedges. It pays to check caviar prices with fancy food markets and caviar dealers (look in the yellow pages under Caviar).

Our favorite champagne with this supper is Billecart Salmon nonvintage brut, or other mellow, toasty bottlings of J. Lassale brut Blanc de Blancs, or Piper-Heidsieck nonvintage extra dry (in the $20 to $30 range).

Roughly, my investment in the most luxurious version of this meal is $150, but it can be as little as $50. We could easily spend more on dinner for two at almost any San Francisco restaurant, but we couldn't dine in our bathrobes. ■

BOB THOMPSON ON WINE
Portly pleasures

Wood port is for rainy days, when smoke rolls out of chimney tops and slinks away, low to the ground, already smelling a bit like cold ashes.

Vintage port is for those same days. It also is the great marker of great milestones, because it lasts so reliably, made strong by a Mediterranean sun, then stronger yet by the addition of brandy.

With January and February still to be borne, wood ports make fine Christmas gifts for now. They get their categorical name, wood port, for slumbering in oak casks through the coming and going of generations of cats at the least, men at the most.

Once upon a time, most all of them were subtitled ruby if made mostly from red grapes and younger stocks, or tawny if they had an important proportion of older stocks or white grapes. Some forgo those distinctions nowadays, going by the simple name of porto if they come from Portugal, or port or port-type if from elsewhere.

By any name, a port without a vintage date on it is ready to drink when it comes out of its gift wrappings, though there is no need to hurry. Some candidates for under the tree (mostly $10 to $20): Cockburn, Croft, Dow's, Fonseca (Tawny or Bin 27), Graham (10-Year Tawny), Quinta de Noval, Sandeman, Taylor Fladgate (First Estate or Ten-Year Tawny), and Warre's. From California: Ficklin's portlike Tinta Port.

Vintage ports, contrarily, go to bottle just two years after the harvest, all rough and out of sorts, needing the time it takes a marriage to season, or a new baby to turn 21. (For example, the Brits think the 1975s are just rounding into form.) Though vintage ports age smoothly, they for-ever taste more of grapes than wood ports do.

In great years, every winery "declares" and bottles vintage port. In more troubled years, only a few may, so some vintages can be scarce, leaving anniversaries to be celebrated otherwise. But if a birth or wedding year coincides with a vintage year, then a gift bottle is perfect for an acquaintance, a case for a friend. In British tradition, fathers buy a cask for each son.

Look for vintage ports from the producers named above, but above all, seek advice from a wine merchant who stocks at least a dozen producers, preferably more.

When *Sunset* cooks gather with family and friends

Our editors and writers share their down-to-earth ways of seasonal entertaining

WHAT WOULD YOU EXPECT IF A *Sunset* food writer invited you home for a holiday party? If it's scary perfection, don't worry. Reality toppled our pedestals at home long ago—and culinary preening is reserved for other occasions.

When we gather families and friends to share the season's festivities, it's their company we want to enjoy. We choose and serve foods that will make friends comfortable, get them involved, break the ice, and reaffirm traditions. We also choose dishes for their flexibility—little parties can grow and big parties can get larger. We think what we've learned—and share here—will fit ideally into situations on your own agenda, and help make this year's holidays the merriest yet.

Spontaneous sangria

Last-minute addition brightens a family brunch

By Betsy Reynolds Bateson

Last year, I hosted my first Christmas brunch for the whole family, with ages ranging from 1, our daughter Amanda, to 84, my grandfather. As a working mom, I

SANGRIA *is a bubbly blend of red fruit juice, lime syrup, and champagne or mineral water.*

had to squeeze menu planning and shopping into lunch breaks, and on one whirl through the market I picked up some red fruit juices, thinking their cheerful color might fit in someplace.

Christmas Eve, my sister called to ask what she could bring. I announced we needed bubbles, and so she arrived with sparkling wine, apple juice, and mineral water. As she set them beside my red juices and a basketful of limes on the counter, an idea clicked—and I rushed to make a fresh lime syrup.

Christmas morning, Rosy Sparkling Sangria was born. It was an instant hit. After I demonstrated how to make the first glass, the family leapt in with their own modifications. The little ones and adults all loved the red-tinted, tart-sweet, fizzy nonalcoholic

versions, and adults also enjoyed the rosy light wine refreshment. With departing farewells came requests to "do that drink again next year," and I realized a tradition had just been born in our own home.

Rosy Sparkling Sangria

Fresh lime syrup (recipe follows)

About 1 quart chilled red fruit juice, Pinot Noir grape juice, or juice blend of cranberries, raspberries, or cherries

About 1 bottle (750 ml.) chilled sparkling wine or champagne

About 1 quart chilled sparkling mineral water or apple juice

For each serving, pour into a 6- or 8-ounce glass 1 to 3 tablespoons fresh lime syrup and about ¼ cup fruit juice. Fill with sparkling wine or mineral water. Makes 12 to 14 servings.

Per serving with sparkling wine: 108 cal. (0 percent from fat); 0.1 g protein; 0 g fat; 19 g carbo.; 0 mg sodium; 0 mg chol.

Fresh lime syrup. In a 2- to 3-quart pan, combine 1 cup **sugar** and 1 cup **water**. Boil

DAN DAN NOODLES *start with coils of egg pasta dropped into a Chinese takeout carton. Dress noodles to taste with browned ground pork, cilantro, green onions, bean sprouts, salty preserved vegetable, tongue-tingling Sichuan peppercorns, and squirts of hot chili oil, soy sauce, and black vinegar. Serve with chopsticks.*

PETER CHRISTIANSEN

Chinese takeout stays home

Guests season their own, so I don't have to worry about fussy eaters

By Linda Lau Anusasananan

over high heat until reduced to 1 cup; let cool.

Add 1 cup freshly squeezed **lime juice** (takes 10 to 12 limes) to the cool syrup. Cover and chill until cold, about 1 hour or up to 2 days. Makes 2 cups.

Per tablespoon: 26 cal. (0 percent from fat); 0 g protein; 0 g fat ; 6.9 g carbo.; 0.1 mg sodium; 0 mg chol.

Asian-style noodles fit my take-it-easy entertaining strategy perfectly. Once the

food is on the table, I relax. Now it's the guests' turn to work, and they treat it more like fun than a chore. From a buffet, they gather ingredients

for their one-dish main course into paper cartons—the kind used by Chinese takeout restaurants. The foundation of the dish is room-temperature noodles. Guests tailor portions to taste with toppings of fresh and preserved vegetables, seasoned meat, and salty, spicy, and tart condiments. Not only does this relieve me of worrying about fussy eaters—they can pick out just what they want—but the disposable cartons and throwaway chopsticks make cleanup a cinch.

In this Chinese noodle dish from Sichuan, toppings for tender egg noodles are fried ground pork, cilantro, green onions, crisp bean sprouts, Chinese black vinegar, numbing Sichuan peppercorns, and pungent preserved vegetables.

When I change a few ingredients in this formula, I have a completely new menu. Sometimes I use rice noodles, cold cooked chicken, sliced cucumbers, and a purchased Sichuan peanut sauce or chili dressing. For a Thai option, I add hot broth, thin beef slices, chopped peanuts, and fried garlic.

Look for the paper cartons in stores that sell gift wrap or restaurant supplies, or ask at a Chinese restaurant if you can buy a dozen.

Dan Dan Noodles

3 pounds fresh or dried thin Chinese egg noodles or capellini

2 tablespoons Oriental sesame oil

1 tablespoon salad oil

3 pounds ground lean pork

⅓ cup Chinese rice wine (Shaoxing) or sake

¼ teaspoon ground white pepper

Salt

¾ cup chopped Chinese preserved vegetable such as Tientsin or Sichuan (optional)

Seasonings (suggestions follow)

1½ cups fresh cilantro (coriander) leaves

1½ cups thinly sliced green onions

1½ pounds bean sprouts, rinsed and drained

In an 8- to 10-quart pan, bring about 5 quarts water to a boil over high heat. Add noodles; cook until just barely tender to bite, about 2 minutes for fresh, about 6 minutes if dried; drain water from pan. Fill pan with cold water; drain noodles, and again fill pan with cold water and add sesame oil. When noodles are cool, lift out 1 handful at a time and loosely coil into mounds on a platter or in a basket. If making ahead, cover and hold at room temperature up to 4 hours.

In a 10- to 12-inch frying pan over medium-high heat, stir salad oil and pork often until meat is crumbly and browned, 10 to 20 minutes. Drain off any fat. Add wine and pepper to meat; bring to a boil, scraping free brown bits. Add salt to taste. Pour into a bowl and serve hot or keep warm on an electric warming tray. If making ahead, cover and chill up to

1 day; reheat to serve.

To serve, arrange noodles, meat, vegetable, and seasonings on a table. Invite guests to add a coil of noodles to a carton or bowl, then top noodles to taste with preserved vegetable, meat, cilantro, green onions, bean sprouts, and seasonings. Makes 12 main-dish servings.

Per serving: 618 cal. (32 percent from fat); 36 g protein; 22 g fat (6.5 g sat.); 67 g carbo.; 95 mg sodium; 207 mg chol.

Seasonings. Present in individual containers **soy sauce, Chinese black** or white **rice vinegar, hot chili-flavor oil,** and **ground Sichuan peppercorns** (recipe follows) or crushed dried hot red chilies.

Ground Sichuan peppercorns. Remove any debris from ¼ cup **Sichuan peppercorns.** In a 6- to 8-inch frying pan over medium-low heat, frequently shake peppercorns until they are fragrant, 2 to 3 minutes. Whirl in a blender until finely ground. Use, or store airtight up to 6 months. Makes 2 tablespoons.

PETER CHRISTIANSEN

SAVORY TART *sports two toppings. Pick your side: cheddar with mushrooms, or chèvre with arugula and porcini.*

Something for everyone

A new family, a new way to cook, a new tart

By Christine Weber Hale

When I was growing up, my family treated eating as a wonderful adventure—an opportunity to experience new foods, different cultures, and interesting flavor combinations. However, when I became host of my own parties, I quickly learned that a culinary onslaught of quail eggs, ancho chilies, and mizuna is not always met with equal enthusiasm. Some of my early exotic menus generated more confusion than appetite. So I moved ahead, working to balance the new, for my enjoyment, with the familiar, for the comfort of my more timid friends.

It was good training for the future. I married into a family with divergent tastes and lots of young nieces and nephews;

my balancing act has expanded to include dishes for a wide range of ages, too. This need to please so many at once inspired my split-personality appetizer tart. Half is topped with tried-and-true cheese and mushrooms; the other half has more daring ingredients.

I make one dish, it bridges all tastes, and everybody is happy.

50/50 Appetizer Tart

1½ ounces (about 1½ cups) dried porcini mushrooms

1 package (17¼ oz.) frozen puff pastry dough, thawed

2 tablespoons butter or margarine

½ pound fresh common mushrooms, rinsed and sliced

4 cloves garlic, minced or pressed

1 tablespoon minced fresh or 1 teaspoon crumbled dried sage

About 1 cup thinly cut strips red bell pepper

1 cup (¼ lb.) shredded cheddar cheese

2 green onions, ends trimmed, chopped

⅓ pound soft chèvre cheese

2 tablespoons prepared pesto sauce

2 to 3 ounces arugula, stems pinched off, rinsed and crisped

Fresh sage sprigs

Place porcini in a small bowl; add boiling water to cover. Let stand until mushrooms are soft, at least 30 minutes or up to 4 hours.

On a lightly floured board, lay out the 2 puff pastry sheets so that they overlap ½ inch on a narrow edge; firmly press edges together. Cut dough to make a 16-inch-long piece; reserve scrap for other uses. Roll out dough to widen to a 13- by 16-inch rectangle; trim edges with a knife to make straight. Gently transfer dough to a 14- by 17-inch baking sheet. Pierce dough all over with a fork. Bake on lowest rack in a 350° oven until puffed and golden brown on bottom, about 20 minutes. Use hot or lukewarm, or let cool, cover, and chill up to 1 day; return to oven for 10 minutes, then continue.

Meanwhile, in a 10- to 12-inch nonstick frying pan over medium-high heat, melt ½ the butter. Add common mushrooms, ½ the garlic, and the minced sage. Stir often until mushrooms are well browned, about 10 minutes. Transfer mixture to a small bowl. Wipe pan clean.

Gently rub porcini in water to release any grit, then lift from water; discard liquid. Pat porcini with towels to lightly dry; set aside any large attractive pieces and mince remainder. In frying pan, melt remaining butter over medium-high heat. Add porcini and remaining garlic. Stir often just until garlic begins to brown, about 7 minutes. If making ahead, cover mixtures and chill up to 1 day.

On warm pastry, lay bell pepper strips in a straight line diagonally from 2 opposite corners. On 1 triangle of pastry, sprinkle cheddar cheese, then scatter common mushrooms and green onions over cheese. Break soft chèvre into small pieces and scatter over the other pastry triangle; spread gently to fill space. Top chèvre with pesto and spread over cheese. Lay arugula leaves on pastry to cover pesto, and scatter with porcini. Bake tart in a 350° oven until cheddar melts, 5 to 10 minutes. Transfer tart to a platter. Garnish with arugula leaves and sage sprigs. Cut into squares. Serves 12.

Per serving: 289 cal. (65 percent from fat); 8.1 g protein; 21 g fat (6.9 g sat.); 18 g carbo.; 220 mg sodium; 21 mg chol.

My favorite mulled wine

Easy to make and inexpensive

By Elaine Johnson

Everyone knows how to make mulled wine, don't they? That's what I thought—until guests started asking what makes my mulled wine so good, and friends who were giving parties kept pulling me over to their stoves for advice.

My first tip for them—a good mix of flavorings—probably isn't too unusual. But a few of the ingredients might be: star anise (sold in the Asian section of many grocery stores), ginger, and plenty of apple and orange slices. The result is reminiscent of sangria, but hot and spiced.

You need a surprising amount of sugar for good mulled wine. Heating brings out tartness and tannins in the wine that are enjoyable at cellar temperature, but are a little potent warm. The sugar smoothes the rough edges and brings out the spice and fruit flavors.

What about the wine? Here's where my pocketbook cheers. Cheaper, gutsy bottles stand up best to the sugar and generous flavorings I like to use. Burgundy-type, red table wine, and Zinfandel all work great, whether closed with corks or screw caps.

Mulled wine will definitely be back in my kitchen this season. The scent of warm spices and wine says welcome when friends walk in the door. More practically, it's easy to make in quantity, relatively inexpensive, and sure to please most guests.

My Favorite Mulled Wine

2.25 liters (about 10½ cups, a 1.5 liter bottle plus a 750 ml. bottle; or 3 bottles, each 750 ml.) full-flavored red wine such as burgundy-type or Zinfandel

About ⅔ cup sugar

16 inches cinnamon stick, total (use long decorative sticks from a gourmet store or Mexican market, or short sticks from the supermarket)

2 whole nutmegs, cracked in large pieces with a hammer

PETER CHRISTIANSEN

SPICES AND FRUIT *perfume hot mulled wine.*

1 tablespoon whole star anise

1 teaspoon whole allspice

1 teaspoon whole cloves

8 quarter-size slices fresh ginger

1 large (about ½ lb.) Granny Smith apple, cored and thinly sliced crosswise

1 medium-size (about ½ lb.) orange, halved lengthwise and thinly sliced crosswise

Colored part of peel from 1 medium-size (about ½ lb.) orange, peeled from fruit in a long spiral

In a 5- to 6-quart pan over medium-low heat, stir wine, ⅔ cup sugar, cinnamon, nutmegs, anise, allspice, cloves, ginger, apple, orange, and orange peel until steaming. To blend flavors, hold at steaming, uncovered, 15 to 20 minutes. Taste and stir in more sugar, if desired. Ladle into mugs and serve, or turn heat under wine to low (below simmering), and keep warm up to 2 hours. Makes 11 cups, about 14 servings, ¾ cup each.

Per ¾ cup: 162 cal. (0.6 percent from fat); 0.5 g protein; 0.1 g fat (0 g sat.); 15 g carbo.; 9 mg sodium; 0 mg chol.

PERFECT FINGER FOOD: *two salads—couscous at left, chicken at right—are surrounded by lettuce leaves. Spoon salads onto leaves to serve—no other utensils are necessary.*

Who knows how many guests there will be?

No forks, no plates—lean salads to nibble can be appetizers or dinner

By Jerry Anne Di Vecchio

To make it onto a party menu in our house, dishes have to meet some tough standards, especially for the come-and-go gathering that we particularly enjoy. Here are the primary criteria: foods stay fresh for several hours; are self-serve; can be eaten with the fingers; require no last-minute attention and few, if any, touch-ups; are as lean as they can be; and, of course, taste great.

During the holiday season, we place added demands on our menus. Many friends have family visiting; our guest lists frequently swell to accommodate them. And the nature of a party can change on a

whim, too. We may decide to snack lightly, then move on to a restaurant, or pitch the tent and stay home. So dishes frequently switch roles from appetizer to whole meal or back again, and leftover elements often get rolled into other occasions.

This pair of salads—one chicken, the other couscous—does a good job shifting gears. Both are extremely low in fat, and the couscous one accommodates my vegetarian friends. The salads are refreshingly seasoned and do well as appetizers. But they can also become an instant meal to share in a communal Middle Eastern style—from a low coffee table without plates or forks. You scoop

small bites of salad onto tender lettuce leaves.

Chicken and Couscous Salads in Leaf Cups

4 cups tiny, torn or cut pieces skinned cooked chicken

Tinted onions (directions follow)

1½ cups orange segments (cut from membrane)

1½ cups chopped fresh cilantro (coriander)

Orange-lime dressing (directions follow)

Spiced couscous (directions follow)

Salt

1 tablespoon finely shredded orange peel (colored part only)

Salad leaves (directions follow)

Thin orange slices (optional)

Mix chicken, tinted onions, orange segments, ¾ cup cilantro, and ½ the orange-lime dressing. Mix remaining dressing with the spiced couscous. Season both salads to taste with salt, then

mound chicken salad and couscous salad in wide shallow bowls, or in separate mounds on a large rimmed platter. Sprinkle remaining cilantro over chicken; sprinkle orange peel over couscous. Mound leaves in a separate container, or arrange around salads. Garnish with orange slices. To serve, invite guests to spoon bite-size portions of salad onto leaves. Makes 6 to 8 main-dish or 12 to 16 appetizer servings.

Per main-dish serving: 419 cal. (17 percent from fat); 32 g protein; 7.7 g fat (1.7 g sat.); 56 g carbo.; 108 mg sodium; 62 mg chol.

Tinted onions. Cut 1 medium-size (5 or 6 oz.) **red onion** into thin, short slivers. Bring 6 cups **water** and ¼ cup **rice vinegar** to boiling in a 3- to 4-quart pan over high heat. Add onion and 1 teaspoon **cumin seed.** Let cook, uncovered, until boil resumes. Drain in a fine strainer; let onion and seed cool. Use, or if making ahead, cover and chill up to 1 day.

Orange-lime dressing. Combine 1½ cups **orange juice** and 1 cup **lime juice** with ¼ cup minced **fresh ginger,** and 1 teaspoon **crushed dried hot red chilies.** Use, or if making ahead, cover and chill up to 6 hours.

Spiced couscous. In a 3- to 4-quart pan, combine 3 cups **regular-strength chicken broth,** 2 tablespoons **mustard seed,** 1½ teaspoons **coriander seed,** 1 teaspoon **cumin seed,** 1 teaspoon **dried thyme leaves,** 1 teaspoon **curry powder,** and ⅛ teaspoon hulled **cardamom seed.** Bring to a boil, cover, and simmer 5 minutes, then add 2 cups **couscous.** Stir, remove from heat, and cover. Let stand until cool. Stir with a fork to separate couscous pieces. Use, or if making ahead, cover and chill up to 1 day.

Salad leaves. Use inner **romaine leaves** and larger, unbruised outer leaves, broken in ½ lengthwise, and tender **butter lettuce leaves;** you will need about 3½ to 3¾ pounds total edible leaves. Rinse leaves, drain, and wrap in towels; enclose in a large plastic bag and chill at least 1 hour or up to 2 days.

ON A CENTURY-OLD *china platter, pineapple, kiwi fruit, and papaya come drizzled with a fresh strawberry sauce.*

The blue platter lives on

Its offerings change with the generations

By Barbara E. Goldman

Propped up on telephone books at my grandparents' dining table, I loved helping myself from my grandmother's blue china platter, just like an adult. Back on that Wisconsin dairy farm, the large platter usually held a roast chicken—one that had met its fate on a backyard stump.

Today the platter plays an important role in my own home in Menlo Park, California—but it's my 3-year-old granddaughter, Zoë, who's

trying to be the big girl. And she can't get enough of the platter's contents—almost invariably an arrangement of fresh fruit that I like to serve for brunch, for an open house, or even for dessert.

My guests seem to welcome refreshing fruit combinations during the holidays, perhaps as a respite from so much rich food. I use tropical fruits, or a citrus assortment of pink and white grapefruit and orange segments scattered with raspberries, blueberries, or halved seedless grapes.

Tropical Fruit Platter with Strawberry Sauce

If fresh strawberries aren't available, use frozen whole strawberries for sauce and thaw to use.

2 cups strawberries, hulled and rinsed

   About 1 tablespoon sugar

   About 2 tablespoons orange-flavor liqueur such as Grand Marnier (optional)

1 medium-size (about 3 lb.) pineapple, peeled, cored, quartered lengthwise, and cut crosswise into ¼-inch slices

2 small (about 2 lb. total) firm-ripe papayas, peeled, halved lengthwise, seeded, and cut crosswise into ¼-inch slices

6 medium-size (about 1½ lb. total) kiwi fruit, peeled and cut crosswise into ¼-inch slices

3 whole strawberries with stems (optional)

In a blender or food processor, whirl hulled strawberries until smooth. Add sugar and Grand Marnier to taste. If making ahead, cover strawberry sauce and chill up to 2 days.

On a large platter, overlap slices of each fruit, grouping each kind separately. Drizzle strawberry sauce over fruit in attractive pattern. Garnish with whole strawberries; if desired, cut each berry into 4 or 5 slices from tip to, but not through, stem end, and flare slightly. Makes 12 servings.

Per serving: 90 cal. (6 percent from fat); 1.2 g protein; 0.6 g fat (0 g sat.); 22 g carbo.; 4.8 mg sodium; 0 mg chol.

HANDWRITTEN, HAND-ILLUSTRATED *cookbook holds the recipe for this velvety pumpkin mousse and rum sauce—plus many other family favorites. The bowls contain a double batch.*

A dessert handed down

A treasured album holds the family's pumpkin tradition

By Hilary Doubleday

The whole story didn't come out until we discovered that my mother's long-kept "secret" recipe wasn't actually a secret. She'd never suggested otherwise, but with her culinary reputation in our family, I had assumed that the pumpkin mousse, part of so many holidays, was her own invention.

The truth emerged when I was offered my position at *Sunset*—to which she had subscribed for years. On hearing my news, she casually remarked, "Well, you know, the pumpkin mousse is a *Sunset* recipe." What a shock! I'd always thought that the mousse recipe was filed away in her head and someday, if I was good and extremely convincing, I might coax her to write it down.

Fortunately, my mother, Françoise Park, came to this decision herself—spurred, no doubt, by frequent long-distance calls from me and my three sisters: "Hello, Mom?… Boy, am I glad I reached you! I have six people coming over for dinner in an hour.… Could you tell me how to make that mousse again?" Assembled in four hand-illustrated books titled "Family Favorites of Françoise and Daughters" are the pumpkin mousse and 50 other recipes. She gave the books to us as Christmas gifts, and they became instant heirlooms. Should disaster strike, I know my copy would be one of the first treasures I would save, and I suspect my sisters feel the same way.

Upon researching the origins of our beloved mousse, I made another discovery. It turns out that my mother's recipe isn't quite identical to the magazine's. Through the years, she has adjusted and modified, perfecting it according to our tastes; as for the sauce—well, that really is hers alone.

Pumpkin Mousse

¾ cup sliced almonds

2 envelopes unflavored gelatin

1 cup firmly packed brown sugar

½ teaspoon *each* ground cinnamon, ground allspice, ground ginger, and ground nutmeg

¼ teaspoon salt

⅔ cup milk

⅓ cup dark rum

4 large eggs, separated

1 can (1 lb.) pumpkin

½ cup coarsely chopped candied ginger

¼ teaspoon cream of tartar

1 cup whipping cream

Rum sauce (recipe follows)

In a 10- to 12-inch frying pan over medium-high heat, stir the almonds until lightly toasted, 6 to 8 minutes. Pour from pan and coarsely chop ½ cup nuts.

In frying pan, mix gelatin with ½ cup of the sugar, cinnamon, allspice, ground ginger, nutmeg, and salt. Stir in milk, rum, and 4 egg yolks. Stir over medium-low heat (mixture must not boil) until just thick enough to coat a metal spoon with a velvety layer, 3 to 5 minutes. Remove from heat; stir in chopped almonds, pumpkin, and candied ginger.

In a deep bowl, combine egg whites and cream of tartar. Whip on high speed until whites are just stiff enough to barely hold their shape. Continue to beat at high speed, gradually adding the remaining ½ cup sugar, then beat until whites hold very stiff peaks. In another deep bowl, whip cream on high speed until it holds soft peaks. With a whisk or rubber spatula, gently fold together pumpkin mixture, egg white meringue, and whipped cream; mix evenly. Pour into a serving bowl. Cover and chill until cool, at least 3 hours or up to 1 day. Wrap sliced nuts airtight.

Uncover mousse and sprinkle with sliced almonds; spoon into bowls. Add rum sauce to taste. Makes 10 to 12 servings.

Per serving without rum sauce: 263 cal. (38 percent from fat); 5.6 g protein; 11 g fat (5 g sat.); 33 g carbo.; 98 mg sodium; 95 mg chol.

Rum sauce. In a 10- to 12-inch frying pan, mix together 4 **large egg yolks,** 1 cup firmly packed **light brown sugar,** 1 cup **whipping cream,** and ½ cup **light rum.** Stir over medium-low heat (mixture must not boil) until sauce lightly coats a metal spoon, about 5 minutes. Pour into a small bowl or pitcher. Cover and chill until cold, at least 2 hours or up to 1 day. Makes about 2⅓ cups.

Per tablespoon: 55 cal. (41 percent from fat); 0.4 g protein; 2.5 g fat (1.4 g sat.); 6 g carbo.; 5.3 mg sodium; 30 mg chol.

Cooked meringue (egg-safe) pumpkin mousse. Follow preceding recipe for pumpkin mousse, but omit fresh egg whites, cream of tartar, and the ½ cup sugar whipped with whites. Use instead 1 package **meringue mix for Pavlova** (4.4 oz.); whip the dried egg white mixture with **water** and **sugar** as directed on package. Fold meringue into the pumpkin mousse. ■

PETER CHRISTIANSEN

CAKE WEDGE *(left) and lemon tart (above) surrounded by dramatic tricolor sauce make shamelessly simple desserts—and homemade or purchased pastries work equally well.*

Sauces with designs on dessert

Stained-glass windows inspire these delicious presentations

GIVE YOUR HOLIDAY desserts three-star-restaurant style with three purchased ingredients and a playful technique. To create the illusion of stained-glass windows on dessert plates, pipe a pattern of thick caramel sauce onto them. Then fill in the spaces with transparent jelly and opaque eggnog. Plain slices of angel food or pound cake or scoops of ice cream look handsome on such a backdrop, and other seasonal desserts, from pumpkin pie to chocolate-frosted Yule logs, work well, too.

To get a head start, decorate the plates several hours in advance. Even if the lines blur slightly on standing, the effect is still appealing.

Stained-glass Dessert Sauce

Just before serving, set desserts on sauced plates.

About ½ cup purchased caramel sauce that is too thick to pour

About 6 tablespoons raspberry or currant jelly

About 6 tablespoons purchased eggnog

Spoon caramel sauce into a zip-lock plastic sandwich bag without pleats. Trim 1 corner from bottom of bag to make a ¼-inch hole. Gently squeeze caramel onto the flat area of 6 to 8 dinner plates, drawing a design with large spaces between borders.

In a 1- to 1½-quart pan over medium-high heat, stir jelly until smoothly melted. Or put jelly in a microwave-safe bowl and heat on full power (100 percent) in a microwave oven; stir every 10 or 15 seconds until jelly is smoothly melted. Let cool until lukewarm but still liquid (if too hot, it will soften caramel).

With a teaspoon, ladle jelly, a little at a time, into some of the spaces created by the caramel, then push jelly with spoon tip to caramel borders; barely fill spaces, don't flood them. Spoon eggnog, a little at a time, into remaining spaces and push with spoon tip to caramel borders. Use, let plates stand at room temperature up to 15 minutes, or chill, uncovered, up to 4 hours. Makes enough to decorate 8 dinner plates.

Per serving, sauce only: 106 cal. (7.6 percent from fat); 0.8 g protein; 0.9 g fat (0.5 g sat.); 25 g carbo.; 83 mg sodium; 7 mg chol. ■

THICK CARAMEL, *squeezed onto plates, separates melted jelly and eggnog that fill between the lines.*

GENTLY PUSH *melted jelly up to, but not into, the edges of the caramel lines; do the same with the eggnog.*

By Christine Weber Hale

The ultimate panettone

It's easier than it looks. Start with store-bought sweet Italian bread. Then follow our step-by-step directions for assembling and filling.

By Elaine Johnson

I f you're making only one dessert this month, this should be the one. Though it looks like an engineering feat, the dessert is actually more show than work, and you do most of the assembly a week ahead. The dessert slices easily, too. The recipe is a creation of Gary Rulli, owner of Pasticceria Rulli in Larkspur, California, just north of San Francisco. Like pastry shops in Italy, Rulli's bakes panettone year-round, but orders skyrocket in December, when the bread (plain, or filled like this) becomes the focus of holiday tables. This month other bakeries in the West create their own dried fruit–studded bread, while many upscale markets and Italian delicatessens import it from Italy year-round.

Frozen Two-tone Panettone

Use either a rounded, shorter panettone (shown at right, about 8 in. wide and 4 in. tall) or a taller cylinder shape (usually about 6 in. wide and 7 in. tall); just be sure to get the 2-pound (1 kg.) size. Panettones may be labeled Turin- or Milan-style, or with other city names; avoid the Genovese, a flatter, dense fruitcake. Allow plenty of space in the freezer.

- 6 large egg yolks
- ½ cup sugar
- 3 tablespoons all-purpose flour
- 1½ cups milk
- 1 strip (¾ in. by 2 in.) lemon peel (colored part only)
- 1 teaspoon vanilla
- 3 ounces bittersweet or semisweet chocolate, chopped
- ½ cup chopped high-quality candied orange peel
- 2 tablespoons dark rum
- 2¼ cups whipping cream
  Nut brittle (recipe follows)
- 1 purchased 2-pound panettone
  Orange syrup (recipe follows)
  Segments from 2 medium-size (about ½ lb. each) oranges, with peel and membrane cut off
  Citrus leaves (optional)

In a bowl of an electric mixer, beat yolks and sugar until thick, then beat in flour. In a 2- to 3-quart pan over medium-high heat, stir milk

JOHN HARDING

At Gary Rulli's Italian pastry shop, Pasticceria Rulli, he and his staff bake 5,000 pounds of panettone each December.

1. With panettone upside down, cut circle ¾ inch from edge through bread to 1 inch from domed top; mark distances with toothpicks on cake, tape on knife.

2. Invert bread. Insert knife horizontally 1 inch from top. Push to ¾ inch from other side. Without enlarging hole, saw across half of bread to ¾-inch wall. Turn blade; repeat.

KEVIN CANDLAND

3. Ease shell from core; set core aside. If needed, reinsert knife through opening in shell to level the inside top of panettone (it should be 1 inch from outer domed top).

4. After spooning chocolate custard into syrup-soaked shell, cover with nut custard to within ½ inch of top. (Panettone sizes vary; save any extra filling for other use.)

5. From flat end of reserved core, cut a slice ½ inch thick; generously brush cut side with orange syrup and push into panettone to seal. Freeze filled panettone until firm.

6. On top of frozen, right-side-up panettone, use mounds of whipped cream to anchor chunks of panettone, nut brittle, and orange segments.

and lemon peel often until simmering, 3 to 4 minutes; discard peel. Beat milk into yolk mixture. Return to pan; whisk over medium-low heat just until custard starts to bubble, 4 to 5 minutes (don't overcook or custard will lump). Remove from heat; stir in vanilla.

Spoon half of custard into a medium-size bowl. To custard remaining in pan, add chocolate; stir until melted. Stir in orange peel and rum. Let custards cool slightly; chill airtight until cold, 45 to 50 minutes.

In bowl of an electric mixer, beat 1¼ cups cream until thick. Working with half of it, stir ½ cup into chocolate custard, then gently fold in the rest. Chop ⅓ of nut brittle and stir into plain custard with ½ cup remaining whipped cream; fold in rest of cream. Chill custards airtight until used, up to 1 hour.

Peel off and discard paper collar from panettone. With a long serrated knife, hollow out panettone as shown above in steps 1, 2, and 3.

Line a rimmed plate or dish with plastic wrap; place panettone shell in it upside down. Brush ⅔ cup orange syrup over inside of shell. Patch knife opening (and any other holes) inside shell with thin slice of panettone core taken from cut side.

As shown in steps 4 and 5, fill panettone with chocolate and nut custards, then seal with slice from bottom of core. Wrap panettone airtight and freeze upside down for at least 8 hours or up to 1 week. Store remaining panettone core and nut brittle airtight up to 2 days; or freeze up to 1 week (thaw to use). Store remaining syrup airtight up to 1 week.

To assemble for serving, tear reserved core into 1- to 2-inch pieces; place in a large bowl, and mix evenly with reserved syrup. In the bowl of an electric mixer, beat remaining 1 cup cream until soft peaks form. Unwrap panettone and place right side up on a platter.

Leaving a border of crust, lay 4 or 5 large dollops of cream on top of panettone. Use cream to anchor panettone chunks, brittle, and orange segments as in step 6. Repeat several times, narrowing layers to form a cone shape. Decorate with citrus leaves. Refrigerate at least 45 minutes or up to 2 hours.

With a sturdy knife, cut panettone gently through toppings, then firmly through base, into wedges. Gently wrap any leftovers airtight and refreeze up to 3 days; (orange pieces may be slightly dry after freezing). Serves 16.

Per serving: 551 cal. (44 percent from fat); 8.5 g protein; 27 g fat (13 g sat.); 68 g carbo; 307 mg sodium; 157 mg chol.

Orange syrup. In a 1- to 1½-quart pan over high heat, bring ¾ cup **sugar,** ½ cup **water,** and 1 tablespoon **light corn syrup** to a boil, stirring often, 3 to 4 minutes. Let cool, then stir in ⅓ cup **orange-flavor liqueur.**

Nut brittle. Place ¼ cup each **hazelnuts, shelled salted pistachios, walnuts,** and **slivered almonds** in a 10- by 15-inch baking pan. Bake in a 350° oven until almonds are golden, 8 to 9 minutes.

In a 1- to 2-quart pan over medium-high heat, stir ⅔ cup **sugar** and 2 tablespoons **corn syrup** often until sugar melts and turns light amber, about 5 minutes. Add warm nuts; protecting hands, stir until syrup is deep amber, 1 to 2 minutes more. Spread candy as thinly as possible on a buttered 12- by 15-inch baking sheet; let cool. Flex pan to loosen candy; break into 1- to 2-inch chunks. ∎

Why?

Why bake with one fat instead of another?

Fats and oils behave differently in baking for many reasons, starting with their sources and structures. Some come from animals, some from plants. Some are natural, some are manufactured. Fats are solid at room temperature, oils are liquid. In baking, the most commonly used are:

Butter. This natural fat is about 20 percent water, but the water is emulsified—suspended throughout the butter.

Margarine. Hydrogenated vegetable oils are processed to resemble butter through the addition of color, flavor, and moisture. Converting oil to a solid fat produces the controversial transfatty acids.

Light butter and margarine. Added water (or other nonfat ingredients) gives them more volume, so cup for cup, you get less fat.

Vegetable shortening. Like margarine, this fat is made from hydrogenated vegetable oils, but as the fat cools and firms, air is incorporated rapidly to make it soft and malleable. The flavor is neutral.

Lard. Rendered (or slowly melted) pork fat has a grainy texture, no water, and a distinctive taste.

Vegetable oils. Most of these oils, which are from seeds, grains, beans, nuts, or fruits, are refined until clear and neutral-tasting.

Why do some recipes use butter and others don't? Are fats interchangeable?

Taste is one factor that determines choice. If you prefer the flavor of butter, use it, especially when its taste is obvious, as in pound cake or shortbread cookies. Otherwise, mechanically, margarine works like butter.

If foods are heavily spiced or seasoned, you can consider other fats in recipes, substituting solid for solid, liquid for liquid.

Solid fats form strong bonds and stay molecularly linked in batters and doughs, especially when beaten. When solid fat is beaten with sugar, the granules of sugar are cut or broken into smaller bits and create minute air cells that the fat traps. When solid fat is beaten with eggs, the stretchy eggs trap air in bubbles that the fat then encloses and distributes evenly. In cakes, these bubbles contribute to fine, light texture. The fat surrounds water from other ingredients and keeps it

Butter

Light butter

Salad oil

Melted margarine

Shortening

Lard

NORMAN A. PLATE

POUND CAKES *are made from the same recipe but with different kinds of fat or oil.*

from moving around in ways that can alter the texture of the baked food.

Solid fats make pastries flaky because rolling stretches lumps of fat into thin sheets that keep dough layers separate; moisture in the baking dough steams, swells, and pushes the layers apart to make flakes. Lard, with its grainy texture and lack of water, makes the flakiest pastry. Solid fats used cold (but not hard enough to tear pastry) also make more noticeable flakes.

Even when melted, solid fats retain some of their ability to bond and hold air, but they become more homogeneously integrated in batters and doughs, and behave differently. If the ratio of fat is high, as in a rich cookie such as a shortbread, the cookie will be shorter in texture—that is, more crumbly to the bite; it may also spread more while baking. In a cake, melted fat won't retain as much whipped-in air.

Oil is distributed throughout doughs and batters more completely than melted solid fat. Oil can't retain air when beaten, it won't hold together and sheet for flakiness, and it is less able to protect gluten from getting wet and tough. Some baked products made with oil, such as cookies with little or no liquid, muffins, or quick breads, may be more tender and feel shorter to the bite. If you use oil in a quick bread recipe that calls for solid fats, the bread may have coarser texture; if you make this substitution in a cookie recipe, the cookies may spread more as they bake, since oil wants to puddle.

"Why didn't my cookies come out when I substituted light margarine for butter?"—*Jay Lee, Concord, California*

Because light versions of butter and margarine contain more water and less fat, by volume, than regular butter or margarine, they change the proportions of a recipe just as

if you'd measured less fat and added more liquid.

"What's the best way to soften butter and margarine?"—*Jay Lee*

Butter and margarine hold beaten-in air best when they are firm but malleable, generally after standing at cool room temperature 30 to 45 minutes. Chilled, the fat is much harder, and you have to beat it more to make it fluffy.

You can speed the softening: Place butter (unwrap, if in foil), ¼ pound at a time, on a microwave-safe plate. Heat in a microwave oven on half-power (50 percent), rotating every 10 seconds, just until soft when pressed, 30 to 50 seconds total.

"Why do some recipes call for unsalted butter but then add salt later on?"—*Julie Scandora, Seattle*

If butter or margarine is unsalted, the cook can control the amount of salt in the recipe. But unsalted butter is usually more expensive. If a recipe calls for salt and unsalted butter, it's more practical to use regular salted butter—and you'll get the same results. However, many cooks strongly disagree, claiming the creamier texture and more delicate flavor of unsalted butter makes it worthwhile. In *Sunset*'s test kitchens we find adequate beating makes salted butter just as creamy, and in blind comparative tastings, texture and flavor differences in baked foods could not be verified.

More questions?

We would like to know what kitchen mysteries you're curious about. Send your questions to Why?, *Sunset Magazine,* 80 Willow Rd., Menlo Park, Calif. 94025. With the help of Dr. George K. York, extension food technologist at UC Davis, *Sunset* food editors will try to find solutions. We'll answer your questions in the magazine. ■

By Linda Lau Anusasananan

STIR-FRY CHOICES *include leftover turkey or other meat, just about any vegetable, and piquant toppings.*

Charting a turkey
stir-fry

Follow these amounts and ingredient choices to serve 2, 4, or 6

FOR A QUICK MEAL, a stir-fry is a good option. However, figuring out the correct proportions of ingredients can be a trial-and-error proposition. Here we chart amounts that make a perfect turkey stir-fry for two, four, and six servings.

Leftover cooked turkey from your holiday meal (or other cooked meat that you have on hand) makes the cooking process especially fast. And a well-seasoned cooking sauce alleviates the need to marinate the meat and seasons the vegetables.

You'll get a good balance of flavor and texture with an assortment of three to four different vegetables. If you run short of time, you can turn to precut vegetables available at most supermarkets. However, the vegetables are sometimes drier than those that you freshly cut.

Some unusual and delicious vegetable combinations with turkey are Japanese eggplant, onion, Anaheim chili, and carrot; yam, red bell pepper, fresh shiitake mushrooms, and kale or purple cabbage; onion, edible pea pods, green olives, and mustard greens; zucchini, yellow bell pepper, onion, and enoki mushrooms; and red onion, green beans, and dried cranberries.

If you're going to serve the stir-fry on top of hot rice or noodles, it's a good idea to double the sauce: the rice and noodles will absorb much of it. You can refrigerate the sauce for a few days.

Sauce. Combine ⅓ cup *each* regular-strength **chicken broth** and **mirin** (sweet sake), ¼ cup **reduced-sodium** or regular **soy sauce**, 3 tablespoons minced **fresh ginger**, 3 cloves minced or pressed **garlic**, 1 tablespoon **cornstarch**, 2 teaspoons **Oriental sesame oil**, and ½ teaspoon **crushed dried hot red chilies** (optional). Makes about 1 cup.

Cooking directions.

1. To a wok or 12-inch frying pan over high heat, add oil. When oil is hot, add assorted vegetables.

2. Stir-fry until hot (vegetable colors will become brilliant, may tinge brown), about 2 minutes.

3. Add broth; cook vegetables, covered, until just tender, 2 to 6 minutes. Remove the lid; cook until liquid evaporates.

4. Stir in sauce and turkey; bring to a boil. Stir in additional choices and cook until all ingredients are hot, 30 seconds to 2 minutes more.

5. Spoon mixture onto a platter; sprinkle with a topping, if desired. Serve rice, noodles, or napa cabbage on the side. ■

By Betsy Reynolds Bateson

STIR-FRY PROPORTIONS AND CHOICES

INGREDIENTS	SERVES 2	SERVES 4	SERVES 6
Cooking oil *Olive, peanut, or vegetable*	2 tsp.	1 tbsp.	1½ tbsp.
Vegetables *Broccoli flowerets, bell pepper wedges (green, red, or yellow), sliced carrots, green beans (cut into 1½-in. pieces), sliced Japanese eggplant, onion wedges, sliced mushrooms (button or shiitake), yams (peeled and thinly sliced), and sliced zucchini*	3 cups	5 cups	7 cups
Broth or water	¼ cup	⅓ cup	⅓ cup
Sauce	½ cup	¾ cup	1 cup
Cooked turkey or meat *In bite-size pieces*	1 cup	2 cups	3 cups
Additions *Anaheim or pasilla chilies (sliced and seeded), edible pea pods (strings removed), mustard greens, kale or purple cabbage (thinly sliced)*	Vary amounts to personal taste		
Toppings *Dried cranberries, pitted calamata or green olives, crushed dried hot red chilies, and enoki mushrooms*	Vary amounts to personal taste		
On the side *Cooked white or brown rice, cooked noodles, or uncooked, thinly sliced napa cabbage*	2 cups	4 cups	6 cups

RUBY GRAPEFRUIT glistens next to crusty, golden brown salmon fillet; grapefruit, capers, and mint flavor the refreshing sauce.

Simple elegance with salmon and grapefruit

Fruit juice and caper sauce is the finishing touch

COMPLEX BUT SUBTLE interplays of textures and flavors bring sophistication to this simple entrée. The season's ruby grapefruit contributes character to crisply coated salmon fillets at two levels. The tender grapefruit segments make a pretty garnish and juicy contrast for the crusty fish. The fruit juice, boiled down to intensify its flavor, spikes the cold sauce, in which the slight bitterness of the grapefruit, the sharpness of the capers, and the refreshing coolness of the mint merge to become a perfect foil for salmon's rich flavor.

You cook the salmon in two easy steps. First, quickly sauté bread crumb–coated pieces just until perfectly browned. You don't have to worry whether the fish is completely cooked because you then pop it into the oven to bake briefly.

Crusted Salmon with Grapefruit

6 slices (about 7½ oz.) firm-textured white bread, crusts removed

3 large (1 lb. each) ruby grapefruit

2 large egg whites

   About 2⅛ pounds boned and skinned 1-inch-thick salmon fillet, cut into 6 equal pieces

2 tablespoons butter or margarine

   Grapefruit caper sauce (recipe follows)

Cut bread into cubes; whirl cubes in a food processor or blender to make coarse, even-size crumbs.

Spread crumbs in an even layer in a 9- to 10-inch-wide pan. Bake in a 325° oven, stirring often, until the crumbs feel dry and crisp but are not browned, 10 to 15 minutes. If making ahead, store airtight up to 1 day.

Cut off and discard peels and white membranes from grapefruit. Cut between membrane and fruit to release segments into a bowl; discard seeds.

In a wide, shallow bowl, beat egg whites to blend. Pour crumbs into another wide bowl. Coat salmon pieces, 1 at a time, with egg whites. Drain briefly, then coat with crumbs. Lay pieces slightly apart on a sheet of waxed paper.

In a 10- to 12-inch nonstick frying pan over medium heat, melt 1 tablespoon butter. Add salmon to fill pan; do not crowd. Cook until salmon is brown on bottom, then turn pieces over and brown bottoms again, about 5 minutes total. As pieces are cooked, transfer to a 10- by 15-inch pan and put into a 325° oven. Melt remaining butter in frying pan, cook remaining salmon, and transfer to oven. Bake salmon until the pieces cooked last are still moist-looking but opaque in center of thickest part, 5 to 8 minutes.

Lift grapefruit segments from bowl and arrange on dinner plates. Place salmon on plates and accompany with grapefruit caper sauce. Serves 6.

Per serving without sauce: 419 cal. (34 percent from fat); 40 g protein; 16 g fat (4.4 g sat.); 27 g carbo.; 325 mg sodium; 108 mg chol.

Grapefruit caper sauce. In an 8- to 10-inch frying pan over high heat, boil 1 cup **ruby grapefruit juice** until reduced to ¼ cup. Let cool. Stir into ¾ cup **reduced-fat** or regular **mayonnaise.** Add 3 tablespoons drained **prepared capers** and 2 tablespoons chopped **fresh** or ½ teaspoon crumbled dried **mint.** If making ahead, cover and chill up to 1 day. Makes 1⅛ cups.

Per tablespoon: 32 cal. (76 percent from fat); 0.2 g protein; 2.7 g fat (0.7 g sat.); 1.9 g carbo.; 91 mg sodium; 9.9 mg chol. ■

By Christine Weber Hale

PETER CHRISTIANSEN

ALMOND-MERINGUE STARS, *hazelnut diamonds, and chocolate-ginger snowballs make a delicious cookie trio to serve at holiday gatherings.*

Holiday heirlooms

Traditional family favorites sweeten the season

BOTH ANNETTE Fullmer, of Alameda, California, and Karol Frietzsche, of San Francisco, celebrate the holidays with special cookie recipes handed down from their grandmothers.

Fullmer was raised in Switzerland, where family members gathered for hot wine and cookies each Christmas Eve after midnight mass. Two of the family's favorite cookies are Cinnamon Stars and Hazelnut Croquants.

The Chocolate-Ginger Balls from Frietzsche's grandmother, Henrietta Biittner, are the most popular holiday cookie among the Biittner clan. Frietzsche adds crystallized ginger to the cookie dough for a new twist.

Cinnamon Stars

2½ cups (about 15 oz.) almonds with skins

3 large egg whites

2½ cups powdered sugar

1 tablespoon ground cinnamon

1 tablespoon kirsch (cherry liqueur), optional

About ⅓ cup granulated sugar

Spread almonds in a 10- by 15-inch pan. Bake in a 350° oven until pale golden beneath skins (cut to test), about 15 minutes; shake pan occasionally during baking. Let cool. Finely grind nuts in a food processor or blender.

In a large bowl, whip egg whites with a mixer until they hold moist, soft peaks. Beating at high speed, gradually add powdered sugar, and continue to beat until whites hold stiff peaks. Spoon out ¾ cup of the whites; set aside.

To bowl, add ground almonds, cinnamon, and kirsch, mixing well. Sprinkle a board with some of the granulated sugar; scrape almond mixture onto it. Sprinkle dough lightly with more granulated sugar and pat flat. Roll dough ⅜ inch thick, using more sugar if mixture

sticks to rolling pin or board. Dip a star-shaped cutter, about 1½ inches wide, in granulated sugar and use to cut out cookies; dip in sugar as needed to prevent sticking. With a spatula, place cookies slightly apart on lightly oiled 12- by 15-inch baking sheets (you'll need 3, or bake in sequence). Dot each cookie with about ½ teaspoon of the reserved whites; spread over cookie.

Bake cookies in a 350° oven until meringue is golden, about 10 minutes. With a spatula, quickly but gently transfer cookies to racks to cool (tops tend to pop off). Serve, or store airtight up to 4 days. Makes about 5 dozen.—*Annette Fullmer, Alameda, California*

Per cookie: 67 cal. (49 percent from fat); 1.6 g protein; 3.7 g fat (0.4 g sat.); 7.6 g carbo.; 3.6 mg sodium; 0 mg chol.

Hazelnut Croquants

2 cups (about 10 oz.) hazelnuts

½ cup (¼ lb.) butter or margarine

¾ cup firmly packed brown sugar

1 large egg

1 teaspoon vanilla

1½ cups all-purpose flour

1 cup (6-oz. package) semisweet chocolate baking chips

Put hazelnuts in a 10- by 15-inch pan. Bake in a 350° oven until nuts are pale golden beneath skins (cut to test), about 15 minutes; shake pan occasionally. Pour nuts onto a towel; fold cloth over nuts and rub briskly to remove as much of the brown skins as possible. Lift nuts from cloth; discard skins.

Coarsely chop nuts. In a blender or food processor, finely grind half the nuts.

With an electric mixer, blend butter, brown sugar, egg, and vanilla until smooth. Add ground nuts and flour; mix well. Evenly press dough over bottom of a lightly buttered 10- by 15-inch pan. Bake in a 350° oven until just firm to touch, about 15 minutes.

Remove from oven. Immediately sprinkle hot cookie with chocolate chips. When chips are soft when pressed, spread evenly over cookie. Quickly sprinkle remaining nuts over chocolate; press down lightly with a wide spatula.

Chill until chocolate is firm, about 15 minutes. With a sharp knife, cut cookie lengthwise in pan into 1-inch-wide strips. At 1½-inch intervals, cut across strips at a 45° angle to create diamond shapes. Serve, or package airtight up to 4 days; freeze to store longer. Makes about 6 dozen.—*Annette Fullmer*

Per cookie: 67 cal. (60 percent from fat); 1 g protein; 4.5 g fat (1.4 g sat.); 6.4 g carbo.; 16 mg sodium; 6.6 mg chol.

Chocolate-Ginger Balls

1   cup granulated sugar

2   large eggs

¼   cup minced crystallized ginger

2   tablespoons butter or margarine

2   teaspoons vanilla

1¼ cups all-purpose flour

½   cup unsweetened cocoa

1   teaspoon baking powder

About ⅓ cup powdered sugar

With an electric mixer, blend granulated sugar, eggs, crystallized ginger, butter, and vanilla until smooth. Combine flour, cocoa, and baking powder; add to sugar mixture and mix well. Cover and chill dough until firm enough to handle easily, about 2 hours.

Roll dough into 1-inch balls, then roll balls in powdered sugar. Set balls about 1½ inches apart on ungreased 12- by 15-inch baking sheets (you'll need 2, or bake in sequence). Bake in a 375° oven until just firm to touch, about 10 minutes. Transfer to racks to cool. Serve, or package airtight up to 4 days; freeze to store longer. Makes about 3½ dozen.—*Karol Frietzsche, San Francisco*

Per cookie: 52 cal. (16 percent from fat); 0.9 g protein; 0.9 g fat (0.5 g sat.); 10 g carbo.; 21 mg sodium; 12 mg chol. ■

By Betsy Reynolds Bateson

PETER CHRISTIANSEN

CANDY'S RICH MAHOGANY *color develops during cooking as sugar caramelizes with butter.*

Toffee tradition

A handcrafted gift with dark chocolate and three kinds of nuts

SEVERAL EVENINGS A WEEK each December, I clear the counters and turn my kitchen into a candy and cookie center. Since I was a teenager, it's been my holiday tradition to make treats for family Christmas stockings, for parties, and for gifts for friends. As my list has grown, recipes like this one for toffee have become indispensable.

With three kinds of nuts and a dark chocolate coating, the buttery toffee is one of my favorites because it makes a lot, requires no detail work, stores well, and, best of all, tastes better than most toffee I can buy.

You'll need a candy thermometer. Once the toffee is cooked, be prepared to spread it out at once; it hardens rapidly.

Almond, Pistachio, and Hazelnut Toffee

About 1¼ cups (10 oz.) butter or margarine

2¼ cups sugar

½   teaspoon salt

½   cup water

1   cup coarsely chopped blanched almonds

½   cup coarsely chopped hazelnuts

1   cup shelled, salted pistachios

1½ cups (9 oz.) semisweet chocolate baking chips

Smoothly line 2 pans, 9 by 13 inches, each with a single piece of foil, crimping edges over pan rims to hold foil in place. Butter foil and set pans aside.

In a 5- to 6-quart pan over medium-high heat, cook 1¼ cups butter, sugar, salt, and water until mixture reaches 250° on a thermometer, 6 to 10 minutes; stir often. Add almonds and hazelnuts; stir until mixture reaches 300°, 4 to 8 minutes longer. Remove from heat and stir in ¾ cup of the pistachios. Protecting hands and working quickly, scrape candy equally into pans and spread evenly.

Let toffee cool until firm to touch, about 2 minutes. Evenly sprinkle with chocolate chips, and let stand until chocolate is softened, about 5 minutes. With a flexible spatula, spread chocolate to cover toffee. Chop remaining pistachios and scatter onto soft chocolate. Chill, uncovered, until chocolate is firm, about 15 minutes.

Lift foil with candy from pans. Break toffee into chunks. Serve, chill airtight up to 2 weeks, or freeze to store longer. Makes about 2¾ pounds.

Per ounce: 159 cal. (62 percent from fat); 1.7 g protein; 11 g fat (4.7 g sat.); 16 g carbo.; 93 mg sodium; 15 mg chol. ■

By Elaine Johnson

HEARTY SOUPS USUALLY owe their heartiness to a lot of red meat, butter, egg yolk, or a smooth roux of flour and butter. Julie Walther's Creamy Winter Squash Soup sticks to your ribs without any of these delicious but calorie-laden adhesives.

Creamy Winter Squash Soup

About 1½ pounds banana squash

1 large (about ½ lb.) russet potato, scrubbed

1 large (about ¼ lb.) carrot

3 slices whole-wheat bread, cut into 1-inch pieces

1 medium-size (5 to 6 oz.) onion, thinly sliced

1 whole chicken breast (about 1 lb.), split and skinned

1½ cups regular-strength chicken broth

2 tablespoons dry sherry

½ teaspoon ground nutmeg

1½ cups nonfat milk

½ cup unflavored nonfat yogurt

Thinly sliced green onions

Salt and white pepper

Scrape and discard seeds from squash. Place squash cut side down in a lightly oiled 9- by 13-inch pan. Pierce potato in several places with a fork and set in pan. Peel carrot and cut into 2- to 3-inch lengths; add to pan. Cover pan snugly with foil. Bake vegetables in a 400° oven until they are tender when pierced, about 45 minutes for squash and carrot, about 1 hour for potato; remove vegetables as cooked and let cool. Meanwhile, spread bread cubes in a 9- by 13-inch pan, and bake in the same oven as vegetables until cubes are toasted, 5 to 8 minutes, turning them over several times. Set the vegetables and cubes aside.

In a 5- to 6-quart pan over medium-high heat, frequently stir sliced onion and

Barrage of white chocolate blasts chocolate cookies

And squash soup richly deceives

IN DECEMBER 1992, WHEN Chefs of the West published Gerry Cutler's recipe for White White Chocolate Cookies, we editorialized that the only remaining challenge was a chocolate cookie with white chips.

Gerald M. Gardner is not one to ignore a thrown gauntlet. He eventually produced the recipe we print here. He adds two cautions: do not attempt to remove cookies from the sheet until they have cooled (they are initially very tender), and do not be surprised if the flavor changes between the first bite and last.

Chocolate Challenge Cookies

1 ounce unsweetened chocolate

¼ cup (⅛ lb.) butter or margarine

1 tablespoon finely ground coffee beans

½ cup sugar

¾ cup all-purpose flour

1 teaspoon baking powder

2 tablespoons milk

1 teaspoon vanilla

¼ cup sweetened shredded dried coconut

¼ cup white chocolate chips

Chop unsweetened chocolate and butter into small pieces. Combine with ground coffee in a metal bowl; nest bowl over hot water and stir often until mixture is smoothly melted. Or put mixture in a microwave-safe bowl and heat in a microwave oven on ½ power (50 percent), stirring at 30-second intervals, until smoothly melted.

In a bowl, stir together sugar, flour, and baking powder. Add chocolate mixture, milk, vanilla, coconut, and white chocolate chips; stir to mix well. Shape dough into 24 equal-size (about 1-in.) balls. Set balls about 3 inches apart on a lightly oiled 12- by 15-inch baking sheet. With your palm, flatten balls to about ¼ inch thick. Bake in a 350° oven until cookies feel firm at edges when lightly touched, 10 to 12 minutes. Let cool at least 10 minutes on pan (cookies tear when hot), then transfer with a spatula to racks to cool. Serve, or store airtight in the refrigerator up to 5 days; freeze to store longer. Makes 2 dozen.

Per cookie: 69 cal. (46 percent from fat); 0.7 g protein; 3.5 g fat (2.2 g sat.); 9.1 g carbo.; 45 mg sodium; 5.6 mg chol.

Gerald M. Gardner

Redmond, Washington

2 or 3 tablespoons water until onion begins to lightly brown, about 10 minutes. Remove onion from pan and set aside.

Add chicken and about ¼ cup water to pan. Simmer, turning chicken often, until pan is dry and chicken is lightly browned, about 8 minutes. Lift out chicken and let cool. Pull meat from bone (it may be pink in center); cut meat into small chunks and discard bone.

Pour broth into pan, add sherry, and stir to free any browned bits; add chicken and nutmeg.

Peel squash and potato. Whirl vegetables with carrot in a blender or food processor until smooth, slowly adding milk. Pour mixture into pan with broth. Stir soup frequently over medium-high heat until simmering. Ladle soup into bowls, and add toasted cubes, yogurt, green onions, and salt and pepper to taste. Makes 6 to 8 servings.

Per serving: 159 cal. (8.5 percent from fat); 14 g protein; 1.5 g fat (0.4 g sat.); 22 g carbo.; 135 mg sodium; 23 mg chol.

Renton, Washington

THIS GLAZED ROAST pork loin can't compete visually with a roast suckling pig with an apple in its mouth, but to chef Don Peterson, it is a much more sensible way to combine meat with fruit. The cranberry glaze and sauce are real contributors to the flavor. And the loin is much easier to carve than a pig. Dried cranberries are now available throughout the year.

Pork Loin Roast with Cranberry-Ginger Glaze

2 cups dried cranberries

¼ cup ginger-flavor liqueur

¾ cup light corn syrup

2 tablespoons balsamic vinegar

¼ teaspoon grated orange peel

1 boned, rolled, and tied pork loin roast (6 lb. with bone, about 4¾ lb. boned)

1¾ cups regular-strength beef broth

1½ tablespoons cornstarch mixed smoothly with ¼ cup water

Salt

In a 2- to 3-quart pan, combine cranberries, ginger liqueur, corn syrup, vinegar, and orange peel. Bring to a boil over high heat; cover and simmer until cranberries are plump, about 10 minutes. Whirl ½ the cranberry mixture in a food processor or blender until puréed smoothly. If making ahead, cover both mixtures and chill up to 1 day.

Place pork loin on a rack in a 10- by 15-inch roasting pan. Bake in a 350° oven until a thermometer inserted in center of thickest part registers 155°, about 1 hour and 10 minutes. After meat has cooked 40 minutes, coat with the puréed cranberry mixture, using all.

Transfer cooked roast to a platter; keep warm and let rest at least 10 minutes. Meanwhile, in a 3- to 4-quart pan, combine remaining whole cranberry mixture and broth. Bring to a boil on high heat. Stir in cornstarch mixture and return to a boil. Pour into a serving bowl. Slice roast, and accompany slices with cranberry sauce; add salt to taste. Makes 12 to 14 servings.

Per serving: 397 cal. (39 percent from fat); 32 g protein; 17 g fat (6.3 g sat.); 28 g carbo.; 84 mg sodium; 95 mg chol.

Mapleton, Utah

EDIBLE FLOWERS HAVE become popular during the last few years, but none is as nourishing as Jane Viehmann's Marigold, a surprising collage of pocket bread, sauerkraut, eggs, and cheese. With one of these under your belt, you can go forth and slay dragons.

Viehmann named the creation for the best of reasons: it reminded her of a marigold. With its breakfast setting and sunny countenance, it reminds us of some lines from a song in Shakespeare's *Cymbeline:*

Hark! hark! the lark at heaven's gate sings…

And winking Mary-buds begin

To ope their golden eyes….

Marigold

⅓ cup drained canned sauerkraut

1 pocket bread (6 in. wide)

½ cup shredded sharp cheddar cheese

2 large eggs

2 teaspoons butter or margarine

Paprika

Put sauerkraut in a strainer and rinse well with cool water. Squeeze dry. Set bread on a microwave-safe plate and scatter sauerkraut over it, then sprinkle with half the cheese.

In a bowl, beat eggs to blend with remaining cheese. In a 6- to 8-inch frying pan over medium heat, melt butter. Pour egg mixture into frying pan. As eggs on bottom set, lift cooked portion with a wide spatula and let uncooked eggs flow underneath. When eggs are almost as firm as you like, set plate with bread in a microwave oven and cook on full power (100 percent) until cheese melts, about 20 seconds. Spoon eggs onto the sauerkraut-topped bread and dust liberally with paprika. Serves 1.

Per serving: 618 cal. (54 percent from fat); 32 g protein; 37 g fat (20 g sat.); 37 g carbo.; 1,057 mg sodium; 505 mg chol.

Escondido, California

By Joan Griffiths, Richard Dunmire

Chinese chicken wings

ENJOY THESE SUCCULent wings as a finger food, or serve them atop mounds of finely shredded crisp iceberg lettuce as a first course or a main dish.

Sticky Spiced Chicken Wings

¼ cup rice wine (Shaoxing or sake)

2 pounds chicken wings, rinsed

2 star anise (or ½ teaspoon crushed anise seed and 1 cinnamon stick, 3 in. long)

1 cinnamon stick (3 in. long)

2 tablespoons dark soy sauce (or 5 teaspoons soy sauce with 1 teaspoon dark molasses)

1 tablespoon sugar

1 green onion, ends trimmed, cut into pieces

Place a wok, 12-inch frying pan, or 5- to 6-quart pan over high heat. After 30 seconds, add wine and chicken. Stir until wine almost evaporates, 6 to 8 minutes. Add 1½ cups water and bring to a boil. Add star anise and cinnamon; cover and simmer 8 minutes. Stir often.

Add soy sauce and sugar. Cover and simmer 10 minutes; stir occasionally. Uncover and stir over high heat until sauce clings to wings, about 15 minutes. Stir in onion, and with a slotted spoon, transfer wings to a platter; discard fat in pan. Makes 4 to 6 appetizer or 2 main-dish servings.—*Bruce Cost, Ginger Club, Palo Alto, California, and Ginger Island, Berkeley*

Per appetizer serving: 180 cal. (55 percent from fat); 16 g protein; 11 g fat (3.1 g sat.); 3.2 g carbo.; 390 mg sodium; 48 mg chol. ■

By Linda Lau Anusasananan

SUNSET'S KITCHEN CABINET

Creative ways with everyday foods—submitted by *Sunset* readers,
tested in *Sunset* kitchens, approved by *Sunset* taste panels

Indian-spiced Scrambled Eggs

Karen E. Bosley, Lake Oswego, Oregon

- 1 teaspoon olive oil
- 1 small (about 4 oz.) onion, chopped
- 2 cloves garlic, pressed or minced
- 3 large (about ¾ lb. total) Roma-type tomatoes
- 1½ teaspoons chili powder
- ½ teaspoon turmeric
- 3 tablespoons chopped fresh cilantro (coriander)
- 8 large eggs
- 1 tablespoon butter or margarine
  Salt and pepper

In a 10- to 12-inch nonstick frying pan over medium-high heat, frequently stir oil, onion, and garlic until onion is lightly browned, about 5 minutes. Meanwhile, core and chop tomatoes. Stir chili powder and turmeric into onion. Add tomatoes and 1 tablespoon cilantro; stir often until most of the liquid evaporates, 8 to 10 minutes. Pour sauce into a bowl; keep warm. Rinse and dry pan.

Beat eggs to blend with ¼ cup water. Melt butter in frying pan over medium heat. Add egg mixture. As eggs set, lift up cooked portion with a wide spatula so uncooked eggs flow underneath. Repeat until eggs are softly set. Top eggs with sauce and remaining cilantro. Add salt and pepper to taste. Serves 4.

Per serving: 223 cal. (57 percent from fat); 14 g protein; 14 g fat (5.1 g sat.); 9.7 g carbo.; 174 mg sodium; 433 mg chol.

SPICY TOMATO SAUCE, *laced with cilantro, enlivens scrambled eggs.*

Curried Apple Raisin Relish

Barbara Keenan, Fort Morgan, Colorado

- 1 teaspoon salad oil
- ¾ cup chopped onion
- ½ teaspoon minced garlic
- ½ teaspoon mustard seed
- ½ teaspoon curry powder
- ¼ teaspoon ground ginger
- ¼ cup cider vinegar
- ¼ cup raisins
- 2 tablespoons firmly packed brown sugar
- 2 large (about 1 lb. total) tart green apples
  Salt

In a 2- to 3-quart pan, combine oil, onion, and garlic; stir over medium heat until onion is limp, about 5 minutes. Add mustard seed, curry powder, and ginger; stir until fragrant, about 30 seconds. Add vinegar, raisins, and sugar; cover and simmer 3 minutes.

Meanwhile, core and finely chop apples. Stir apples into pan. Cover and cook over medium heat, stirring often, until apples are very hot, 6 to 8 minutes. Add salt to taste. Serve warm or cool. If making ahead, cover and chill up to 3 days. Makes about 2½ cups.

Per ¼ cup: 57 cal. (11 percent from fat); 0.4 g protein; 0.7 g fat (0.1 g sat.); 13 g carbo.; 2 mg sodium; 0 mg chol.

APPLE AND RAISIN *relish makes a delicious accent for baked ham.*

Pasta and Bean Soup

Gina Stanziano Matthews, Palo Alto, California

- 1 large (about ½ lb.) red onion, chopped
- 1 teaspoon olive oil
- 1 cup chopped celery
- 4 cloves garlic, chopped
- 2½ quarts regular-strength chicken broth
- 1½ cups dried small pasta shells
- 3 to 4 cups cooked or canned white beans, drained
- 1 cup shredded carrots
- 1 box (10 oz.) frozen petite peas
  Grated parmesan cheese

Set aside ⅓ cup onion. In a 6- to 8-quart pan, stir remaining onion, oil, celery, and garlic over medium-high heat until onion is lightly browned, 5 to 8 minutes. Add broth and bring to a boil. Stir in pasta and beans; cover and simmer until pasta is tender to bite, 5 to 7 minutes. Add carrots and peas; bring to a boil.

Ladle soup into wide bowls. Sprinkle with reserved onion. Add parmesan cheese to taste. Serves 6 to 8.

Per serving: 246 cal. (12 percent from fat); 14 g protein; 3.2 g fat (0.7 g sat.); 41 g carbo.; 141 mg sodium; 0 mg chol.

BEANS AND PASTA *merge with vegetables in a healthful soup.*

Enchiladas Carnitas

Jane King, Davis, California

1½ pounds boned pork butt or shoulder, fat trimmed

1 large (½ lb.) onion, chopped

1 large (¼ lb.) carrot, chopped

1 teaspoon chili powder

½ teaspoon dried oregano leaves

3 cloves garlic, minced or pressed

1 jar (1 lb. 5 oz.) tomatillo salsa

12 corn tortillas (6 to 7 in. wide)

1 pound jack cheese, shredded

Cut pork into 1½-inch chunks. In a covered 5- to 6-quart pan over medium heat, cook pork in ¼ cup water 8 to 10 minutes. Uncover; stir often over high heat until drippings are very brown, 10 to 12 minutes. Add 4 cups water, onion, carrot, chili powder, oregano, and garlic; stir brown bits free. Simmer, cov- ered, until meat is very tender when pierced, about 1 hour. Uncover; stir of- ten over high heat until liquid evapo- rates, 20 to 25 minutes. Cool; shred the meat.

In an 8- to 10-inch frying pan over medium heat, warm salsa. Dip tortillas, 1 at a time, into salsa. Spoon ½₂ of the meat mixture and 1 tablespoon cheese down center of each tortilla; roll to en- close. Lay seam down in a 9- by 13- inch casserole. Top enchiladas with re- maining salsa and cheese. If making ahead, cover and chill up to 1 day. Bake, uncovered, in a 400° oven until filling is hot, about 20 minutes (40 min- utes, if chilled). Serves 6.

Per serving: 622 cal. (48 percent from fat); 44 g protein; 33 g fat (17 g sat.); 37 g carbo.; 1,215 mg sodium; 156 mg chol.

BRAISE PORK, *then roll in tortillas and bake with salsa to make enchiladas.*

Citrus Avocado Salad

J. Hill, Sacramento

2 large (2 lb. total) ruby grapefruit

2 large (1½ lb. total) oranges

1 large (10 oz.) firm-ripe avocado

8 large (about 5 oz. total) radicchio leaves, rinsed and drained

¼ cup sliced almonds, toasted

2 tablespoons slivered green onion

Dressing (recipe follows)

With a sharp knife, cut peels and membranes from grapefruit and or- anges. Cut between inner membranes to release segments; discard seeds and save membranes. Pit and peel avo- cado; quarter lengthwise. From wide base of each quarter, make cuts ¼ inch apart up to ½ inch from tip; press wedge gently to fan slices. Set 1 avo- cado fan and 2 radicchio leaves on each plate; squeeze membrane juice over avocado. Add citrus segments, al- monds, and onion equally to salads; moisten with dressing. Serves 4.

Per serving: 311 cal. (52 percent from fat); 4.4 g protein; 18 g fat (2.5 g sat.); 38 g carbo.; 15 mg sodium; 0 mg chol.

Dressing. In a 7- to 8-inch frying pan over low heat, stir 2 tablespoons *each* **jalapeño jelly** and **white wine vine- gar,** 3 tablespoons **lime juice,** and 1 clove minced **garlic** until jelly melts. Off the heat, whisk in 2 tablespoons **salad oil,** ½ teaspoon **ground mustard,** ¼ teaspoon **crushed dried hot red chilies,** and 1 tablespoon minced **fresh cilantro** (coriander). Use warm.

COLORFUL WINTER SALAD *has tart, warm jalapeño jelly dressing.*

Speedy Chocolate Orange Mousse

Marilou Robinson, Portland

1 can (12 oz.) evaporated nonfat milk

1 teaspoon unflavored gelatin

6 ounces semisweet chocolate, cut into chunks

2 tablespoons orange-flavor liqueur

Thin orange slices, cut in half crosswise

Pour ½ cup milk into a 1½- to 2-quart pan and sprinkle with gelatin; let stand about 1 minute to soften gelatin. Stir over low heat until gelatin melts. Add remaining milk and chocolate. Stir over low heat until chocolate melts, about 5 minutes. Add liqueur. Whirl in a blender or food processor to blend well. Pour into small bowls. Cool, cover, and chill until firm, at least 2 hours or up to 1 day. Garnish desserts with orange slices. Serves 4.

Per serving: 302 cal. (39 percent from fat); 10 g protein; 13 g fat (7.6 g sat.); 40 g carbo.; 117 mg sodium; 3.8 mg chol.

Compiled by Linda Lau Anusasananan, Paula Freschet

ORANGE-SCENTED *chocolate mousse takes only minutes to prepare.*

Articles Index

Index of Recipe Titles

General Index

If you are not already a subscriber to *Sunset Magazine*
and would be interested in subscribing, please call
Sunset's subscriber service number, 1-800-777-0117.